For Congress and the Nation

A view of the Main Building of the Library of Congress made in 1898 from the grounds of the U.S. Capitol by the American Architect and Building News Company. Authorized in 1886, the building was officially opened in 1897 and immediately hailed as a national monument. One contemporary guidebook boasted: "America is justly proud of this gorgeous and palatial monument to its National sympathy and appreciation of Literature, Science, and Art. It has been designed and executed entirely by American art and American labor and is a fitting temple for the great thoughts of generations past, present, and to be." Visitors to the new building saw a white exterior of New Hampshire granite, decorated with Corinthian columns, topped with a gleaming gold dome and the Torch of Learning at the center and apex. The architects were John L. Smithmeyer and Paul J. Pelz.

For Congress and the Nation

A Chronological History of the Library of Congress

by John Y. Cole

Library of Congress   Washington   1979

Library of Congress Cataloging in Publication Data

Cole, John Young, 1940–
For Congress and the Nation.

Bibliography: P.
Includes index.
1. United States. Library of Congress.—History.
I. United States Library of Congress. II. Title.
Z733.U6C565   027.5753   76-608365
ISBN 0-8444-0225-7

ENDPAPERS: *An 1888 drawing of the Library of Congress building prepared by architects John L. Smithmeyer and Paul J. Pelz. When the structure was completed in 1897, its dome had been raised and several ornamental features had disappeared. (See page 52.)*

For sale by the Superintendent of Documents, U.S. Government Printing Office
Washington, D.C. 20402

Stock Number 030-003-00018-7

Contents

v

Preface

In 1950, the sesquicentennial year of the Library of Congress, the eminent librarian S. R. Ranganathan paid the Library and the U.S. Congress a unique tribute:

> The institution serving as the national library of the United States is perhaps more fortunate than its predecessors in other countries. It has the Congress as its godfather. . . . This stroke of good fortune has made it perhaps the most influential of all the national libraries of the world.[1]

A quarter of a century later, the Library built by the U.S. Congress has achieved an even greater degree of preeminence: it is the largest library in the world and the scope of its services is unmatched by any other research library. The most remarkable feature of the Library of Congress, however, is its dual nature as both a legislative library for the American Congress and a national library for the country at large. In this sense, the Library of Congress brings together the concerns of government, librarianship, and scholarship—an uncommon combination, perhaps, but one that has been of great benefit to American society and culture.

The dual nature of the Library of Congress stems from events in the early years of the 19th century, when the Library began its gradual expansion into an institution that served both the Congress and the rest of the nation. The extension of the services of the Library of Congress to the nation was a direct result of the expansion of the scope of the Library's collections; in this sense, the functions of the Library have derived from its collections, not vice versa.

There were two events of great importance in the development of the Library's collections during the 19th century, events that shaped

the future of the institution. The first was the purchase by Congress, in 1815, of the personal library of former President Thomas Jefferson. The Jefferson collection provided the Congress with "a most admirable substratum for a National Library."[2] Furthermore, in offering to sell his library to the government, Jefferson used a phrase that applies equally well today in justifying the comprehensive nature of the Library of Congress: "There is . . . no subject to which a member of Congress may not have occasion to refer."[3] The second "event" was the 32-year administration of an ardent collection-builder, Ainsworth Rand Spofford, who served as Librarian of Congress from 1865 to 1897 and applied Jefferson's rationale on a grand scale. Spofford was responsible for the copyright law which has done so much to mold the Library and its collections and for the monumental Library building, completed in 1897, which permanently separated the Library from the Capitol. In 1898 Spofford provided the best description of his own librarianship when he explained to John Russell Young, the new Librarian of Congress: "I fought to bring us oceans of books and rivers of information."[4]

Thirteen years ago Douglas W. Bryant, associate librarian of Harvard University, accurately observed: "The major functions of the Library of Congress might have been assigned to three or four separate agencies. . . . an explanation of why they have been combined would call for a study of history rather than of administrative

---

1. S. R. Ranganathan, "The Library of Congress among National Libraries," *ALA Bulletin* 44 (October 1950): 356.

2. *Annals of Congress* 28 (January 26, 1815): 1106.

3. Thomas Jefferson to Samuel H. Smith, September 21, 1814, Jefferson Papers, Library of Congress.

4. Ainsworth Rand Spofford to John Russell Young, February 16, 1898, Library of Congress archives.

logic. . . ."[5] In this volume I have attempted to document the story of how the Library of Congress acquired the many functions it now performs. The explanation of why the Library developed in this manner is, it seems to me, implicit in the facts as they are outlined: the growth of the Library of Congress cannot be separated from the growth of the nation it serves.

The emphasis in this volume is on the *origins* of the Library's principal collections, services, and administrative units. The early development of the collections is outlined in considerable detail; in later years, only those acquisitions which seemed to be of special significance are included. The names of Library officials, consultants, donors, and other persons are mentioned sparingly, only because the inclusion of all the persons who have made important contributions to the Library's development would have been impossible.

I wish to express my thanks to Paul L. Berry, director of the Reference Department, and to John Charles Finzi, assistant director, for encouraging this endeavor. I also am grateful to Helen Anne Hilker, interpretive projects officer, for her careful reading of the manuscript and her many useful suggestions. Numerous Library of Congress specialists were consulted with regard to entries in their areas of interest, and their help is appreciated very much. In the end, however, a volume of this nature has to be a highly subjective interpretation of an institution's history, and the author bears full responsibility for the inclusion or omission of specific events, as well as for the wording and the accuracy of individual entries.

It is my hope that this book, prepared in the year of the 175th anniversary of the founding of the Library of Congress, somehow conveys the personality and the significance of an extraordinary American institution.

JOHN Y. COLE
Reference Department
December 1975

5. U.S., Library of Congress, *Annual Report of the Librarian of Congress, 1962*, p. 89.

Symbols

AC	*Annals of Congress*
AL	*American Libraries*
ALA	American Library Association
ALAB	*American Library Association Bulletin*
AR	*Annual Report of the Librarian of Congress*
ARL	Association of Research Libraries
ARS	Ainsworth Rand Spofford Papers, Library of Congress
CG	*Congressional Globe*
CLR	Council on Library Resources, Inc.
CR	*Congressional Record*
GO	General Order, Librarian of Congress
GW	George Watterston Papers, Library of Congress
HP	Herbert Putnam Papers, Library of Congress
HRA	U. S. House of Representatives, Legislative Branch Appropriations Hearings
HRD	U.S. House of Representatives Document
HRED	U.S. House of Representatives Executive Document
HRH	U.S. House of Representatives Hearings
HRMD	U.S. House of Representatives Miscellaneous Document
HRR	U.S. House of Representatives Report
JCC	*Journals of the Continental Congress, 1774-1789,* 34 vols. (Washington: Government Printing Office, 1904-37.)
JRY	John Russell Young Papers, Library of Congress
LCA	Library of Congress Archives, General Records and Correspondence
LCA-L	Library of Congress Archives, Librarians' Letterbooks
LCA-M	Library of Congress Archives, "Extracts From the Minutes of the Joint Library Committee, 1861–1898"
LCA-R	Library of Congress Archives, Rare Book and Special Collections Division
LCA-T	Library of Congress Archives, Trust Fund Board Records
LCIB	*Library of Congress Information Bulletin*
LCR	Library of Congress Regulation
LJ	*Library Journal*
LQ	*Library Quarterly*
LRTS	*Library Resources & Technical Services*
LT	*Library Trends*
PR	Press Release, Library of Congress
QJ	*Quarterly Journal of the Library of Congress*
SA	Special Announcement, Librarian of Congress
SAR	Smithsonian Institution, *Annual Report of the Board of Regents*
SD	U.S. Senate Document
SED	U.S. Senate Executive Document

SER   U.S. Senate Executive Report

SH   U.S. Senate Hearings

SMD   U.S. Senate Miscellaneous Document

SO   Special Order, Librarian of Congress

SR   U.S. Senate Report

Stat.   *U.S. Statutes at Large*

SUM   U.S. President, *The State of the Union Messages of the Presidents, 1790–1966*, ed. Fred L. Israel, 3 vols. (New York: Chelsea House, 1966)

TJ   Thomas Jefferson Papers, Library of Congress

TR   Theodore Roosevelt Papers, Library of Congress

WDJ   William Dawson Johnston, *History of the Library of Congress, 1800-1864*, vol. 1 (Washington: Government Printing Office, 1904)

WM   William McKinley Papers, Library of Congress

x

Illustrations

Chronology 1774–1975

1774 AUGUST 31. As the opening session of the Continental Congress approaches, the directors of the Library Company of Philadelphia order that "the Librarian furnish the gentlemen, who are to meet in Congress, with the use of such Books as they may have occasion for, during their sitting, taking a receipt for them." (JCC 1:27)

SEPTEMBER 6. The Continental Congress orders that "the thanks of the Congress be returned to the Directors of the Library Company of Philadelphia for their obliging order." (JCC 1:27)

1782 NOVEMBER 12. Theodorick Bland, Jr., delegate to the Continental Congress from Virginia, offers a motion that the Congress import books from Europe for the use of "the United States in Congress." (Papers of the Continental Congress, item 186)

1783 JANUARY 24. A committee of delegates, chaired by James Madison of Virginia, reports favorably on Bland's motion. Easy access to "authors on the law of Nations, Treaties, Negotiations, etc." is termed "indispensable" for Congress, and it is observed that the want of this information has been "manifest in several important acts of Congress." The committee urges that no time "be lost in collecting every book & tract which related to American antiquities & the affairs of the U.S.," since the most valuable of these works are not only becoming "extinct" but are also needed as to protect the United States against possible claims from "Spain or other powers which had shared in the discoveries & possessions of the New World." Over 250 titles in the subjects of law, history, politics, and geography are recommended. The motion to adopt the committee report is defeated primarily because of the "inconvenience of advancing even a few hundred pounds" during the present wartime fiscal crisis. (JCC 24:83–92, 25:858–59)

1789 MARCH 4. The First Congress of the United States begins its sessions in the City Hall in New York City, where the

1789 legislators are granted access to the New York Society Library, located in the same building. (WDJ:17)

AUGUST 6. Elbridge Gerry, a Representative from Massachusetts to the First Congress of the United States, offers a motion "that a committee be appointed to report a catalogue of books necessary for the use of Congress, with an estimate of the expense, and the best mode of procuring them." The motion is tabled. (AC 1:705)

1790 APRIL 30. In the second session of the First Congress, Representative Gerry's motion is called up and Gerry is appointed to head the committee. (AC 2:1550)

JUNE 23. On behalf of his committee, Gerry recommends that Congress establish a library for the use of the legislative and executive departments. A sum not exceeding $1,000 should be appropriated immediately, as well as $500 annually in the future, to be "applied to the purpose by the Vice-President, Chief Justice and Secretary of State of the United States." Without a library, Gerry observes, officials will be deprived of necessary books "or be obliged at every session to transport to the seat of the General Government a considerable part of their personal libraries."

(Gazette of the United States, June 26, 1790; AC 2: 1647)

1791 JANUARY 19. The First Congress, meeting in Philadelphia for its third session, receives a letter from the directors of the Library Company of Philadelphia offering the free use of their library "to the members of both Houses of Congress." (AC 2:1872)

1800 APRIL 24. President John Adams approves an "act to make provision for the removal and accommodation of the Government of the United States," which establishes the Library of Congress. Five thousand dollars is appropriated "for the purchase of such books as may be necessary for the use of Congress" after it moves to the new capital city of Washington. The books will be housed in "a suit-

3

"able apartment" in the Capitol, and a joint congressional committee will oversee the purchase of the books, furnish a catalog, and "devise and establish" the Library's regulations.

(2 Stat. 55)

JUNE 20. The Joint Library Committee orders books for the new Library from the London firm of Cadell & Davies, booksellers.

(LCA)

MAY 2. The first books and maps for the new Library arrive in Washington. The collection, consisting of 152 works in 740 volumes and three maps, is soon stored in the office of the secretary of the Senate.

(TJ)

DECEMBER 7. Secretary of the Senate Samuel A. Otis reports on the books and maps "purchased in consequence of an act of Congress, passed 24th April, 1800." The Senate agrees to appoint a committee "to join such gentlemen as shall be appointed by the House of Representatives" in considering "the future arrangement of said books and maps." The House of Representatives immediately appoints a similar committee.

(AC 11:10–11)

DECEMBER 21. The Senate approves a bill providing for an annual Library appropriation and the appointment of a Librarian by the President of the United States.

(AC 11:19; WDJ:29)

DECEMBER 21. John Randolph of Virginia presents a detailed report representing the views of the committee members from the House of Representatives. It is recommended that the books and maps be placed in the room that was occupied by the House of Representatives during the last session of the Sixth Congress; that they be combined with the separate collections heretofore kept by the House and by the Senate; and that "for the time being," the secretary of the Senate and the clerk of the House of Representatives be in charge of the new Library.

(AC 12:1292–94; WDJ:27–29)

DECEMBER 31. The House of Representatives approves a bill providing that the unexpended balance of the previous appropriation be used to support the Library and that the Librarian be appointed by the president of the Senate and the Speaker of the House of Representatives.

(AC 11:352–54)

JANUARY 26. President Thomas Jefferson approves a compromise act of Congress "concerning the Library for the use of both Houses of Congress." Books and maps will be purchased using the unexpended balance of the previous appropriation "together with such sums as may hereafter be appropriated to the same purpose." The Librarian, who will be paid "a sum not exceeding two dollars" per day, will be appointed by the President of the United States. Expenditure of funds will be supervised by a joint committee consisting of three members of the Senate and three members of the House of Representatives. The Library "shall be placed in the Capitol"; its rules and regulations will be established by the president of the Senate and the Speaker of the House of Representatives. The use of the Library, "for the time being," is restricted to members of Congress and the President and Vice President of the United States.

(2 Stat. 128)

JANUARY 29. President Jefferson appoints John J. Beckley, clerk of the House of Representatives, to be the first Librarian of Congress. Beckley will serve concurrently in both jobs.

(LCA)

APRIL. Publication of the first Library catalog, *Catalogue of the Books, Maps, and Charts Belonging to the Library of the Two Houses of Congress,* printed by William Duane. The catalog lists the collection of 964 volumes according to their size and appends a list of nine maps and charts.

(LCA)

APRIL 14. In response to a request for advice concerning additional book purchases, Jefferson replies to Joint Library Committee Chairman Abraham Baldwin: "I have prepared a catalogue for the Library of Congress in con-

1802

formity with your ideas that books of entertainment are not within the scope of it, and that books in other languages, where there are not translations of them, are not to be admitted freely." (TJ)

1805

JANUARY 2. President Jefferson approves an act of Congress stipulating that 300 copies of the laws of the United States and of the journals of Congress are to be "placed in the Library of Congress," not to be taken out of the Library "except by the President and Vice President of the United States and members of the Senate and House of Representatives, for the time being." (2 Stat. 308)

1806

JANUARY 20. Library Committee Chairman Samuel Latham Mitchill urges the expansion of the Library: "Every week of the session causes additional regret that the volumes of literature and science within the reach of the national legislature are not more rich and ample." The New York Senator, characterized by contemporaries as a "living encyclopedia" and a "chaos of knowledge," argues that "steps should be taken to furnish the Library with such materials as will enable statesmen to be correct in their investigations and, by a becoming display of erudition and research, give a higher dignity and a brighter luster to truth." (AC 15:54–55)

FEBRUARY 21. President Jefferson approves an act of Congress that "continues" the earlier appropriation "made to purchase books for the use of Congress." An additional $1,000 a year for a period of five years is authorized for this purpose, its expenditure to be supervised by the joint committee. (2 Stat. 350)

MARCH 14. The Senate rejects a House of Representatives proposal that the privilege of taking books out of the Library be extended to the secretaries of state, treasury, war, and navy and to the attorney general. (AC 15:184)

MARCH 31. Senator John Quincy Adams, a member of the Joint Library Committee, notes in his diary an agree-

5

CATALOGUE.

No.	FOLIO's.	No. of Vols.	Value, as near as can be estimated.	
			WHOLE SET. Dollars.	EACH BOOK. Dollars.
1	Fathers Paul's Council of Trent,	1	4	
2	Blair's Chronology, (not to issue,)	1	35	
3	Helvicus's Chronological Tables,	1	3	
4	Booth's Diodorus Siculus,	1	10	
5	Appian's History of the Civil Wars of the Romans,	1	4	
6	Machiavel's Florentine History,	1	3	
7	Duncan's Cæsar,	1	32	
8	Du Halde's History of China,	2	24	12
10	De Soli's Conquest of Mexico,	1	4	
11	Rapin's History of England,	5	50	10
16	Lord Herbert's Life of Henry VIII.	1	2	
17	Rushworth's Historical Collections,	8	24	3
25	Lord Clarendon's History of the Rebellion,	4	24	6
29	Guthrie's Geography,	1	13	
30	Bayle's Dictionary,	5	30	6
35	Postlewayte's Dictionary of Commerce,	2	24	12
37	Beawes' Lex Mercatoria,	1	12	
38	Domat's Civil Law,	2	12	6
40	Grotius, by Barbeyrac,	1	14	
41	Puffendorf, by ditto,	1	24	
42	Sidney on Government,	1	10	
43	Bacon's Works,	5	55	11

The first page of the 1802 catalog, prepared by Librarian John Beckley and printed by William Duane of Washington City. Volumes were listed by size. As described in the catalog, the Library's 964-volume collection consisted of 212 folios, 164 quartos, 581 octavos, and 7 duodecimos, plus 9 maps and charts. Rare Book and Special Collections Division.

1806

ment "that the principal part of the fund appropriated this year should be expended by Dr. Mitchill, Mr. Clay, and myself, during the recess, in collecting books in Boston, New York, and Philadelphia, as the occasion may offer." John Quincy Adams, *Memoirs*, ed. Charles Francis Adams, vol. 1 (Philadelphia: J. B. Lippincott, 1874), p. 424.

1807

APRIL 8. Death of John Beckley, clerk of the House and Librarian of Congress.

APRIL 21. Jefferson explains to Henry Dearborn, his secretary of war, that he is considering the separation of the offices of Librarian of Congress and clerk of the House of Representatives. However, he remains "a little puzzled . . . between doubt and inclination" on the matter. (TJ)

NOVEMBER 7. President Jefferson appoints Patrick Magruder, a Washington newspaperman who was named clerk of the House of Representatives on October 26, 1807, to the post of Librarian of Congress. (LCA)

1809

FEBRUARY 6. The House of Representatives approves a resolution that directs the clerk of the House to deposit, in the Library of Congress, "two sets of the journals and of all printed reports and documents laid before Congress, or either House, at each session." (AC 19:1375)

1810

MAY 1. The President approves an act that authorizes the financial agent of the Joint Library Committee to use the books in the Library in accordance with the "same terms, conditions, and restrictions as members of Congress." (2 Stat. 612)

1811

DECEMBER 6. President James Madison approves an act of Congress that renews the Library's $1,000 annual appropriation for a period of five years. (2 Stat. 667)

1812

The first classified catalog is issued, listing 3,076 volumes (in 18 classes, subarranged by size) and 53 maps, charts,

6

A contemporary sketch of Patrick Magruder (1768–1819), the second Librarian of Congress, who served in the post from 1807 to 1815. Like John Beckley (1757–1807), the first Librarian of Congress, Magruder served simultaneously as clerk of the House of Representatives. Both men were appointed by President Thomas Jefferson. LC–USZ62–6004

RULES
AND
REGULATIONS

To be observed in the LIBRARY of CONGRESS.

I. THE Library shall be opened every day during the session of Congress, and for one week preceding and subsequent thereto, Sundays excepted, from nine o'clock in the morning, to three o'clock in the afternoon, and from five o'clock to seven in the evening.

II. IN the recess of Congress, it shall be opened three days in every week, during the hours aforesaid, to wit; on Tuesday, Thursday and Saturday.

III. IT shall be the duty of the Librarian to label and number the Books, place them on the shelves, and preserve due lists and catalogues of the same. He shall also keep due account and register of all issues and returns of books as the same shall be made, together with regular accounts of all expences incident to the said Library, and which are authorized by law.

IV. BOOKS, to be issued by the Librarian pursuant to law, shall be returned as follows:

A *Folio*, *within three*
A *Quarto*, *within two* } WEEK.
An *Octavo or Duodecimo*, *within one*

And no member shall receive more than one folio, one quarto, or two octavo's or duodecimo's, within the terms aforesaid, unless where so connected as to be otherwise useless.

V. FOR all books issued, a receipt or note shall be given, of double the value thereof, as near as can be estimated, conditioned to return the same, undefaced within the term above mentioned, or to forfeit the amount of such note: at the expiration of which, unless application has been made by another person for the same book, and the Librarian requested to take a memorandum thereof, the said Librarian, upon the books being produced to him, may renew the issue of the same for the time and on the conditions aforesaid: *Provided*, That every receipt or note shall contain a further forfeiture or penalty for every day's detention of a book beyond the specified term, that is to say : for

A *Folio—three dollars per day*,
A *Quarto—two dollars per day*,
An *Octavo—one dollar per day.——*Which forfeiture or penalty may, for good cause, be remitted by the President of the Senate and Speaker of the House of Representatives for the time being, in whole or in part, as the case may require.

VI. WHEN a member shall prefer to take a book for the limited time, without removing it from the Library, he shall be allowed to do so without giving a receipt or note for the same, and to preserve his priority for the use of such book for the time limited, in like manner as if he had withdrawn the book from the Library, and given a receipt or note therefor. And the Librarian shall keep due account and entry of all such cases.

VII. BOOKS returned shall be delivered to the Librarian, to be examined whether damaged or not.

VIII. IF a book be returned damaged, the party returning it shall not be entitled to receive another until the damage for the first shall be satisfied.

IX. NO book shall be issued within one week of the termination of any session of Congress.

X. ALL books shall be returned three days before the close of a session, whether the time allowed for the use thereof be expired or not.

The early rules and regulations of the Library were stringent. These rules, which also specified the duties of the Librarian, were published in the Library's 1808 catalog. LCA–R; LCMS–29074-7

7

1812

and plans. An adjustment in the Library's rules exempts members of Congress from overdue fines. Other borrowers must provide a receipt or note "of double the value" of the book; however, their overdue fines are reduced to one dollar, fifty cents, and twenty-five cents a day for folios, quartos, and octavos, respectively.　　　　(LCA–R)

MARCH 2.　President Madison approves a joint resolution of Congress that authorizes the judges of the Supreme Court to use the books in the Library.　(2 Stat. 786)

1813

APRIL 27.　American forces capture York (Toronto), the capital of Upper Canada, and burn the Parliament buildings—including the small library of the Legislative Assembly.

1814

AUGUST 24.　After capturing Washington, the British burn the U.S. Capitol, destroying the Library of Congress. (WDJ:65–66)

SEPTEMBER 21.　Thomas Jefferson, in retirement at Monticello, offers to sell his personal library to the Library Committee of Congress in order to "recommence" the Congressional Library. At the same time he forwards a catalog of the books and explains that he is at work "making an alphabetical index of the authors' names." In his letter to the committee, the former President describes his collection and why it would be useful to Congress:

You know my collection, its condition and extent. I have been fifty years making it, and have spared no pains, opportunity or expense, to make it what it is. While residing in Paris, I devoted every afternoon I was disengaged, for a summer or two, in examining all the principal bookstores, turning over every book with my own hand, and putting by everything which related to America, and indeed whatever was rare and valuable in every science. Besides this, I had standing orders during the whole time I was in Europe, on its principal book-marts, particularly Amsterdam, Frankfort, Madrid and London, for such works relating to America as could not be found in Paris. So that in that department particularly, such a collection was made as probably can never again be effected, because it is hardly probable that the same opportunities, the same time, industry, per-

On August 24, 1814, the British captured Washington and destroyed the U.S. Capitol, including the Library of Congress. The notion that the invaders used the Library's books to kindle the fire in the Capitol was false but persistent. This drawing was published in Harper's New Monthly Magazine in December 1872.

8

severance and expense; with some knowledge of the bibliography of the subject, would again happen to be in concurrence. During the same period, and after my return to America, I was led to procure, also, whatever related to the duties of those in the high concerns of the nation. So that the collection, which I suppose is of between nine and ten thousand volumes, while it includes what is chiefly valuable in science and literature generally, extends more particularly to whatever belongs to the American statesman... I do not know that it contains any branch of science which Congress would wish to exclude from their collection; there is, in fact, no subject to which a member of Congress may not have occasion to refer. (TJ)

1814

SEPTEMBER 24. Georgetown bookseller and binder Joseph Milligan informs his longtime customer Thomas Jefferson: "Your truly magnanimous offer of the Monticello library to Congress will be very acceptable. If Congress should purchase it, to literary men it would be a great privilege to be permitted at all times of the year to have free access, not to take away the books, but to read in the Library and make extracts. Therefore the place of Librarian would be well to be a distinct office from the Clerk of the House of Representatives." (TJ)

NOVEMBER. Joseph Milligan provides the Joint Library Committee with an evaluation of Jefferson's books; the price of the 6,487 volumes will be $23,950. (wDJ:84)

DECEMBER 3. The Senate approves a bill to purchase Jefferson's library. (AC 28:120)

1815

JANUARY 26. By a vote of 71–61, the House of Representatives approves the purchase of Jefferson's library. The *Annals of Congress* record that "those who opposed the bill did so on account of the scarcity of money and the necessity of appropriating it to purposes more indispensable than the purchase of a library; the probable insecurity of such a library placed here; the high price to be given for this collection; its miscellaneous and almost exclusively literary (instead of legal and historical) character, etc. . . . To those arguments, enforced with zeal and vehemence, the friends of the bill replied with fact, wit, and argument, to show that the purchase, to be made on terms of long credit, could not affect the present resources of the United States; that the price was moderate, the library more valuable from the scarcity of many of its books, and altogether a most admirable substratum for a National Library." (AC 28:1105–06)

JANUARY 28. After an investigation relating to the loss of the Library in 1814 and the use of the funds under his control, Patrick Magruder resigns his position of clerk of the House of Representatives and, by inference, the office of Librarian of Congress. (*American State Papers, Miscellaneous* 2:253–68)

JANUARY 30. President Madison approves an act of Congress appropriating $23,950 for the acquisition of Jefferson's library. (3 Stat. 195)

MARCH 3. President Madison approves an act of Congress authorizing the President of the United States "to cause a proper apartment to be immediately selected and prepared for a library room" to house "the library lately purchased from Thomas Jefferson." (3 Stat. 225)

MARCH 21. George Watterston, a local novelist and journalist, is appointed by President Madison as the new Librarian of Congress—the first Librarian who does not also serve as clerk of the House of Representatives. (LCA)

MARCH 25. In a letter to Madison, Watterston thanks the President for the appointment and reminds him of the action needed to comply with the act of March 3. The new Librarian suggests a library room on the third floor of the "present Capitol"—Blodgett's Hotel at 7th and E Streets NW. The room is soon prepared and occupied. (James Madison Papers; wDJ:121–23)

APRIL 26. Librarian Watterston writes to Jefferson: "if you think the plan you have followed in the arrangement of the present library be the most judicious, you would oblige me by having the books packed up according to that arrangement. I have long thought the arrangement of the old Library was incorrect and injudicious." (TJ)

MAY 7. In a letter to Watterston, Jefferson explains his classification scheme and tells the Librarian: "you will receive my library arranged very perfectly in the order observed in the catalogue, which I have sent with it." (TJ)

MAY 8. Jefferson reports to his friend Samuel Harrison Smith: "Our tenth and last waggon load of books goes off today. . . . It is the choicest collection of books in the United States, and I hope it will not be without some general effect on the literature of the country."
(Jonathan Bayard Smith Papers, Library of Congress)

JULY 31. The daily National Intelligencer of Washington proclaims: "In all civilized nations of Europe there are national libraries, the selection and increase of which occupy much of governmental attention. In a country of such general intelligence as this, so laudable an example should by all means be instituted, and the Congressional or National Library of the United States [should] become the great repository of the literature of the world."

SEPTEMBER 15. Librarian Watterston publishes a notice in the National Intelligencer asking that "American authors, engravers, and painters" transmit copies of their works to the Library to serve "not only as a literary history of this now interesting country, but [also] to exhibit the progress and the improvement of the arts."

OCTOBER 13. Watterston explains to Jefferson: "I have preserved your arrangement as one I think excellent and that I had previously thought of adopting." (TJ)

NOVEMBER. The Library adopts the classification scheme devised by Thomas Jefferson. The new Catalogue of the Library of the United States: To Which Is Annexed, a Copious Index, Alphabetically Arranged, although pre-

The 1815 purchase of Thomas Jefferson's private library provided the Congress with "a most admirable substratum for a National Library." Furthermore, the collection was already arranged according to Jefferson's personal classification scheme. Jefferson explained his system to Librarian of Congress George Watterston in this letter "on the arrangement of libraries." TJ

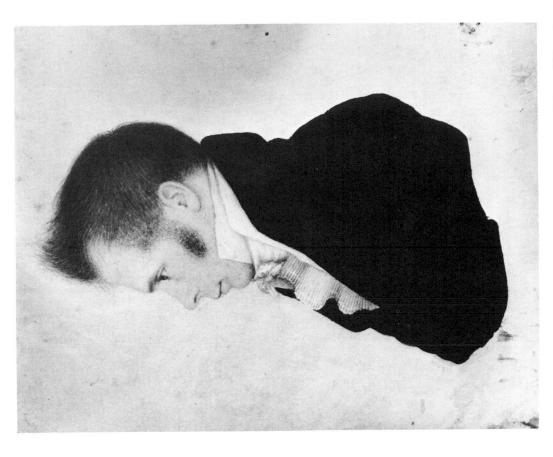

11

1815 pared by Librarian Watterston, is based on Jefferson's catalog of his personal library. The arrangement, which follows Sir Francis Bacon's classification of knowledge, is alphabetical by title within each of 44 basic divisions. Appended to the catalog is a list of "rules and regulations to be observed in the library of Congress." Six hundred copies are printed at a cost of $2.25 each. (LCA–R)

1816 JANUARY 26. The Joint Committee on the Library recommends a $10,000 appropriation for the purchase of books and maps, independent of the annual $1,000 appropriation which it submits "to Congress to make perpetual." Only such an expenditure will "place within the reach of every member of Congress all the most valuable books in every department of arts and sciences, of which now there is such a lamentable deficiency." The committee points out that the "merit" of the new catalog "is altogether due to Mr. Jefferson and not to the librarian of Congress," and is especially critical of the catalog's cost. Nevertheless, an increase in the salary of the Librarian is recommended. Finally, the committee also observes "not without astonishment, that by an act passed the 26th of January 1802, the President of the United States solely. It is difficult to conceive why an officer of both Houses of Congress . . . should not be appointed by the authority to which he ought to be amenable." It therefore recommends that, in the future, the Joint Library Committee make the appointment

(14/1 SR 26)

JANUARY 29. Watterston writes Jefferson: "The Library Committee are dissatisfied with me for having the catalogue printed without having written to consult their *superior judgment*, but the members generally speak very highly of your arrangement and the disposition of the books." (TJ)

APRIL 16. President Madison approves an act which raises the salary of the Librarian of Congress to $1,000 per

1816

year, retroactive to March 21, 1815. The "privilege of using books in the library" is extended to the U.S. attorney general and the members of the diplomatic corps.

(3 Stat. 283)

1817

JANUARY 6. In order to "stamp the Congressional Library with that degree of usefulness contemplated in its establishment," the Joint Library Committee invites the chairmen of other House and Senate committees to recommend books and maps for purchase. It also directs that a box be placed in the Library "where may be deposited by the members of both Houses, the titles of such books as they may be desirous to procure." A final recommendation is that the "heads of Departments" be given the privilege of using the books "on the same terms on which members of Congress are permitted to use them." (14/2 SR 34:3-4)

JANUARY 9. The Senate approves a bill authorizing the Library Committee to select, for deposit in the Library of Congress, copyright deposits sent to the Department of State.

FEBRUARY 18. Unhappy with the Library's temporary quarters, Library Committee Chairman Eligius Fromentin, Senator from Louisiana, introduces a resolution advocating a separate building for the Library of Congress, to be situated "on Delaware Avenue, north of the Capitol."

(WDJ:158)

FEBRUARY 22. Senator Fromentin's resolution is "determined in the negative."

(AC 30:131)

MARCH 25. In a letter to the *National Intelligencer*, appearing under the caption "National Library," and signed "W," Librarian Watterston regrets the failure of the "proposition to erect a building for the reception of the Library of the United States." He points out that "in all other countries," such a structure would be "an object of national pride."

(AC 30:144)

1818

APRIL 18. The annual salary of the Librarian is raised to $1,500.

(3 Stat. 431)

DECEMBER 3. President James Monroe approves an act authorizing the Joint Library Committee "to cause suitable apartments, in the north wing of the Capitol, to be fitted up and furnished for the temporary reception of the Library of Congress." The same act appropriates $2,000 "to the further purchase of books for the said library." By the end of the year, the Library has been moved back into the Capitol.

(3 Stat. 477; WDJ:127)

1820

APRIL 11. President Monroe approves an act of Congress that inaugurates a separate annual appropriation exclusively for the purchase of books and maps. The allocation is $2,000.

(3 Stat. 555)

1822

APRIL 30. Representative Enoch Lincoln of Maine introduces a resolution that would require the deposit of all manuscript records of the government in the Library of Congress. The resolution is tabled.

(AC 39:1743)

AUGUST 28. The *National Intelligencer* expresses the wish that the Library of Congress become "something more national and truly literary in its arrangements and objects than it has hitherto been."

1824

FEBRUARY 24. The House Ways and Means Committee reports that the collections of the Library are "defective in all the principal branches of literature" and notes that its present appropriation is so small that purchases are generally confined to "works of the day." It recommends that the annual appropriation for the acquisition of books be increased to $5,000, "a sum very little exceeding the amount which individual taste and liberality often bestow upon private selections." The committee also suggests that the Library continue to import most of its books from England.

(18/1 HRR 69)

1824

MAY 26. President Monroe approves an act of Congress that increases the annual appropriation to the Library for the purchase of books to $5,000. (4 Stat. 60)

AUGUST 17. The Library is moved from the north wing into a spacious new room designed by Architect of the Capitol Charles Bulfinch in the center of the west front of the Capitol. (WDJ:128–29)

1825

DECEMBER 22. A fire, started by a candle left burning in the gallery, is controlled before it can do serious damage to the Library's 14,000-volume collection. The fire was first noticed by Representative Edward Everett who observed, from the foot of Capitol Hill, "a bright light from some of the windows of the Capitol." (WDJ:132–34)

DECEMBER 24. The *National Intelligencer* describes the firefighting: "An engine and hose were brought and by the very active exertions of the fireman, aided by a number of members of Congress, who vied with one another in their exertions to save the Library, the flames were extinguished in less than an hour. . . . Among the members earliest aroused and most active were Mr. Houston, Mr. Webster, Mr. Dwight, and Mr. Wickliffe."

1826

MAY 18. After spending the entire day working in the Library, historian Jared Sparks writes in his journal: "On American History the library is exceedingly meagre, containing nothing but the commonest books; but on American politics it is full, particularly to the year 1808, when Mr. Jefferson left the government. It was his habit to preserve pamphlets and papers, and they are all deposited in this library." Herbert B. Adams, *The Life and Writings of Jared Sparks*, vol 1 (Boston: Houghton Mifflin, 1893), pp. 461–62.

DECEMBER 13. Upon request, Watterston provides a list of "books it would be expedient to remove from the Library as being imperfect." The Librarian, however, respectfully informs the new Library Committee chairman —Representative Edward Everett of Massachusetts—that making such decisions "may be leaving too much to the taste & discretion of the Librarian." (GW)

1827

FEBRUARY 22. Watterston informs Everett that the document rooms of the Library "have been required by the Senate for Committee rooms," and asks that the Library Committee find additional space for the documents "before the adjournment of Congress." (GW)

FEBRUARY 24. Lamenting that "the most important sources of our early history are deposited in the archives of foreign governments," Chairman Everett reports a resolution urging that "proper measures be adopted, at the discretion of the President, to procure from the public offices in England copies of documents illustrative of the history of America." The resolution fails. (19/2 HRR 91)

1828

MAY 24. President John Quincy Adams approves an act of Congress that authorizes the Librarian of Congress to employ an assistant at an annual salary of $800, retroactive to March 4, 1827. Watterston names Edward B. Stelle to the position of Assistant Librarian. (4 Stat. 301; WDJ:179–80)

MAY 24. President Adams approves a joint resolution that provides for the distribution of duplicate copies of public documents in the Library to members of Congress, state legislative libraries, universities and colleges, "incorporated Atheneums," and to the U.S. Military Academy at West Point. Also, the Joint Library Committee is authorized to "remove from the library of Congress, and dispose of in such manner as they think expedient, any duplicate, imperfect, or damaged, or other work or works, not wanted for the use of the library." (4 Stat. 321)

1829

FEBRUARY 12. Because it is "very desirable that a prompt and regular supply of the laws of the several states" be sent to the Library, the Library Committee reports favor-

The fourth Librarian of Congress, John Silva Meehan (1790–1863), held the office from 1829 to 1861, serving under nine Presidents. LC-USZ62-43063

1829

ably on a House resolution that would provide for the receipt of such documents on a "standing order" basis. No action is taken, however.

(20/2 HRR 77)

MAY 28. Newly elected President Andrew Jackson, a Democrat, replaces Librarian of Congress Watterston, a Whig. The new Librarian is John Silva Meehan, a local printer and publisher. The library has a collection of approximately 16,000 volumes.

(LCA)

JUNE 9. Writing in the Washington *National Journal*, Watterston protests Jackson's action: "This is one of the most extraordinary removals as well as appointments which the weak and tyrannical heads of the present Administration have yet made. We regard this act as a gross outrage on the rights of Congress and on open violation of law."

JULY 11. To demonstrate why "none could immediately, and very few after an apprenticeship of several years, be properly qualified" to be Librarian of Congress, Watterston outlines the Librarian's duties in the *Washington City Chronicle*: "Custom has rendered it necessary for the Librarian, when called upon by members, to furnish such information as they may require, and which may be obtained in the Library. The mere knowledge of the location of a book is but a small part of his duty. He is frequently called upon for facts, dates, passages, acts, official communications, and even lines of poetry. The Librarian, too, must have a knowledge of bibliography and be able to point out the best and rarest editions, as well as to furnish lists of books to the committee."

JULY 21. Former Congressman Henry Clay consoles Watterston, terming the latter's removal "a step in keeping with the despotism which now rules at Washington," having as a precedent "that act by which the famous Alexandrian library was reduced to ashes." Moreover, the Congressman is "inexpressibly grieved by the reflection

1829

that friendship for me may have been one of the causes which led to the exercise of vengeance upon you." (GW)

1830

JANUARY 9. "For the convenience of readers," Librarian Meehan is instructed to place the latest numbers of periodicals received by the Library on a special table. (WDJ:353)

JANUARY 13. President Jackson approves a joint resolution that grants the use of the books in the Library of Congress to the secretary of state, the secretary of the treasury, the secretary of war, the secretary of the navy, the postmaster general, the secretary of the Senate, the clerk of the House of Representatives, the chaplains of Congress, and "ex-Presidents (when in the District of Columbia)." (4 Stat. 429)

FEBRUARY. At the request of the Joint Library Committee, ex-Librarian Watterston accounts for the books "charged as missing by the Keeper of the Library," an accusation Watterston regards as wholly erroneous. He also explains: "The manuscript catalogue of the Library was given me by Mr. Jefferson, if I could save it from the printer. It was of no use to him or the Library, and I therefore claim it as my property." (GW)

FEBRUARY 9. For the third time in five years, Representative Charles Wickliffe of Kentucky introduces a resolution instructing the Joint Library Committee "to inquire into the expediency of separating the law books from the other books in the Library of Congress and placing them under the superintendence of the Supreme Court." (WDJ:248)

FEBRUARY 15. The National Journal opposes Wickliffe's proposal because "the members themselves are often in want of books of jurisprudence, and should not be deprived of those which are now in the Library of Congress."

MARCH 13. The Joint Library Committee votes to deposit surplus books with the Washington Library Company, the city's only circulating library. The volumes will be returned to the Library of Congress "when required." (WDJ:400)

MARCH 20. The Library Committee instructs Librarian Meehan to procure Burr's County Atlas of the State of New York and the "best maps of the several States" not already in the Library. (WDJ:340)

APRIL 28. In a speech of the House of Representatives, Congressman John Holmes of Maine continues the criticism of President Jackson's removal of Watterston: "The greatest outrage of all is that the President has invaded our dominions and actually removed, and in the recess too, an officer of the two Houses of Congress!" (Register of Debates 6:393)

MAY 21. Obadiah Rich, 12 Red Lion Square, London, is designated to purchase the English books on a list recently prepared by the Library Committee. He is also authorized to purchase "at his discretion, valuable books not contained in the Library nor in said list, to an amount not exceeding £100 sterling." (WDJ:226)

JULY 26. Librarian Meehan reports to Chairman Everett: "We are still engaged in cleaning the books and arranging them for the catalogue. I find it a very laborious task this warm season. The mercury in our thermometer stands at 90° this moment (2 P.M.) and has not been below 82° during the last two weeks." (GW)

1831

MARCH 1. The Library Committee agrees "that each member of the Committee be authorized, during the recess, to make purchases for the Library on his own selection and judgment to any amount not exceeding $50." (GW)

1832

MARCH 31. The Library Committee instructs Meehan to "strictly enforce" the rule that all visitors to the Library should be introduced by a member of Congress. (WDJ:376)

1832

JUNE 23. The Library Committee authorizes Meehan "to visit the public libraries at Baltimore, Philadelphia, New York, West Point, and Boston to instruct himself in their modes of managing libraries for preservation, exhibition, use, etc." His "reasonable expenses for traveling" will be paid out of the Library fund.

(WDJ:214)

JULY 14. President Jackson approves "an act to increase and improve the law department of the Library of Congress." The Librarian is instructed to prepare a separate "apartment" for the law collection. The justices of the Supreme Court, who "shall have free access to the said law library," are empowered to make rules and regulations for the use of the collection provided that those rules do not restrict the access of the President or Vice President or of members of Congress. A separate appropriation for the purchase of lawbooks is established: $5,000 will be spent "for the present year" and a "further annual sum of one thousand dollars" for the next five years. The Librarian shall purchase the books "under such directions, and, pursuant to such catalogue as shall be furnished him by the Chief Justice of the United States." Section three of the act clearly states, however, "that the law library shall be part of the Library of Congress." (4 Stat. 579)

1834

JUNE 19. The President approves a joint resolution of Congress which stipulates that 25 copies of every work printed by "order or at the expense of the United States" will be placed at the disposition of the Library Committee to be disposed of in return for donations to the Library.

(4 Stat. 743)

1835

JANUARY 31. The Library Committee votes not to sponsor a petition from William Elliot proposing the publication of his list "of all the books deposited for copyright in the Department of State, alphabetically and analogically arranged." (WDJ:372)

FEBRUARY 21. A writer in a local literary magazine, the *Champagne Club*, criticizes the use of the Library—which is conveniently located between the two Houses of Congress—as a society meeting place: "Almost thrown into asphyxia, a few days ago, by the upas eloquence of a member from the far West, I instinctively sought the Library of Congress as a means of relief. A group of laughing, chatting ladies were *nonchalantly* turning over the elephant sheets of Audubon's ornithology; a sort of *obligato* amusement, like a flute accompaniment in a concerto, for all the fashionable idlers, who put to test the urbanity of the Librarian." (WDJ:381)

1836

JANUARY 16. The Library Committee directs Librarian Meehan to subscribe to all the newspapers of Washington City "not yet taken."

(WDJ:346)

JANUARY 30. In an address before the American Historical Society, Secretary of War Lewis Cass advocates the expansion of the Library "in *all* the departments of human learning, as will render it worthy of the age and country, and elevate it to an equality with those great repositories of knowledge which are among the proudest ornaments of modern Europe."

(LCA)

MARCH 15. The Library Committee recommends the purchase of the 25,000-volume personal library of the "late Count Bourtoulin of Florence," which is being offered at "fifty or sixty thousand dollars." This noted collection of early Italian, Greek, and Latin works includes "419 copies of Aldine editions, 368 from the Bodoin press, and many hundred volumes printed in the fifteenth century." Committee Chairman William C. Preston, Senator from South Carolina, notes that "it is most complete in those departments where the library of Congress is deficient, particularly the ancient authors, belles lettres, literary history, the fine arts, and the standard productions of France and Italy." Senator Preston strongly urges its purchase, citing Jefferson's "very wise and pointed statement that there was 'no subject to which a member of Congress may not have occasion to refer.'" (24/1 SR 242:2–5)

1836

JUNE 4. With a vote of "ayes 16, noes 17," the Senate rejects the purchase of the Bourtoulin library. On the motion of Henry Clay, who voted with the majority, the resolution is "laid on the table." (CG 24/1:422)

1837

JANUARY 10. The first exchange of official publications with foreign nations is authorized by the Library Committee. The Librarian is authorized to "exchange Gales and Seaton's State Papers . . . and other public documents with the French Government." (WDJ:253-54)

MARCH 3. President Jackson approves an act which appropriates, for the next fiscal year, $5,000 for the purchase of lawbooks. Included is a stipulation that the chief justice of the United States shall furnish a catalog of the law collection. (5 Stat. 163)

NOVEMBER 13. An anonymous letter to the *National Intelligencer* criticizes the arrangement of the Library's published catalog: "The supplements to the present catalogue are growing much too numerous and embarrassing; but by far the most important reason for an entirely new catalogue is the very imperfect character of the present one. The principle on which it is framed is defective, not to say preposterous. . . . The method followed has been the very difficult one of a classification of the subject-matter—a method frequently doubtful, and always perplexed and embarrassing, and which is followed by a list of authors, attempted to be adapted to it. Now, let the inverse order be followed, and all will be found lucid and harmonious."

1838

JULY 9. President Martin Van Buren approves an act of Congress that authorizes the Joint Library Committee to publish the papers of James Madison, which have been deposited in the Department of State library. (5 Stat. 309)

1839

FEBRUARY 15. The Senate approves a resolution directing the Librarian to prepare "a catalogue of all the laws and of all the legislative and executive journals and documents of the several States and Territories now in the Library." Its sponsor, Senator William Allen of Ohio, explains: "It is a remarkable fact that you can lay your hands on all the proceedings of the English Parliament in our Library, and yet you can not find the journals and public documents complete of any State in the Union." (CG 25/3:196)

1840

JUNE 5. The Joint Library Committee reports favorably on a memorial of Alexandre Vattemare of Paris regarding the establishment of a system of international exchange of public documents. The committee emphasizes that "it is very desirable that we should have the means within the reach of Congress of as minute a knowledge as authentic records can furnish in regard to foreign governments." (26/1 SD 521)

JULY 20. President Martin Van Buren approves a joint resolution of Congress that authorizes the exchange of duplicate documents and books for their equivalents in foreign countries. (5 Stat. 409)

1841

JANUARY 14. The President approves a joint resolution of Congress directing that one copy of the catalog of the Library of Congress "be presented to each of the incorporated universities, colleges, athenaeums, and historical societies in the United States, not exceeding three hundred in number, and to the American Antiquarian Society." (WDJ:367)

1842

FEBRUARY 19. The House of Representatives approves a joint resolution passed the previous day by the Senate that authorizes the removal of the Law Library from the main Library to a room on the floor below—on the ground floor and near the Supreme Court. (CG 27/2:255)

MARCH 11. Library Committee Chairman Preston asks historian George Bancroft to recommend book purchases for the Library since "we have a very scant bibliographical store of knowledge on the committee." (LCA)

1842

AUGUST 26. President John Tyler approves an act authorizing the publication of "an account of the discoveries made by the Exploring Expedition under the command of Lieutenant Wilkes," under the direction of the Joint Library Committee. The committee is also placed in charge of the "objects of natural history" gathered by Wilkes.

(5 Stat. 534)

1843

JANUARY 20. The President approves an act of Congress that authorizes the distribution of copies of the Library's printed catalog "to each of the colleges and universities in the United States that has not already been furnished with the same and to each person entitled to the use of the Library."

(5 Stat. 648)

OCTOBER 9. Meehan sends the Library's New York Customs House agent a personal check for $11.93 to pay "for books from London and Havre" during the months of August and September 1843. The Librarian explains that the usual cashier's check is not being sent because "my messenger is sick and we are all so busy in the Library, fitting it up, that I have not been able to get down to the Bank myself."

(LCA-L)

1844

JANUARY 3. An anonymous letter to the *National Intelligencer* suggests that the Library remain open daily even during congressional recess and that its usual closing time of 3 P.M. be extended: "Would it not be liberal and better comport with the spirit of the times if Congress would appoint one or two assistant librarians and otherwise make provision which would render the National Library accessible at all hours and until 8 o'clock at night to all persons employed in the Departments?"

JUNE 7. The Joint Library Committee rejects the proposed purchase of the 10,000-volume library of the Durazzo family of Genoa—one of the choicest private libraries of Europe. On behalf of the committee, Representative George P. Marsh of Vermont reports that although "it would be a highly desirable acquisition to a well endowed literary institution, it is not . . . suited to the purposes of Congress."

(28/1 HRR 553)

1844

JUNE 7. Representative Marsh and the Library Committee recommend governmental support for a National Institute for the Promotion of Science, noting that the city of Washington "as the seat of the National Government, and its consequent exemption from the influence of sectional partialities and jealousies, is indicated as the most favorable point in our country for the formation of a national museum."

(28/1 HRR 368)

1845

JANUARY 8. Senator Rufus Choate, chairman of the Joint Library Committee, argues in favor of establishing the projected Smithsonian Institution as the national library, since the small annual appropriation allowed the Library of Congress could never enable it "to fulfill the functions of a truly great and general public library of science, literature and art."

(CG 28/2:105–6; WDJ:410)

1846

MARCH 3. Senator James A. Pearce of Maryland, the new Joint Library Committee chairman, reports favorably on a plan of lawyer Thomas F. Gordon to compile and publish "a series of indices to the congressional records, comprehending the executive documents, reports of the committees, and journals of both houses of Congress." Senator Pearce terms the existing indices "entirely insufficient . . . being crude, meagre, and deficient."

(29/1 SR 84)

APRIL 23. Representative George Perkins Marsh, in his speech on the bill for establishing the Smithsonian Institution, points out that the collection of the Library of Congress has "been almost wholly purchased and selected from the best European sale catalogues, and yet there is no one branch of liberal study . . . in which it is not miserably deficient."

(CG 29/1:852–53)

AUGUST 10. President James Polk approves an act of Congress that establishes the Smithsonian Institution, "for the

increase and diffusion of knowledge among men." A Board of Regents will govern the institution and make, from the interest of the bequest of James Smithson, "an appropriation not exceeding an average of twenty-five thousand dollars annually, for the gradual formation of a library composed of valuable works pertaining to all departments of human knowledge." One section of the act authorizes the Library of Congress, along with the Smithsonian Institution, to receive as a deposit one copy of each copyrighted "book, map, chart, musical composition, print, cut, or engraving."

(9 Stat. 102)

1846

1847

JANUARY 25. A Board of Regents committee considering the organization of the Smithsonian Institution agrees on a compromise regarding the development of a large library; a collection of 100,000 volumes is planned, despite the committee's "own deliberate conviction that a library of more than half that size could not, with the present means of our Institution, advantageously be purchased."

(1847 SAR:24)

1848

JUNE 26. The President approves an act authorizing the Joint Library Committee to establish exchange agencies for participation in a large-scale system for the exchange of public documents.

(9 Stat. 240)

JULY 25. The Joint Library Committee appoints Alexandre Vattemare to be its agent in "carrying into effect" the newly authorized donation and international exchange system, which will have its headquarters in Paris.

(13/1 HRMD 99)

AUGUST 4. The Library Committee authorizes Librarian Meehan to purchase "all the constitutions and laws of Mexico, and also to subscribe for a newspaper published in Vera Cruz and for one published in the City of Mexico."

(WDJ:247)

AUGUST 4. Senator Pearce informs Joseph Henry, secretary of the Smithsonian Institution, that the Joint Library

James Alfred Pearce (1805–1862), senator from Maryland and chairman of the Joint Committee on the Library from 1845 until his death. Senator Pearce was devoted to the Library and exercised tight control over its operations, even selecting the books for its collections. According to the Reminiscences (1886) of Washington journalist Ben Perley Poore, in 1857 Pearce refused to order the newly established Atlantic Monthly for the Library for fear of engendering "sectional differences" between the North and the South. LC-USZ62-61725

Charles Coffin Jewett (1816–1868), Librarian of the Smithsonian Institution from 1847 until 1854, when he was dismissed by Smithsonian Secretary Joseph Henry. Jewett attempted to develop the Smithsonian into a national library and bibliographic center; the keystone in his plan was to be a centralized cataloging system for American libraries based on the distribution of catalog entries produced at the Smithsonian from stereotype plates. LC–USZ62–13081

1848

Committee has subscribed $250 for a bibliographic account of books relating to or printed in America before 1700, which the Smithsonian proposes to sponsor and which is to be prepared by Henry Stevens, an American-born book-dealer in London, under the title Bibliographia Americana. Senator Pearce adds, however, that for this sum the committee also expects Stevens to include "such books on America, in the Library of Congress, as are within the period proposed by him."

(1848 SAR:60)

AUGUST 12. President Polk approves an act of Congress that authorizes the Joint Library Committee to "print and publish" the papers and manuscripts of Thomas Jefferson and Alexander Hamilton.

(9 Stat. 284)

NOVEMBER 22. Librarian Meehan informs chairman Pearce: "Mr. Vattemare was in the Library yesterday and took leave of me. He said he was going to S. Carolina and intended to visit Canada, but would not again visit Washington. He wanted to know how he should draw the remaining money appropriated for his exchanges, and I advised him that it could be done only on your order, but at the same time told him not to annoy you with his wants. He said, therefore, that he would write to me, and present his wishes in that way to you. I agreed to his proposal, as he would annoy us both if I did not."

(LCA–L)

DECEMBER 13. Smithsonian Librarian Charles Coffin Jewett presents a list of about 3,000 bibliographies for purchase: "by procuring the books necessary for carrying out the plan of making the library a center of bibliographical reference we shall furnish one class of books most immediately important to American scholars. . . . to place American students on a footing with those of the most favored country of Europe is the design of the Smithsonian library."

(1848 SAR:42–43)

1849

MAY 8. Testifying in London before the Select Committee on Public Libraries of the House of Commons, book dealer Henry Stevens assures the committee that the

1849

Library of Congress "is free to all the world," that any "stranger" or "native of the United States of any class" may walk right in. *Report From the Select Committee on Public Libraries; Together With the Proceedings of the Committee, Minutes of Evidence, and Appendix* (London: The House of Commons, 1849), p. 98.

1850

JANUARY 1. In a survey of American libraries, issued as an appendix to the 1849 Smithsonian annual report, Jewett finds the 84,000-volume Harvard University library to be the largest in the United States. With its collection of 50,000 volumes, the Library of Congress ranks second—along with the Boston Atheneum, the Library Company of Philadelphia, and Yale. (1849 SAR:A3–A191)

JANUARY 2. Jewett points out the value of a comprehensive collection of copyright deposits: "To the public the importance, immediate and prospective, of having a central depot, where all the products of the American press may be gathered year by year and preserved for reference, is very great." He also describes his major goal, which is to secure, through the Smithsonian, "a general uniformity among the various libraries in the preparation of catalogs; and to establish a system of *stereotyping them by separates titles*; which will enable each library to print annual editions of its catalogue; incorporating the titles of the last accessions to the collection; and which will enable us, by means of the same titles, to print a general catalogue of all the libraries." (1849 SAR:35–37)

FEBRUARY 12. President Zachary Taylor approves a joint resolution that authorizes the Library Committee to acquire the manuscript of Washington's Farewell Address "if the purchase of it can be effected on fair and just terms." On the same day, the manuscript is purchased at an auction by James Lenox of New York for $2,300. (9 Stat. 560; WDJ:34?)

FEBRUARY 13. The Joint Library Committee orders Meehan to purchase immediately "all works of any reputation touching the modern history, existing conditions, and prospects of Hungary and Germany." (WDJ:247)

1850

AUGUST 16. Secretary Henry asks six "literary" gentlemen—Edward Everett, Charles Folsom, George Livermore, Joseph G. Cogswell, Samuel F. Haven, and Edward E. Hale—to examine Jewett's plan "to form a general catalogue of the various libraries of the United States." Two propositions are to be studied, "a plan for stereotyping catalogues of libraries by separate titles in a uniform style," and "a set of general rules to be recommended for adoption by the different libraries of the United States in the preparation of their catalogues." (1850 SAR:80)

SEPTEMBER 30. President Millard Fillmore approves an act of Congress that increases the annual appropriation for the purchase of lawbooks to $2,000. (9 Stat. 523)

OCTOBER 26. The commission appointed by Secretary Henry reports favorably on both of Jewett's proposals—the stereotyped catalog plan and the system of uniform cataloguing rules. In order that "a beginning might be made in the execution of the plan under circumstances highly favorable to its success," the commission recommends that the Smithsonian regents obtain permission to "prepare a catalogue of the library of Congress" according to Jewett's plan. The commissioners note that "an alphabetical catalog of this library is now very much wanted," and is now "a matter of absolute necessity." Moreover, such a step would "afford the best opportunity for commencing an arrangement by which the various libraries of the country will be brought into a mutually beneficial connection with each other on the plans proposed by Professor Jewett." (1850 SAR:81–83)

1851

DECEMBER 24. Librarian Meehan writes Senator Pearce: "It is my melancholy duty to inform you that a fire originated in the principal room of the Library of Congress this morning, about half past seven o'clock, and that nearly everything in the room was destroyed before the flames were subdued." The fire destroyed approximately 35,000 of the Library's 55,000 volumes, including nearly two-thirds of Jefferson's library.

DECEMBER 25. In a lengthy article about the fire, the *National Intelligencer* reports: "The contents only of the principal hall were consumed, the north room and the law library not having been visited by the fire owing to the thickness of the intervening walls. . . . We must express our unqualified admiration for and warm thanks to the firemen and other citizens who, in such a freezing night, turned out to save from destruction, if possible, the property of their fellow-citizens, and with an energy and perseverance beyond all praise continued their exertions till noon the next day, when the fire at the Capitol was at length subdued."

(LCA-L)

DECEMBER 26. After changing its wording from "the National Library" to "the Library of Congress," the House of Representatives approves a joint resolution authorizing an investigation into the origin of the fire.

(CG 32/1:153–54)

DECEMBER 27. Architect of the Capitol Thomas U. Walter reports that the fire was caused by faulty chimney flues and that "no human forethought or vigilance could, under the circumstances, have prevented the catastrophe."

(*Washington Republic*)

DECEMBER 29. Librarian Meehan explains that the Library's copy of "Birds in America," which was "selected for us by Mr. Audubon and bound . . . under his own care and supervision," fortunately was "saved and uninjured."

(LCA-L)

JANUARY 10. *To-Day: A Boston Literary Journal*, edited by Charles Hale, reports: "They celebrated the Christmas holidays at Washington by burning up the Congress Library—a valuable collection of miscellaneous and law books. . . . Valuable as it was, there were circumstances attending its collection which diminish the feeling of regret for it. It was collected by different committees,—of course without any continued system, and it exhibited quite curiously the whims of Congresses and Congressmen. . . . Any private person, with the $250,000 spent for this Library, would have had a collection of four times its value. But 'Uncle Sam' never gets his money's worth."

(10 Stat. 1)

JANUARY 13. President Fillmore approves an appropriation of $5,000 "in discharge of the expenses incurred in the extinguishment of the late fire in the Library Room," and $10,000 for the purchase of books to replace those lost in the fire.

(10 Stat. 1)

JANUARY 15. Meehan sends a list of desired books to the firm of Rich Brothers in London, informing his agents that at a recent meeting of the Library Committee "it was decided to commence operations, without delay, for restoring the Library to its great usefulness, and for extending it in every department of literature." He also warns the booksellers that "you have great competition here . . . and we expect that you will maintain in our approaching dealings the superiority that your house has maintained for promptness, accuracy, cheapness, and fidelity."

(LCA-L)

JANUARY 23. President Fillmore approves an act appropriating $1,200 to provide a temporary room for the Library.

(10 Stat. 1)

JANUARY 27. Architect of the Capitol Walter presents a plan for the repair and enlargement of the Library. The cost will be $72,500. Because of the "irreparable loss the country has sustained by the destruction of the old Library," fireproof materials are to be used throughout. The new Library will "embrace the entire western projection" of the Capitol.

(32/1 SR 63)

MARCH 10. Impatient with the normal parliamentary pace, Representative Thomas Clingman of North Caro-

1851

1852

lina argues: "We ought certainly to make an appropriation for the Library. We all feel the want of it, and we had better make an appropriation at once, and let the men go to work." (cg 32/1:710)

MARCH 19. President Franklin Pierce approves an appropriation of $72,500 for the "repair of the Congressional library room, which was lately destroyed by fire." The work shall "be subject to such a modification of the details as may be consistent with the general arrangements of the plan, and necessary and proper in the opinion of the President of the United States." (10 Stat. 2)

APRIL 14. An anonymous contributor to the *National Intelligencer* expresses doubt that the Library of Congress should become "the great library of reference and research for the country—the National Library." The writer speculates that "it would be difficult, perhaps it would defeat its chief end, to subject it to the regulations which would be indispensable to the proper conducting of a National Library."

AUGUST 20. In his annual report, Secretary Henry warns that, with reference to the Smithsonian library, "the idea ought never to be entertained that the portion of the limited income of the Smithsonian fund which can be devoted to the purchase of books will ever be sufficient to meet the needs of the American scholar." In fact, Henry looks to a restored Library of Congress—rather than the Smithsonian—as the appropriate foundation for "a collection of books worthy of a Government whose perpetuity principally depends upon the intelligence of the people." (1851 SAR:22)

AUGUST 31. President Pierce approves an appropriation of $75,000 for the purchase of books for the Library "and for the contingent expenses thereof, and for purchase of furniture." The same measure repeals the foreign exchange act of June 26, 1848. (10 Stat. 76)

DECEMBER 18. Meehan describes the operations of the Library to W. A. Adamson, a Canadian librarian. The Library has a staff of five and is open every day when Congress is in session, as well as three days a week during the recess. (LCA-L)

DECEMBER 28. Architect Walter reports to the House of Representatives that his original estimate "for the repairs of the Congressional Library" was too low, and that a deficiency appropriation of $20,500 is necessary. (32/2 HRED 18)

MARCH 3. The Library Committee delegates to the Librarian responsibility for preparing lists of books, according to the Library's "chapters or departments," that are needed "for the purpose of collecting a Library for the Congress of the United States on the most complete and systematic plan." (WDJ:308)

MARCH 3. President Pierce approves an appropriation of $3,000 for the preparation and publication of a general catalog which the Library Committee has agreed will be prepared according to the stereotype plate system of Smithsonian Librarian Jewett. (10 Stat. 189)

JUNE 15. Librarian Meehan explains to Vattemare why Congress rescinded the law under which he was appointed the Library's international exchange agent: "The committee have been greatly disappointed in not receiving from the Government of France, or from any other government, through your agency, complete copies of the official reports," as would enable the committee to acquire the same satisfactory knowledge of foreign public affairs "as is given of our public affairs in the printed documents of the United States." (LCA-L)

JULY 6. Assistant Librarian Stelle reports to Meehan that President Pierce, in the company of British scientist Sir Charles Lyell, inspected the nearly completed new Library

The new Library room, restored "in the most elegant manner" following the disastrous fire of December 24, 1851, was opened on August 23, 1853. Designed by Architect of the Capitol Thomas U. Walter, the new Library in the west front of the Capitol was said to be "the largest room made of iron in the world." It measured 91 feet long, 34 feet wide, and 38 feet high. Each of the galleries encircling the room was 9 feet 6 inches high, rendering the use of stepladders unnecessary. According to historian William Dawson Johnston, "The furniture of the new room was made expressly for the Library, in harmony with the surroundings; the coloring of the room, of the pilasters and panels was a neutral hue tinged with pale green and burnished with gold leaf." LC-USZ62-1818

24

APRIL 21. Representative John Taylor of New York complains to the House that the Library is too lax in enforcing its own rules, specifically that one copy of each work be kept "*constantly* therein," and that all books be returned "within a definite time." (CG 33/1:963)

1854

MAY 20. A special committee of the Smithsonian Board of Regents chaired by Senator Pearce, who serves on the board as well as on the Joint Library Committee, concludes its investigation of whether the Smithsonian funds should be spent on a large library. By a 6 to 1 vote, the committee agrees: "The 'increase and diffusion of knowledge among men' are the great purposes of this munificent trust. . . . Neither of these purposes could be accomplished or materially advanced by the accumulation of a great library . . . (this) would be the *hiving* of knowledge, not its increase and diffusion." (*Proceedings of the Board of Regents up to July 8, 1854;* 1853 SAR:83)

MAY 31. President Pierce approves a $1,700 appropriation to purchase Spanish and Mexican lawbooks. (10 Stat. 290)

MAY 31. The President approves a $5,000 appropriation for the preparation of the stereotype catalog. (10 Stat. 290)

JULY 8. By a vote of 6 to 4, the Smithsonian Board of Regents affirms the power of Secretary Henry "to remove" his assistants. (*Proceedings of the Board of Regents up to July 8, 1854;* 1853 SAR:96)

JULY 10. Secretary Henry dismisses Jewett. (1854 SAR:21)

JULY 27. Hector Bossange, a Paris bookdealer, is appointed as the first Library purchase agent on the European continent. (WDJ:351)

1853

room "a few days ago," and Sir Charles pronounced it "the most beautiful room in the world." (LCA-L.)

AUGUST 23. The new fireproof Library is opened in the west front of the Capitol, adjacent to the rotunda. (LCA)

SEPTEMBER 16. Jewett tells the first national conference of librarians, meeting in New York City, that "a great central library is an important national object; as necessary to secure the literary independence of this people as was the war of the Revolution to secure its political independence." (*Norton's Literary Gazette* 3:172)

SEPTEMBER 17. The Librarians' convention unanimously adopts a resolution stating that "in no way can the government better promote the progress of learning through the whole country than by placing a central national library under the administration of the Smithsonian Institution." (*Norton's Literary Gazette* 3:175)

1854

JANUARY. The Library of Congress catalog prepared according to Jewett's stereotyped block system is published. Only the first chapter in the Library's classification scheme, Ancient History, is included. (LCA)

MARCH 30. A memorial from the American Association for the Advancement of Science is presented by Senator Everett and referred to the Library Committee. Prepared in response to the association's August 1853 resolution on the subject, the memorial advocates "a geographical library" at the Library of Congress, pointing out that "there is not in the United States nor on this continent a single collection of geographical materials which is even tolerably complete." Signers include Alexander D. Bache, superintendent of the U.S. Coast Survey, Matthew F. Maury, superintendent of the Naval Observatory, geographer A. H. Guyot, historian Peter Force, and Lieutenant Edward B. Hunt of the U.S. Army, originator of the proposal. (CG 33/1:789; WDJ:340-46)

1854

AUGUST 4. The President approves an act of Congress which increases the annual salary of the Librarian of Congress to $1,800.

(10 Stat. 546)

1855

FEBRUARY 6. After studying the expenditure of Smithsonian funds, the Senate Judiciary Committee supports Secretary Henry. Furthermore, it asserts that if money were to have been appropriated to collect an "immense library at Washington," it would "have been far better to buy the books and place them at once in the Congress Library."

(1855 SAR:84)

FEBRUARY 15. While the Smithsonian controversy continues, Norton's Literary Gazette takes an optimistic view regarding the eventual creation of a national library "on a far more secure and extended basis than that of the Smithsonian endowment," maintaining: "Let the matter be properly brought before our National Legislature, and the same liberality will be evinced that has been so freely displayed for the encouragement of scientific and geographical expeditions." (Norton's Literary Gazette, n.s., 2:67)

1857

MARCH 3. The President approves an increase in the annual salary of the Librarian to $2,160.

(10 Stat. 643)

JANUARY 28. President Pierce approves a joint resolution that transfers responsibility for the international exchange of books and documents and for the distribution of public documents, heretofore functions of the Library of Congress, to the State Department and the Bureau of Interior, respectively.

(11 Stat. 253)

JUNE 12. The Joint Library Committee rejects a resolution which would extend borrowing privileges to the judges and solicitor of the Court of Claims, noting: "The list of those who are entitled to take books from the Library of Congress is very large; and the privilege is often abused by those who are entitled to it, using it for the supply of others than themselves and their own families."

Senator Pearce points out, however, that visitors are permitted in the Library and that they are "allowed the use of books by reading them while there, and the means of making notes of what they read are readily furnished. They are also cheerfully aided by the Librarian and assistants in making researches."

(35/1 SR 328)

1857

JUNE 21. Meehan informs Edward G. Allen, 12 Tavistock Row, Covent Garden, that he has been appointed the Library's London acquisitions agent—and thus the Library's principal source of books.

(LCA-L)

1859

FEBRUARY 5. President James Buchanan approves an act of Congress that repeals the copyright deposit provision of the act of August 10, 1846. The deposit amendment, which had no enforcement provision, was largely ineffective. The repeal was urged by Secretary Henry and agreed to by Librarian Meehan.

(11 Stat. 379; LCA; QJ 28:121)

1860

DECEMBER. The Law Library is moved into the old room of the Supreme Court, on the east side of the Capitol basement.

(WDJ:250)

1861

MARCH 8. Library Committee Chairman Pearce informs newly elected President Abraham Lincoln that for the last 15 years the President "has always deferred to the wishes of Congress" regarding the appointment of the Librarian of Congress, and that the present wish of the Library Committee is to retain Librarian Meehan and his entire staff. Pearce trusts these "men of books" will be "unaffected by political changes & safe from the influence of political partisanship which has heretofore had no influence in the Republic of letters." Pearce's statement is endorsed by Senators William P. Fessenden and Jacob Collamer of the Library Committee.

(Abraham Lincoln Papers, Library of Congress)

MAY 24. President Lincoln appoints a political supporter, John G. Stephenson, a physician from Terre Haute,

1861

Ind., to be Librarian of Congress. He also appoints as his secretary of the interior Caleb B. Smith, an Indiana Republican, who—together with Indiana Senator Henry S. Lane —had advocated Stephenson's appointment as Librarian.

(LCA; Lincoln Papers, Library of Congress)

MAY 28. Meehan informs London book agent Edward Allen that: "my duties as Librarian of Congress will terminate on the last day of the present month. Your letters of business must therefore be addressed to John G. Stevenson [sic.] Esq. who will be my successor. Your agency will not be in any way disturbed by this change as your appointment is in the hands of the Library Committee."

(LCA-L)

JUNE 3. John G. Stephenson assumes his duties as Librarian. The Library's annual appropriation totals $17,000 and its book collection contains approximately 70,000 volumes.

(LCA)

SEPTEMBER. After dismissing Stelle, Librarian Stephenson hires Ainsworth Rand Spofford, a Cincinnati bookseller and newspaperman, to be the new Assistant Librarian.

(LCA)

SEPTEMBER 25. Chairman Pearce complains to fellow Library Committee member William Pitt Fessenden about the behavior of Librarian Stephenson, who has dismissed most of the old Library employees. Moreover, "the Librarian complains of disorder & neglect in the library, which I think he fancies . . . [and] he is disposed to take too much authority on hand in the purchase of books. He has no right to purchase any book without the order of the Committee or chairman, which I learn he has sometimes done."

(William Pitt Fessenden Papers, Library of Congress)

NOVEMBER. A new general catalog is published. Its arrangement is the same as previous catalogs, but the number of subject subclasses has increased to 175.

(LCA-R)

John G. Stephenson (1828–1883), the fifth Librarian of Congress. Stephenson served from 1861 until the last day of 1864. Photographic portrait by L. C. Handy Studios. LC-USZ62-57283

27

1861

DECEMBER 16. A handwritten annual report for the past year, prepared by Assistant Librarian Spofford, is critical of most aspects of the Library and its operations and solicits the attention of the Joint Library Committee "to repair its deficiencies and to promote its usefulness to those who are entitled to its benefits." An inventory of the Library's 70,000 volumes has revealed over 1,300 missing "or drawn out and unreturned books." Of these, "856 are charged to persons no longer members of Congress or of the Government; 276 volumes are charged to persons belonging to the so-called seceded states."

(LCA)

1862

JANUARY 31. Ralph Waldo Emerson visits the Library. As recorded in Emerson's journal, Assistant Librarian Spofford states that the Library has "been under Southern domination, and as under dead men." This is the reason why the medical and theological collections are so large, while modern literature is "very imperfect." Ralph Waldo Emerson, *Journals*, ed. Edward Waldo Emerson and Waldo Emerson Forbes, vol. 9 (Boston: Houghton Mifflin Company, 1913), pp. 395–96.

MAY 7. The Librarian is authorized to spend a sum not exceeding $100 to procure pamphlets relating to "the present war."

(LCA-M)

1863

JANUARY 7. Another handwritten annual report, this one covering the year 1862 and signed by Librarian Stephenson, contains many concrete proposals for the improvement of the Library. It also asserts that although the Library collection of 79,214 volumes is the fourth largest in the United States, "in its collective value it is second."

(LCA)

MAY–JULY. Librarian Stephenson serves as a volunteer aide-de-camp at the battles of Chancellorsville and Gettysburg.

NOVEMBER. In an article on "The Public Libraries of the United States" published in the *National Almanac and Annual Record for 1864* (Philadelphia: 1864), Assistant

Ainsworth Rand Spofford (1825–1908), who served as the Assistant Librarian from 1861 to 1865, as Librarian of Congress from 1864 to 1897, and as Chief Assistant Librarian from 1897 until his death. More than any other individual, Spofford was responsible for transforming the Library of Congress from a legislative library into an institution of national significance. LC-BH826-452-A

1863

Librarian Spofford asserts: "The United States will never possess a public library which can be called national, until Congress shall take a more liberal view of the value and importance of such a collection." (ARS)

1864

June 13. Spofford informs Assistant Secretary of State William Seward: "If a system of exchange of public documents could be established with the various European Governments, there would accumulate a great mass of material of a kind that would be of great value to Congress. ... The Vattemare Agency, however, was long ago proved to be a failure and a successful exchange must, if at all, be made in some other way." (LCA-L)

June 25. President Lincoln approves an expenditure of $4,000 for "a complete file of selections from European periodicals from 1861 to 1864 relating to the rebellion in the United States." The same act adds a third laborer to the Library's staff, which now totals eight—the Librarian, three Assistant Librarians, three laborers, and one messenger. (13 Stat. 145)

July 2. The President approves an act of Congress that authorizes a $1,000 appropriation to purchase from Edward Everett Hale a collection of 101 manuscript and printed maps relating to the French and Indian War and the American Revolution. The maps formerly belonged to English map publisher William Faden. (13 Stat. 344)

September. The Library's first alphabetical author catalog is published. In the preface, Assistant Librarian Spofford explains that the classified arrangement has been abandoned because "the chief desideratum, next to accuracy of description, is facility of reference, and to this end all minor considerations should be sacrificed." (LCA-R)

October 22. In justifying his budget request for the expansion of the Library, Assistant Librarian Spofford in-

1864

forms the secretary of the treasury that "the sum of $160,-000, although large in itself, is not so in comparison with the great object of providing safe and permanent room for this rich historical collection." He points out that the new reading room of the British Museum cost half a million dollars and that "the Boston Public Library Building cost, exclusive of ground, $240,000." (LCA-L)

November 11. Spofford sends 16 letters—most of them from Senators and Congressmen—to President Lincoln in support of the Assistant Librarian's "fitness for the position of Librarian of Congress, shortly to be vacated." Spofford feels the endorsements are necessary because he has "no special (i.e. recent) political 'claims'—having made it my business to attend to the duties of my position to the engrossment even of my leisure time." (National Archives and Records Service, Record Group 59)

December 22. Spofford forwards to President Lincoln eight letters and a petition signed by Members of Congress endorsing his application for Librarian, explaining that these papers, together with those sent in November, "make up 22 Senators and 87 representatives who have signified their preference in the matter." (National Archives and Records Service, Record Group 59)

December 22. Librarian Stephenson submits his resignation, effective December 31, 1864. (LCA)

December 31. Lincoln appoints Spofford to be the sixth Librarian of Congress. The Library has a staff of seven, a collection of approximately 82,000 volumes, and an annual appropriation of approximately $20,000, which includes $2,000 to purchase lawbooks and $5,000 to purchase books for the general collections. (LCA)

1865

March 1. In his annual report for 1864, Smithsonian Secretary Henry takes note of recent developments at the Library of Congress and ponders "whether, since Congress

1865

has appropriated $160,000 to the enlargement of the accommodation for its own library, it may not be expedient to request that the Smithsonian collection be received and arranged as one of its departments, while the free use and general control of the same shall still be retained by the Institution."

MARCH 2. President Lincoln approves the $160,000 appropriation for the expansion of the Library's room. Two new fireproof wings will be added and the Joint Library Committee will exercise final approval over any modifications in the construction plan.
(1864 SAR:59)

MARCH 3. After a recommendation from the Librarian, the copyright law is changed to require, once again, the deposit of copyrighted materials in the Library of Congress. The law states that one printed copy of every copyrighted "book, pamphlet, map, chart, musical composition, print, engraving, or photograph" must be sent to the Library for its use.
(13 Stat. 540)

OCTOBER 25. Librarian Spofford sends a letter to the officials of eight southern states, asking them to send "copies of your Legislative Documents and Laws to the National Library in Washington."
(LCA-L)

DECEMBER 20. The Library Committee, at Spofford's suggestion, votes that the Librarian "prepare hereafter an annual report of the condition of the Library for the Library Committee."
(LCA-M)

1866

FEBRUARY 8. Spofford sends letters to the governors of 10 northern states requesting that all laws, legislative journals, and official reports published in their states be sent to the Library of Congress.
(LCA-L)

FEBRUARY 21. Representatives of the Library Committee agree to confer "with the sub-committee of the Board of Regents of the Smithsonian Institution upon the proposed

30

Joseph Henry (1797–1878), secretary of the Smithsonian Institution from its founding in 1846 until his death. Henry opposed Charles Coffin Jewett's plans to develop the Smithsonian into a national library, looking instead to the Library of Congress as a more appropriate foundation for such an institution. Henry supported Spofford's efforts in this direction, personally suggesting the transfer of the Smithsonian library to the Library of Congress. Congress approved such a transfer in April 1866. LC-USZ62-14760

1866

removal of the library of that institution to the Capitol, and its incorporation with the Library of Congress."

(LCA-M)

APRIL 5. President Andrew Johnson approves an act of Congress that transfers the 40,000-volume library of the Smithsonian Institution to the Library of Congress. The Smithsonian retains use of the collection "in like manner as it is now used;" the general public shall have access to it "for purposes of consultation." The Smithsonian deposit is especially strong in scientific works and in publications of learned societies.

(14 Stat. 13)

APRIL 7. President Johnson approves a $1,500 appropriation "for purchasing files of leading American newspapers."

(14 Stat. 14)

MAY 26. Spofford asks historian George Bancroft, American minister to Germany: "What, in your opinion, would be the reasonable pecuniary value of the Force Library, including . . . the MS materials for the American Archives, if purchased by the Government?"

(LCA)

JUNE 6. Bancroft replies, informing the Librarian that $100,000 was a "liberal price, but not extravagant" for Peter Force's personal library of Americana. Moreover, "such a collection can never again be made and therefore it is of the utmost importance to secure it. . . . Congress will never again have another such opportunity."

(John A. G. Creswell Papers, Library of Congress)

JULY 25. The President approves the purchase, for $5,000, of the private law library of James L. Petigru of South Carolina.

(14 Stat. 365)

DECEMBER 3. In the first published annual report of the Librarian of Congress, Spofford asserts that the recent acquisition of the Smithsonian library "will insure the rapid growth of a great and truly national library." He also

39TH CONGRESS, } SENATE. { MIS. DOC.
2d Session. { No. 6.

LETTER

FROM

THE LIBRARIAN OF CONGRESS,

TRANSMITTING

His first annual report.

DECEMBER 20, 1866.—Ordered to be printed.

LIBRARY OF CONGRESS,
Washington, December 3, 1866.

SIR: In compliance with the instructions of the Joint Committee of both houses of Congress on the Library, the undersigned has the honor to submit the following report, for the year ending December 1, 1866:

The progress of the new library extension during the vacation of Congress, though not so rapid as was expected at the commencement of the work, has resulted in the completion of one entire wing, measuring ninety-five feet in length by thirty feet in width, which is now opened and fully occupied with books. It is expected that the remaining wing will be completed and occupied during the coming month. The modifications of the original plan, heretofore sanctioned by the committee, have added greatly to the architectural effect of both wings of the new library, by reducing the projection of the galleries, and securing additional shelf-room for books. The light and ventilation are superior to those features in the main library, while the economy of space has been so closely consulted in the details as to give an increase of 3,800 linear feet of shelving in each wing, over that which exists in the main library. The total length of iron shelving in the library is now 21,360 feet, which will afford space for about one hundred and seventy thousand volumes. Adding the shelf accommodation of the law library room (formerly occupied by the Supreme Court) and the long attic room communicating with the upper gallery of the main library, the entire length of shelving at command is 26,148 feet, or nearly five miles. These accommodations afford space for the safe-keeping of about 210,000 volumes. The fact that the whole library is now impregnably fireproof, being constructed of solid iron material throughout, and that future accessions to its stores, as well as the present accumulation of valuable works, are secure from a casualty which has twice consumed our national library, is a matter for sincere congratulation.

Librarian Spofford's first annual report was the first annual report of the Librarian of Congress to be published. His reports rarely exceeded five pages in length and always emphasized "the progress of the Library." LCA-R

1866

asks Congress for an amendment to compel publishers to deposit books in compliance with the 1865 copyright law.

(1866 AR:3, 5)

DECEMBER 12. The Library Committee approves new rules proposed by the Librarian: 1) direct access to alcoves and galleries will be limited to members of Congress, except for those alcoves "devoted to light reading"; and 2) all engravings and works of art will be constantly protected and used only with special permission from the Librarian.

(LCA-M)

1867

JANUARY 25. Librarian Spofford presents a detailed report on the contents of archivist Peter Force's unparalleled private library of books, pamphlets, manuscripts, newspapers, and maps. Noting that "the largest and most complete collection of books relating to America in the world is now gathered on the shelves of the British Museum," he challenges Congress to "repair this deficiency" by appropriating $100,000 to purchase the Force library.

(LCA-R)

JANUARY 26. The Library Committee approves the establishment of a small, separate periodical reading room for members of Congress.

(LCA-M)

FEBRUARY 7. The Librarian informs the Library Committee chairman that the annual newspaper appropriation needs to be increased to include the periodicals regularly purchased by the Library: "The wants of Congress for all the leading journals, magazines & reviews covering the departments of law, commerce, finance, & literature require the Librarian to subscribe annually for an increased number."

(LCA-L)

FEBRUARY 18. President Johnson approves an amendment to the copyright law that provides a $25 penalty for failing to deliver copyrighted articles to the Library of Congress within one month of publication. (14 Stat. 395)

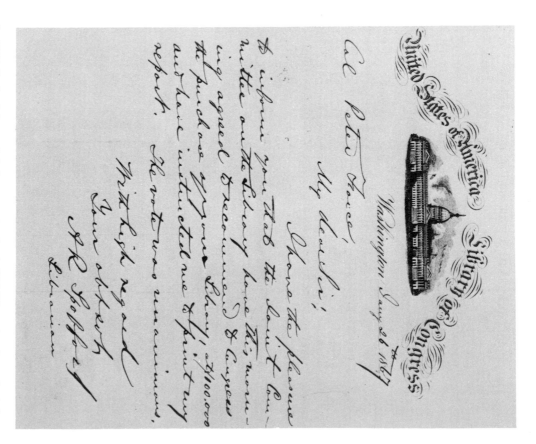

In 1867 Spofford persuaded Congress to spend $100,000 to purchase the private library of Peter Force, which became the foundation of the Library's Americana and incunabula collections. In this letter the Librarian informs Force that the Joint Committee on the Library has recommended the purchase. LCA; LC-USP6-6660.A

1867

JUNE. Spofford charges George Bancroft $25 for the transcription of two of General Nathanael Greene's letter-books in the Force collection. (LCA)

DECEMBER 1. The Librarian reports to Congress that "among the governments which have responded affirmatively to the circular proposing an exchange of government publications are those of Great Britain, Russia, Denmark, Belgium, the Netherlands, Greece, Switzerland, Chile, and Costa Rica." (1867 AR:5)

1868

FEBRUARY 5. When questioned by E. D. Morgan, the new chairman of the Library Committee, Librarian Spofford defends his purchase of De Miller's *Abuses of the Sexual Function*, which was acquired so that the Library could "keep up with the progress of medical science." (LCA)

MARCH 10. Spofford sends Morgan a bill drawn up by the Librarian to "carry out the purpose" of the March 2, 1867, resolution concerning the exchange of public documents with foreign governments. The resolution "has remained inoperative because the Congressional printer did 'not consider that it directed him to print any additions to the documents.'" (National Archives and Records Service, Record Group 128)

JULY 23. The President approves a joint resolution of Congress intended to "carry into effect the resolution approved March 2, 1867," regarding international exchange. (15 Stat. 260)

1869

JUNE. The emperor of China sends a gift of 933 volumes to the U.S. government, a donation that forms the nucleus of the Library's Chinese collection. The volumes were sent in exchange for publications and several varieties of seeds presented to the Chinese government through the U.S. delegation at Peking. (LCA)

OCTOBER 26. Addressing the general meeting of the American Social Science Association in New York City,

1867

FEBRUARY 18. Spofford obtains Library Committee approval for a proposed exchange of government documents with foreign governments "through the already organized agency for exchanges of the Smithsonian Institution; the works obtained in exchange to be placed in the Library of Congress." (LCA-M)

MARCH 2. The President approves a joint resolution stipulating that the Public Printer provide 50 extra copies of U.S. government publications to the Joint Library Committee, which is authorized to exchange those documents —through the Smithsonian Institution distribution system—for public documents published in foreign nations "and especially by foreign governments." The works received from abroad will be deposited in the Library of Congress. (14 Stat. 573)

1868

MARCH 2. The President approves an act of Congress that appropriates funds for the purchase of the Peter Force library, which becomes the foundation of the Library's Americana and incunabula collections. (14 Stat. 457)

MARCH 13. Additional rules are approved by the Library Committee: 1) manuscripts and rare materials may not be withdrawn from the Library by anyone; and 2) persons under 16 years of age will not be permitted to use the Library. (LCA-M)

1869

MAY 16. Smithsonian Institution Secretary Henry distributes a circular to foreign governments informing them that "a law has just been passed by the Congress of the United States authorizing the exchange, under the direction of the Smithsonian Institution, of a certain number of all U.S. official documents for the corresponding publications of other governments throughout the world; the returns to be placed in the National Library at Washington." (1881 SAR:746–48)

Spofford asserts that there are two things the "National Library" still needs "to complete its usefulness. First, the completion (now nearly accomplished) of its printed catalogue of subjects, which will furnish a complete key to unlock its treasures; and secondly, to be thrown open to readers during the evening as well as during the hours of business."

(*Journal of Social Science* 2:11)

NOVEMBER 29. After an extensive survey, Boston Public Library superintendent Justin Winsor determines that the Library of Congress, with a collection of 175,000 volumes, is the largest in the United States.

(Boston Public Library, *Annual Report*: 112–33)

DECEMBER. A two-volume *Catalogue of the Library of Congress; Index of Subjects* is published. In the preface, Spofford explains that: "The one thing needful in a catalogue of subjects is instant facility of reference; and if a scientific arrangement of topics is sometimes sacrificed to this end, the student whose time is saved will be little disposed to quarrel with the bridge that carries him safely over."

(LCA-R)

DECEMBER 1. Spofford reports to Congress that he has been forced to depart from his usual cataloging procedure because of the "heavy accessions of pamphlets acquired with the Force collection and the Smithsonian library"; instead of being prepared for the printed catalog, these pamphlets have been cataloged on cards. He also notes that the hours of the Library have been extended: it is now open every weekday from 9 A.M. to 4 P.M., even when Congress is not in session.

(1869 AR:2, 4)

FEBRUARY 24. By a vote of 4 to 1, the Library Committee rejects the Librarian's proposal to keep the Library open during the evening.

(LCA-M)

APRIL 9. In a lengthy letter to Representative Thomas A. Jenckes of Rhode Island, chairman of the Committee on Patents, Spofford outlines "some leading reasons why the

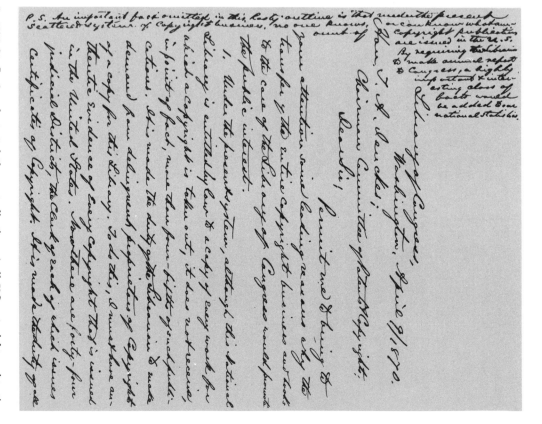

In 1870 Spofford orchestrated the centralization of all U.S. copyright registration and deposit activities at the Library of Congress, viewing copyright deposit as the most practical method of acquiring a comprehensive collection of American publications. The Librarian states his case in this letter to Representative Thomas A. Jenckes of Rhode Island. LCA

1870

transfer of the entire copyright business to the Library of Congress would promote the public interest." In the Librarian's view, "the advantage of securing to our only National Library a complete collection of all copyright entries can scarcely be over-estimated. . . . We should have one comprehensive library in the country, and that belonging to the country, whose aim it should be to preserve the books which other libraries have not the room nor the means to procure." (LCA-L)

MAY 20. Educator Francis Lieber donates three volumes to the Library. He inscribes them "To the National Library," and explains to Spofford: "It is not the official name, but I take the liberty. It is the name you have come to. Library of Congress was good enough in Jeffersonian times, but it is not now after the war and for the current age." (ARS)

JULY 8. President Ulysses S. Grant approves an act of Congress that centralizes all U.S. copyright registration and deposit activities at the Library of Congress. The Librarian "shall perform all acts and duties required by law touching copyrights" and the Library will receive two copies of all copyrighted items. The Librarian's salary is raised to $4,000. Pre-1870 copyright records and deposits are also to be sent to the Library. The $25 penalty for failure to forward deposits remains in force. (16 Stat. 198)

1871

MARCH 1. The Library Committee votes to recommend a $25,000 appropriation to purchase 2,000 mounted photographs from "Mr. Brady's historical gallery of portraits." (LCA-M)

DECEMBER 1. Spofford reports to Congress that the increased receipts resulting from the new copyright law "will soon compel the provision of more room for books." As one alternative, he suggests a separate building. (1871 AR:4-5)

1872

FEBRUARY 14. In response to a request from Librarian John Shaw Billings of the Surgeon General's Office, Spofford begins transferring copyright deposits in medical subjects to the Surgeon General's library. (LCA)

FEBRUARY 19. The Library Committee authorizes Spofford to "print a weekly statement of all copyrights entered." At the same meeting, the committee considers a petition of T. N. Hornsby of Kentucky asking Congress to establish a "bureau of poets and poesy," but no action is taken. (LCA-M)

SEPTEMBER 17. Spofford sends a letter to officials of 26 "leading" American cities, asking that copies of their city documents be furnished to the Library; "some of the previous years" are requested, "as well as the current and future publications." (LCA-L)

DECEMBER 2. Spofford points out that severe overcrowding has now made the Library "comparatively an unfit place for students." Furthermore, "without calculating upon specially large accessions," he estimates that the Library will contain 2,500,000 volumes by the year 1975. The Librarian has become convinced of "the absolute necessity of erecting a separate building for the Library and the copyright department conjoined," and therefore presents an "outline of a plan for such an edifice." (1872 AR:6–11)

1873

FEBRUARY 7. The Joint Library Committee reports that "after attentive consideration of the subject-matter," it finds "the question of international copyright attended with grave practical difficulties and of doubtful expediency, not to say of questionable authority." (42/3 SR 409)

MARCH. For the sum of $1,000, the Library purchases a collection of nearly 1,500 books and pamphlets relating to Abraham Lincoln from Andrew Boyd of Albany, N.Y. (LCA)

35

1873

MARCH 3. The President approves an appropriation of $5,000 for a commission which will select a plan and "supervise the location and erection of a building" for the Library of Congress. The same act authorizes a competition to design plans for the structure. (17 Stat. 485)

MARCH 3. President Grant approves an act of Congress that authorizes the publication of French documents relating to the discoveries and explorations made in the United States by the French government from 1614 to 1752. The volumes will be edited by Pierre Margry but published under the direction of the Joint Committee on the Library—and the supervision of Spofford. (17 Stat. 485)

APRIL 23. The Library pays $800 for a copy of John Eliot's *Indian Bible*, which was printed at Cambridge, Mass., in 1663. (LCA)

JUNE 18. Two boxes of U.S. documents are sent to the government of Norway through the Smithsonian Institution exchange system, the first American shipment in compliance with the House resolution of March 2, 1867. (1881 SAR:774)

1874

JUNE 25. Composing two speeches in Cleveland, Congressman James A. Garfield laments in his diary: "Every day I miss Spofford and our great Library of Congress." (Garfield Papers, Library of Congress)

MAY 6. The Library Committee authorizes the Librarian to subscribe to at least two newspapers from each state. These newspapers are to reflect differing political views. (LCA-M)

JUNE 10. Spofford submits a plan to Senator Matthew H. Carpenter, president pro tempore of the Senate, for the compilation of "a complete index of subjects to the documents and debates of the U.S. Congress." (43/1 SMD 125)

JUNE 18. The President approves an amendment to the copyright law transferring responsibility for prints and labels for articles of manufacture from the Library of Congress to the Patent Office. (18 Stat. 78)

JULY. The Library subscribes to more than 100 daily newspapers from throughout the United States. (1901 AR:191)

1875

OCTOBER 1. A Smithsonian circular, sent to the foreign ministers of 26 nations, provides additional details about the international exchange program and stipulates that the Smithsonian Institution, on behalf of the Joint Library Committee, "is prepared to deliver the publications of the United States, free of charge for freight, to any person in the city of Washington, or in New York who may be designated by the governments which enter into the arrangement." (1881 SAR:768–69)

NOVEMBER. The Japanese government accepts the Smithsonian Institution's proposal for the exchange of documents, an event which marks the beginning of the Library's Japanese collection. (LCA)

1876

JANUARY 1. Spofford reports to Congress that the Library has exhausted all shelf space and that "books are now, from sheer force of necessity, being piled upon the floor in all directions." He notes that unless Congress takes quick action on a new Library building, its Librarian soon will be placed "in the unhappy predicament of presiding over the greatest chaos in America." He also urges Congress to authorize the Library to employ "a competent historical scholar," since "it is very important that every manuscript or written paper in the Library which can throw any light on any portion of American history, should be systematically arranged and indexed." (1875 AR:6–10)

MARCH 13. President Grant approves a joint resolution of Congress recommending, on the occasion of "the ap-

On December 23, 1873, the special commission planning a new Library building announced that this Italian Renaissance design submitted by the firm of Smithmeyer & Pelz of Washington, D.C., had won first prize. A total of 27 architects submitted designs, all in accordance with general specifications prepared and issued by Spofford in August 1873. These specifications stated in part: "The general plan of the building will embrace a circular reading room in the center, of one hundred feet diameter, with alcoves radiating from the circumference of the inner circle outward. The exterior walls are to be within a space of 270 by 340 feet. The ele-

vation is not to exceed 60 to 65 feet. . . . No dome nor towers of greater height than 70 feet can be admitted on account of the proximity of the projected building to the Capitol. . . . All parts of the building are to be of fireproof materials, no wood being employed in any part of the structure. . . . The front of the edifice will look out upon a park the dimensions of which are about 500 by 800 feet, lying directly east of the Capitol and having Greenough's statue of Washington in its center." LCA; LC–USZ62–3765

37

To the dismay of Spofford, the results of the 1873 competition were inconclusive; the new Library building was not authorized until 1886, and its final design not approved until 1889. Between 1874 and 1886, Smithmeyer and Pelz, at the request of the Joint Library Committee, submitted drawings in several architectural styles—each appropriate to a different site. This Victorian Gothic design for "the Proposed National Library" was, according to Smithmeyer, "calculated to be erected solitarily on the grand Judiciary Square" near Capitol Hill. LC–USZ62–46793

38

1876

proaching Centennial Anniversary of our National Independence," that local communities "cause to have delivered" historical sketches of their various counties or towns. Copies should be filed both in the county clerk's office and in the Library of Congress, so that "a complete record may thus be obtained of the progress of our institutions during the First Centennial of their existence."
(19 Stat. 211)

MAY 29. Spofford declines to sign a call for a conference of librarians at Philadelphia because he has "always entertained insuperable objections to figuring in conventions (usually mere wordy outlets for impracticables and pretenders)." He does state, however, that he might "find it possible to look in upon the Conference." (ALA archives)

JUNE 8. The Joint Library Committee, chaired by Senator Timothy O. Howe of Wisconsin, reports that the congressional failure to provide "additional accommodations for the National Library" is "absurd . . . almost insane, if not wicked." The committee's report points out that the books stacked on the Library's floors are scarcely more available "than if they were still in the book-stalls from which they were gathered." Moreover, "the evil is constantly growing with each year's accumulations [and] that growth cannot be prevented, even if we refuse further appropriations for the purchase of books." The committee recommends a Library building on the grounds of the Botanic Garden, at the foot of Capitol Hill. (44/1 SR 387)

AUGUST 3. The President approves a joint resolution of Congress which establishes a commission "to have resort to such means as will most effectively restore the writing of the original manuscript of the Declaration of Independence." Commission members are the Librarian of Congress, the secretary of the interior, and the secretary of the Smithsonian Institution.
(19 Stat. 216)

OCTOBER. In an article about reference works published in the Bureau of Education's *Public Libraries in the*

United States, Spofford explains that the "most useful librarian" is the one who helps the reader "put his finger on the fact he wants just when it is wanted." In the Library of Congress, he explains, a good selection of reference books "is placed on shelves in an accessible portion of the main library," while the rest of the 300,000 volumes are stored in alcoves and kept under lock and key. Spofford also contributes, to the same volume, articles on periodicals, binding and preservation, library bibliography, and "The Library of Congress, or National Library."
(19 Stat. 211)

OCTOBER 6. Discussing copyright at the organizational conference of the American Library Association in Philadelphia, Spofford states that two objectives have not yet been attained: a new Library building to house the great increase in accessions and the publication of a periodical list of copyright publications. (LJ 1:89)

1877

JANUARY 12. Librarian Spofford writes the Wisconsin State Historical Society: "This Library is in want of Western Newspapers, as well as of portions of files of many Eastern ones. If you have such to offer in exchanges for any of the List inclosed, please send a memorandum of Journals and prices." (LCA)

JANUARY 31. On behalf of an ALA committee, Melvil Dewey publishes a report on cooperative cataloging that poses the question: "Is it practicable for the Library of Congress to catalogue for the whole country?" (LJ 1:171)

MARCH 3. The President approves an appropriation of $1,000 for the Library of Congress to index the "resolves, ordinances, and acts of the Continental Congress and the Congress of the Confederation" before their publication.
(19 Stat. 406)

JUNE 2. While visiting the Library, President Rutherford B. Hayes arranges for an exchange between the Executive Mansion Library and the Library of Congress. Over 100 volumes of congressional and state documents and

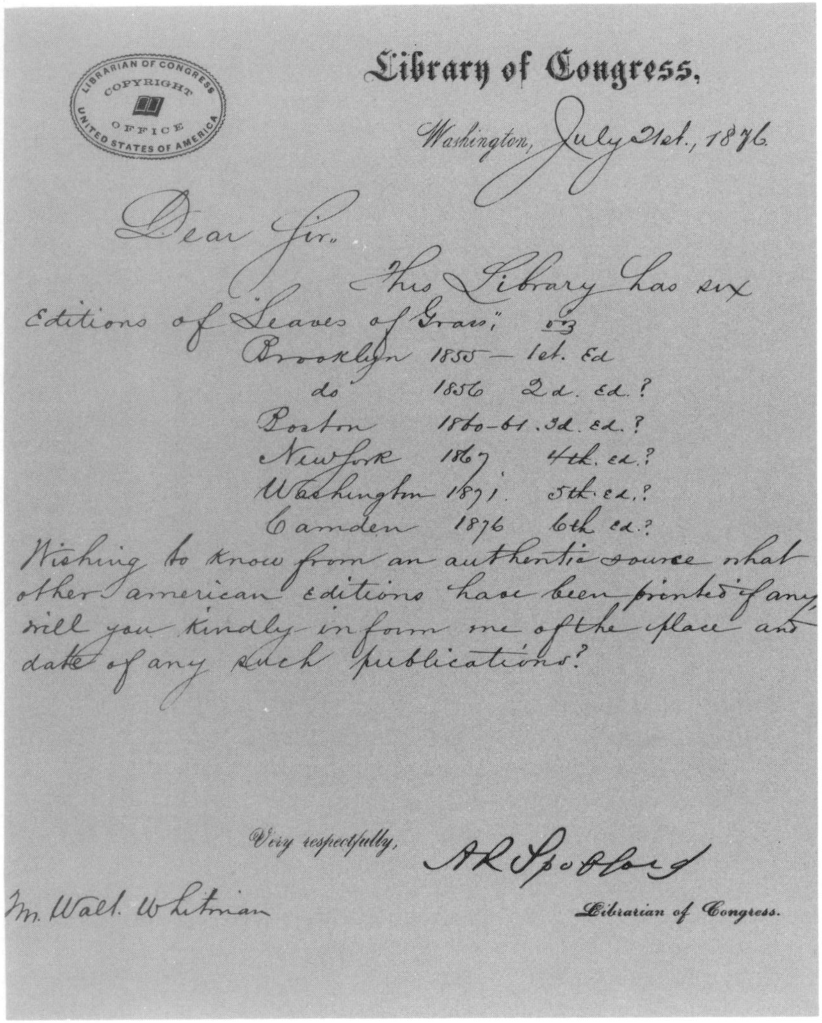

Library of Congress,

Washington, July 21st, 1876

Dear Sir,

The Library has six
Editions of *Leaves of Grass*:

Brooklyn	1855 — 1st Ed.
do	1856 2d. ed.?
Boston	1860–61. 3d. ed.?
New York	1867 4th. ed.?
Washington	1871. 5th ex.?
Camden	1876 6th ex.?

Wishing to know from an authentic source what
other American editions have been printed if any,
will you kindly inform me of the place and
date of any such publication?

Very respectfully,

A R Spofford

Librarian of Congress.

Mr Walt Whitman.

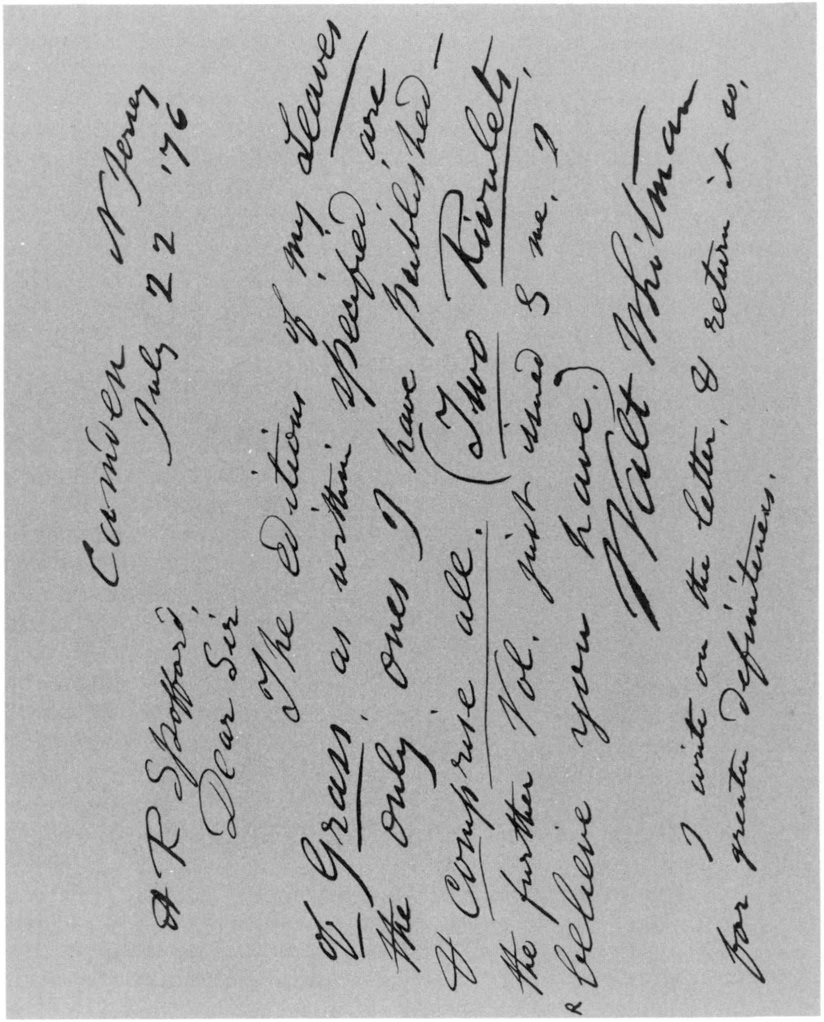

Camden   N Jersey
July 22 '76

A R Spofford
Dear Sir

The Editions of my *Leaves
of Grass*, as within specified, are
the only ones I have published—
& *comprise all*. (Two Rivulets,
the further Vol. just issued to me, I
believe you have.)

Walt Whitman

I write on the letter, & return it so,
for greater definiteness.

By 1876 Spofford was spending most of his time on "the new building question" or on copyright matters. In this letter the Librarian asked "an authentic source" about the various American editions of Leaves of Grass. Whitman replied on the back, noting, "I write on the letter, & return it so, for greater definiteness." ARS; LCMS-40972-2

1877

1,000 pamphlets are transferred to the Library of Congress in exchange for a selection of "Duplicates of Miscellaneous books." (Hayes Papers, Hayes Library, Fremont, Ohio)

DECEMBER 3. In his first annual message, President Hayes recommends that Congress approve construction of a fire-proof Library building, since "the question of providing for the preservation and growth of the Library of Congress is . . . one of national importance." (SUM 2:1354-55)

1878

JANUARY 2. Librarian Spofford complains that "the measure of silence which should be enforced for the protection of readers is rendered impossible for want of space in which members of Congress or other investigators can be isolated from the crowd of sightseers which sometimes throng every public place in the Capitol." He also is politely indignant about congressional delays regarding a separate building, claiming that unless there soon is action, "Congress will hardly be held to have discharged the trust reposed in it as the custodian of what President Jefferson called with prophetic wisdom the Library of the United States." (1877 AR:7-8)

1879

OCTOBER 22. The Library purchases over 2,500 Chinese and Manchu works assembled by Caleb Cushing, the first American minister to China. (LCA)

1880

MARCH 11. Samuel L. Clemens sends his nephew, with a written introduction, "to burrow a little" in Spofford's "grand literary storehouse." (ARS)

MAY 5. Concluding a lengthy speech in which he strongly urges a new Library building, Senator Daniel W. Voorhees of Indiana declares: "Let us therefore give this great national library our love and our care. Nothing can surpass it in importance. Knowledge is power, the power to maintain free government and preserve constitutional liberty. Without it the world grows dark and the human race takes up its backward step to the regions of barbarism. I cannot

1880

believe that the plain and imperative duty of Congress on the subject of its Library will be longer neglected." (CR 10:3004)

1881

JANUARY 6. President-elect Garfield telegraphs Spofford, asking him to send "by Express inaugural addresses of J. Q. Adams, Jackson, Harrison, Polk, Taylor, and Buchanan." The same day, Spofford forwards the addresses of all but the last, explaining that he will "send copy of Buchanan as soon as copied." The Librarian also expresses his "cordial satisfaction that a man of ideas can be & has been elected President of the United States." (Garfield Papers, Library of Congress)

DECEMBER 6. In his first annual message, President Chester A. Arthur urges approval of a new Library building. (SUM 2:1450)

1882

FEBRUARY 20. On behalf of the Library Committee, Senator George F. Hoar of Massachusetts recommends Senate approval of a $20,000 appropriation for the purchase of the military papers, maps, and letterbooks of the comte de Rochambeau—the entire collection to be preserved in the Library of Congress. (47/1 SR 187)

MARCH 13. In response to a request from the Joint Select Committee on Additional Accommodations for the Library, Gen. Montgomery C. Meigs, former engineer of the Capitol extension, states his views regarding "a proposed plan for raising the dome of the Capitol 50 feet, in order to secure additional space in and near the rotunda for the Library." Meigs labels the proposed plan "a dangerous and perhaps fatal enterprise." (47/1 SMD 65)

MARCH 25. In persuading Joseph M. Toner to donate his 40,000-volume private library to the Library of Congress, Spofford writes that although the chairman of the Joint Library Committee, Senator John Sherman, "conceives that there is full power vested in the Committee under existing laws to receive and provide for the separate custody of any donations of books," Senator Sherman nevertheless suggests "that it would be eminently proper that a special act should be passed, recognizing and accepting the gift on behalf of the Government."

(47/1 SR 578)

APRIL 4. The Joint Committee on the Library recommends an $8,000 appropriation to purchase the Supreme Court records and briefs belonging to the estate of the late Senator Matthew H. Carpenter: "It is understood that there are only three sets of these documents in existence, and that they would be of great and constant value in the law department of the Library, for the use and reference of the courts, the bar, and the public."

(47/1 SR 369)

MAY 16. Senator Sherman, on behalf of the Joint Library Committee, reports favorably to the Senate regarding acceptance of the Toner library. Sherman notes that the Toner collection represents "the first instance in the history of this government of the free gift of a large and valuable library to the nation," and expresses the committee's hope that "an example so laudable may be productive of many similar literary and scientific benefactions in the future."

(47/1 SR 578)

MAY 19. President Chester A. Arthur approves a joint resolution of Congress that authorizes the Librarian of Congress to accept the gift of the Toner library.

(22 Stat. 382)

AUGUST 7. The President approves the purchase, from Henry Stevens of London, of the Benjamin Franklin collection. The Library of Congress is to receive the printed books, pamphlets, and newspapers "and one of the typewritten copies of the manuscripts"; the remaining manuscripts are "to be preserved in the Department of State."

(22 Stat. 302)

OCTOBER. The Joint Select Committee on Additional Accommodations for the Library of Congress sends architect

John L. Smithmeyer to Europe to examine the buildings of the British Museum and the "national libraries at Paris, Berlin, Munich, and Vienna and the new library at Rome."

(Paul J. Pelz Papers, Library of Congress)

OCTOBER 26. In an anonymous article in Nation magazine, John Shaw Billings, librarian of the Surgeon-General's Office, attacks Spofford's general plan to consolidate all governmental libraries in the proposed national library building.

(Nation 35:350–51)

JANUARY 29. The Library Committee postpones "consideration of the consolidation of the Army and Medical Museum Library with the Congressional Library." (LCA-M)

MARCH 3. President Arthur approves an act of Congress providing funds for the purchase of the Rochambeau collection of manuscripts and maps and the Carpenter collection of Supreme Court records and briefs. (22 Stat. 603)

AUGUST 15. In a letter to the annual ALA meeting, Spofford states his firm opposition to a plan advocated by Chicago librarian William Frederick Poole for the new Library of Congress building: "I am not willing to have the interior plans of a library building of national importance dwarfed to the dimensions of a prolonged series of packing-boxes."

(LJ 8:270)

A gift of 375 volumes from Sultan Abdul-Hamid II of Turkey establishes the nucleus of the Turkish collection. Acquired through the efforts of Representative Abram S. Hewitt of New York, the volumes each contain the cover inscription, in three languages, "To the national library of the United States of America, through the Honorable A. S. Hewitt . . . 1884 A.D."

(LCA)

JANUARY 30. Spofford notes the acquisition, "without any expense whatever to Library funds," of 3,000 volumes of bound newspapers and nearly 3,000 volumes of govern-

1884

ment documents, transferred from the Department of State and from the War Department. (1883 AR:4–5)

FEBRUARY 7. Senator Justin S. Morrill of Vermont, characterizing the Library as "the property of the nation, open to all the people without any ticket of admission," pleads for a new building, informing the Senate: "Our duty is obvious, and neglect [of the Library] cannot escape reproach." (CR 15:243)

FEBRUARY 23. The Library Committee rejects proposals "from some quarters" to curtail the future growth of the Library because "the Government of the United States is too far committed by the legislation of Congress to the encouragement of literature and fine arts through a system of copyright; because any supposed limitation which should fix the wants of the national legislature for books and information by any arbitrary standard is fallacious and impossible; and because to arrest the progress of this great repository of learning (more than half of which has been gathered without expense to the taxpayers) would be a step backward." (LCA; LCIB April 15–21, 1947)

APRIL 18. The Library Committee votes adversely on a bill which would give copyright protection to newspapers. (LCA-M)

MAY 23. The Library Committee recommends the purchase, through the secretary of state, of copies of documents in European archives relating to the Paris Peace Treaty of 1783. The project of "obtaining copies of all documents in the European archives illustrative of the early history of the United States" will be carried out by B. F. Stevens, U.S. despatch agent in London.
(LCA-M; 48/1 SMD 84)

1885

JANUARY 23. On the motion of Senator Hoar, the Library Committee stipulates "that no copies of manuscript matter in the Library of Congress be permitted to be made except by the authority and under the direction of the Librarian,

Inquiry card.

Library of Congress: Department of Anonymous Books.

Washington, D. C. 188

Who was the author of

Name in full

Authorities

☞ Please fill blanks, and return to the address given.

The Librarian used a special postcard to obtain information about "anonymous books." LCA

43

1885

and that the Librarian be authorized to establish suitable regulations and restrictions for the inspection and use by the public of such manuscript matter."

(LCA-M)

JUNE. George H. Boehmer reports on his recent six-month visit to Europe "as special European agent of the Library of Congress for exchanging the official publications of the United States Government for like publications of foreign Governments." Boehmer, head of the Smithsonian exchange office, stated that he had visited the governments of 19 countries, "obtaining immediate results far above all expectations, and securing the promise of further valuable returns." One difficulty he had to overcome was frequent misunderstanding "as to the true position of the Library of Congress as regards this exchange, as well as to its relative position to the Government of the United States."

(1885 SAR:49–50)

DECEMBER 8. In his first annual message, President Grover Cleveland asks Congress to take prompt action in providing a new Library building.

(SUM 2:1553–54)

1886

MARCH 4. The Joint Committee on the Library looks with disfavor upon an inquiry from Houghton, Mifflin & Co. "as to whether the Committee would favorably consider an application for permission to print the Records of the Virginia Company." Senator Hoar moves to refer to Spofford the general question of allowing valuable public records to be printed by private persons.

(LCA-M)

MARCH 15. Spofford reports to Congress that the preparation and printing of the Library's new general catalog "has been long interrupted because of the engrossing and rapidly increasing business of the copyright department." The last catalog volume was published in 1880. He also suggests a permanent overseas agent as "the only efficient guarantee of realizing from the system of international exchanges what we have a right to expect."

(1885 AR:5–7)

1886

MARCH 15. The Honorable Lambert Tree, U.S. Minister to Belgium, signs the Brussels Conventions, providing for the international exchange of official documents, scientific and literary publications, and parliamentary journals among the signatory nations—which also include Belgium, Brazil, Spain, Italy, Portugal, Serbia, and Switzerland. The agreements thus formalize the arrangement whereby the Smithsonian Institution serves as the official U.S. agency for the shipping and receipt of documents on behalf of the Library of Congress.

(LCA)

APRIL 15. President Grover Cleveland approves an act of Congress authorizing the construction of a new building for the Library of Congress, to be located directly across the east plaza from the Capitol. It will be in the Italian Renaissance style, in accordance with a design prepared by the Washington architectural firm of Smithmeyer & Pelz. A sum of $5,000 is appropriated to begin construction.

(24 Stat. 12)

JULY 31. The President approves the legislative, executive, and judicial appropriations act for fiscal 1887, which includes $2,500 for the Librarian of Congress "to continue the preparation of the historical manuscripts in the Library known as Force's American Archives." (24 Stat. 172)

1887

AUGUST 5. James G. Blaine sends Spofford a reference question from Bar Harbor, Maine: "Can you tell me the origin and application of the phrase 'wood & water?' I bother you because I know no other place to apply—Too great acquisition of knowledge pays a penalty." (ARS)

AUGUST 8. Senator Morrill, dismayed by delays in the construction of the new Library, complains to Secretary of the Interior L. Q. C. Lamar: "I really had hoped to see the building completed within my lifetime, but I now fear that I shall never see it done."

(LCA)

1888

FEBRUARY 16. More delays and alleged improprieties by architect Smithmeyer lead the House of Representatives to

44

appoint a special committee to investigate contracts for the construction of the Library building. (50/2 HER 3795)

MARCH 8. "Following a brief and convincing statement by Mr. Hoar as to the absolute need for a new catalogue of the Library of Congress," the Library Committee votes to recommend an $18,000 appropriation for the preparation and printing of such a catalog. (LCA-M)

JUNE 19. In a House of Representatives debate about the new Library, Congressman Newton W. Nutting of New York advocates a monumental building: "The structure which emphasizes the value that we set upon the education of our people, upon the means which can put our people in a position to understand the principles upon which our Government is founded, ought to be our largest and best building." Representative Thomas Holman of Indiana protests: "Our library was only intended to be the Library of Congress. The movement now on foot is the first attempt to create a national library in imitation of European monarchies." (CR 19:5392–93)

JULY 11. President Cleveland approves the legislative, executive, and judicial appropriations act for fiscal 1889, which stipulates that hereafter the Law Library "shall be kept open every day so long as either House of Congress is in session." (25 Stat. 256)

JULY 27. The Joint Committee on the Library, now chaired by Senator William M. Evarts of New York, recommends that "a systematic effort should be made to collect and to preserve all manuscript papers which may be offered to the Government, and to make provision for the purchase of manuscripts deemed of special value." Once the new Library building is opened, a special "department of manuscripts" should be established. The committee notes that "little has yet been done by the General Government" in preserving valuable historical manuscripts,

e.g., "Where are the papers, public and private, left by the Presidents of the United States since the time of Monroe?" (50/1 SMD 165)

SEPTEMBER 12. Architect of the Capitol Edward Clark testifies before the special House investigating committee that Smithmeyer was responsible for the placement of the new Library's foundation and for the grading which "set the building on a mound." Clark personally preferred a plan prepared by landscape architect Frederick Law Olmsted which provided for grading "in a manner corresponding" to the Capitol grounds and placing the building on the site "without shutting out the whole view of the Capitol Building from Pennsylvania Avenue—the main approach from Capitol Hill." (50/2 HRR 3795:139)

OCTOBER 2. The President approves a sundry appropriations act for fiscal 1889 which includes $500,000 for the continuation of work on the new Library building. Construction is placed under the direction of Gen. Thomas L. Casey, chief of the U.S. Army Engineers, who will be assisted by Bernard R. Green. (25 Stat. 505)

JANUARY 15. The Brussels Conventions of 1886, after appropriate ratifications, are proclaimed and become effective. (LCA)

MARCH 2. President Cleveland approves a sundry appropriations act for fiscal 1890 that provides for a new Library building costing approximately $6 million. (25 Stat. 939)

MAY 29. The Library Committee discusses the need for an index of public documents. Spofford states that he would always be ready to give advice on such an undertaking, but he does not think that the committee "could well ask him, in addition to his many other duties, to take the general supervision of such a work." No action is taken. (LCA-M)

AUGUST 28. At 3 P.M. and without a formal ceremony, the cornerstone for the new building is finally laid. It is placed in the northeast corner of the building. (LCA)

FEBRUARY 28. Spofford reports to Congress that "the great portion of the Library now unprovided with shelf room renders the embarrassment of producing books with promptitude extreme." He estimates that the Library now contains about 650,000 books and about 207,000 pamphlets. (1890 AR:3)

MARCH 3. President Benjamin Harrison approves an amendment to the copyright law that affords protection to works of foreign origin under certain conditions of reciprocal protection and requires deposit of these works in the Library of Congress. A weekly Catalogue of Title-Entries for copyright deposits is authorized. To be compiled by the Librarian of Congress, it will be published by the Treasury Department for the purpose of preventing the importation of pirated works from abroad. (26 Stat. 1106)

OCTOBER 7. President Daniel Coit Gilman of Johns Hopkins University looks to the Library of Congress to free university libraries from the necessity of maintaining comprehensive collections: "For the publications of a single country, it may be enough if there are one or two storehouses, like the library of Congress, the British Museum, the National Library of Paris, and the like, where completeness is the aim. Among other libraries some principle of differentiation must be worked out."
Cornell University, Exercises at the Opening of the Library Building (Ithaca, 1891), p. 46.

MARCH 24. President Harrison approves an act authorizing the Librarian to exhibit "at the World's Columbian Exposition such books, papers, documents, and other artifacts from the Library of Congress that may relate to Christopher Columbus and the discovery and early history of America." (27 Stat. 394)

46

APRIL 12. The President approves a joint resolution of Congress authorizing access to the "scientific and literary" collections of government institutions, including the Library of Congress, to "the scientific investigators and to students of any institution of higher education now incorporated or hereafter to be incorporated under the laws of Congress or of the District of Columbia." (27 Stat. 395)

APRIL 30. Spofford points out his need for additional staff, explaining that "the constant wants of Congress, of the Departments and Bureaus of the Government, and of the public resorting to the Library for books and information, require the incessant and careful attention of the Librarian and his assistants, in addition to the time and labor demanded to keep the catalogue of the Library to date with its large annual accessions from copyright and other sources, and the steady work involved in the binding and rebinding books and periodicals." (1891 AR:5)

MAY 19. Spofford asks the House Committee on Appropriations for more positions to help "the necessities of public service in my office as register of copyrights." He points out that the Library has a maximum force of only "28 assistants, three of whom are employed in the law library, while the Boston Public Library, with half the number of books, has 89 assistants, and the British Museum Library, with twice as many books, but no copyright business, has 95 assistants." (1893 HRA:193)

JULY 19. The Library Committee recommends the purchase, for $75,000, of the "library of historical manuscripts and printed books belonging to the estate of the late George Bancroft." In his will Bancroft gave "the Government the first option to purchase his collection"; the committee feels "the Government would not be unwise in preserving a monument to the industry of a man of letters, enriching itself with the very words and deeds out of which rose the fabric of American Independence." (52/1 HRR 1947)

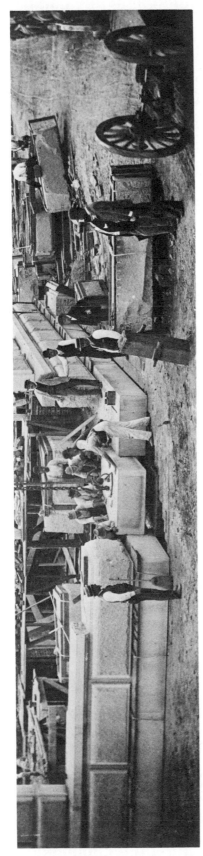

The cornerstone for the new building was laid at 3 P.M. on August 28, 1890, apparently without greater formality than a photograph for the record. LC–USP6-2232-A

A construction photograph taken from the U.S. Capitol on November 25, 1892. The third story of the outer walls was under way and scaffolding had been erected for the construction of the dome. The south portion of the building, to the right in this photograph, blocked the whole view of the Capitol from Pennsylvania Avenue, seen extending to the southeast. LC–USP6-6516-A

47

1893

JANUARY 31. A "List of Books, Pamphlets, and Periodicals Relating to Banking and Finance in the United States," prepared by Spofford for Secretary of the Treasury Charles Foster, is published as part of a Senate document.

(52/2 SED 38)

APRIL 1. The George Bancroft collection is acquired by the Lenox Library.

(LCA)

JULY 10. In an address before the World's Library Congress held at the Columbian Exposition in Chicago, Spofford notes that the "wise and liberal provision" of Congress will soon provide the Library with an edifice which "for capacity, for convenience, and for architectural beauty, promises to be worthy of the nation and of the age."

(U.S. Bureau of Education, *Report of the Commissioner of Education for 1892–93*, p. 708)

OCTOBER 28. Spofford reports to Congress that any "enumeration of the books and other publications in the vast collections of the Library" is impossible, since those collections are "now scattered in sixteen separate halls and storage rooms in the Capitol."

(1892 AR:3)

DECEMBER 4. General Casey reports to Congress the completion of the 195-foot-high dome, including the Torch of Learning at its apex, all of which has been coated with 23-carat gold leaf.

(53/2 HRMD 7)

1894

JANUARY 9. The Library acquires, as a copyright deposit, a paper print of the *Edison Kinetoscopic Record of a Sneeze*, January 7, 1894, the earliest motion picture in the Library's collections.

(LCA)

JANUARY 26. General Casey and Superintendent of Construction Green meet with a committee from the National Sculpture Society, consisting of John Q. A. Ward, Augustus Saint-Gaudens, and Olin L. Warner, to plan the sculpture for the Library's interior.

(LCA)

MAY 4. President Cleveland approves a joint resolution of Congress that appropriates $6,800 for the employment of additional Library clerks, needed because the copyright work "is several months in arrears."

(28 Stat. 582)

JUNE 15. The newly established District of Columbia Library Association elects Librarian Spofford as its first president.

(ARS)

1895

MARCH 2. President Cleveland approves the legislative, executive, and judicial appropriations act for fiscal 1896 which includes the stipulation: "The Librarian of Congress shall make to the next regular session of Congress a full report touching a complete reorganization of the Library of Congress, and whether a separation of the law library is desirable, and whether a separation of the new Library building."

(28 Stat. 764)

OCTOBER. Approximately 70 tons of unclassified copyright deposits are transferred from the southern crypt under the Capitol to the basement of the new Library building.

(55/2 HRR 23)

DECEMBER 2. In his special report on reorganization, Spofford recommends an expansion of the Library into nine separate departments: printed books, periodicals, manuscripts, maps and charts, works of art, cataloging, binding, copyright, and superintendence of the building and grounds. He emphasizes the need for "separating the functions of register of copyrights from those of Librarian of Congress," and details the duties of each. The job of Librarian is characterized as one in which the incumbent must act "as the custodian, the protector, the enlarger, and, to a considerable extent, the interpreter of the great collection confided to his charge." Spofford feels the Law

1895

Library should remain in the Capitol "so long as the Supreme Court continues its sessions in the Capitol."

(54/1 sd 7)

1896

FEBRUARY 7. The Librarian presents to the House Committee on Appropriations his 1897 budget requests "in accordance with the requirements of Library service in the new building." He requests 97 positions; 58 for the general Library administration and the remainder for the proposed copyright department, to be headed by a register of copyrights.

(1897 HRA:121–22)

APRIL 2. One week after the death of General Casey, President Grover Cleveland approves a joint resolution of Congress "authorizing and directing Bernard R. Green to exercise the duties and powers heretofore conferred upon the late Thomas L. Casey in relation to the construction and completion of the Library of Congress." Green's annual salary will be $5,000.

(29 Stat. 470)

MAY 5. The U.S. Senate adopts a concurrent resolution providing that the Joint Committee on the Library be authorized to hold hearings, during the recess of Congress, "for the purpose of inquiring into the condition of the Library of Congress, and to report upon the same at the next session of Congress, with such recommendations as may be deemed advisable; also to report a plan for the organization, custody, and management of the new Library building and the Library of Congress."

54/2 SR 1573:i

MAY 21. The Senate debates the provision in the 1897 appropriations conference report which calls for a separate register of copyrights, to be selected by the Library Committee. Senator Orville H. Platt of Connecticut claims "there is no power under the Constitution giving Congress the right to appoint a legal and constitutional officer of this Government." The conference report is rejected.

(CR 28:5496–5507)

Thomas Lincoln Casey (1831–1896), U.S. Army Corps of Engineers, who completed the construction of the Washington Monument and the State, War, and Navy Building (now the Executive Office Building) and in 1888 was placed in charge of constructing the Library of Congress. This sketch is reproduced from Harper's Weekly, December 20, 1884. LC-USP6-6503-A

MAY 28. President Cleveland approves the legislative, executive, and judicial appropriations act for fiscal 1897, which includes funds for 30 "assistants" for the general Library and 12 copyright clerks who will work "under the direction of the Librarian of Congress." (29 Stat. 140)

JUNE 3. President Cleveland approves an act of Congress establishing a free public library in the District of Columbia. (29 Stat. 244)

AUGUST. In a *Library Journal* article titled "The American National Library," publisher R. R. Bowker asserts: "It is time to recognize, in name, the fact that the Library of Congress, so called, is now the library of the nation as well as of Congress; and as part of the plan of reorganization it should undoubtedly be designated as the National Library." (LJ 21:357)

NOVEMBER 16. The Joint Committee on the Library, chaired by Senator George Peabody Wetmore, starts its inquiry into "the condition" of the Library and its future organization. (54/2 SR 1573:i)

NOVEMBER 21. Spofford begins four days of testimony before the Joint Committee on the Library concerning the history of the Library, its present operations, and his recommendations for its future. In response to a question from Representative Lemuel E. Quigg of New York, the Librarian expresses regret that during his administration the Joint Committee on the Library "has not taken more interest" in Library matters, and he wonders "whether something in the nature of a joint commission of trustees, acting with the Congressional committee, or something else similar in character, might tend to a closer and more constant supervision of this growing institution." (54/2 SR 1573:112–13)

NOVEMBER 26. Spofford testifies that the administration of the copyright law requires over 75 percent of his time

50

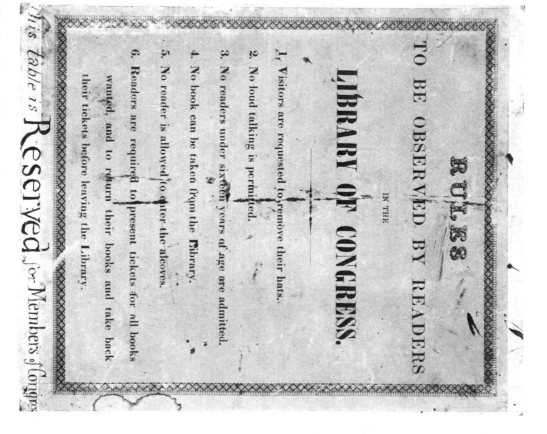

This broadside, which was prominently displayed in the Library room in the Capitol, outlines the basic rules observed by the public in the last decades of the 19th century. LCA

and the full-time efforts of 24 of the Library's 42 employees.
(54/2 SR 1573:127–32)

DECEMBER 1. Melvil Dewey, director of the New York State Library, and Herbert Putnam, librarian of the Boston Public Library, are among the witnesses testifying on behalf of the American Library Association. Dewey maintains: "We shall never accomplish our best results in librarianship till we can have at the National Library in Washington a center to which the libraries of the whole country can turn for inspiration, guidance, and practical help." His specific recommendations include a new system of card catalogs, a new classification scheme, centralized cataloging and card distribution, an interlibrary loan system, a national reference and copying system, and governance by a board of regents. Dewey also hopes that "with the new order will come a new name, for the Library of Congress conveys a false impression, as much as it would to call the British Museum the parliamentary library."
(54/2 SR 1573:139–50)

DECEMBER 2. As the hearings continue, Putnam states his view that the Library of Congress, as the national library, should stand "foremost as a model and example of assisting forward the work of scholarship in the United States." Commissioner of Education W. T. Harris advocates the employment of a "series of experts in the Congressional Library who should devote their time to examining all sources of information" in order to respond to congressional requests "no matter how special the subject is."
(54/2 SR 1573:220, 254)

DECEMBER 7. The hearings end. Herbert Putnam supplements his previous testimony with a letter to Chairman Wetmore. The Boston librarian emphasizes that on one point the witnesses were very strongly in unison—that the enlargement of the scope function and equipment of the Library should at all events mean this: That while personal mediation between the reader and the books should be retained, while, indeed, every effort should be made (in the direc-

tions indicated by Commissioner Harris) to extend the area of personal mediation, nevertheless an endeavor should now be made to introduce into the Library the mechanical aids which will render the Library more independent of the physical limitations of any one man or set of men; in other words, that the time has come when Mr. Spofford's amazing knowledge of the Library shall be embodied in some form which shall be capable of rendering a service which Mr. Spofford as one man and mortal can not be expected to render.
(54/2 SR 1573:228)

DECEMBER 7. Superintendent Green presents a detailed report to Congress about the construction of the building, emphasizing that the structure "is a product of American talent and skill in architecture and art and practically so in workmanship." He includes a list of 22 sculptors and 20 artists, "all of whom are citizens of the United States," who furnished the special sculptures and mural paintings necessary "to fully and consistently carry out the monumental design and purpose of the building." (54/2 HRD 20)

DECEMBER 8. Librarian Spofford presents his budget request for fiscal 1898 to the House Committee on Appropriations. He also asks the committee to avail itself of the testimony recently taken by the Joint Committee on the Library which "is now being printed." (1898 HRA:85)

DECEMBER 19. In the House of Representatives debate on the legislative appropriation bill, the Committee on Appropriations presents a bill that gives the Librarian of Congress sole authority to establish rules and hire employees. Representative Quigg counters with amendments representing the position of the Joint Committee on the Library, which has not yet had an opportunity to prepare its recommendations. The Library Committee proposes a Library "director," appointed by the President and confirmed by the Senate, but serving under the supervision and direction of the Library Committee. Representative Alexander M. Dockery of the Appropriations Committee rebuts this approach. He insists that the Library "should be presided over by some executive officer with authority to appoint and remove his employees." He opposes giving

A Smithmeyer and Pelz adaptation of their 1873 plan that illustrates the basic design finally accepted by the Congress. Construction engineers Casey and Green made several changes, however, omitting certain ornamental features, then raising the dome to a height of 195 feet and covering it with 23-carat gold leaf. LC–USZ62–46799

the Library Committee authority over the Librarian: "In organizing this great library in that gorgeous new building, let us not make the grave mistake of also organizing a scramble for 187 offices to be disposed of under the direction and control of the joint committee of the two Houses of Congress, to the detriment of public service."

(CR 29:311–19)

JANUARY. An editorial in *Library Journal*, the official ALA organ, contends that "the future of the national library in its new home is really *the* library question of the year." It also is critical of Spofford, who "has not trained himself as an executive for this kind of work, nor been able to keep in touch with the modern developments of library organization and practice. Nor has he benefited, as was to be hoped, by recent experience; to cite a single instance, copyright checks are still unbanked and used, without proper safeguards, to pay off the minor bills of the Library." The continuing legislative debates regarding the organization of the Library are described in an article titled "A Congressional or a National Library?" contributed anonymously by Edith E. Clarke of the Public Documents Library in Washington. The article concludes by calling on Congress to "renounce the right, now 96 years old, which it holds in the Library of Congress," and to constitute the Library as an executive establishment governed by a board of regents, "as the Smithsonian Institution is organized."

(LJ 22:3–4, 7–9; LCA)

JANUARY 18. Librarian Spofford presents a statement describing the special rooms and facilities needed in the new building for the proper functioning of the Library.

(54/2 SD 65)

JANUARY 20. The legislative branch appropriation bill is considered by the Senate after several amendments in committee. Senator Shelby M. Cullom of Illinois explains that the committee finally decided against a board of directors for the Library, but the arrangements in the pending bill for governing the Library could still be considered "some-

what tentative." The Senate amendments call for the confirmation of the Librarian by the Senate and for the Librarian to make the rules and regulations of the Library "to be approved by the Joint Committee of the Library." Senator Wilkinson Call of Florida, however, is unhappy: "By this bill, when enacted into law, Congress forever puts it out of their power to control the Library. It now loses its name and function of a Congressional library and becomes a national or Presidential Library, beyond the control of Congress, except by the President's consent." The bill passes as reported.

(CR 29:975–77)

FEBRUARY. The new building is completed and ready for occupancy.

(1897 AR:5)

FEBRUARY 17. The House of Representatives concurs in a conference report, approved two days earlier by the Senate, which compromises on differences concerning the Library. Representative Dockery notes with approval that while the House agreed to the Senate's confirmation of the Librarian, the conference bill now "gives the Joint Committee on the Library no supervision of the regulations to be made by the Librarian." He also states that the "time has come when the national library should be in charge of a management fully abreast with the progress of the times," even employing, perhaps, a graduate of one of the new schools "whose sole function, I am advised, is to equip gentlemen for the discharge of the duties of librarian."

(CR 29:1945–47)

FEBRUARY 19. The reorganization and expansion of the Library of Congress is approved by President Grover Cleveland as part of the legislative, executive, and judicial appropriations act for fiscal 1898, which will become effective on July 1, 1897. Under the provisions of the new law, the President's appointment of a Librarian of Congress must be approved by the Senate; the Librarian is given sole authority and responsibility for making the "rules and regulations for the government" of the Library, including the selection of the staff; and all appointments will be made "by reason of special aptitude for the work of the Library." The annual salary of the Librarian is established at $5,000 and the size of the Library staff is increased from 42 to 108. Separate "departments" are established for copyright, law, cataloging, periodicals, manuscripts, music, graphic arts, and maps and charts. Provision is made for a congressional reference library in the Capitol, and for reading room attendants in the Main Reading Room and in the separate reading rooms in the Main Library for the House of Representatives and the Senate. A separate position of register of copyrights is created; the register will serve "under the direction and supervision" of the Librarian. The superintendent of building and grounds, a presidential appointment with an annual salary of $5,000, is authorized to hire a separate staff. Bernard R. Green is designated as the first superintendent, effective March 4, 1897.

(29 Stat. 538)

MARCH 3. The report of the Joint Committee on the Library on its recent inquiry is published, along with the testimony it gathered. The committee notes that heretofore it has had "authority to approve such rules and regulations as have been made by the Librarian of Congress, but the provision of law under which the Joint Committee has hitherto passed upon said rules and regulations would appear to be repealed by the more recent act (February 19, 1897) which places this power in the hands of the Librarian of Congress." For this reason, the Joint Committee does not deem it necessary to report a plan for the "organization, custody, and management" of the Library. It does, however, suggest that funds be appropriated so that the Library "may be opened at night for the use of the general public."

(54/2 SR 1573:i–ii)

MARCH 15. Opening of a special session of Congress, called by newly inaugurated President William McKinley to deal with tariff revision. The extra session delays the transfer of the main Library from the Capitol to the new building.

(1897 AR:5)

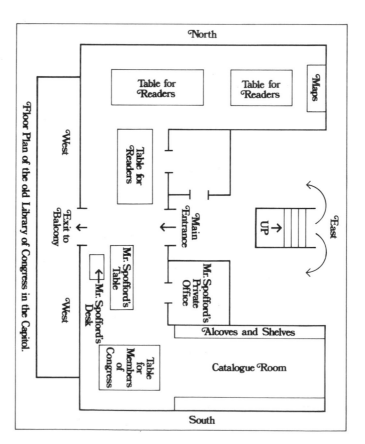

Floor Plan of the old Library of Congress in the Capitol.

Shelf space within the Library proper was exhausted by 1876, when Spofford reported that "books are now, from sheer force of necessity, being piled upon the floor in all directions." By 1897 the collections of the Library had overflowed into over a dozen different locations throughout the Capitol, including the attic and the cellar. In addition, 42 employees had to find work space. The only privacy was in Spofford's private office, noted on this floor plan, but it also served as the Library's rare book room.

This drawing by W. Bengough appeared in Harper's Weekly on February 27, 1897. Spofford is depicted on the far right, emerging from his desk area with a book for a reader. The man on the left holding the lamp is David Hutcheson, Assistant Librarian. LC–USZ–62–3868

55

An 1897 photograph of the new Library of Congress Building, opened to the public on November 1, 1897. Horatio Greenough's statue of George Washington is in the right foreground. Architectural critic Montgomery Schuyler praised the structure as "a national possession, an example of a great public building monumentally conceived, faithfully built, and worthily adorned." Professional librarians also recognized the significance of the structure. In the February 13, 1897, issue of The Critic, Amherst librarian William I. Fletcher maintained: "With the occupancy of this magnificent building, the Library of Congress should enter on a new career. It should now become in name, as it must in fact, the National Library."

The extensive interior decoration in the new building, which combined sculpture, mural painting, and architecture on a scale unsurpassed in any other public building, was possible only because General Casey and Bernard Green efficiently kept construction costs to a minimum. Edward Pearce Casey (1864–1940), hired as architect of the building in 1892, was in charge of interior design and decoration. More than fifty American painters and sculptors contributed works of art to the facade and interior. LC–USP6–6534–A

56

1897

APRIL 10. The systematic transfer of materials into the new building commences with the move of the Toner collection out of a crypt beneath the Capitol. (55/2 HRD 23)

APRIL 22. Superintendent Green reports to Congress that the net cost of the new building was $6,032,124.54, a sum $200,000 less than the total construction appropriation.
(55/1 SD 55)

MAY 4. Journalist and former diplomat John Russell Young, a personal friend of President McKinley, makes the following diary entry: "Saw the President. . . . he said that he would have an important nomination very soon, namely that of Librarian of Congress. Would like to nominate Mr. Spofford, but was afraid he could not. I presume he had me in mind, but I made no suggestion.—Would rather be paralyzed than in any way disturb Spofford. (JRY)

MAY 28. Spofford notes a substantial increase in copyright business, "notwithstanding the prolongation of the commercial and industrial depression in the country." The international copyright law of 1891 is the prime reason. The Librarian terms the completion of the new building a "proper subject of congratulation to Congress and to the American people."
(1896 AR:3–5)

JUNE 30. President McKinley nominates John Russell Young to be Librarian of Congress and Bernard R. Green to be superintendent of the Library building and grounds. Both nominations are approved by the Senate. (CR 30:2159)

JUNE 30. The Washington *Evening Star* reports that the Young nomination has met with "general commendation" in Congress, and that the new Librarian is "a man of wide knowledge, marked polish of manner, and of broad and liberal views." Furthermore, there exists "a thorough and amicable understanding" between Young and Spofford, who will be appointed Chief Assistant Librarian. According to the *Star*, the 72-year-old Spofford informed the

57

Edwin H. Blashfield's painting The Evolution of Civilization in the collar of the dome of the Main Reading Room. The twelve figures represent "the twelve countries, or epochs, which have contributed most to the development of present-day civilization in this country." Chronologically arranged, the figures depict: Egypt (Written Records), Judea (Religion), Greece (Philosophy), Rome (Administration), Islam (Physics), The Middle Ages (Modern Languages), Italy (Fine Arts), Germany (Art of Printing), Spain (Discovery), England (Literature), France (Emancipation), and America (Science). LC-USP6-6543-M

President that he was not a candidate for renomination as Librarian, and Young accepted the nomination only after he learned that it would be "absolutely acceptable" to Spofford.

JULY 1. John Russell Young takes office as the new Librarian of Congress. He immediately appoints Spofford to be Chief Assistant Librarian.

(LCA; 1897 AR:3)

JULY 12. Melvil Dewey writes Young:
Many librarians have expressed themselves strongly against any appointment except of an experienced technical librarian. I have said from the first that I could easily conceive of a strong administration man being put at the head who might be better for the country than any of the professional librarians. I profoundly hope that you are the man needed for the wonderful work that is possible. May I ask you to glance over my testimony before the joint committee last December for what I believe the true ideal for the library that ought to lead the world.

(LCA)

JULY 22. Thorvald Solberg, a Boston book dealer and acknowledged copyright expert, takes office as the first register of copyrights.

(1897 AR:13)

JULY 31. The Library is closed to all "except those having business with the copyright department," and preparations for the move of the shelved and classified volumes begin. The books will be transported across the east plaza of the Capitol in horse-drawn wagons.

(1897 AR:5–6)

AUGUST 2. Because the Library is not part of the classified civil service, a special board consisting of Spofford, Register of Copyrights Solberg, and Superintendent of the Reading Room David Hutcheson is appointed by Young to examine potential appointees to permanent Library positions.

(55/2 SD 42)

AUGUST 13. Librarian Young responds to Dewey, informing him that he would have declined the post of Librarian "if it would have 'interfered' with Mr. Spofford," but "that

John Russell Young (1840–1899), Librarian of Congress from 1897 until his death. Young was in charge of the Library when it was moved from the Capitol into the new building. A skillful and innovative administrator, he successfully established the Library of Congress as an apolitical institution. On June 12, 1898, the Librarian confided to his diary: "I am trying to build the library far into the future, to make it a true library of research." LC-USZ62-60114

1897

gentleman was more than solicitous that I should succeed him." (LCA-L)

AUGUST 18. Young asks his assistants to consider the possibility of inaugurating "a special service for the blind," which "would go far towards the complete idea of a national library." (LCA)

AUGUST 25. Young asks the Department of State to obtain "information in regard to the rules and regulations governing the great national libraries of other countries for use in reorganizing the Library of Congress." (LCA)

SEPTEMBER 13. Chief Assistant Librarian Spofford recommends against placing rare printed books in the custody of the "Keeper of the Manuscripts," pointing out that "in all great National Libraries, the head of the Manuscript department has nothing to do with printed books." He explains to Young that the "department of rare books and Americana should be in direct charge of the one in the Library who knows their pecuniary and comparative and intrinsic value, and who alone could discriminate from the great mass for special care and treatment." The rare book collection should consist primarily of early Americana, incunabula, and first or very rare editions of notable writers. (LCA)

SEPTEMBER 15. J. C. M. Hanson, formerly of the University of Wisconsin library, begins work as superintendent of the Catalogue Department. (LCA)

NOVEMBER 1. At 9 A.M. the monumental new Library building officially opens for service to the public. The south gallery of the second floor, 217 feet long by 85 feet wide, has been set aside for "a series of graphic-art exhibitions." The building itself, with its elaborate sculpture work and interior decoration, is widely praised in the press. The Washington *Evening Star* also reports that "the first volume asked for about three minutes after the door

Melvil Dewey (1851–1931), director of the New York State Library and a leading figure in the American library movement. Dewey strongly advocated an expanded national role for the Library of Congress, urging the institution to become "a center to which the libraries of the whole country can turn for inspiration, guidance, and practical help, which can be rendered so economically and efficiently in no other possible way." LC-USZ62-40188

One of the new services inaugurated by Librarian Young was a reading program for the blind. A special reading room for the blind was opened on the ground floor in the northwest pavilion on November 8, 1897. LC-BH836-215

60

1897

was opened was 'Roger Williams' Year Book,' of so recent a date that it had not been received."

NOVEMBER 8. A reading room for the blind is opened and a special program of readings is inaugurated. One of the first programs features poet Paul Laurence Dunbar, a Library staff member, who reads from his works.

(1898 AR:40; LJ 22:764)

NOVEMBER 20. The transfer of Library materials into the new building is completed. Superintendent Green estimates that a total of 800 tons of material was moved and that at least two-fifths of it was not in the Library proper, but scattered in various locations throughout the Capitol.

(55/2 3RD 23)

NOVEMBER 25. On this Thanksgiving holiday, over 4,700 visitors tour the new Library building.

(55/2 3RD 23)

NOVEMBER 27. R. R. Bowker asks Young to consider requesting the transfer of the office of the Superintendent of Documents to the Library of Congress.

(LCA)

DECEMBER 1. Charles Martel, formerly of the Newberry Library, begins his duties as assistant to the superintendent of the Catalogue Department.

(LCA)

DECEMBER 6. In his first annual report, Librarian Young notes that "now, when the work of organization is in a plastic condition, before what is done hardens and consolidates and becomes difficult of undoing, no step should be taken without considering not alone what is most convenient today, but what will be most useful a hundred years from today." With regard to the impending reclassification of the collection, he asserts one "inflexible" rule: "no method of classification should be favored which would disintegrate the general collection." The Librarian also advocates the transfer of historical manuscripts from the Department of State to the Library of Congress and

Bernard R. Green (1843–1914), Casey's assistant and successor as superintendent of construction, who completed the building for $200,000 less than the sum appropriated for its construction. Green served as superintendent of the building and grounds from 1897 until his death. LC–USP6–6496–A

61

1897

decries the use of cheap, nondurable paper by publishers, warning that many of the works coming into the Library "threaten in a few years to crumble into a waste heap, with no value as record."

(1897 AR:17–21, 31, 49)

DECEMBER 6. In his first annual message, President William McKinley congratulates Congress for its "foresight and munificence" in providing a Library building for its "noble treasure-house of knowledge" and expresses his hope that the legislators "will continue to develop the Library in every phase of research to the end that it may be not only one of the most magnificent but among the richest and most useful libraries in the world."

(SUM 2:1880)

DECEMBER 6. Representative Dockery introduces a bill providing 1) that the Library of Congress "shall be known as and styled as the 'national library'"; 2) that the Librarian of Congress be designated "the Director of the National Library"; and 3) that all U.S. citizens over the age of 12 and residing in the District of Columbia be entitled "to withdraw books from the national library." (LCA)

DECEMBER 13. The Joint Committee on the Library, chaired by Congressman Quigg, recommends that the third section of Representative Dockery's bill "be stricken out," but with that change, the bill be approved. No action is taken, however.

(55/2 HRR 34)

DECEMBER 14. In response to a request from Senator Henry Cabot Lodge, the chief clerk of the Library reports that the Library received 2,872 applications for positions, from which Librarian Young made 65 probationary appointments.

(LCA-L)

1898

JANUARY. J. C. M. Hanson and Charles Martel begin work on reclassifying the Library's collections according to a new classification scheme.

(LCA)

62

LIBRARY OF CONGRESS, WASHINGTON.

February 16, 1898.

Sir:

The Library of Congress has been removed from the Capitol to the new Library Building. The books, pamphlets, serials, manuscripts, and other collections are now in process of arrangement.

Its original classification by Thomas Jefferson contemplated a National Library, universal and representative in its character, with all knowledge for its province. The policy of Mr. Jefferson has been followed until its inception was a collection of less than 8,000 volumes, has become nearly 800,000, and ranks among the great libraries of the world.

The new Library has space for four and a half millions of books. The increase from 1861 to the present day has been more than tenfold—that is to say from 75,000 to 800,000 in one generation alone. There is no sign of a diminishing ratio, and it is believed that it could be increased through the advice and co-operation of gentlemen in our foreign service. Public documents, newspapers, serials, pamphlets, manuscripts, broadsides, chap-books, ballads, records of original research, publications illustrative of the manners, customs, resources, and traditions of communities to which our foreign representatives are accredited, the proceedings of learned, scientific, or religious bodies, the reports of corporations such as railways, canals, or industrial companies, legislative records and debates, public decrees, church registers, genealogy, family and local histories, chronicles of country and parish life, folk-lore, fashions, domestic annals, docu-

1898

JANUARY 7. "On behalf of the American home," the National Women's Christian Temperance Union urges "that no intoxicants shall be offered in our National Library."

(LCA)

FEBRUARY 16. Young addresses a circular letter to U.S. diplomatic and consular representatives throughout the world, asking them to send to the national library newspapers, serials, pamphlets, documents, manuscripts, or reports, or "whatever, in a word, would add to the sum of human knowledge." Reviewing and approving the text of the letter, Assistant Librarian Spofford reminds the Librarian: "I fought to bring us oceans of books and rivers of information."

(1898 AR:83; LCA)

FEBRUARY 26. Librarian Young organizes a separate Order Department.

(1898 AR:75)

FEBRUARY 28. Despite his "hearty support" of the concept, Young explains to the University of California librarian that interlibrary loans are not possible because the Joint Committee on the Library has always held "that the laws governing the Library of Congress do not permit of the books belonging to the Library being sent out of the District of Columbia."

(LCA)

MAY 14. In a cooperative undertaking with the Copyright Office, the Catalogue Department begins preparing book entries for copyright deposits for the *Catalogue of Title-Entries*.

(1898 AR:21–22)

JUNE 12. Librarian Young writes in his diary: "I am trying to build the library far into the future, to make it a true library of research."

(JRY)

JULY. The Government Printing Office begins printing, on cards, 50 copies of each entry from the *Catalogue of Title-Entries*, listing copyright deposits. The printed cards enable the Library to establish three new dictionary cata-

ments illustrative of the history of those various nationalities now coming to our shores, to blend into our national life, and which, as a part of our library archives, would be inestimable to their descendants—whatever, in a word, would add to the sum of human knowledge, would be gratefully received and have due and permanent acknowledgment.

Opportunities for securing the original or a copy of useful manuscripts or rare editions would be welcome. Those and the other publications suggested might be brought to our attention with the view of purchase from the Library funds, or securing by exchange, buying what may have a special value, or exchanging from our collection of duplicates. In the process of selection or inquiry, nothing should be deemed trivial, remembering that what in its day was an apparently worthless publication, of the time of the English Commonwealth, the American Revolution, or our recent Civil War, may hereafter be priceless in its value.

This is written in the interest of the National Library, and with the belief that the suggestion alone is necessary to secure your co-operation in the development of one of the most important branches of our public service.

Yours respectfully,

[signature]

Librarian of Congress.

Librarian Young's interest in international matters and belief that the National Library should contain foreign materials as well as Americana led him to send this letter to U.S. diplomatic and consular representatives around the world. By December nearly three hundred volumes and pamphlets from 20 embassies and consulates had been received. LCA

logs, one for the use of the public and two for the cataloging staff. In its July issue the *Library Journal* approves this innovation and comments: "No arrangements have yet been made, we believe, for furnishing the printed catalog cards outside the library, but it is to be hoped that this feature may ultimately be extended, so that from the national library may be furnished, at a price repaying cost, entries of all copyright American books."

(LCA; LJ 23:272)

JULY 7. President McKinley approves a joint resolution of Congress authorizing the Librarian of Congress to accept the Gardiner Greene Hubbard collection of engravings as a gift from his widow, Gertrude M. Hubbard.

(30 Stat. 751)

AUGUST 1. Two employees from the Government Printing Office begin "work on the repair of manuscripts" in the Library.

(1899 AR:8)

AUGUST 18. Librarian Young alerts the staff to a new development: since "the Government has taken possession of Manila under circumstances that look to its permanent retention," he asks that additional books about the Philippines be purchased immediately.

(LCA)

OCTOBER 1. The Library opens for evening hours on a regular basis.

(30 Stat. 284)

NOVEMBER 6. An accidental explosion and fire at the entrance of the Law Library, still located in the Capitol, damages over 1,000 books.

(1898 AR:39)

DECEMBER 9. J. C. M. Hanson asks Young to request five new cataloging positions every year for the next three years, pointing out that the Library has only five catalogers "engaged permanently on actual cataloging work," whereas the Boston Public Library has 18 and the New York Public Library, 15.

(LCA)

DECEMBER 12. In his annual report, Young points out that the bibliographic bulletins issued during the past year, e.g., the lists of books on Cuba and Hawaii compiled by Assistant Librarian A. P. C. Griffin, were printed "in the belief that Congress might value the information thus presented," adding: "It has been our aim to anticipate the wants of Congress upon subjects of legislation and to hold the resources of the Library ever at the command of those for whom it was founded." He also reports that "the work of reclassification began with chapter 38, containing works on writing, printing, bibliography, and library science, and is now complete." The Librarian feels his paramount duty is "the strengthening of the Library as a collection of books," and he looks forward to the day when the Library receives, in addition to copyright deposits, increased congressional appropriations for books, and "gifts from private sources." He concludes by describing his hopes for the Library's future: It should be our aim to broaden the Library, safeguard its integrity as a library of reference, and bring it home to the people as belonging to them—a part of their heritage—to make it American in the highest sense, seeking whatever illustrates American history—the varied forms of American growth, theology, superstition, commonwealth, building, jurisprudence, peace, and war. And, while accepting this as the chief end of the Library, it is no less incumbent to seek out and gather in the learning and piety of every age. With the considerate care of Congress and a due appreciation of what has been done and what may so readily be done by the American people, there is no reason why the Library of Congress should not rival those noble establishments of the Old World, whose treasures are a people's pride and whose growth is the highest achievement of modern civilization.

(1898 AR:12–13, 22, 46–47)

JANUARY 8. Herbert Friedenwald, superintendent of the Manuscripts Department, departs for Puerto Rico for the purpose of collecting "rare manuscripts, books, and maps pertaining to that island."

(1899 AR:37)

JANUARY 17. After a year of serious illness, Librarian Young dies.

(JRY)

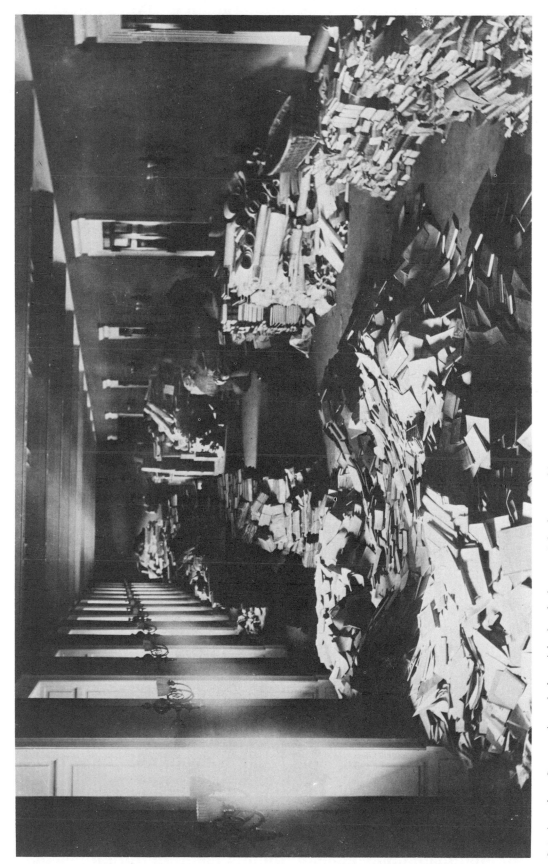

Superintendent Green estimated that eight hundred tons of books, pamphlets, maps, manuscripts, prints, pieces of music, and other materials were moved into the new building. These copyrighted deposits were awaiting sorting, counting, and classification. LC–USZ62–38245

65

1899

JANUARY 18. Spofford becomes Acting Librarian of Congress.
(LCA)

JANUARY 23. William Coolidge Lane, ALA president, urges President McKinley to appoint an experienced library administrator as the next Librarian of Congress, for the Library—as the national library—should "stand at the head of American libraries as the best organized and best equipped of all." The Harvard librarian also points out that, under the right leadership, the Library "can be made a leading factor in the educational and intellectual life of the country, and will exercise an important influence on the progress of the library movement."
(LJ 24:99)

JANUARY 28. In a letter to President McKinley, Acting Librarian Spofford argues against the rumored appointment of the Library's chief clerk, Thomas Alvord, as the next Librarian since "he who stands at the head of America's foremost library must mingle with the foremost men of science and literature, native and foreign, who resort to it, or correspond with it, on terms of something like equality."
(WM)

FEBRUARY 4. President McKinley authorizes Lane to offer the librarianship to Herbert Putnam, superintendent of the Boston Public Library.
(WM)

FEBRUARY 8. Putnam accepts the nomination and then, in a telegram to the President, declines it unless Congressman Samuel J. Barrows "withdraws his candidacy." (WM)

FEBRUARY 15. President McKinley nominates Representative Samuel J. Barrows to be Librarian of Congress.
(CR 32:1891)

FEBRUARY 28. Senator Henry C. Hansborough of North Dakota, on behalf of the Joint Committee on the Library,

66

Herbert Putnam (1861–1955), Librarian of Congress from 1899 to 1939 and Librarian Emeritus until his death. The first experienced librarian to direct the Library of Congress, Putnam inaugurated a host of national library services and permanently linked the policies of the Library of Congress to the broader interests of American librarianship. LC-BH833-32

reports adversely on the Barrows nomination.
(U.S. Senate, *Journal of Executive Proceedings*, vol. 31, pt. 2, p. 1344)

MARCH 3. Senator George F. Hoar of Massachusetts advises the President: "I am satisfied Mr. Barrows will be almost unanimously rejected if a vote [is] taken now. If, on full inquiry, you can find a competent skilled librarian, I hope one may be appointed; otherwise, that Mr. Barrows may be considered again hereafter." (WM)

MARCH 3. The President approves an act of Congress authorizing the construction, with funds donated by Andrew Carnegie, of a new building for the Public Library of the District of Columbia. The plans for the new structure render Young's earlier plan for a reading room for children in the Library of Congress "unnecessary." (30 Stat. 1372; 1899 AR:18)

MARCH 4. The 55th Congress adjourns without taking any action on the Barrows nomination. (CR 32:2870)

MARCH 7. In a letter to McKinley, Representative Barrows declines the President's offer of a recess appointment as Librarian, citing the opposition in the Senate to his nomination. (WM)

MARCH 7. ALA President Lane again urges the President to appoint Putnam. (LJ 24:101)

MARCH 13. President McKinley, during the congressional recess, appoints Putnam to be Librarian of Congress. (LCA)

APRIL 5. Herbert Putnam takes the oath of office as the eighth Librarian of Congress. The Library has a book collection of approximately 900,000 volumes, a staff of 134, and an appropriation in fiscal 1898 of approximately $280,000. The superintendent of the building and grounds has a staff of 99. (LCA; 1899 AR:1–5, 27)

JUNE 9. James H. Canfield, president of Ohio State University, urges, in a letter to Putnam, that the Library of Congress catalog all of its current receipts and print catalog cards for these books "in quantities sufficient to supply the various libraries of the country." (LCA-L)

JUNE 12. Putnam informs Canfield that the Library "should be undertaking such a service on a large scale," but that "it can do so adequately and conveniently only with a printing plant of its own." (LCA-L)

OCTOBER 10. Putnam submits his estimated budget for the next fiscal year to the secretary of the treasury. He asks for five new "departments of work not covered by the present organization": a reading room for current newspapers and periodicals, a department for ordering (purchasing), one for documents and exchanges, another for bibliography, and a "reference room" for the Smithsonian collection. He requests an increase in the staff from 134 to 230 employees. The Librarian informs Congress that the collection is "exceedingly defective," and "may be built up only by incessant solicitation, exchange, and purchase." For this reason, he recommends $50,000 be spent on purchases but warns: "Were it not for the difficulty of handling a larger amount of accessions with the force provided for I should recommend the expenditure of a much larger sum." Putnam notes that the entire Library must be reclassified, since the present classification is "meager, rigid, and inelastic." Finally, he includes funds to purchase an electric automobile to replace the Library's one wagon and two horses. (1899 AR:27–40)

DECEMBER 4. In his first annual report, Putnam pays tribute to Young's "enthusiasm, learning, and geniality of character," as well as the former Librarian's "high intentions" for the Library of Congress. (1899 AR:3)

DECEMBER 4. In a letter to Charles H. Hastings, president of the Bibliographical Society of Chicago, Librarian Putnam explains his concept of reference work: "I think students with a purpose should receive at the hands of librarians not merely advice as to consulting the catalogues, but counsel as to the authoritative works on special subjects; and guidance as to unexpected sources of information. . . . I think that students who are engaged upon work tending to public improvement should receive the utmost assistance; and the cost of such assistance is very properly a 'charge on the public'; particularly is this of force in municipal and governmental libraries." (LCA-L)

DECEMBER 6. President McKinley sends the Senate the nomination of Herbert Putnam as Librarian of Congress "to which office he was appointed during the last recess of Congress." (CR 33:99)

DECEMBER 12. The U.S. Senate confirms, without debate, the nomination of Herbert Putnam to be Librarian of Congress. (CR 33:236)

JANUARY. The Library publishes the Preliminary List of Books by Negro Authors, for the Paris Exposition and Library of Congress, compiled by Daniel Murray of the Library of Congress reading room service. (1900 AR:18)

JANUARY 20. Putnam asks the House Appropriations Subcommittee to substitute the words "division" and "chief" for "department" and "superintendent," respectively, in the budget estimate it is considering. (1900 HRA:18)

JANUARY 22. A separate periodical-newspaper reading room is opened. (1900 AR:22)

JANUARY 26. In a letter to George F. Bowerman of the New York Tribune, Putnam reassures the journalist: "to ... I believe in Congress. I believe in the men who in Congress are controlling these matters. I believe in their fairness. I believe in their common sense. My experience during the past eight months has confirmed my general belief and has given me a particular confidence.

I have already had occasion to submit recommendations and I have been delighted with the courtesy, consideration, and fairness with which they have been received. . . . I fully believe that Congress will do whatever is necessary for the Library. (LCA)

FEBRUARY. Writing in the Atlantic Monthly, Putnam assesses the collections and services of the Library, "an appreciation of which must precede any serviceable discussion of the future." He concludes with a summary of the "negative aspects" of the situation: "The Library of Congress is not now, as a collection, an organic collection, even for the most particular service it has to render; it is not yet classified, nor equipped with the mechanism necessary to its effective use; the present organization is but partial; and the resources have yet to be provided not merely for the proper development of the collection, but for the work of bringing the existing material into condition for effective service." (Atlantic Monthly 85:145–58)

FEBRUARY 12. The House Appropriations Committee approves a "reorganization of the Library" as described in Putnam's budget request. (56/1 HRR 289)

APRIL 6. Putnam asks Melvil Dewey if he is in the process of revising his decimal classification scheme. The Librarian explains that he is not inquiring because of any mere abstract interest, "but because we are about to reclassify. If by any possibility I can justify the use of D.C. I shall prefer to use it." He notes however, that "in its present form, the arguments against its use in this Library seem insuperable." (LCA-L)

APRIL 17. President McKinley approves the legislative, executive, and judicial appropriations act for fiscal 1901. The new law authorizes the establishment of new divisions for bibliography, documents, ordering, and binding in the Library of Congress, as well as a new division for the administration of the Smithsonian deposit. An increase in the annual salary of the Librarian to $6,000 also is included. (31 Stat. 86)

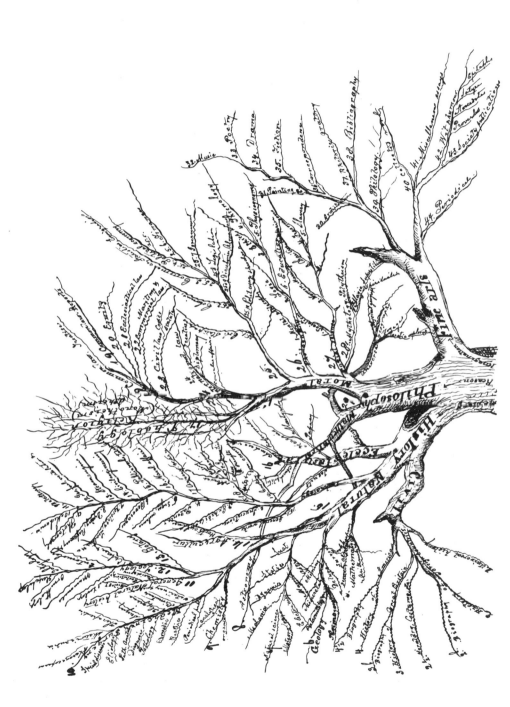

This "tree of classification," anonymously penned in the 1890's, illustrates the classification system used in the Library of Congress until 1897. Its caption reads: "The Library is divided into 44 chapters. The system of classification was originally prepared by President Jefferson, but has been modified since. It is based upon Lord Bacon's division of knowledge, the subjects classed according to the faculties of the mind employed on them."

Librarian Young made the decision to reclassify the collections, and work was started under the direction of J. C. M. Hanson and Charles Martel. Librarian Putnam restudied the question and finally decided that the Library could not use any scheme in current use. Instead, an entirely new system was to be developed, based on the special character of the Library's collections and the conditions of their use. The first new classification schedule was published in 1901. LCA; LC–USZ62–6015

69

JUNE. Librarian Putnam departs for a European trip to "stimulate" the Library's exchange agreements and reorganize its overseas purchase methods.

OCTOBER 1. Putnam informs the secretary of the treasury that he is holding the position of chief of the Manuscripts Division vacant "until the salary shall be placed at a sum which will enable me to secure for it a thoroughly adequate person." (1900 AR:10)

OCTOBER 19. The Librarian tells William I. Fletcher, librarian of Amherst College, that after intensive study he has reached the reluctant conclusion that the Library cannot use any classification scheme in current use, and "to modify may be less satisfactory than to devise newly for ourselves." (LCA-L)

OCTOBER 20. In a letter to Library Committee Chairman Wetmore, the Librarian emphasizes that the specialty of the Library of Congress is Americana and that the Library is "a bureau of information" for Americana that serves both the entire country and the entire world, "for of all American libraries it will sustain the most active and intimate relations with libraries abroad, and through the Smithsonian with all learned societies abroad." (LCA-L)

DECEMBER. A branch of the Government Printing Office is established within the Library to print catalog cards and continue the repair of historical documents. (LCA)

DECEMBER 4. Putnam explains that his annual statistics of reading room use are "given only in accordance with custom," for "the service of a library such as this is not to be measured by the number of readers nor by the number of books issued." He also notes that the Library has expanded its foreign newspaper collection "to include those which would exhibit most accurately the current political, industrial, and commercial intelligence of the various countries in whose activities Congress and the public

might be interested." As a consequence, over 120 foreign newspapers are now received on a current basis. (1900 AR:15, 23, 33–37)

JANUARY. The reclassification of the Library's collections resumes. The Library publishes the first new classification schedule, *Class E and F: America: History and Geography; Preliminary and Provisional Scheme of Classification*, prepared by Chief Classifier Charles Martel. (LCA)

JANUARY. The Library begins printing cards for all books being cataloged or recataloged. (LCA)

MARCH. The Library publishes its first manuscript calendar: *A Calendar of Washington Manuscripts in the Library of Congress*, compiled under the direction of Herbert Friedenwald. (LCA)

MARCH 2. President McKinley approves a joint resolution of Congress directing the public printer to furnish the Library of Congress with two copies of all congressional and executive documents for its own use and up to 100 copies for use in international exchange. (31 Stat. 1464)

MARCH 3. The President approves the legislative, executive, and judicial appropriations act for fiscal 1902. The new law includes a provision extending access to governmental libraries to "scientific investigators and duly qualified individuals" from the "several States and Territories" as well as from the District of Columbia. Librarian Putnam interprets this law as authority for the Library of Congress to inaugurate an interlibrary loan service. (31 Stat. 960; LCA)

APRIL. The electric automobile is purchased for $2,000, enabling the Library "to make a delivery twice daily at any point within the ordinary limits." (LCA; 1901 AR:44, 51)

MAY. The Library publishes *A Check List of American Newspapers in the Library of Congress*, compiled under the direction of A. B. Slauson, chief of the Periodicals Division. The volume lists nearly 400 daily newspapers that are permanently retained. (LCA)

JUNE. *A Union List of Periodicals, Transactions, and Allied Publications Currently Received in the Principal Libraries of the District of Columbia* is published. Putnam notes that "this is the first cooperative publication of the Library, and the beginning of what we trust will be an effective cooperation among the Federal libraries at Washington." (1901 AR:37)

JULY. The Library publishes *A List of Maps of America in the Library of Congress,* by Philip Lee Phillips, chief of the Division of Maps and Charts. The 1,000-page catalog, described by its compiler as "a subject-chronological monograph," is preceded by a lengthy list of works relating to cartography. Since the Library of Congress "contains the largest single collection in existence of maps relating to America," Putnam feels the volume is an extremely important contribution to cartography. (1901 AR:39-40)

JULY 4. At the annual meeting of the American Library Association, held in Waukesha, Wis., Putnam addresses himself to the subject of "what may be done for libraries by the nation" and declares: "If there is any way in which our National Library may 'reach out' from Washington, it should reach out." One proposal discussed by the Librarian is a general distribution of printed catalog cards, an idea suggested "a half a century ago by the Federal Government through the Smithsonian Institution," and advocated by Professor Charles C. Jewett. (LJ 26:9-14)

OCTOBER 15. Putnam explains to President Theodore Roosevelt why "a national library for the United States should mean in some respects more than a national library in any other country has hitherto meant." The Librarian notes that other libraries must "look to the National Library" for standards and leadership in uniformity of methods, cooperation in processing, interchange of bib-

---

DISTRIBUTION OF CATALOGUE CARDS.

The Library of Congress,

WASHINGTON, D. C.,

October 28, 1901.

THE Library of Congress is now prepared to furnish a copy or copies of any of the catalogue cards (a) which it is currently printing; (b) which it has heretofore printed, so far as copies of these can be supplied from stock.

The Library is currently printing cards for the following classes of accessions:

(a) Books currently copyrighted under the laws of the United States.
(b) Miscellaneous material, both current and non-current, so far as acquired by it.
(c) The printed books in its present collection as these are reached in the process of reclassification.

The cards already printed have included the following:

(a) Copyrighted books since July 1, 1898.
(b) Miscellaneous accessions since January 1, 1901, and in part since January 1, 1900.
(c) The two groups in the existing collection already reclassified, to wit: Bibliography and Library Science; American History. (The group next to be dealt with is Political and Social Science.)

Samples of the printed cards are enclosed herewith. They are author cards merely. Subject headings will, however, be suggested on cards in the following groups at least:

1. Copyrighted books;
2. Bibliography and Library Science;
3. American History, and
4. Each new group as reclassified.

In the Library of Congress these subject headings are prefixed, with pen or typewriter, to the author cards in order to form subject cards.

Subscription Price.

The charge will be based upon the cost (including handling) of the extra copies, plus 10 %. What this charge will be will depend upon the number of copies subscribed for, both in the aggregate and by any particular library. For a single copy of a single card it will not exceed two cents.

Orders.

1. Orders will be accepted in any form which specifically identifies the book (i. e. the card desired). For copyrighted books the most convenient form of order would be a checked copy of the Weekly Bulletin of copyright entries, containing the titles desired. This Bulletin is a publication of the Treasury Department It is available to any subscriber at a cost of $5 per year. Subscriptions for it should be addressed to the Treasury Department, at Washington.

2. The Publishers' Weekly contains almost all the titles in the Bulletin that would interest the ordinary library, and many of the uncopyrighted books also. Orders may be sent in in the form of a checked copy of the Publishers' Weekly.

In 1901, finding that the Library of Congress could no longer ignore "the opportunity and the appeal" of the idea of centralized cataloging, Putnam began the sale and distribution of the Library's printed catalog cards. In the announcement he explained: "American instinct and habit revolt against multiplication of brain effort and outlay where a multiplication of results can be achieved by machinery. This appears to be a case where it may." LCA

liographic service, and, in general, the promotion of efficiency in services.

OCTOBER 28. A circular announcing the sale and distribution of Library of Congress printed catalog cards is sent to over 500 American libraries. Putnam notes that "a centralization of cataloguing work, with a corresponding centralization of bibliographic apparatus, has been for a quarter of a century an ambition of the librarians of the United States" and terms the new card service "the most significant of our undertakings of this first year of the new century." Certain libraries, such as the New York Public Library, will receive depository copies of every card printed in exchange for a copy of every card they print. A separate Card Section, under the direction of Charles H. Hastings, is established.

(1901 AR:29–37, 69–73)

DECEMBER 2. The Library publishes its annual report for 1901, a 380-page volume featuring a "manual" that describes its history, organization, facilities, collections, and operations. Putnam reports an increase in the Library's total appropriation to over $500,000; approximately $60,000 of this sum is for the purchase of library materials. Furthermore, the Library of Congress has become the first American library to contain over one million volumes. The Librarian declares that "the purpose of the administration is the freest possible use of the books consistent with their safety; and the widest possible use consistent with the convenience of Congress." He also explains that since the Library is in the legislative branch of the government, "the regulations adopted by the Executive Departments, including the rules for the government of employees, are not mandatory upon the Library. But as the Library has in its administration many activities properly executive . . . many such regulations are in fact accepted by the authorities of the Library as having an analogy useful to its purpose."

(1901 AR:203–7)

DECEMBER 3. In his first state of the Union message, President Theodore Roosevelt calls the Library of Con-

THE LIBRARY OF CONGRESS

IS OPEN EVERY WEEK DAY FROM 9 A.M. UNTIL 10 P.M.

On Saturday morning, Dec. 28th, beginning at 9 a. m., special facilities will be offered for inspecting the administrative portions. Visitors are recommended to begin with the basement (ground floor) and circle the floors in succession.

The departments of special interest will then be reached in the following order:

Basement—to the right: Copyright Office, Bindery, Printing Office, Music Division, Reading Room for the Blind.

Second (main) **floor**—to the right: Representatives' Reading Room, Senators' Reading Room, Periodical Reading Room, Catalogue Division, Division of Bibliography, Order Division, Division of Manuscripts, Division of Maps and Charts; then through north bookstack to the Main Reading Room and return to hallway. Librarian's Office to the right.

Third floor—to the right: Exhibits of prints, Division of Prints, and then through east wing to the Pavilion of the Seals, where the members of the Historical Association gather at 10.30 o'clock. After the papers here, return to the main hallway through the Division of Documents and the northwest exhibit rooms.

The Public Restaurant is on the floor above the third floor, and is reached only by the elevators.

DECEMBER 28, 1901.

The new Library building was a popular tourist attraction and meeting site. This handout (above) was prepared for a meeting of the local history society, held in the northeast pavilion (the Pavilion of Seals) on December 28, 1901. Visitors were invited to walk through this prints exhibit on the third floor on their way to the meeting. The painting at the end of the gallery, "The Arts" by Kenyon Cox, is 34 feet long and over 9 feet high. LC-US262-37241

73

The lavish House of Representatives Reading Room on the main floor of the southwest gallery. Frederick Dielman's mosaic panel "Law" can be seen over the marble fireplace at the north end of the gallery. LC-USZ62-051467

74

1901

gress "the one national library of the United States' and a library that "has a unique opportunity to render to the libraries of this country—to American scholarship—service of the highest importance." (SUM 2 2049)

1902

JUNE 28. The President approves an act of Congress authorizing the Library to sell copies of its "card indexes" and other publications "to such institutions and individuals as may desire to buy them." All proceeds shall be deposited in the U.S. Treasury. (32 Stat. 419)

JUNE 30. The first complete count of the books and pamphlets in over three decades is completed, showing an aggregate total of 1,114,111 volumes. (1902 AR:17)

SEPTEMBER 14. As authorized in its last appropriation, the Library begins Sunday hours, remaining open from 2 until 10 P.M. (1902 AR:41)

NOVEMBER 29. Charles H. Hastings reports that depository sets of all cards printed by the Library are being sent to 21 libraries throughout the United States and Canada to make the collections of the Library of Congress more widely known, to promote bibliographical work and uniformity in cataloging, and to facilitate the ordering of cards from libraries in different regions. (1902 AR:103)

DECEMBER 1. In his annual report, Putnam announces the appointments of several subject specialists, including two new division chiefs: Oscar George Theodore Sonneck of the Music Division and Worthington Chauncey Ford of the Manuscripts Division. The Librarian explains that only experts such as these "can realize the need of the inquirer, can assume for the time being his point of view, can translate the language of the classification and the catalogue." He also reports that the Library's Orientalia collection of nearly 10,000 volumes is now "believed to be the largest representation in this country of the literature of the Far East." (1902 AR:12, 13, 19)

1903

JANUARY 27. The Librarian informs the Library Committee that to make the Library of Congress a general circulating library for the public would "tend rather to the injury than the aid of serious research in this Library, including its use by Congress." He points out that this function "can be more effectively dealt with by the Public Library of the District." (1907 AR:158)

FEBRUARY 25. President Roosevelt approves the legislative, executive, and judicial appropriations act for fiscal 1904. The new law authorizes U.S. government agencies to transfer to the Library of Congress "any books, maps, or other material no longer needed for its use and in the judgement of the Librarian of Congress appropriate for the uses of the Library." (32 Stat. 854)

MARCH 9. An executive order issued by President Roosevelt directs the transfer of the records and personal papers of Washington, Madison, Jefferson, Hamilton, Monroe, and Franklin from the State Department to the Library of Congress, "to be there preserved and rendered accessible" for historical and "other legitimate uses." (1903 AR:24–25)

JUNE. Librarian Putnam begins a one-year term of office as president of the American Library Association. (HP)

JULY. The Kohl collection of manuscript copies of maps significant in the history of cartography is transferred from the Department of State to the Library. (LCA; 1903 AR:30)

1904

JANUARY 24. A cylinder recording of the voice of Kaiser Wilhelm II is made. This recording, presented to the Library shortly thereafter, is the first phonograph record acquired by the Library of Congress. (LCA; Library Trends 21:53)

1904

APRIL. Publication of *History of the Library of Congress, 1800–1864*, volume 1, by William Dawson Johnston of the Catalogue Division. The volume is planned as part of a "general history of American libraries." (1904 AR:90)

APRIL 20. The Louisiana Purchase Exposition at St. Louis opens. The Library of Congress exhibit, which emphaizes the "National Library," marks "the first direct participation of the Library in any of the great international expositions." (1904 AR: 227–87)

JULY 11. Putnam informs the staff that he "will at any season and with or without special appointment, be glad to see any member of the force who desires to confer with him, whether the matter concern his status or prospects, or the duties or privileges or comforts of the service, or be purely personal." (so)

OCTOBER. In cooperation with the New York State Library and the American Library Association, the Library publishes the *A.L.A. Catalog: 8,000 Volumes for a Popular Library*. (LCA)

DECEMBER 5. Putnam explains that his annual reports are lengthier than those of the British Museum or the Bibliothèque nationale only because the Library of Congress is pursuing activities "of which their operations afford no example." The Librarian includes in this year's report a description of the recent purchase of a 4,000-volume collection of Indica, formerly the personal library of Albrecht Weber, professor of Sanskrit at the University of Berlin. He points out that the Library could not "ignore such an opportunity to acquire a unique collection which scholarship thought worthy of prolonged, scientific, and enthusiastic research, even though the immediate use of such a collection may prove meager." Another new activity is announced: the publication of historical texts from the Library's collections, beginning with

1904

the Journals of the Continental Congress and the Records of the Virginia Company. The manuscripts will be published to "save excessive wear and tear upon the originals," to "enable the texts to be studied by investigators who cannot come to Washington," and "to promote a proper understanding and representation of American history." (1904 AR:8, 27–31, 64–70)

1905

MAY 31. Putnam convenes, in New York City, the first in a series of conferences to consider revision of the copyright laws. (1905 AR:88)

JULY 5. The Librarian justifies the liberal interlibrary loan policy of the Library of Congress, explaining that if a volume be lost in the process: "I know of but one answer: that a book used is, after all, fulfilling a higher mission than a book which is merely being preserved for possible future use." (LJ 30:C30)

DECEMBER. The Library's program for copying manuscripts in foreign archives that relate to American history officially begins. Planned by Putnam, J. Franklin Jameson of the Carnegie Institution, and officials of the American Historical Association, the project starts with records in the British Museum and the Bodleian Library in Oxford. The documents to be transcribed were selected by Charles M. Andrews of Bryn Mawr and the work is performed by the London firm of B.F. Stevens and Brown. (1905 AR:56–58)

DECEMBER 5. Superintendent Green recommends the "occupation of the southeast court" for storage of the rapidly growing bound newspaper collection. All other adequate shelving is in use. (1905 AR:103)

1906

MAY 17. H. G. Wells is among the luncheon guests entertained by Librarian Putnam at his "Round Table," an informal dining room on the top floor of the Library. A few months later, Wells describes the event in his book

Workmen erecting mahogany display cases in the south gallery or Print Room. The coffered skylight in this room is decorated with gilt "cherub's wings." The design in the stained glass lists the names of the signers of the Declaration of Independence. Photograph by Flynn Photo Company (ca. 1905). LC-USZ-62-3865

77

The Great Hall of the Library of Congress. The entrance to the Main Reading Room is through the marble arch at the lower right. The staircases were designed by Philip Martiny. The floor consists of red and yellow Italian marble; brass inlays representing the signs of the zodiac are arranged in a square pattern enclosing the large rayed disc, or sun, as the centerpiece. LC-USZ62-36227

1906

The Future in America: "I found at last a little group of men who could talk. It was like a small raft upon a limitless empty sea. I lunched with them at their Round Table, and afterwards Mr. Putnam showed me the Rotunda."

(LCA)

MAY 23. President Roosevelt, in an executive order, directs "further transfers of historical material from the Department of State" to the Library, including the papers of Jefferson Davis and material relating to the Whiskey Rebellion and the Burr Conspiracy. (1906 AR:26–27)

JUNE 6. The patent committees of the House of Representatives and the Senate, sitting as a joint committee, begin hearings on the general revision of the U.S. copyright law. The hearings are held in the Library's Senate Reading Room and Librarian Putnam is the first witness. Other witnesses include R. R. Bowker, Victor Herbert, and John Philip Sousa.

(1906 AR:14–15; 1965 AR:2–3)

JUNE 30. The President approves an act of Congress appropriating funds for the civil expenses of the government in fiscal 1907. The new law includes funds enabling the Library of Congress to prepare a new index to the *Statutes at Large* and "to prepare such other indexes, digests, and compilations of law as may be required for Congress and other official use." The same law gives the Library responsibility for publishing the *Catalogue of Title-Entries* of copyright deposits, which is prepared by the Copyright Office. Since July 1891 the *Catalogue* has been published by the Treasury Department.

(34 Stat. 697)

JULY 7. Register of Copyrights Solberg explains to James Bain, librarian of the Toronto Public Library, why he has changed the organization of the *Catalogue* of copyright deposits: "I want to make it so complete a bibliographical record of copyright registrations that it will be indispensable to most libraries."

(Copyright Office archives)

1907

AUGUST 5. Librarian Putnam reluctantly accepts the resignation of David Hutcheson, who served as Chief Assistant to Librarian Spofford from 1874 to 1897 and then as superintendent of the Reading Room until the present time. Hutcheson's reasons for resigning are "advancing age, fatigue of long service, and premonitions of ill health." (1907 AR:10–12)

NOVEMBER 4. Putnam receives approval from the attorney general to use the following wording for gifts or bequests to the Library: "To the United States of America, to be placed in the Library of Congress and administered therein by the authorities thereof." (LCA)

DECEMBER 2. The Librarian announces the first large acquisition of Japanese books. The 9,000 volumes were carefully selected in Japan by Kan-Ichi Asakawa, a Yale University professor, to provide the Library with a good "working" collection for the student of Japanese literature, history, and institutions. (1907 AR:24–29)

DECEMBER 7. President Roosevelt asks Putnam to send him a report "upon the subject of a Hall of Records" or archive building for governmental departmental papers, a proposal recently presented by J. Franklin Jameson of the Carnegie Institution of Washington. (LCA)

DECEMBER 20. Putnam informs the President that a separate government archives building should be constructed "for the accommodation of administrative records of the various departments which ought not to be destroyed, but which are not appropriate for the collections of the Library." (LCA)

DECEMBER 24. Upon learning of Putnam's endorsement of an archives building, Jameson thanks the Librarian and restates the position held by both: ". . . that there is no conflict at all between the desirability of gathering into the Library of Congress as much as it cares to house of those manuscript-materials which are primarily his-

1906

OCTOBER. President Roosevelt congratulates Putnam "upon having concluded to purchase" the private library of G. V. Yudin of Siberia, which contains over 80,000 volumes of Russian literature. The President notes that the acquisition will give the Library of Congress "preeminence in this particular field, not only in the United States, but as far as I know, in the world generally outside of Russia; and this in a field not yet developed at all in America." (LCA)

NOVEMBER. The Library publishes the *A.L.A. Portrait Index* for the American Library Association. (LCA)

DECEMBER 3. Putnam notes the expansion of "cooperation in cataloging among departmental libraries." Uniform cataloging rules for the Library of Congress, the libraries of the Department of Agriculture and the Geological Survey, and the Washington Public Library now make it possible for the cards prepared in one of these libraries to "be fitted into the catalogues of any of the other three." (1906 AR:56)

DECEMBER 8. Putnam explains to Representative Henry H. Bingham of Pennsylvania, chairman of the Legislative Appropriation Subcommittee, that, in addition to lending books to Congress and other borrowers designated by statute, the Library lends "to any person engaged in a serious investigation calculated to advance the boundaries of knowledge." (1907 AR:158–59)

1907

APRIL. The last shipment of the Yudin library arrives from Siberia. Since the sum paid for the collection "scarcely exceeded a third of what the owner himself had expended," Putnam considers the acquisition "primarily a gift." (1907 AR 20–24)

JUNE 30. The Librarian reports that the Library's reference service through correspondence is growing rapidly; perhaps as many as 10,000 letters a year are received. (1907 AR:77–78)

torical, and the necessity (and utility to historical scholars incidentally) of providing a better storehouse for the main masses of administrative papers."

(LCA)

MAY 22. The President approves the legislative, executive, and judicial appropriations act for fiscal 1909, which includes $320,000 for the construction of a new bookstack in the Library's southeast courtyard. (35 Stat. 184)

JULY. The American Library Association publishes the American edition of the Anglo-American cataloging rules, which represent a compromise between cataloging rules developed by the Library of Congress and those used by other libraries. The editor is J. C. M. Hanson, chief of the Library of Congress Catalogue Division. (1908 AR:45–47)

AUGUST 11. Death of Ainsworth Rand Spofford, Chief Assistant Librarian of Congress. Librarian Putnam notes that Spofford's title during the last eleven years "did not obscure his greater office, that of Librarian Emeritus, nor the distinction to the Library or the honor to himself of the service which for thirty-two years he had rendered as its Librarian-in-chief." (1908 AR:7)

NOVEMBER. The Library purchases, from Albert Schatz of Rostock, Germany, Mr. Schatz's famous collection of over 12,000 early opera librettos. (LCA: 1909 AR:38)

NOVEMBER 12. Putnam presides over a memorial meeting honoring Spofford, held in the Library's Senate Reading Room. (LCA)

DECEMBER. The Library publishes the first issue of its List of Subject Headings, compiled by the Catalogue Division. (1909 AR:52)

DECEMBER 7. In his annual report for 1908, Putnam notes the promotion of Chief Bibliographer Appleton P. C. Griffin to the post of Chief Assistant Librarian. (1908 AR:8)

DECEMBER 7. Because the Library of Congress has now become "national in aim and scope," Putnam suggests that the libraries of U.S. government departments and agencies should, as far as practicable, 1) limit their collections to their special fields of service; 2) interchange with the Library of Congress information about material in the collections of each institution; 3) recommend to the Library of Congress the acquisition of material . . . "fundamental in their work but beyond their means"; and 4) fully utilize the cataloging information and classification schemes of the Library of Congress. (1908 AR:60–63)

DECEMBER 29. The Librarian accepts a complete set of the world's largest printed encyclopedia, the 5,041-volume *Tu Shu Tsi Cheng*, presented by the Chinese government "with the acknowledgements of China to the United States for the remission of the 'Boxer indemnity.'" (1909 AR:21–23)

MARCH 4. President Roosevelt approves the legislative, executive, and judicial appropriations act for fiscal 1910. The new law authorizes the Librarian of Congress to transfer surplus materials to other governmental libraries within the District of Columbia as well as to the public library and also "to dispose of or destroy such material as has become useless." (35 Stat. 845)

MARCH 4. The President approves an act of Congress which amends and consolidates the copyright law; the revision is based primarily on a bill prepared by the Copyright Office. Major changes from the 1870 law provide that copyright can be secured by publication of a work with notice of copyright and make copyright available for unpublished works designed for exhibition or performance, such as lectures, dramatic works, and musical compositions. Also included in the law is authorization for the Librarian of Congress to determine what copyright deposits "shall be transferred to the permanent collections of the Library of Congress, including the law library, and

1909

what other books or articles shall be placed in the reserve collection of the Library of Congress for sale or exchange, or be transferred to other governmental agencies in the District of Columbia for use therein."

(35 Stat. 1075; 1906 AR:111–25)

JUNE 30. Oscar G. T. Sonneck, chief of the Music Division, reports to Putnam on his success in soliciting gifts of original music manuscripts to the Library, noting that "it is gratifying to see the repeated appeals to possessors of the original manuscripts of American composers gradually becoming effective."

(1909 AR:36)

AUGUST. The Library publishes O. G. T. Sonneck's 255-page *Report* on "*The Star-Spangled Banner," "Hail Columbia," "America," and "Yankee Doodle.*" In the preface the author states that although the *Report* is "not intended for popular consumption, it may be used for popular consumption with reasonable assurance of accuracy."

(LCA)

AUGUST. The Library publishes the first volume of *A List of Geographical Atlases of America in the Library of Congress,* which contains analytical descriptions of over 3,200 atlases. The compiler, Philip Lee Phillips, chief of the Division of Maps and Charts, explains in the preface that heretofore atlases have not received bibliographic attention equivalent "to their importance in literature and as contributions to knowledge."

(LCA)

DECEMBER. Superintendent of the Reading Room William Warner Bishop opposes the development of a separate "central storage library and bureau of information" which would lend books to college libraries—a proposal of Harvard Librarian William C. Lane. Bishop maintains that the Library of Congress already is "on the way toward becoming a national lending library and bureau of information."

(LJ 34:527–32)

1910

JANUARY. The Library publishes the first issue of the *Monthly List of State Publications,* compiled by the Division of Documents.

(1910 AR:42–43)

MARCH. The catalog card program is expanded to include the printing of cards from copy prepared by libraries outside of the District of Columbia.

(1910 AR:72)

MARCH. The new bookstack in the southeast courtyard is completed. It contains 44 miles of shelving and, according to Superintendent Green, will accommodate about 946,000 volumes of books and 94,000 volumes of newspapers. The total size of the Library's book collection is approximately 1,800,000 volumes.

(1910 AR:18, 80–81)

APRIL 27. Mrs. John Boyd Thacher places a valuable collection of 840 15th-century books on deposit at the Library of Congress. The volumes were collected by her late husband, a former mayor of Albany, N.Y.

(LCA; 1910 AR:23–24)

MAY. The Library publishes *American and English Genealogies in the Library of Congress,* which lists over 3,700 titles.

(LCA)

MAY 13. Bibliographer and historian Henry Harrisse dies, bequeathing to the Library of Congress his personal library of maps, manuscripts, and rare books, along with a full set of his personal writings.

(1915 AR:31–35)

OCTOBER. J. C. M. Hanson, chief of the Catalogue Division, resigns to become associate director of the University of Chicago Library. Putnam notes that the full significance of Hanson's achievements "can be realized only by those who understand what an exact, full, and scientific catalogue—an author and a subject catalogue—means for

1910

a collection of books already the third largest in the world."

(1910 AR:7–8)

NOVEMBER 29. Putnam requests a salary increase for the office of Librarian of Congress: "The position justifies the increase, and really, in its own interest, permanently requires it." He adds: "Librarians in general are not people given to luxuries; they are content to live modestly; but they ought not to have to live penuriously."

(1912 HRA:13)

1911

MARCH 4. The Librarian announces that he has arranged for the continuation of service to Congress. "whenever either House of Congress is sitting. . . . This service is to cover, of course, all all-night sessions, the morning of holidays, and Sunday mornings when Congress is sitting even when eulogies are being delivered."

(so 86)

APRIL 6. In response to the introduction in Congress of several bills on the subject, Putnam submits a special report "relative to legislative reference bureaus." Included are materials describing legislative reference services in several states, particularly New York and Wisconsin. Putnam states that the "main object is the improvement of legislation," and emphasizes the specialized nature of the bureaus, which undertake "not merely to classify and catalogue, but to draw off from a general collection the literature—that is, the data—bearing on upon a particular legislative project. It indexes, extracts, compiles. . . . To printed literature it often adds written memoranda as to fact and even opinion as to merit." Finally, it organizes and concentrates "all the data pertinent to a question in such form as to be readily responsive." The Librarian informs the Senate that the Library would "gladly undertake" such work, but that it is beyond the abilities of the institution with its present organization. It would require "an enlargement of its present Divisions of Law, Documents, and Bibliography, and in addition the creation of a new division under the title of a Legislative or Congres-

sional Reference Division." He concludes by emphasizing "that for the work to be scientific (i.e. having only truth as its object) it must be strictly nonpartisan."

(62/1 SD 7:2–3)

APRIL 25. After receiving the Librarian's special report, the Senate Library Committee asks Putnam for his version of a satisfactory bill for the establishment of a legislative reference bureau.

(LCA)

DECEMBER 4. In his annual report for 1911, Putnam notes that the Library recently declined to accept custody, from another government department, of the records of the American military occupation of Cuba from 1898 to 1902; the reason was that "such papers should go to a national archives repository."

(1911 AR:26)

1912

JANUARY. The Library publishes a general handbook that describes its organization, collections, and services. The author, William Warner Bishop, superintendent of the Reading Room, emphasizes that since 1897 the Library, "while rendering greatly increased service to Congress, has begun a career of service to the whole nation."

(LCA)

JANUARY 8. Chief Clerk Allen R. Boyd announces that the Library's new photostat and flexotype machines "are now available" for use.

(GO 229)

JANUARY 25. Putnam shows copies of maps, prints, and newspaper pages made by the new photostat machine to members of the House of Representatives Appropriations Subcommittee. He asks the subcommittee to approve a small appropriation for the salary of the machine operator, who makes copies of items from the collections for the public.

FEBRUARY 26. The House Library Committee holds hearings to consider a bill that would establish a congressional

preserve "such of the papers as he may deem to be of historical interest." (1912 AR:34–35)

APRIL. A collection of nearly 10,000 volumes and pamphlets of Hebraica, gathered by Ephraim Deinard, is donated to the Library by Jacob H. Schiff of New York City. Putnam terms it a notable foundation which will be expanded "into a significant department embracing all Semitica." (1912 AR:7, 23–25)

MAY. The Library publishes the *Guide to the Law and Legal Literature of Germany*, by Law Librarian Edwin M. Borchard, the first in a series of guides to the laws of foreign countries. (1912 AR:65–66)

MAY 20. Putnam sends a circular letter to American universities that explains a new plan for collecting and cataloging the doctoral dissertations submitted to those universities. The dissertations will be sent to the Library, which will catalog them and then publish, beginning in 1912, an annual list of American doctoral dissertations. (1912 AR:86–88)

AUGUST 20. President Taft approves an act of Congress accepting a bequest from Mrs. Gardiner Greene Hubbard which will provide for the future growth of the Hubbard collection of engravings. (37 Stat. 319)

AUGUST 24. The President approves an act of Congress extending copyright protection to motion pictures as a distinct form. Because of the flammability of nitrate film stock, the Library begins retaining printed descriptions of motion pictures—but not the films themselves—as evidence of copyright. Before this act, motion pictures were deposited as photographs in paper print form. (37 Stat. 488; LCA)

NOVEMBER 19. J. Pierpont Morgan informs President Taft: "I herewith present to the United States of America,

reference bureau in the Library of Congress. Representative John M. Nelson of Wisconsin, the sponsor of the bill, reads several endorsements, including one from Governor Woodrow Wilson of New Jersey, then introduces James Bryce, British ambassador to the United States. Ambassador Bryce explains that he agreed to testify on behalf of the bill only after he became satisfied that the subject of a legislative reference bureau "was one of entirely nonpartisan character, which did not raise any domestic political issue upon which the parties were divided in this country, when it was in fact a matter deemed to be of common concern." Another witness, Frederick A. Cleveland, chairman of President Taft's Commission on Economy and Efficiency, endorses the idea of specialized aid to government agencies: "It is the German idea, of having scientific staff back of the line; and to my mind it is the one thing that has made Germany more proficient than any other nation in its governmental processes." Charles A. McCarthy of the Wisconsin legislative reference department answers questions and emphasizes the need for close supervision of a legislative reference bureau: "It must be checked so it will not go to sleep and become a great big bureau of red tape and checked so that it cannot be made a football of politics." (1912 HRH:7, 33, 45)

FEBRUARY 27. At the conclusion of the hearings, Representative Nelson addresses the committee: "I plead for the individual Member of Congress. He needs information and data upon legislation upon which he is to vote upon bills that he intends to submit upon legislation pending; and I trust that this committee will not urge upon Congress a one-sided bill, one that will simply look after a committee or a party leader, but that we will have an institution here that will look to the collective efficiency, and will enlarge the individual capacity of every Member of the House for legislative service." (1912 HRH:114)

MARCH 16. President William H. Taft issues an executive order directing the Librarian of Congress to review documents not wanted by the executive agencies in order to

1912

to be placed in the Library of Congress . . . a complete bound set of letters and documents from the Signers of the Declaration of Independence, which, it seems to me, is more fittingly preserved in the National Library than in that of any individual."

NOVEMBER 20. Putnam directs employees that in answering telephone calls they are first to announce the name of their division, because "the exclamations, 'Hello!' 'What is it?' etc., now much in use are unnecessary." (1913 AR:60)

1913

FEBRUARY 4. The Senate Library Committee holds hearings to consider two bills: the first, sponsored by Senator Robert M. LaFollette of Wisconsin, would create a "legislative drafting bureau," and a Legislative Reference Division in the Library; the second, introduced by Senator Robert L. Owen of Oklahoma, would "establish the Legislative Reference Bureau of the Library of Congress and the congressional corps of legislative investigators." Librarian Putnam states his opposition to including bill-drafting in the proposed bureau: "I can see many reasons why it should be separate and apart from the organization of the legislative reference bureau. I may go further and say that it preferably should be, and that impression is confirmed by my attendance in the hearings before the House." (62/3 SR 1271:30)

FEBRUARY 18. The House Library Committee recommends the creation of a legislative reference service that does not include the bill-drafting function. It recommends that the director be appointed by the Librarian of Congress, subject to the approval of the Joint Committee on the Library. (62/3 HRR 1533)

FEBRUARY 20. On behalf of the Senate Library Committee, Elihu Root of New York reports favorably on Senator LaFollette's bill, making only minor amendments. (62/3 SR 1271)

LIBRARY OF CONGRESS

INTER-LIBRARY LOANS

MEMORANDUM

Under the system of inter-library loans the Library of Congress will lend certain books to other libraries for the use of investigators engaged in serious research. The loan will rest on the theory of a special service to scholarship which it is not within the power or the duty of the local library to render. Its purpose is to aid research calculated to advance the boundaries of knowledge, by the loan of unusual books not readily accessible elsewhere.

The material lent can not include, therefore, books that should be in a local library, or that can be borrowed from a library (such as a state library) having a particular duty to the community from which the application comes; nor books that are inexpensive and can easily be procured; nor books for the general reader, mere text books, or popular manuals; nor books where the purpose is ordinary student or thesis work, or for mere self-instruction.

Nor can it include material which is in constant use at Washington, or whose loan would be an inconvenience to Congress, or to the Executive Departments of the Government, or to reference readers in the Library of Congress.

Genealogies and local histories are not available for loan, nor are newspapers, for they form part of a consecutive historical record which the Library of Congress is expected to retain and preserve. And only for very serious research can the privilege be extended to include volumes of periodicals.

A library in borrowing a book is understood to hold itself responsible for the safe-keeping and return of the book at the expiration of 10 days from its receipt. An extension of the period of loan is granted, upon request, whenever feasible. It is expected that books so lent will not be taken from the building of the borrowing library. Exceptions to this rule must be authorized by the Library of Congress.

All expenses of carriage are to be met by the borrowing library.

Books will be forwarded by express (charges collect) whenever this conveyance is deemed necessary for their safety. Certain books, however, can be sent by mail, but it will be necessary for the borrowing library to remit in advance a sum sufficient to cover the postal charges, including registry fee.

The Library of Congress has no fund from which charges of carriage can be prepaid.

MARCH, 1913.

Herbert Putnam

LIBRARIAN OF CONGRESS

The Library of Congress began lending books to other libraries in 1901. Four years later, Librarian Putnam justified the Library's relatively liberal policy by explaining that if a book is lost in the process, "I know of but one answer: that a book used is, after all, fulfilling a higher mission than a book which is merely being preserved for possible future use." In 1913 the Librarian outlined the Library's loan policies in the general memorandum illustrated here. LCA

1913

MARCH 14. President Woodrow Wilson approves the legislative, executive, and judicial appropriations act for fiscal 1914. The new law directs the American Printing House for the Blind of Louisville, Ky., to deposit in the Library of Congress one copy of each embossed book that it manufactures with federal financial assistance. (37 Stat. 739)

JULY 10. Because of the "great changes to be made in the laws of the Nation" under President Wilson's New Freedom program, the Senate Library Committee urges that a legislative reference bureau be established in the Library of Congress "as quickly as possible." (63/1 SR 73)

1914

JANUARY. The Library publishes a two-volume *Catalogue of Opera Librettos Printed Before 1800*, which lists 6,450 librettos from the Library's collection. (LCA; 1914 AR:114–16)

JUNE 15. As the Senate debate over the legislative branch appropriations bill draws to a close, Senator LaFollette offers the following amendment, which is agreed to: "Legislative reference: To enable the Librarian of Congress to employ competent persons to prepare such indexes, digests, and compilations of law as may be required for Congress and other official use pursuant to the Act approved June 30, 1906, $25,000." (CR 51:10467)

JUNE 26. Disagreements regarding the functions of the proposed legislative reference bureau are finally resolved when the House of Representatives votes, 140 to 94, to accept the Senate amendment to the appropriations bill. In the debate, Representative James W. Good of Iowa assures his colleagues that the Librarian of Congress will give this rather small appropriation a "broad interpretation." (CR 51:11207–9)

JULY 1. Putnam establishes the Division of Semitica and Oriental Literature. (1914 AR:30)

1914

JULY 16. President Wilson approves the legislative, executive, and judicial appropriations act for fiscal 1915, which includes the $25,000 for "legislative reference" in the Library of Congress. (38 Stat. 454)

OCTOBER 22. Death of Bernard R. Green, superintendent of the Library building and grounds. (1914 AR:facing p. 6)

DECEMBER 22. Librarian Putnam establishes a special "Legislative Reference Roll" of selected staff members throughout the Library. Its members are "at any and every moment" subject to call for reference work in response to a congressional request. (SO 101)

1915

MARCH 4. President Wilson approves the legislative, executive, and judicial appropriations act for fiscal 1916, which broadens the functions of the Library's Legislative Reference Service. Beginning on July 1, 1915, the service is authorized "to gather, classify, and make available in translations, indexes, digests, compilations, and bulletins, and otherwise, and data for or bearing upon legislation, and to render such data available to Congress and committees and Members thereof." (38 Stat. 997)

APRIL 19. President Wilson nominates Frank L. Averill to be the new superintendent of the Library building and grounds. (1915 AR:7)

APRIL 23. Mr. Averill assumes his duties as superintendent. (1915 AR:8)

AUGUST. Putnam reports that the new Legislative Reference Service is anticipating questions from Congress concerning conservation, immigration, railroad securities, federal aid in roadmaking, publicity in campaign contributions, and a national budget system. (*American Political Science Review* 9:544)

AUGUST. Reading Room Superintendent William Warner Bishop resigns to become librarian of the University of

Herbert Putnam and the officers of the Library on the steps of the Main Building, 1914. Front row, from left: Thorvald Solberg, register of copyrights, Allen R. Boyd, chief clerk, Jessica L. Farnum, secretary of the Library, Appleton P. C. Griffin, Chief Assistant Librarian, Putnam, Bernard R. Green, superintendent of the building and grounds, and John V. Würdemann, captain of the watch.

Second row: Francis H. Parsons, assistant in charge of the Smithsonian Deposit, Gaillard Hunt, chief of the Division of Manuscripts, Herman H. B. Meyer, chief of the Division of Bibliography, William Warner Bishop, superintendent of the Reading Room, David E. Roberts, assistant in the Division of Prints, Oscar G. T.

Sonneck, chief of the Division of Music, Charles H. Hastings, chief of the Card Division, and Oswald Welti, assistant in the Division of Maps.

Back row: William Adams Slade, chief of the Division of Periodicals, Arthur Kimball, in charge of the Binding Office, Israel Schapiro, in charge of the Semitic Division, Henry J. Harris, chief of the Division of Documents, Ernest Bruncken, assistant register of copyrights, J. David Thompson, in charge of the Legislative Reference Service, Frederick W. Ashley, chief of the Order Division, Samuel M. Croft, in charge of the Mail Division, Charles Martel, chief of the Catalog Division, and Clarence W. Perley, chief classifier. LC-USZ62-6013A

86

1915

Michigan. Bishop's departure, Putnam points out, adds one more name to the list of accomplished men and women "who have graduated from our service into positions of importance elsewhere." (1915 AR:18–19)

DECEMBER 17. The U.S. Senate confirms the appointment of Frank L. Averill as superintendent of the Library building and grounds. (CR 53:399)

1916

APRIL 11. Two drafts of President Abraham Lincoln's Gettysburg Address, believed to be the original and second drafts, are presented to the United States government by the descendants of John Hay and placed in the custody of the Library of Congress. (1916 AR:47–49)

1917

JANUARY. The Library receives the first installment of the gift of the Theodore Roosevelt Papers, the first group of presidential papers received directly from a former President. (LCA)

MAY 24. Mr. and Mrs. Joseph Pennell, the authorized biographers of James Whistler, present a valuable collection of prints and sketches by Whistler to the Library, along with a collection of books and research materials about the artist and his era. (1917 AR:21–22)

OCTOBER. Putnam becomes the director of the American Library Association War Service, which supplies reading matter to American troops training for or engaged in the war, with its general headquarters at the Library of Congress. (1919 AR:8–11)

DECEMBER 3. Because of overcrowded conditions in the stacks, Superintendent Averill recommends the construction of a new bookstack in the northeast courtyard. (1917 AR:213–14)

1918

FEBRUARY. The Library publishes a *Guide to the Cataloguing of Periodicals*, prepared by Mary Wilson MacNair of the Catalogue Division. Its purpose is to provide guidance to catalogers "without intrenching on the exercise of good judgement on their part." (LCA)

APRIL. The Library publishes the 750-page *Handbook of Manuscripts in the Library of Congress*, which describes the resources of the Manuscripts Division "in a comprehensive way for the practical use of the writer, reader, scholar, and student." (LCA)

JULY 25. Putnam distributes a letter addressed to "the loyal staff of the Library of Congress." He explains: You have much to discourage you in the present situation. Your expenses are increasing; your salaries aren't. . . . If you can't live on your salary here you can't be blamed for taking a higher one elsewhere. But don't for a moment believe that—outside of the fighting ranks themselves—there is any "war work" more necessary or more patriotic than that you are doing here. . . . To thank you for it would seem to imply that it is a loyalty merely to me or to the Library, whereas it is the higher loyalty to a cause and a principle. But I want you to know how clearly I realize it, how deeply I value it, and how sure I am that in the end, and upon the final reckoning, it will secure the recognition it deserves. (LCA)

NOVEMBER. The Library publishes *Dramatic Compositions Copyrighted in the United States, 1870 to 1916*, prepared by the Copyright Office. (LCA)

1919

MAY 7. Robert Todd Lincoln, son of President Abraham Lincoln, deposits a major collection of his father's papers in the Library. (LCA; 1948 AR:14)

1920

DECEMBER 20. In his annual report for 1920, Richard A. Rice, acting chief of the Prints Division, notes the acquisition of over 300 original daguerreotype portraits of prominent Americans made between the year 1845 and 1853 by the studio of photographer Mathew B. Brady of Washington, D.C., and New York. The collection was transferred to the Library from the U.S. Army War College. (1920 AR:77; LCA)

1921

SEPTEMBER 29. President Warren G. Harding issues an executive order directing the transfer of the original copies of the Declaration of Independence and the Constitution of the United States from the Department of State to the Library. The order was issued "at the instance of Dr. Gaillard Hunt, formerly Chief of the Division of Manuscripts, but now Editor for the Department of State and in charge of its Library and Archives," and upon the recommendation of Secretary of State Charles Evans Hughes.

(1921 AR:28)

SEPTEMBER 30. The Declaration of Independence and the Constitution are transferred to the Library. (1921 AR:28)

1922

MARCH 22. The President approves the legislative branch appropriations act for fiscal 1923, which includes $12,000 to provide "a safe, permanent repository of appropriate design" for the Declaration of Independence and the Constitution in the Library.

(42 Stat. 422)

MAY 9. Representative Robert Luce of Massachusetts, on behalf of the House Library Committee, reports in favor of a bill which would abolish the office of the Library's superintendent of building and grounds and transfer its responsibilities to the Architect of the Capitol and the Librarian of Congress. Congressman Luce explains that Librarian Putnam favors the bill.

(67/2 HRR 995)

MAY 18. President Harding nominates Harriet de Kraft Woods to be superintendent of the Library building and grounds.

(CR 62:7198)

MAY 20. The U.S. Senate confirms the nomination of Mrs. Woods.

(CR 62:7342)

MAY 31. The resignation of Frank L. Averill as superintendent becomes effective and Mrs. Woods assumes the post.

(1922 AR:11)

1922

JUNE 29. President Harding approves an act of Congress abolishing the office of superintendent of the Library building and grounds as an independent office. Responsibility for the structural work, repairs, physical equipment, and operation of the mechanical plant is transferred to the Architect of the Capitol. The Librarian of Congress becomes responsible for the custody and safeguarding of the building, its "housekeeping," and for the work of the disbursing office. The Librarian will appoint an administrative assistant to serve as disbursing officer and assist him in carrying out the other new responsibilities. The law becomes effective on July 1, 1922.

(42 Stat. 715; 1922 AR:7–12, 193–95)

JULY 11. Putnam appoints Mrs. Woods to be his administrative assistant, thereby filling the post provided in the law approved on June 29, 1922.

(1922 AR:11)

1923

JANUARY 23. Robert Todd Lincoln donates the Abraham Lincoln Papers to the Library on the condition that they be kept sealed "until the expiration of twenty-one (21) years from the date of my death." (1923 AR:43; 1948 AR:14)

MAY 27. Death of David Hutcheson, who retired from the Library in 1907. Putnam observes that Hutcheson's death "should be recorded as the severance from our companionship of one of the last surviving veterans of the old regime, who had rendered to the Government and to the public many years of the most sterling service." (1924 AR:5)

DECEMBER 3. In his annual report for 1923, Putnam addresses himself to "general considerations regarding the shelving of books in any large, growing library," but emphasizes the "imperative need" for a new bookstack in the northeast courtyard of the Library of Congress. The Librarian also discusses a pending reclassification of civilian employees in government service, stressing the need to improve the salaries of the Library's professional staff—

1923

for it is upon the professionals "that the future of the Library as a learned institution must rest."

(1923 AR:4–7, 112–19, 196–210)

1924

FEBRUARY 7–9. The Library sponsors three chamber music recitals, which are held at the Freer Gallery in Washington, D.C., and supported by Elizabeth Sprague Coolidge "in connection with her gift to the Library of the original scores of the compositions which had received awards in her Berkshire festivals." Putnam hails the event as "the first notable recognition by our Government (apart from its maintenance of the collection in the Library) of music as one of the finer arts—entitled to its concern and encouragement."

(1924 AR:4–5)

FEBRUARY 28. In the presence of President Calvin Coolidge, Secretary of State Hughes, and a representative group of Congressmen, Putnam places the Declaration of Independence and the Constitution in a specially designed shrine for protection and exhibition. The ceremony takes place "without a single utterance, save the singing of two stanzas of 'America.'"

(1924 AR:4)

DECEMBER 1. In his annual report for 1924, Putnam explains to Congress that James B. Wilbur of Manchester, Vt., has initiated a gift of utmost significance for the Library: "He is himself meeting the cost of reproducing, by photostat, groups of source material outside of our regular scheme, the resultant copies being added to our collection."

(1924 AR:11)

DECEMBER 4. In a letter to the Speaker of the House, Representative Frederick H. Gillett of Massachusetts, Putnam transmits an offer from Elizabeth Sprague Coolidge to give to the Congress a sum of $60,000 for the construction and equipping of an auditorium, connected to the Library of Congress, which shall be planned for the performance of chamber music and dedicated to it. The Librarian recommends approval of the offer and explains that space

Elizabeth Sprague Coolidge (1854–1953), who in 1925 donated funds to build an auditorium for the performance of chamber music and established an endowment to aid in the "study, composition, and appreciation of music." Her encouragement led to the creation of the Library of Congress Trust Fund Board. Portrait by John Sargent. LC–USP6–1532A

President Calvin Coolidge and his wife, Grace Goodhue Coolidge, at the dedication of the "shrine" in the Library's Great Hall where the Declaration of Independence and the Constitution were placed for protection and exhibition. Librarian Putnam is on the left. The documents were transferred to the National Archives in 1952. National Photo Company. LC–USZ62–57285

1924

is available for the auditorium in the northwest courtyard, adjacent to the Music Division. A secondary purpose of the auditorium will be its use for staff assemblies and meetings. (68/2 HRD 472)

1925

JANUARY 19. Through a deed executed by the Northern Trust Company of Chicago, Mrs. Coolidge establishes an endowment, to be paid annually to the Librarian of Congress, to aid the Music Division "in the development of the study, composition, and appreciation of music." These funds, estimated to yield a net income of $28,200 a year, will enable the division to conduct festivals of music, give concerts, and award prizes for original compositions. In addition, the chief of the division will receive an honorarium "in recognition of the special labor (much of it outside official hours and routine), special responsibility, and inevitable personal expense, imposed upon him in the suitable execution of these purposes." (LCA; 1925 AR:3–5)

JANUARY 23. President Calvin Coolidge approves a joint resolution of Congress accepting the gift from Elizabeth Sprague Coolidge for the construction of the auditorium at the Library of Congress. (43 Stat. 788)

MARCH 3. President Coolidge approves an act of Congress creating a Library of Congress Trust Fund Board, which is authorized "to accept, receive, hold, and administer such gifts or bequests of personal property for the benefit of, or in connection with, the Library, its collections, or its service." The board consists of three ex officio members—the secretary of the treasury, the chairman of the Joint Library Committee, and the Librarian of Congress—and two public members appointed by the President of the United States. The total of the principal sums given or bequeathed to the board is limited to the sum of $5 million. (43 Stat. 1107; 1925 AR:5–6, 91–93)

MARCH 4. The President approves the legislative appropriations act for fiscal 1926, which includes $345,000 to begin construction of a bookstack in the Library's northeast courtyard. (43 Stat. 1286)

AUGUST 10. In a letter to Andrew W. Mellon, secretary of the treasury and chairman of the Library of Congress Trust Fund Board, James B. Wilbur establishes an endowment for the acquisition, in photocopy, of "manuscript material on American history in European archives." (LCA-T; 1925 AR:6–7)

OCTOBER 28–30. The first Library of Congress festival of chamber music is held. It takes place in the newly completed Coolidge Auditorium, located in the northwest courtyard of the Library. (1925 AR:2–3, 294–97)

DECEMBER 7. In his annual report for 1925, Putnam describes Mrs. Coolidge's gift and endowment as "absolutely consistent with the scheme and policy of the Library as the National Library and an agency of the Federal Government, which is, not to duplicate local or ordinary effort, nor supplant it where the project is within its proper fields and abilities, but to do for American scholarship and cultivation what is not likely to be done by other agencies." He asserts that the Coolidge gift and the Wilbur and Coolidge endowments have initiated a "new era" for the Library. The Librarian also announces the gift, from the Victor Talking Machine Company, Camden, N.J., of "an 'Art-Victrola,' electrically run, and an initial selection of 412 double-face disks." In the same report, Superintendent of the Reading Room Frederick William Ashley expresses concern about "the space-consuming growth of the public card catalogue." Ashley suggests that a practical way out of the difficulty probably will be reached "by printing in book form large portions of the card catalogue (subject groups or country groups or accession-period groups) and removing from the public catalogue the corresponding card entries." (1925 AR:5–7, 99, 146–49)

The first Library of Congress festival of chamber music was held in the newly completed Coolidge Auditorium on October 28–30, 1928. This photograph of the Budapest String Quartet performing in the Coolidge Auditorium was taken in the 1940's. LC–USP6–1753C

92

JANUARY. William Dawson Johnston begins his duties as a Library of Congress representative in Europe, with headquarters in Paris. His assignment is to establish and maintain contacts "with dealers, collectors, scholars, and learned institutions," and to "be in touch with the foreign book market for the acquisition of not only the individual book but also for collections en bloc." (1926 AR:29–30)

JANUARY 2. In a letter to Putnam, publisher R. R. Bowker presents the Library of Congress Trust Fund Board with funds to establish an endowment to further "the bibliographic service of the Library." (1926 AR:1–2, 354–55)

APRIL 16. Chief Assistant Librarian Appleton P. C. Griffin dies. (1926 AR:7–9)

APRIL 23. Joseph Pennell dies, bequeathing most of his estate to the United States government to be used for the promotion of collections and services in the Division of Prints in the Library of Congress. Pennell chose the U.S. government as beneficiary "because the United States is spending money on prints and encouraging art and artists." (1926 AR:3–5, 338)

OCTOBER-NOVEMBER. James B. Childs, chief of the Documents Division, visits Germany, Lithuania, Russia, and Latvia "to form new connections" for the acquisition of government publications. (1927 AR:60–61)

DECEMBER 6. In his annual report for 1926, Putnam warns that the nearly completed new bookstack "will not be likely to take care of the accessions beyond the coming decade." The book collection now totals over 3.5 million volumes. (1926 AR:6, 15)

FEBRUARY 10. President Coolidge approves an act of Congress which authorizes the Librarian of Congress to prepare a biennial index to the legislation of the

states "together with a supplemental digest of the more important legislation of the period." (44 Stat. 1066)

FEBRUARY 18. Mrs. John Boyd Thacher dies, bequeathing to the Library the collection of incunabula, autographs, early printing, and manuscripts acquired by her husband and deposited at the Library. (1927 AR:25–29)

MARCH. The new bookstack in the northeast courtyard is completed. The first separate custodial unit for the Library's rare books is located on the top floor of the new stack; Putnam assigns V. Valta Parma to be "keeper of the Rare Book Room." (1927 AR:11, 171)

MARCH. The House of Representatives publishes the 1,115-page Documents Illustrative of the Formation of the Union of the United States, compiled and indexed by the Legislative Reference Service. (69/1 HRD 398)

APRIL. Putnam announces two new endowments "for the perfection of the service" of the Library of Congress. He explains that "both of the gifts . . . are for the maintenance of 'chairs'; the one in American history, the other in the fine arts." The donors are, respectively, William Evarts Benjamin of New York City and the Carnegie Corporation. A "chair," according to the Librarian, will take the form of an honorarium paid directly to a division chief, in this case the chiefs of the manuscripts and fine arts divisions, for their work in "interpreting" the collections to the inquiring public. (1927 AR:4–5, 279–84)

APRIL 1. Putnam promotes Frederick W. Ashley, superintendent of the reading room, to the position of Chief Assistant Librarian. (1927 AR:12)

JUNE. The endowment by William Evarts Benjamin for a chair of American history enables Putnam to appoint, on a full-time basis, a well-known historian to the post of chief of the Manuscripts Division. J. Franklin Jameson of the Carnegie Institution is named as chief. (1928 AR:1, 337)

JUNE 23. Speaking at the annual ALA conference, H. H. B. Meyer, acting director of the Legislative Reference Service, cautions other librarians: "The inhibitions of the Library of Congress should be recognized, for if they are, much time will be saved. There are certain things which the Library of Congress can do and ought to do because of its immense resources, or its peculiar organization. There are other things which it can do, but ought not do, because other agencies exist nearer at hand to do them. Lastly there are still other things which it cannot do at all. It is astonishing how many persons do not recognize this last limitation."

(ALAB 21:336)

AUGUST. The Library publishes *An Account of Government Document Bibliography in the United States and Elsewhere*, by James B. Childs, chief of the Documents Division.

(LCA)

SEPTEMBER 1. The Library initiates two large projects, both funded for a five-year period by John D. Rockefeller, Jr., with a gift totaling $700,000. The first will enable the Library to acquire, on a greatly expanded scale, copies and facsimiles of source materials in foreign archives for the study of American history. The second provides for the further development of the Library's bibliography apparatus, in particular the National Union Catalog. Termed for convenience "Project A" and "Project B," the projects are directed by Samuel Flagg Bemis and Ernest C. Richardson, respectively.

(1927 AR:5–6; 1928 AR:228–50)

NOVEMBER 18. In a letter to Putnam, Archer M. Huntington, of New York City, presents the Library of Congress Trust Fund Board with funds to establish an endowment for the purchase of books relating "to Spanish, Portuguese, and South American arts, crafts, literature, and history."

(1927 AR:9–10; LCA-T)

FEBRUARY-APRIL. Charles Martel, chief of the Catalogue Division, joins two former Library of Congress colleagues —William Warner Bishop and J. C. M. Hanson—in Rome to install in the Vatican Library "the methods of cataloguing in vogue in American libraries." The enterprise is paid for by the Carnegie Corporation.

(1928 AR:11)

MARCH 6. President Coolidge approves an act of Congress increasing the salary of the Librarian of Congress to $10,000, effective July 1, 1928.

(45 Stat. 197)

APRIL. Under the supervision of Samuel F. Bemis, director of Project A, the Library begins microfilming French documents relating to American history at the Archives nationales in Paris. The camera, the first owned by the Library, is known as a "Lemare apparatus" because of accessories designed by Paul Lemare, a Paris optician.

(LCA; 1928 AR:236)

APRIL 24. In a letter to Putnam, Archer M. Huntington donates funds to the Library of Congress Trust Fund Board to establish a chair of Spanish and Portuguese literature.

(LCA-T; 1928 AR:3)

MAY. Using funds donated by "public-spirited citizens," Putnam establishes an American folk song project in the Music Division. The project will collect and preserve the folk songs and ballads now "endangered by the spread of the radio and phonograph, which are diverting the attention of the people from their old heritage."

(LCA; 1928 AR:143–44)

MAY 21. President Coolidge approves an act of Congress authorizing the purchase—at a cost not to exceed $600,000 —of land directly east of the Library to be used as a site for a Library annex building.

(45 Stat. 622)

MAY 28. In a speech before the American Library Association, Putnam explains that in addition to the system of chairs—which is associated with administrative duties within established divisions—the Library is employing subject specialists who serve as general "consultants."

(1928 AR:329–43)

1928

JULY 1. Librarian Putnam establishes a division of Chinese literature, which he plans to make into "the center on this hemisphere for the pursuit of oriental studies." The Sinologist Arthur W. Hummel is placed in charge. (1928 AR:6-8)

DECEMBER 11. Over 100 private citizens meet and organize "The Friends of Music in the Library of Congress"; the first president is Nicholas Longworth of Ohio, Speaker of the House of Representatives. (1929 AR:160-61)

1929

APRIL 5. Friends and colleagues of Herbert Putnam present him with a festschrift, *Essays Offered to Herbert Putnam*, edited by William Warner Bishop and Andrew Keogh and published by Yale University Press, on the occasion of his 30th anniversary as Librarian. The Library has, in fiscal 1928, an appropriation of over $1 million, a book collection of over 3 million volumes, and a staff of nearly 800 persons. (1928 AR:16, 23; LCA)

SEPTEMBER 10. The Beethoven Association of New York donates funds to the Library of Congress Trust Fund Board to establish the Sonneck Memorial Fund, which will be used "in the aid and advancement of musical research." The fund is named for Oscar G. T. Sonneck, a former officer of both the association and the Library. (LCA-T)

OCTOBER 29. In a letter to Putnam, Harry F. Guggenheim, president of the Daniel Guggenheim Fund for the Promotion of Aeronautics, Inc., provides funds for the endowment of a chair of aeronautics and for the purchase of aeronautical material. (LCA-T; 1929 AR:8-9)

1930

JANUARY 1. The Library establishes a new Aeronautics Division. (1930 AR:3)

FEBRUARY 7. Representative Ross A. Collins of Mississippi concludes a one-hour speech in the House of Representatives advocating the purchase of the Otto H. F. Vollbehr collection of incunabula for the Library of Congress: "It is a matter of grave doubt if the foreign governments will ever allow another Gutenberg Bible to leave their borders. These cradle books, representing as they do, the earliest efforts of culture, thought, and printing should be preserved and kept by the United States Government for the people of America." The collection, which contains over 3,000 items and includes one of the three perfect vellum copies of the Gutenberg Bible, costs $1 million. (CR 72:3251-57)

APRIL 1. As the result of a cooperative project with the American Library Association, the Library begins supplying Dewey decimal classification numbers on its printed cards. David J. Haykin is in charge of the project. (1930 AR:266-69)

APRIL 4. Associate Supreme Court Justice Harlan F. Stone testifies before the House Appropriations Subcommittee in support of a larger appropriation for the purchase of lawbooks. He explains that he and Justice Louis D. Brandeis are both eager for the Library of Congress to develop "a great collection which will be of service to men interested in the law, and to scholars, for all time." (1931 HRA:232-34)

APRIL 16. The Carnegie Corporation gives the Library $5,000 to begin organizing a collection of pictorial archives of early American architecture. (1930 AR:4, 235-36)

APRIL 22. Register of Copyrights Thorvald Solberg retires. (1930 AR:21-23)

JUNE 4. The House Library Committee reports in favor of acquiring the Vollbehr collection. On behalf of the committee, Representative Robert Luce of Massachusetts points out that the purchase of such cultural rarities would, however, set a new precedent, for heretofore the United States government has not "to any significant degree engaged in aiding the arts from the Public Treasury, in other words, subsidizing culture." (71/2 HRR 1769)

In 1930 Congress appropriated one million dollars for the purchase of the Otto H. F. Vollbehr collection of incunabula, which included a perfect vellum copy of the Gutenberg Bible. Here Librarian Putnam and Dr. Vollbehr pose with several of the 3,000 volumes in the collection. LC-USZ62-57287

1930

JUNE 9. In a debate in the House of Representatives, Congressman Albert Johnson of Washington maintains that "even if times are hard," Congress should purchase the Gutenberg Bible and the other Vollbehr rarities because "it is all for the United States of America which is going to live we hope for thousands of years." (CR 72:10347)

JUNE 13. President Herbert Hoover approves an act of Congress which authorizes the extension and remodeling of the east front of the Library and the appropriation of up to $6 million for the construction of an annex building, to be located on the land east of the Library acquired by the act of May 21, 1928. (46 Stat. 583)

JUNE 16. Testifying in favor of the Vollbehr purchase, Putnam reminds the Senate Library Committee that in 1815, the government paid Thomas Jefferson $24,000 for his library, and "in proportion to the resources of the country that sum was not much short of the million and a half" asked for the Vollbehr collection. Moreover, "what was true of that purchase is certainly true of the one before you. It would form 'a most admirable substratum for a [greater] national library,' such as yours is not yet, but should develop into." (71/2 SR 965)

JULY 3. President Herbert Hoover approves a supplemental appropriation act which includes $1 million to purchase from Otto H. F. Vollbehr his collection of incunabula. (46 Stat. 860)

1931

MARCH 3. The President approves an act of Congress which authorizes a separate annual appropriation to the Library of Congress to "provide books for the use of the adult blind readers of the United States." (46 Stat. 1487)

JULY 1. Putnam gives Herman H. B. Meyer, director of the Legislative Reference Service, the additional responsi-

bility of directing the Books for the Adult Blind project, authorized under the act of March 3, 1931. (1931 AR:395-96)

SEPTEMBER. In his new book *The Epic of America*, historian James Truslow Adams pays tribute to the Library of Congress "as a symbol of what democracy can accomplish on its own behalf." Adams notes that although many have made gifts to the Library, it was "created by ourselves through Congress, which has steadily and increasingly shown itself generous and understanding toward it. Founded and built by the people, it is for the people. Anyone who has used the great collections of Europe, with their restrictions and red tape and difficulty of access, praises God for American democracy when he enters the stacks of the Library of Congress."

1932

APRIL 1. The Library publishes the first issue of *Key to Symbols in Union Catalogs*. The symbols for nearly 350 libraries are listed; the system is based on a scheme devised by Frank Peterson of the University of Nebraska Library. (LCA)

MAY 10. The Library broadens the Division of Chinese Literature into the Orientalia Division. (LCA)

SEPTEMBER 1. The Library creates a Union Catalog division to continue the work of Project B, which has been "brought to completion." (1932 AR:74)

DECEMBER 29. The Library becomes a charter member of the Association of Research Libraries. (LCA)

1933

JANUARY 25. Putnam presents a request to the House Committee on Appropriations for the restoration of funds to the budget of the Legislative Reference Service: "The period of the depression has been a time of intensive use of the resources of the Library of Congress, and the problems arising out of reconstruction will call for the most

1933

careful and comprehensive study by the Legislative Reference staff."

(1934 HRA:99)

FEBRUARY 10. Because he "knows of no greater contribution this Government has made to the public than the Library of Congress," Representative Simeon D. Fess of Ohio urges his fellow congressmen to appropriate funds to construct the Library's annex. Fess, chairman of the Joint Committee on the Library, notes that the institution is "generally regarded as a national library in view of the fact that it serves more than the Members of Congress. However, it is specially designated as the 'Library of Congress,' and I presume it will always so remain."

(72/2 SD 185:1, 12)

1934

FEBRUARY 15. At hearings before the House Committee on Appropriations subcommittee, Putnam states that the Library's collection is now the largest in the world, but he cautions the Congressmen that the methods of counting used by the British Museum and the Bibliothèque nationale "are somewhat different from ours, and it is not safe to undertake comparisons."

(1935 HRA:197–98)

FEBRUARY 24. The Library of Congress Trust Fund Board approves the use of an endowment from James B. Wilbur of Manchester, Vt., to establish a chair of geography and to strengthen service "in the treatment of source material for American history."

(LCA·T; 1933 AR:3)

MARCH. The extension of the east front of the Library building is completed, providing new, specially designed quarters for the Rare Book Room.

(1935 HRA:160–62)

MAY 9. President Franklin D. Roosevelt approves an act of Congress adding "sound reproductions for the use of the blind" to the Library's service for the blind program.

(48 Stat. 678)

1934

MAY 17. In response to a letter from Putnam protesting that no National Industrial Recovery Act funds were available to continue work on the Library's annex, President Roosevelt states that "the condition of the Public Works fund will not permit" such an allotment at this time. The President assures the Librarian, however, that the matter will receive careful attention "if an additional appropriation is voted by Congress."

(LCA)

JUNE 19. President Roosevelt approves an act of Congress establishing the National Archives of the United States. The act stipulates that "all archives or records belonging to the Government of the United States (legislative, executive, judicial, and other) shall be under the charge and superintendence of the Archivist." A National Archives Council is created to advise the archivist and "define the classes of material which shall be transferred to the National Archives Building and establish regulations governing such transfer." The council is composed of the secretaries of each of the executive departments of government, the chairman of the House and Senate Library committees, the Librarian of Congress, the secretary of the Smithsonian Institution, and the archivist. The same act creates a National Historical Publications Commission, chaired by the archivist. The chief of the Manuscripts Division of the Library of Congress is a commission member.

(48 Stat. 1122)

JULY 23. By terms of an agreement with the National Park Service and the American Institute of Architects, the Library of Congress becomes the repository for photographs and drawings from the Historic American Buildings Survey.

1935

JANUARY 21. In a letter to Carl H. Milam, secretary of the American Library Association, Putnam rejects the notion of locating a federal library bureau in the Library of Congress, asserting that the functions of such an agency "would tend to confuse and impede the service to learning

(LCA; 1934 AR:136–37)

98

An aerial view of the Main Building, looking west, taken in 1933. The east side of the building was being extended to provide new quarters for the rare book collection. The new Library annex, authorized in 1930, would be located east of the Main Building and adjacent to the Folger Shakespeare Library (lower right). The Supreme Court building (upper right) was nearly complete. LC–USZ62–61723

99

1935

which should be the primary duty of our National Library." Instead, the Librarian feels the bureau "should be associated with one of the executive departments of the government." (LCA)

MARCH 6. Former Supreme Court Justice Oliver Wendell Holmes dies, bequeathing his private library to the Library of Congress. (1935 AR:14–15)

APRIL 8. Radio station WMAL of Washington, D.C., broadcasts part of a concert by the Kolisch Quartet from the Coolidge Auditorium, the first radio broadcast of a Library chamber music concert. (LCA; 1935 AR:154)

JUNE. The Library of Congress supplies approximately 25,000 duplicate volumes from its law collections to the newly established Supreme Court library. (1935 AR:104–5)

JUNE 6. President Roosevelt approves an act of Congress increasing by $2,866,340 the limit on funds to be appropriated for the construction of the Library's annex, a limit fixed in the act of June 13, 1930. (49 Stat. 326)

JUNE 12. The Architect of the Capitol awards the contract to construct the Library of Congress Annex. (1935 AR:1–2)

JULY 8. President Roosevelt approves the legislative branch appropriation act for fiscal 1935. The new law authorizes the Legislative Reference Service "to gather, classify, and make available, in translations, indexes, digests, compilations, and bulletins and otherwise, data for or bearing upon legislation, and to render such data available to Congress." (49 Stat. 459)

AUGUST. The Library opens a separate "Reading Room for American Local History and Genealogy." (1936 AR:270–72)

1935

NOVEMBER. The Library publishes a *Guide to the Diplomatic History of the United States, 1775–1921,* by Samuel F. Bemis and Grace Gardner Griffin. The authors dedicate the volume to Herbert Putnam, "that organizer of opportunity." (LCA; 1936 AR:251)

DECEMBER. The Library receives, as a gift from Gertrude Clarke Whittall, four Stradivari instruments. (LCA; 1935 AR:156)

1936

JANUARY. The Library publishes the first issue of the *Digest of Public General Bills,* prepared by the Legislative Reference Service. (1936 AR:252)

JANUARY 3. Herman H. B. Meyer, director of the Books for the Adult Blind, reports to Putnam that "the most important feature of the year's work for the blind has been the rapid development of the Talking Books." One result has been the inauguration of a new annual publication, *Talking Book Titles.* (1935 AR:256, 288–89)

MARCH 1. At the suggestion of the Association of Research Libraries, the Library establishes an interlibrary loan clearinghouse. (LCA; 1936 AR:50–51)

MARCH 2. In a letter to Putnam, Gertrude Clarke Whittall donates funds to the Library of Congress Trust Fund Board to establish the Gertrude Clarke Whittall Foundation. The primary purpose of the Library's Whittall Foundation will be the maintenance of the Stradivari instruments recently given to the Library by Mrs. Whittall and support for concerts in which those instruments will be used. (LCA-T; 1936 AR:131–32)

APRIL 1. Chief Assistant Librarian Frederick W. Ashley retires. (1936 AR:2)

APRIL 13. President Roosevelt approves a joint resolution of Congress authorizing the Librarian to accept the prop-

1936

erty bequeathed to the United States in the will of Joseph Pennell. (49 Stat. 1206; 1936 AR:4–6)

JUNE 20. The President approves an act of Congress authorizing the Library to receive 150 copies of all government publications; up to 125 of these copies may be used for "distribution, through the Smithsonian Institution, to such foreign governments as may agree to send to the United States similar publications of their governments for delivery to the Library of Congress." (49 Stat. 1545)

NOVEMBER 17. Archer M. Huntington donates funds to the Library of Congress Trust Fund Board to "equip and maintain" in the Library a room to be known as the Hispanic Society Room of Spanish and Portuguese Arts and Letters and to establish and maintain a chair of poetry of the English language. (LCA-T; 1937 AR:4–5)

1937

JANUARY 14. The Library receives the gift of a fifth Stradivarius string instrument from Gertrude Clarke Whittall. (LCA; 1937 AR:5)

MAY. The Library publishes the first issue of a *Select List of Unlocated Research Books*, prepared by the Union Catalog Division. (1937 AR:49)

JUNE 23. Describing the new Library Annex at an American Library Association meeting, Martin A. Roberts, superintendent of the reading room, points out that the new building, with its 249 miles of shelves, will hold about 10 million volumes—or about twice as many as the main Library building. (1937 AR:354–59)

SEPTEMBER 17. Putnam appoints reading room superintendent Martin A. Roberts to be Chief Assistant Librarian. (1937 AR:v)

1938

JANUARY 3. In his annual report for 1937, Librarian Putnam notes that Joseph Auslander, lecturer on poetry at Columbia University and poetry editor of the *North*

Gertrude Clarke Whittall (1867–1965), who from 1935 to 1938 donated five Stradivari instruments to the Library, established a foundation to support concerts in which the instruments were to be used and donated funds to build a pavilion in which they were to be housed.

American Review, has been engaged for the present year to serve as the Library's first consultant in poetry.
(1937 AR:4–5)

MARCH. A five-year juvenilia bibliographic project is inaugurated, using funds donated by J. K. Lilly, Jr.
(LCA; 1938 AR:8, 346)

MARCH 1. Using funds received from the Rockefeller Foundation, the Library establishes a Photoduplication Service for the purpose of "competently supplying distant investigators with microfilm and other photoduplicates of materials otherwise not available for use outside of Washington." Ten thousand dollars of the total Rockefeller Foundation grant of $35,000 is to be used to establish a revolving fund to operate the laboratory; the remaining $25,000 is to be used to purchase equipment. Union Catalog director George F. Schwegmann is appointed by Putnam to direct the Photoduplication Service as well.
(LCA; 1938 AR:312)

JUNE 15. Putnam asks President Roosevelt to approve the recently passed act of Congress creating the office of Librarian Emeritus, thereby enabling the Librarian to "turn over the administrative duties" to his successor after July 1.
(1938 AR:13)

JUNE 20. President Roosevelt approves an act of Congress providing that "upon separation from the service, by resignation or otherwise, on or after July 1, Herbert Putnam, the present Librarian of Congress . . . shall become Librarian Emeritus." Putnam's annual salary as Librarian Emeritus will be $5,000.
(52 Stat. 808)

AUGUST. A revised edition of The Constitution of the United States of America (Annotated), compiled by the Legislative Reference Service, is published as Senate Document no. 232, 74th Congress, 2d session. The 1,246-page document is the first revised edition to be prepared by the Library of Congress.
(91/2 SR 1229:8–9)

NOVEMBER 1. The Carnegie Corporation gives the Library a three-year grant totaling $13,500 for the development of its Indica collection and "for the promotion of a greater interest at large in the study of India." This undertaking, to be carried out under the auspices of the American Council of Learned Societies, is designated Project F.
(LCA; 1938 AR:9)

NOVEMBER 30. Card Division Chief Charles H. Hastings retires.
(1938 AR:11)

DECEMBER. The Library begins to move staff and materials into its new Annex building.
(1938 AR:1)

JANUARY 3. In his annual report for 1938, Putnam notes that since his successor as Librarian has not yet been named, he is "still exercising the functions of that office, though earnest for those which may be my privilege as Librarian Emeritus." A feature of the report is an appendix, prepared by chief reference librarian William Adams Slade, titled "Some Notes on the Library of Congress as a Center of Research, Together With a Summary Account of Gifts Received From the Public in the Last Forty Years."
(1938 AR:13, 450–65)

JANUARY 27. In a statement addressed to Putnam, the American Council of Learned Societies pays special tribute to the Librarian: "You, and the collaborators and associates whom you have chosen, have made the Library of Congress a national institution, the peer in all respects of its great prototypes, the British Museum and the Bibliothèque Nationale. You have made it an indispensable instrument on the American continent for the promotion of learning and the increase of knowledge."
(1939 AR:2–5)

The Annex Building in 1938 as it neared completion. With its capacity of 10 million volumes, the Annex was intended to serve primarily as a giant bookstack. This photograph, taken from the roof of the Supreme Court Building, includes the Folger Shakespeare Library on the left.

103

JANUARY 30. In its request for funds for fiscal 1940, the Library asks for $1,000 to initiate a program of "microfilming the more important newspaper files in the Library to preserve them from complete loss through disintegration."

(1940 HRA:30)

MARCH 6. Librarian Putnam opens the Whittall Pavilion, which was built, decorated, and furnished with funds donated by Gertrude Clarke Whittall for the purpose of housing the Stradivari instruments. The pavilion is located in the northwest courtyard, adjacent to the Coolidge Auditorium.

(LCA: 1939 AR:439)

APRIL 5. On the 40th anniversary of Putnam's taking the oath of office as Librarian of Congress, the reading rooms in the new Annex are opened to the public and the associates of the Librarian's Round Table honor the Librarian with a special luncheon. Dr. Waldo G. Leland, permanent secretary of the American Council of Learned Societies, presides over the luncheon and the ceremonies.

(LCA: 1939 AR:367)

MAY 11. In a letter to President Roosevelt, Supreme Court Justice Felix Frankfurter endorses the President's suggestion that Archibald MacLeish would make a good Librarian of Congress, primarily because "only a scholarly man of letters can make a great national library a general place of habitation for scholars." Furthermore, the Library of Congress "is not merely a library and in the immediate future even more so than in the past it will be concerned with problems quite outside the traditional tasks associated with collecting, housing, and circulating books."

(Felix Frankfurter Papers, Library of Congress)

JUNE 7. President Roosevelt nominates poet and writer Archibald MacLeish to be Librarian of Congress.

(CR 84:6774)

JUNE 13. The Senate Committee on the Library, chaired by Alben W. Barkley of Kentucky, holds hearings on the

104

MacLeish nomination. The nominee is the sole witness.

(LCA; CR 84:7710–13)

JUNE 18. Meeting in San Francisco at its annual conference, the American Library Association adopts a resolution opposing the nomination of Archibald MacLeish to be Librarian of Congress because "the Congress and the American people should have as Librarian . . . one who is not only a gentleman and a scholar but who is also the ablest library administrator available."

(CR 84:8216)

JUNE 19. The Senate Library Committee continues its hearings. Representatives of the ALA testify against Senate confirmation of MacLeish.

(LCA; CR 84:7710–13)

JUNE 20. On behalf of the Senate Committee on the Library, Senator Barkley presents an executive report favoring MacLeish's confirmation.

(CR 84:7549)

JUNE 29. By a vote of 63 to 8, the U.S. Senate confirms President Roosevelt's nomination of Archibald MacLeish to be Librarian of Congress.

(CR 84:8221)

JULY 1. As provided in the legislative branch appropriations act for 1939, the Library establishes the Hispanic Foundation, a "center for the pursuit of studies in Spanish, Portuguese, and Hispanic American culture."

(LCA; 1940 AR:61)

JULY 10. Archibald MacLeish takes the oath of office as the ninth Librarian of Congress. The Library has a book collection of approximately six million volumes, a staff of 1,100, including buildings and grounds employees, and, in fiscal 1939, a direct appropriation of approximately $3 million.

(LCA; 1939 AR:15; 1940 AR:372–73)

JULY 18. President Roosevelt approves a joint resolution of Congress authorizing the construction of the

1939

Franklin D. Roosevelt Library at Hyde Park, N.Y., which will house the Roosevelt Papers.　　　(53 Stat. 1062)

OCTOBER 1.　Herbert Putnam becomes Librarian Emeritus.　　　(LCA)

OCTOBER 2.　Librarian MacLeish assumes his duties　　(LCA)

OCTOBER 12.　Librarian MacLeish dedicates the Hispanic Room to "the preservation and the study and the honor of the literature and scholarship of those other republics which share with ours the word American." The room, decorated in the style of the late Spanish renaissance by Philadelphia architect Paul Philippe Cret, is "made possible by the generous cooperation of the Hispanic Society of America."　(PR, "Remarks of Archibald MacLeish . . .")

OCTOBER 17.　With the approval of President Roosevelt, a Library of Congress Works Projects Administration (WPA) project is organized to continue the editorial work formerly performed by the staffs of the national Historical Records Survey and the Federal Writers' Project, including the editing of the American Guide series.

(LCA; 1941 AR:176–80)

OCTOBER 28.　Horace I. Poleman, director of Project F, leaves on an acquisitions trip to India, Ceylon, Burma, Siam, Indochina, Java, and Bali. He takes with him a "portable microfilming apparatus" furnished by the American Council of Learned Societies.　(LCA; 1939 AR:73–74)

NOVEMBER.　The Librarian asks a special committee of staff members to examine the Library's acquisitions policies.　　　(LCA; 1945 AR:121)

NOVEMBER 19.　Speaking on the occasion of the laying of the cornerstone of the Franklin D. Roosevelt Library in Hyde Park, N.Y., Librarian MacLeish urges greater

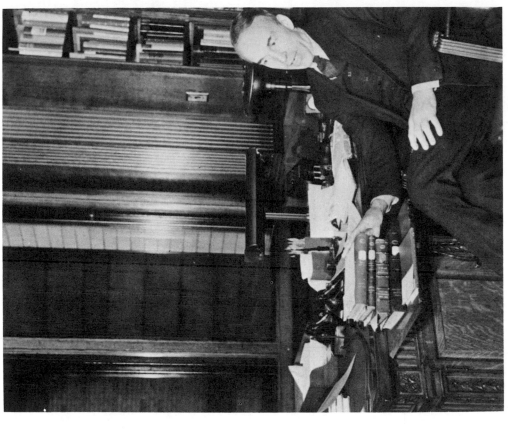

Archibald MacLeish, Librarian of Congress from 1939 to 1944, initiated and supervised a major administrative reorganization. At the end of his five-year term, I am proudest of the change which has drawn into the active administration of the Library of Congress an increasing number of the members of its staff."

1939

cooperation among libraries: "The unit for scholarly purposes is no longer the individual library, but libraries as a whole." (PR, "Remarks of Archibald MacLeish . . .")

NOVEMBER 28. The British ambassador to the United States, the 11th marquess of Lothian (Philip Henry Kerr), deposits the Lincoln Cathedral copy of Magna Carta in the Library of Congress for temporary safekeeping. In his remarks accepting its wartime custody, Librarian MacLeish emphasizes that "the institutions of representative government are the protectors, and the only possible protectors, of the charters of the people's rights."
(PR, "Remarks of Archibald MacLeish . . .")

DECEMBER. The Rockefeller Foundation gives the Library a two-year grant of $22,000 to support the Library's Hispanic Foundation.
(LCA; 1941 AR:326)

DECEMBER 1. Librarian MacLeish appoints Luther H. Evans, a political scientist and director of the Historical Records Survey, to be director of the Library's Legislative Reference Service.
(1940 AR:31)

DECEMBER 19. The Library's committee on acquisitions policy, which has been aided by specialists from the academic community, reports that the Library "is not maintaining its proper position in respect to the completeness or quality of its holdings." Roughly speaking, of the 40 principal subjects in the Library's classification system, 12 are considered strong, 13 are adequate, and 15 are inadequate. The committee recommends that the annual appropriation for general book purchases be increased dramatically.
(LCA; 1941 AR:82–83)

1940

JANUARY 2. With the approval of the House Committee on Appropriations, MacLeish submits a supplemental budget request. It calls for a net addition to the Library's appropriation of $1,062,421.
(76/3 HRD 549)

Canons of Selection

I

THE LIBRARY OF CONGRESS SHOULD POSSESS IN SOME USEFUL FORM ALL BIBLIOTHECAL MATERIALS NECESSARY TO THE CONGRESS AND TO THE OFFICERS OF GOVERNMENT OF THE UNITED STATES IN THE PERFORMANCE OF THEIR DUTIES.

II

THE LIBRARY OF CONGRESS SHOULD POSSESS ALL BOOKS AND OTHER MATERIALS (WHETHER IN ORIGINAL OR IN COPY) WHICH EXPRESS AND RECORD THE LIFE AND ACHIEVEMENTS OF THE PEOPLE OF THE UNITED STATES.

III

THE LIBRARY OF CONGRESS SHOULD POSSESS, IN SOME USEFUL FORM, THE MATERIAL PARTS OF THE RECORDS OF OTHER SOCIETIES, PAST AND PRESENT, AND SHOULD ACCUMULATE, IN ORIGINAL OR IN COPY, FULL AND REPRESENTATIVE COLLECTIONS OF THE WRITTEN RECORDS OF THOSE SOCIETIES AND PEOPLES WHOSE EXPERIENCE IS OF MOST IMMEDIATE CONCERN TO THE PEOPLE OF THE UNITED STATES.

From the Annual Report of the Librarian of Congress, 1940

The development of statements of the Library's objectives was a major accomplishment of MacLeish's administration. These "Canons of Selection" applied to the Library's acquisition of material by purchase but not to its acquisition by gift or copyright deposit.

JANUARY 3. Alan Lomax, assistant in charge of the Archive of American Folk Song, reports a dramatic increase in acquisitions, which he feels has been stimulated by "a developing consciousness of the significance of a native culture." Lomax also notes an expansion in the range of material collected, pointing out that Sidney Robertson, John Lomax, Herbert Halpert, and he "have explored fields of foreign minority music with recordings of Finnish, Serbian, Russian, Polish, Portuguese, Cuban, and Mexican songs and dances."

(1939 AR:218–25)

JANUARY 22. The Librarian's new in-service training committee inaugurates a series of lectures for the staff concerning the organization and functions of the Library.

(GC 938)

FEBRUARY. MacLeish gives the Library of Congress WPA project a new purpose: "to collect, preserve, and organize" the research materials gathered and produced by Federal Project Number One, the principal arts program of the WPA. Arts projects around the nation are instructed to begin sending their research materials and products to the Library.

(LCA; 1941 AR:176–80)

FEBRUARY 28. MacLeish appears before the House Subcommittee on the Legislative Branch Appropriation to explain his budget request for fiscal 1941, which totals $4.2 million. The new Librarian describes the staff and outside advisory committees he has appointed and will appoint to evaluate the Library's operations, but he emphasizes that his first priority is to improve the "salary situation." With regard to the increase requested for the Legislative Reference Service, the Librarian explains: "The assumption upon which we proceeded . . . is that the Congress has a right to scholarly research and counsel in law and history and economics at least as equal to that of people who come before committees . . . [and] it is our obligation to present that kind of research and that kind of counsel."

(1941 HRA:2, 3, 93)

MARCH 13. The House Committee on Appropriations, chaired by Representative Louis C. Rabaut of Michigan, recommends an appropriation of $3,458,498 for the Library. In its detailed and sympathetic report, the committee feels it "should frankly state its pleasure at the industrious and intelligent manner in which Mr. MacLeish has entered upon his duties." It notes that "many important needs of the Library have been deferred heretofore from year to year due to inadequacy of space and other reasons." The committee feels that "first and foremost in consideration of the needs is the necessity of preventing any further arrearage in the matter of processing material coming into the Library each year and attacking [the] accumulated arrearage; and, second, the preservation and putting into condition of material already in the Library." In all, the committee approves 130 of the 287 new positions requested by MacLeish. The proposed establishment of a research staff for a new economics and history section in the Legislative Reference Service is not allowed, pending "more experienced and mature study" of the proposal, for "if Congress needs the services of research experts along the lines indicated in addition to those that are already to be found in the Federal service, there is a serious question as to whether those experts should be a part of the Library of Congress." The proposed increase in the fund for the purchase of books, from $118,000 to $393,000, is not allowed because "in the matter of priorities the preservation of existing collections by putting them in proper shape . . . is more important at this time."

(76/3 HRR 1764:8–10, 14–16)

MARCH 21. The Carnegie Corporation donates $40,000 to the Library "for the support of projects and undertakings proposed and recommended by the Librarian of Congress."

(LCA; 1940 AR:30)

APRIL. At the request of the Librarian, the Civil Service Commission agrees "to conduct a survey of the Library in order to adjust existing inequalities of classification, to correct the allocation of positions where duties had undergone a gradual change over a period of years, and to bring the classification of all positions into line with that of the government service generally."

(1941 AR:332)

APRIL 1. MacLeish appoints Arthur A. Houghton, Jr., "one of the most distinguished American collectors of rare books," to be curator of the rare book collection.

(LCA; 1940 AR:33)

APRIL 4. Representative Ross Collins of Mississippi, speaking in the House of Representatives, urges that a new building for the Army Medical Library be provided on Capitol Hill near the Library of Congress and the Folger Shakespeare Library: "While the nations of the world are engaged in self-destruction, let us build here on this very Capitol Hill a vast educational center such has never before been contemplated. . . . we possess already the nucleus of an American Acropolis."

(CR 86:4019)

APRIL 10. MacLeish appoints a special Librarian's Committee to analyze the operations of the Library, particularly those related to processing activities. Committee members are Carleton B. Joeckel, chairman, professor of library science at the University of Chicago, Paul North Rice, chief of the Reference Department, New York Public Library, and Andrew D. Osborn, chief of the Serial Division, Harvard College Library. The work of the committee is supported by a grant from the Carnegie Corporation.

(SO 163; 1940 AR:2-3)

APRIL 10. Lewis Hanke, director of the Library's Hispanic Foundation, begins a three-month visit to South America "to build up as complete a collection as possible of Hispanic materials."

(GO 942)

APRIL 16. The Librarian's Committee begins work. Joeckel, Rice, and Osborn are to be assisted by Keyes D. Metcalf, director of the Harvard University Library, Francis R. St. John, assistant librarian, Enoch Pratt Free

Library, and L. Quincy Mumford, executive assistant in charge of the preparation division, New York Public Library.

(LCA; 1940 AR:2-3)

APRIL 19. MacLeish announces that the Library has just "received funds which will enable it to embark upon a field of cultural activity heretofore unexplored by libraries." A Carnegie Corporation grant of $41,520 "will provide for the installation in the Music Division of a complete sound laboratory for duplicating phonograph recordings, making master recordings, originating broadcasts, and for making transcriptions for radio broadcasts. In addition, the purchase of a sound truck and six portable receivers will make field recordings possible."

(PR, "Sound Laboratory . . ."; 1940 AR:134)

MAY 31. Speaking before the American Library Association, MacLeish asserts that librarians "must become active and not passive agents of the democratic process."

(ALAB 34:385-88)

JUNE 15. Death of Chief Assistant Librarian Martin A. Roberts.

(1940 AR:33)

JUNE 15. The Librarian's Committee submits a detailed, 300-page report to MacLeish. The major conclusion is that "the Library cannot be an efficient operating agency until its organic structure has been thoroughly overhauled." The committee outlines a reorganization plan that reduces the span of administrative control "at all levels in the hierarchy." It emphasizes that the reorganization should be accompanied by a restatement of the Library's objectives and notes that a study of those objectives is already in progress. Cataloging arrearages are a subject of special concern, and the Library is urged to emphasize its own cataloging needs rather than those of other institutions. Among its many specific recommendations, the committee suggests a program of continuing research "directed at the solution of internal problems of administration and technique," the preparation of

the collections and chief of the book services are created. Appointees to these positions are Alvin W. Kremer and Robert C. Gooch, respectively. (GO 964; 1940 AR:17–19)

JULY 1. The Photoduplication Service is expanded to include the functions formerly performed by the photostat section of the Chief Clerk's Office and is placed in the Reference Department. (GO 965)

JULY 1. MacLeish appoints Robert A. Voorus to be director of the project Books for the Adult Blind. Voorus formerly was the Library's chief clerk and the associate director of the project. (GO 965A)

SEPTEMBER. Using Carnegie Corporation funds and with the cooperation of the U.S. Census Bureau, the Library establishes a Census Library Project to collect and make available "the printed and other materials relating to population, including the official census documents, for all countries of the world." The first project director is Jesse H. Shera of Miami University, Oxford, Ohio. (LCA; 1940 AR:30)

SEPTEMBER 1. The Library establishes a program of resident fellowships for young scholars "who will spend a year in the Library on leave from their institutions." In making the funds available for the fellowships, the Carnegie Corporation acts from the conviction "that American cultural institutions can be greatly strengthened if scholars will accept a responsibility for the collections of the national library and if the national library will accept a responsibility for the instruction of scholars in the services it is expected to render." The first fellows are appointed in the subjects of modern European history, population, romance languages and library science, geology, and Slavic languages and literature. (1941 AR:44–46)

SEPTEMBER 1. L. Quincy Mumford, executive assistant in charge of preparation in the New York Public Library,

procedure manuals for each division, and the conversion of the Smithsonian Division "from an office of record into a science and technology reading room." (LCA; 1941 AR:25–30)

JUNE 18. President Roosevelt approves the legislative branch appropriations act for fiscal 1941, which includes $3,560,298 for the Library—an increase of over $400,000. (54 Stat. 462)

JUNE 28. MacLeish announces that beginning on July 1, 1940, or as soon thereafter as possible, three new departments will be established—the Administrative, Processing, and Reference Departments. Existing divisions and units will be assigned to these departments as appropriate. The Librarian describes the organization of the new Administrative Department. It will be headed by Verner W. Clapp, who will also serve as the Library's budget officer, and will consist of the following units: the Secretary's Office, which will be in charge of the Library's general files and correspondence; the Personnel Office, the Accounts Office, the Disbursing Office, the Mail and Delivery Service, the Publications Office, the Supply Office, and the Office of the Superintendent of Library Buildings and Grounds. (GO 962)

JUNE 29. Librarian MacLeish describes the organization of the new Reference Department, which will perform the functions of 1) reference work throughout the Library; 2) servicing of books to readers; 3) selection of books for the Library; and 4) the care and custody of the collections. Luther H. Evans, retaining his duties as chief of the Legislative Reference Service, a division of the Reference Department, is placed in charge of the new department. David C. Mearns, retaining his duties as superintendent of the reading rooms, is given the task of planning the details of the new administrative structure of the Reference Department. Also, "to aid in the establishment of a central custodial agency and the centralized oversight of all reading rooms," the positions of keeper of

begins a special one-year tour of duty as director of the Processing Department in the Library of Congress.

(1940 AR:31–32; GO 981)

OCTOBER. The Library establishes a "central process file" to facilitate the searching of purchase recommendations, new accessions, and books in the cataloging process.

(1941 AR:212)

OCTOBER 14. The Budapest String Quartet presents its first concert as the Library's "resident" chamber ensemble. For two periods of three months each during 1940 and 1941, the quartet will reside in Washington and use the Stradivari instruments for frequent public performances in the Coolidge Auditorium. This new endeavor is supported by the Library's Gertrude Clarke Whittall Foundation.

OCTOBER 22. Using funds transferred from the Department of State, the Library begins work on a "comprehensive guide to the official publications of the Latin American governments."

(1940 AR:136, 501)

OCTOBER 31. The Librarian appoints Luther H. Evans to be Chief Assistant Librarian and director of the Reference Department.

(GO 992)

NOVEMBER 1. The Librarian designates certain staff members as associate fellows of the Library of Congress, enabling those staff members "to be relieved of their routine duties one day a week" to survey the collections in their fields, initiate orders for books, and undertake special reference services.

(GO 990)

NOVEMBER 15. In his 555-page annual report for 1940, MacLeish summarizes the condition of the Library, its needs, and the "action taken and plans prepared to meet those needs." He finds the Library's general collections "preeminent" in American history, bibliography, library science, the publications of learned societies, economics,

political science, and related social sciences, but "weak" in specific fields of European literature and social science, history other than that of the United States, education, modern anthropology, and "most technology." The Librarian presents a comprehensive statement of the Library's acquisition policies ("The Canons of Selection") and of its research objectives ("The Canons of Service"). He defines the Library of Congress as "a people's library which provides to the people, through their representatives in Congress and their officers of government, as well as directly, the written record of their civilization." In the same report, Chief Assistant Librarian Evans defines the specific purpose of the Legislative Reference Service as assisting "Members and Committees of Congress in securing information and in doing research which they require in their capacity as members and agencies of the national legislature."

(1940 AR:3–29, 89)

DECEMBER. The Library administration decides to take preliminary steps "toward the safe-guarding of the collections against possible air raid damage."

(1941 AR:12)

DECEMBER 1. The Library establishes, as an "experimental division" in the Reference Department, a one-year project for the study of wartime communications. Headed by Harold D. Lasswell, the project is funded by a $20,000 grant from the Rockefeller Foundation.

(GO 1041; 1941 AR:13, 326)

DECEMBER 1. Political scientist Ernest S. Griffith assumes his duties as the new chief of the Reference Department's Legislative Reference Service.

(GO 997)

DECEMBER 18–21. The Library celebrates the 75th anniversary of the proclamation of the 13th amendment, which ended slavery in the United States, with a festival of music and a series of exhibits "dealing with the long struggle of the Negro race for freedom." The four concerts in the festival, sponsored by the Library's Gertrude Clarke Whittall Foundation, feature soprano Dorothy Maynor, tenor

1940

Roland Hayes, the Budapest String Quartet, and the Golden Gate Quartet. (1941 AR:159–61)

DECEMBER 23. The Librarian describes the organization and functions of the Library's new Processing Department. The department consists of the following divisions: Accessions, Card, Catalog Preparation and Maintenance, Descriptive Cataloging, and Subject Cataloging. (GO 1004)

1941

JANUARY. The American Council of Learned Societies, in cooperation with the Library of Congress and with financial support from the Rockefeller Foundation, begins a project of microfilming "the most valued British manuscripts and other early records." The Library will receive the negative microfilm produced by the project. (LCA; 1942 AR:99)

JANUARY 1. The Library of Congress radio research project begins operation. Funded for one year by a $23,320 grant from the Rockefeller Foundation, its purpose is "to find, through experiment and research, radio forms by which pertinent parts of the record of American culture maintained in the Library of Congress may be made available to the American people." (1941 AR:172–76, 326)

FEBRUARY 22. Physicist Dayton C. Miller dies, bequeathing to the Library his unusual collection of approximately 1,500 flutes, his unexcelled library of flute music and literature on the flute, and funds to support and expand the entire collection. (LCA; 1941 AR:121–22)

FEBRUARY 27. Robinson Jeffers reads his poems in the Coolidge Auditorium, inaugurating a series of readings by distinguished American poets titled "The Poet in a Democracy." The series is supported by a gift from Mr. and Mrs. Eugene Meyer of Washington, D.C. (LCA; 1941 AR:23, 159)

1941

APRIL 16. MacLeish announces the establishment of a new "experimental division" of library cooperation "with the aim of eliminating duplication of effort and coordinating certain activities of American libraries." The undertaking, financed for one year by the Carnegie Corporation, will be directed by historian and archivist Herbert A. Kellar. (PR 12; 1941 AR:15–17)

JUNE. Jerrold Orne, special assistant to the Librarian, reports on a recently completed project of selecting and preparing materials from the collections for possible evacuation in the event of wartime emergency. The four-month project was carried out by over 700 staff members who volunteered their time and efforts outside of normal duty hours. (1941 AR:156–57)

JUNE. The Library announces that it has discontinued publication of A List of American Doctoral Dissertations, an annual prepared since 1912, because of "duplication" with a similar list published by the Association of Research Libraries. (LCA; 1941 AR:205)

JULY 3. The Library of Congress WPA project is terminated as a result of a sharp reduction in funds supporting all WPA projects in the District of Columbia. (LCA)

AUGUST. Artist Ezra Winter's four murals illustrating "the basic ideas of the Jeffersonian creed" are hung in the Jefferson Room, the south reading room of the Annex. (PR 36)

AUGUST. A central serial record is established in the Processing Department. (LCA; 1944 AR:15)

AUGUST 5. MacLeish announces the establishment of the Gertrude Clarke Whittall Foundation Collection of Musical Autographs in the Music Division. The first purchase is a collection of original manuscripts by Beethoven, Brahms, Michael Hayden, Mozart, Schubert, Wagner, and

Weber, which was formerly in the possession of the late Dr. Jerome Stonborough of Vienna. (PR 28)

SEPTEMBER. The Library and the University of North Carolina inaugurate a joint project to microfilm the legislative journals of the American states. (1942 AR:96–97)

SEPTEMBER 10. The Library sets aside a "democracy alcove," containing a selection of books and writings about American democracy, for the use of readers in the Main Reading Room. (PR 30)

OCTOBER. President Roosevelt directs MacLeish to assume, in addition to his duties as Librarian of Congress, supervision of the government's newly established Office of Facts and Figures. (1942 AR:15)

DECEMBER 8. The Librarian designates Joseph Auslander, the consultant in poetry, to be the Library's gift officer "with the special assignment of organizing the Library's policy and practice with respect to securing gifts of important collections." (GO 1092)

DECEMBER 15. Because of the wartime emergency, the Library begins providing "a 24-hour service to the Government," which requires temporary curtailment of the hours of service to the general public. (GO 1070)

DECEMBER 23. The Declaration of Independence and the Constitution are removed from the Shrine for safekeeping. (LCA)

DECEMBER 26. The attorney general of the United States rules that the Librarian of Congress has complete control of the Declaration of Independence and the Constitution of the United States and that he can "without further authority from the Congress or the President take such action as he deems necessary for the proper protection and preservation of these documents." Late in the day the

documents, under Secret Service protection, are taken away from Washington for safekeeping in an unnamed repository. (LCA; QJ 2:64–75)

DECEMBER 29. The Library materials prepared earlier in the year for possible evacuation are sent to safer locations. Over 4,700 packing cases, the equivalent of 26 freight-car loads, are shipped. (LCA; QJ 2:74)

JANUARY 1. The Rockefeller Foundation gives the Library a one-year grant of $11,000 to support the activities of the Library's Hispanic Foundation. (LCA)

JANUARY 1. The Librarian appoints an information officer "to establish wider contacts with the press and to inform the public on the various activities of the Library." (1942 AR:55)

JANUARY 16. Librarian MacLeish announces that Thomas Mann, "whose devotion to the cause of democracy led him to self-imposed exile from Nazi Germany," has joined the Library staff as the consultant in German literature. (PR 44)

JANUARY 23. The first issue of a Library of Congress newsletter for staff members appears under the title Staff Information Bulletin. (1942 AR:55)

JANUARY 26. Herman H. Henkle, former director of the School of Library Science, Simmons College, assumes his duties as the new director of the Processing Department. (GO 1081)

FEBRUARY 1. The Maps Division installs a special display of maps in the Speakers' Lobby of the House of Representatives, so that each day members of Congress "can tell at a glance where the war fronts are and how the war is going in each sector." (LC Staff Information Bulletin Feb.–March 1944:11)

FEBRUARY 10. The Library centralizes all binding operations in a new Binding Office under the supervision of the keeper of the collections. (1942 AR:153–54)

FEBRUARY 12. MacLeish announces that the Library has made a special collection of material pertaining to air raid precautions and civil defense available to the public in the Thomas Jefferson Room. (PR 51)

MARCH 14. The Library accepts ownership of the American Imprints Catalog compiled by the Historical Records Survey, "the most complete register of Americana and the history of American printing ever assembled and organized for use." (LCA; 1942 AR:48)

APRIL. Uruguayan poet Emilio Oribe records one of his latest poems at the Library, inaugurating the Archive of Hispanic Literature on Tape. The poem is dedicated to Librarian MacLeish. (LCA; QJ 14:52)

APRIL 1. Using funds donated by the Trust Fund for Netherlands-American Cultural Activities, the Library organizes the Netherlands study unit to evaluate and expand the collections relating to the Netherlands. (1942 AR:29)

APRIL 23. MacLeish announces the formation of the Librarian's Council, composed of distinguished librarians, scholars, and book collectors, who will make recommendations "for the conduct of our services, the development of our collections, and the initiation and control of bibliographical studies." (GO 1110; 1942 AR:19–20)

MAY. Completion of the first year of "exploratory operation" of the central charge file, which contains a record of the location of 10,000 to 12,000 books which are off the shelves while "being used by research workers and members of the staff within the Library." (LC Staff Information Bulletin 1:17, p. 1)

MAY. The first issue of a Library of Congress newsletter announcing public events in the Library appears under the title of Monthly Public Information Bulletin. (1942 AR:55)

MAY 11. The Library of Congress, the Association of Research Libraries, and the American Library Association sign an agreement with Edwards Brothers of Ann Arbor, Mich., for printing A Catalog of Books Represented by Library of Congress Printed Cards, 1898-1942. (LCA)

MAY 18. Librarian MacLeish announces a new program of "selecting motion pictures for preservation" in the Library's collections. A three-year grant from the Rockefeller Foundation will enable the Library to retain the services of the Museum of Modern Art in New York as its agent to screen and select for permanent preservation certain films deposited for copyright. The Librarian expects the new arrangement to "gradually build up in the national library a collection of the most important films produced by the American motion picture industry." (PR 67; 1943 AR:213–14)

MAY 25. Acting Librarian of Congress Luther H. Evans announces the creation of a staff advisory committee "to provide a mechanism for the sifting and crystallization of employee opinion as to measures which the Library administration might appropriately take for the improvement of the operations of the Library." (GO 118)

MAY 26. Acting Librarian Evans announces that the Library has centralized the servicing of microfilm to readers in the Microfilm Section of the Rare Book Room. (GO 1120)

MAY 27. MacLeish announces that the Library has been granted permission to microfilm nearly 3,000 rare Chinese books which were "sent some months ago to this country for safe-keeping during the war." (PR 70)

JUNE. The U.S. Office of Facts and Figures is combined with other agencies to form the Office of War Information. Librarian MacLeish undertakes part-time duties with the new agency as its assistant director in charge of policy matters.

JUNE 26. At the annual meeting of the American Library Association, held in Milwaukee, ALA president Charles H. Brown introduces Librarian of Congress MacLeish as "a man of whom we librarians are very proud," and the Librarian of Congress receives a thunderous ovation. MacLeish delivers an address entitled "Toward an Intellectual Offensive."
(LCA; ALAB 36:P38)

JULY 1. Project F, the development of Indic studies, is established within the Library as the Indic Section of the Orientalia Division, with Horace I. Poleman as section head.
(1942 AR:29)

JULY 5. The Library announces the publication of its first checklist of recorded material in the Archive of American Folk Song. The catalog, which lists over 10,000 titles, was the collaborative work of the Library of Congress and the Works Projects Administration, under the general direction of Harold Spivacke, chief of the Music Division.
(PR 77)

OCTOBER 9. The executive committee of the Librarian's Council begins to formulate plans for a cooperative acquisitions project among American research libraries. The meeting is held at the home of the council chairman, Wilmarth S. Lewis, in Farmington, Conn. The Library of Congress is represented at the meeting by Librarian MacLeish, Chief Assistant Librarian Luther H. Evans, also director of the Reference Department, David C. Mearns, reference librarian, and Frederick R. Goff, acting chief of the Rare Book Collection. Keyes Metcalf of Harvard University is designated chairman of a special committee which will draw up a specific proposal; other committee

members are Julian P. Boyd of Princeton University and Librarian of Congress MacLeish.
(LCA; 1943 AR:41–42)

OCTOBER 16. The Library establishes an Exhibits Office and a Committee on Exhibits.
(GO 1160)

NOVEMBER 17. Thomas Mann, consultant in German literature, presents the first in a series of lectures in the Coolidge Auditorium. His topic is "The Theme of the Joseph Novels."
(LCA)

DECEMBER. In his preface to A Catalog of Books Represented by Library of Congress Printed Cards Issued to July 31, 1942, published by Edwards Brothers of Ann Arbor, Mich., MacLeish places the projected 160-volume work in historical perspective:
What will touch the imagination of imaginative users (readers there will be none) is the fact that this enormous work is not merely a catalog of books, but a source book for the study of catalogs. It is indeed, if I may be permitted the respectful use of the metaphor, a kind of kitchen midden of American librarianship. Among the academic clam shells here are the meaningful artifacts—the hopes and ambitions, the failures and the successes, of some very great Americans—Americans who are no less great because few of their fellow countrymen have heard their names. Charles C. Jewett, Ainsworth Rand Spofford, Richard Rogers Bowker, Melvil Dewey, and Herbert Putnam, the Librarian of Congress, are not, perhaps, household names in the United States, but they have done far more for the enduring life of their country than many whose first names and photographs are familiar around every wood-burning stove in the forty-eight states.

JANUARY 1. The Library assumes sole responsibility for the volunteer braille transcribing service that had been conducted jointly by the American Red Cross and the Library since 1918.

MARCH. The Library publishes the first volume of Eminent Chinese of the Ch'ing Period, 1644-1912, edited by Arthur W. Hummel, chief of the Asiatic Division. The work was prepared during the years 1934 to 1942 by over
(GO 173)

fifty scholars in a project sponsored by the Library and the American Council of Learned Societies.
(1943 AR:65–66)

MARCH 17. The Library announces the gift of a "magnificent collection of rare books and manuscripts" from Lessing J. Rosenwald of Jenkintown, Pa. Over 500 choice rare books are in the Rosenwald collection, including over 200 incunabula. (PR 122; 1943 AR:173–76)

APRIL. In connection with its celebration of the bicentennial of Thomas Jefferson's birth, the Library publishes *The Declaration of Independence: The Evolution of the Text*, by Julian P. Boyd, librarian of Princeton University. (1943 AR:66–67)

APRIL 11. Death of Law Librarian John T. Vance. (1943 AR:86–87)

APRIL 12–19. The Declaration of Independence, temporarily removed from its wartime storage site, is displayed in the newly opened Jefferson Memorial. (QJ 2:73–74)

APRIL 25. Librarian MacLeish announces the purchase of over 9,000 negative plates and photographs by Arnold Genthe, "a pioneer in the field of photography." The Librarian also announces that a new Library Committee on Photographs has been appointed "to insure the proper development" of the Library's photographic archive. (PR 130; 1943 AR:209))

MAY 1. The Library opens its first national print exhibition. Arranged by the Division of Fine Arts, the exhibit features prints selected by a jury composed of representatives of the National Gallery of Art, the National Collection of Fine Arts, the Corcoran Gallery of Art, and the Phillips Memorial Gallery. Purchase prizes from the Pennell Fund enable the Library to acquire 35 of the prints for its collections. (LCA; 1943 AR:57)

MAY 12. The Library administration begins holding informal monthly meetings with the professional staff.
(SO 33)

MAY 25. The Library announces that Eldon R. James, former librarian of the Harvard Law School, has been appointed Law Librarian. (PR 136)

JUNE. The Library announces its first request to U.S. motion picture producers for the deposit of recent motion pictures that have documentary significance or "significance as records of the time." (PR 139)

JUNE 30. The Librarian announces the organization of a new Acquisitions Department "to provide an administrative organization for the more effective development of the Library's collections." All acquisition, selection, and accessioning functions performed by the Reference and Processing departments and the Law Library are transferred to the new department, effective July 1, 1943. A new Exchange and Gift Division is created to "receive all materials acquired through gift, exchange, copyright, transfer, and deposit" and to assume related responsibilities regarding acquisitions and the development of the Library's collections of governmental publications. Verner W. Clapp is named director of the department; he will also serve as chairman of the new interdepartmental Acquisitions Committee. (GO 1188)

JUNE 30. MacLeish explains that as part of the latest organizational change, Reference Department Director Luther H. Evans will devote himself exclusively to his duties as Chief Assistant Librarian, "in which capacity he will serve as the general Executive Officer of the Library of Congress." Evans' "return to his duties as Chief Assistant Librarian will make it possible to dissolve the Administrative Department, since the Divisions composing this Department are instruments of Library-wide administration and are naturally attached to the office of the

Library's Executive Officer. No change is contemplated in the organization of the Divisions composing the Administrative Department, except that they will henceforth report to Dr. Evans' office." David C. Mearns will assume the post of director of the Reference Department.

(GO 1189)

JULY. The Library publishes the first issue of its *Information Bulletin*, which combines and supersedes the *Staff Information Bulletin* and the *Monthly Public Information Bulletin*.

(1944 AR:113)

JULY 1. Poet and literary critic Allen Tate begins his one-year term as the Library's consultant in poetry. He will also advise the Library regarding "its program of acquisitions in English letters generally."

(PR 135)

JULY 3. Librarian MacLeish announces that—with the exception of the Exhibits Office—the divisions, offices, and services formerly constituting the Administrative Department will report directly to the Office of the Chief Assistant Librarian. The Exhibits Office is transferred to the Reference Department.

(GO 1190)

JULY 8. The Librarian establishes an interdepartmental processing committee.

(GO 1192)

JULY 16. President Roosevelt issued a directive to the Librarian of Congress and the archivist of the United States "to draw up plans for a national motion picture repository."

(1945 AR:34–35)

JULY 17. The Librarian designates a special committee to continue work on the reorganization of the Reference Department, which is to be shaped into two "services": the circulation—or issue—service and the reference—or bibliographical—service.

(GO 1195)

AUGUST 26. MacLeish announces that "beginning with the current fiscal year, the Library will report its acquisi-

116

Card Division employees filling orders from libraries throughout the nation for Library of Congress printed catalog cards. This file was located on the third floor of the Annex.

tions of new materials in quarterly supplements to the Annual Report." During its first year, the *Quarterly Journal of Current Acquisitions* will be edited by Allen Tate, consultant in poetry. The issue reporting acquisitions from July to September 1943 will appear on November 1.   (GO 1202)

AUGUST 31. The experimental division for the study of wartime communications completes "the third and final year of its scheduled term" and is dissolved.   (1943 AR:18)

OCTOBER. In response to demands for a microfilm edition of the Thomas Jefferson Papers, the Library begins microfilming its Jefferson collection.   (1944 AR:121)

OCTOBER 18–NOVEMBER 19. In order to discuss possible changes in descriptive cataloging rules, the Library holds a series of conferences with catalogers and Library administrators in 15 cities throughout the United States. The Library is represented by Herman H. Henkle, director of the Processing Department, and Lucile M. Morsch, chief of the Descriptive Cataloging Division.   (LCA; 1944 AR:78)

OCTOBER 30. In his annual report for 1943, MacLeish describes the "psychological reason" for the appallingly low salaries in libraries throughout the country, including the Library of Congress: "Professional work in the law, or professional work in finance, or professional work in economics is assumed to exceed in value professional work in the assembling, organization, interpretation, and service of the printed materials without which the work of the specialists in law or finance or economics would be impossible."   (1943 AR:74)

DECEMBER. The Library purchases, from the Phelps Publishing Co. of Springfield, Mass., over 10,000 photographic negatives and transparencies recording all aspects of the Civil War and made under the direction of Mathew B. Brady.   (LCA)

1943

DECEMBER 31. Register of Copyrights Clement L. Bouvé retires.   (1944 AR:132–33)

1944

JANUARY 1. The Library assumes custody of the Office of War Information collection of nearly 300,000 photographs, which includes the file organized by Roy E. Stryker in the Farm Security Administration from 1936 to 1942 for the "photo-documentation of America."   (LCA; 1946 AR:256)

JANUARY 3. Over 230 staff members are detailed for three weeks to the Office of the Keeper of the Collections to perform "certain operations preliminary to an inventory of the classified collections"—primarily the preparation of charge records and shelfreading. Over 200,000 charges for the central charge file are prepared.   (GO 1208; LCIB Feb.–March 1944:1)

JANUARY 24. A staff of six begins an inventory of the classified book collections, the first since a partial inventory was made in 1928–29.   (LCIB Feb.–March 1944:6)

MARCH 7. The Librarian creates the position of selection officer in the Acquisitions Department. The selection officer "will examine all incoming unsolicited acquisitions, and will indicate the disposition of each piece or group of material, within the limits of approved processing policies."   (GO 1217; 1944 AR:17)

MARCH 25. The Reference Department is reorganized; the objective of the reorganization is the "increased usefulness of the Library to its readers." Three principal services are created: the Legislative Reference Service; the Public Reference Service, which contains the General Reference and Bibliography, Aeronautics, Manuscripts, Maps, Music, Orientalia, Prints and Photographs (formerly Fine Arts), and Rare Books Divisions, along with the Hispanic Foundation and a proposed Slavic center; and the Circulation Service, containing the Stack and Reader Division, which has custody of the general book collection, and the Serials and the Loan Divisions. A science division will be created "as soon as conditions permit." The numerous transfers of functions within the reorganization include the assignment of processing responsibilities for special format and language materials to the Manuscripts, Maps, Prints and Photographs, and Orientalia Divisions.

(GO 1218; 1944 AR:17–25)

MARCH 30. The Librarian establishes an interdepartmental Committee on Bibliography and Publications to recommend policies "for the development of a bibliographical and publishing program in consonance with the Library's objectives." The new committee replaces the Advisory Committee on Publications and the Committee on Bibliography.

(GO 1219; 1944 AR:109)

APRIL 1. The Librarian establishes a chair of Latin American studies.

(1944 AR:26)

MAY 26–27. The Fellows of the Library of Congress in American Letters hold their organizational meeting. The members are Van Wyck Brooks, Katherine Garrison Chapin, Paul Green, Katherine Anne Porter, Carl Sandburg, Allen Tate, Willard Thorp, and Mark Van Doren.

(1944 AR:38)

JUNE. The Descriptive Catalog Division begins reclassifying the last large segment of books still arranged according to the Jeffersonian scheme used by the Library in the 19th century.

(LCIB June 1944:12)

SEPTEMBER 20. The Librarian announces that "with the approval of the War Department and the Joint Chiefs of Staff," the Declaration of Independence and the Constitution of the United States will once again be placed on public display in the Library, beginning October 1.

(PR 208)

OCTOBER. MacLeish describes the Library's reorganization in a lengthy article in *Library Quarterly*. He begins

by describing the Library as he found it: "The Library of Congress in 1939 was not so much an organization in its own right as the lengthened shadow of one man—a man of great force, extraordinary abilities, and a personality which left its fortunate impression upon everything he touched. Only a man of Herbert Putnam's remarkable qualities could have administered an institution of the size of the Library of Congress by direct and personal supervision of all its operations, and only if his administration were based upon the intimate familiarities of forty years." He concludes by expressing his hope and belief that the reorganization "has provided a sensible, orderly, and manageable structure, strong enough to support the great future of which the Library of Congress is so manifestly capable—whatever else the reorganization of the Library has accomplished, it has given, I trust, an increasing number of men and women the sense of participating creatively and responsibly in a work which all of them may well feel proud to share." (LQ 14:277–315; 1945 AR:107–42)

OCTOBER. The Library announces the publication of *Library and Reference Facilities in the Area of the District of Columbia*, compiled in the Reference Department's Legislative Reference Service.

(LCA; PR 203)

OCTOBER. The Library and the National Gallery of Art agree to a cooperative arrangement for the acquisition and servicing of printed materials in the field of art.

(LCA; 1944 AR:95–97)

OCTOBER 1. The Declaration of Independence and the Constitution are placed back in the Shrine for public display.

(LCA)

NOVEMBER 13. Librarian MacLeish announces that a recent $47,800 grant from the Rockefeller Foundation will enable the Library to take the initial steps toward the establishment of a Slavic center. The first project will be the preparation of a Slavic union catalog.

(PR 218)

On December 26, 1941, less than three weeks after the attack on Pearl Harbor, the Declaration of Independence and the Constitution were sent to Fort Knox, Ky., for safekeeping. The documents were returned to the Library in September 1944 and once again placed on public display. In this September 1944 photograph, the Declaration of Independence is examined by, from left to right, David C. Mearns, director of the Reference Department, Librarian MacLeish, and Verner W. Clapp, director of the Acquisitions Department.

119

NOVEMBER 29. The Library announces the establishment, with a $100,000 grant from the Rockefeller Foundation, of the Library of Congress Grants-in-Aid for Studies in American History and Civilization. (PR 222; 1945 AR:105–6)

DECEMBER 19. Librarian MacLeish resigns to become assistant secretary of state.

DECEMBER 20. Luther H. Evans, Chief Assistant Librarian, becomes Acting Librarian of Congress. (1945 AR:11)

FEBRUARY 1. Acting Librarian Evans appoints Sam Bass Warner, former head attorney for compliance in the War Production Board and Harvard Law School professor, to be register of copyrights. (1945 AR:149)

FEBRUARY 1. The Library announces the completion of the microfilming of its unique collection of *Slave Narratives*, which consists of 17 volumes of transcripts based on interviews with former slaves. The interviews were conducted by the WPA Federal Writers' Project. (PR 237)

FEBRUARY 4. The Library announces that the vault of the Bullion Depository of the U.S. Mint at Fort Knox, Ky., was the wartime repository for the Declaration of Independence and the Constitution of the United States. Before this disclosure, the location was regarded as a military secret. (PR 231)

FEBRUARY 21. Barney Balaban, president of Paramount Pictures, Inc., gives the Library a contemporary manuscript copy of the original enrolled copy of the Bill of Rights. The gift is one of the 13 engrossed copies of the proposed amendments to the Constitution which were sent on October 2, 1789, to the 11 states and to Rhode Island and North Carolina. (LCA; PR 240)

MARCH. The Library publishes the first issue of the *United States Quarterly Book List*, a guide to books published in the United States, which is prepared for distribution to Latin America through the Department of State. The *Book List* was undertaken at the request and with the financial support of the State Department, in accordance with a recommendation by the Interdepartmental Committee on Cooperation with the American Republics for carrying out the obligation of the United States under Article XXII of the Buenos Aires Convention of 1936. (1945 AR:89–90)

MARCH 3. Senator Claude Pepper of Florida opens an exhibit commemorating the centennial of Florida's admission to the Union, the first in a series of Library exhibits honoring significant anniversaries in the histories of the American states and territories. (PR 230; 1945 AR:85)

APRIL 25. The United Nations Conference on International Organization, meeting in San Francisco, opens its conference library—which was organized and assembled by the Library of Congress in cooperation with the Department of State and other American libraries. (1945 AR:80–83)

JUNE. The Library purchases the personal library of Sheikh Mahmud al-Imam Mansuri of Cairo, which contains over 5,000 books and manuscripts and greatly strengthens the Arabic collections. (QJ 3, Feb. 1946:37)

JUNE 18. President Harry S. Truman nominates Acting Librarian Luther H. Evans to be Librarian of Congress. (CR 91:6241)

JUNE 28. The Senate Library Committee, chaired by Alben W. Barkley of Kentucky, holds hearings on the Evans nomination and listens to testimony from the nominee. On behalf of the committee, Senator Barkley submits an executive report to the Senate favoring confirmation. (LCA; CR 91:6929)

1945

JUNE 29. The U.S. Senate confirms, without objection, President Truman's nomination of Luther H. Evans to be Librarian of Congress.

(CR 91:7006)

JUNE 30. Luther H. Evans takes the oath of office and becomes the 10th Librarian of Congress. The Library has a book collection of over 7 million volumes, a staff of over 1,200, and an appropriation in fiscal 1945 of over $4 million.

(LCA; 1945 AR 210)

JULY. With the approval of the War Department, a special Library of Congress "mission in Europe" begins its task of obtaining "multiple copies of European publications for the war period" for distribution to American libraries and research institutions.

(1946 AR:264-67)

JULY. In a report to President Truman titled *Science, the Endless Frontier,* Vannevar Bush, director of the Office of Scientific Research and Development, suggests that "federal aid for the library system of the country might well have as its central object the strengthening of the Library of Congress so that it could foster programs of cooperation."

(1946 AR:340)

JULY 1. The Library assumes responsibility for preparation, by its Hispanic Foundation, of future volumes of the *Handbook of Latin American Studies.* The *Handbook* previously was prepared under the direction of the Joint Committee on Latin American Studies of the National Research Council, the American Council of Learned Societies, and the Social Science Research Council.

(1946 AR:243)

JULY 7. Librarian Evans reorganizes the Legislative Reference Service so that it may perform "the enlarged functions" made possible by increased appropriations for fiscal 1946.

(GO 1261)

1945

July 21. In a radio address, Librarian Evans defines his new task: "The library resources of the Nation, at the head of which stands the Library of Congress, must be built up in such a way that this Nation possesses the printed, the pictorial, the cartographic and the other material which will be needed by its Government and its people." (1945 AR:21)

July 22. The Librarian announces a further expansion of the Library's collecting activities for motion pictures. (PR 271)

August 20. The Library establishes a Near East section in the Orientalia Division. (LCA; 1946 AR:253)

August 27. Acting Librarian of Congress David C. Mearns announces that, effective immediately, the Library's work week has been shortened to five days a week, eight hours a day. (GO 1265)

September 19. At a meeting called by Librarian Evans, representatives from library and research associations, the War Department, and the Library of Congress formulate plans for a cooperative overseas acquisitions program which will focus on "locating and forwarding the bookstocks believed to be accumulated in Germany (especially in the Russian Zone) as a result of prewar orders placed by American libraries." With the approval of the Department of State, the Library of Congress Mission to Europe will serve as the "procuring arm" of the project, and the War Department will provide the Library's agents with the necessary credentials. (1946 AR:263–67)

October. The Library publishes *Sixty American Poets, 1896–1944*, with the selection and critical notes by Allen Tate, consultant in poetry, 1943–44, and a bibliography of the writings of each poet, compiled by Frances Cheney of the General Reference and Bibliography Division. (LCA)

1946

January 1. The Library begins cooperating with the Office of Technical Services of the Department of Commerce in a project to reproduce declassified reports of wartime scientific and technical research. (1946 AR:258)

January 11. In ceremonies at the Library, the Lincoln Cathedral copy of Magna Carta is turned over to the British Ambassador to the United States, John Balfour, for return to England. (1946 AR:247–48)

February 7. Librarian Evans "re-establishes" the Administrative Department in a changed form, naming it the Department of Administrative Services. The new department has responsibility for the Library's Accounts, Disbursing, Personnel, Supply, and Tabulating Offices, as well as for the Secretary's Office, Library Buildings and Grounds, and the Photoduplication Service. The department has been reestablished because of the need to reduce the span of control over these administrative functions and to "coordinate and improve" administrative services to the other departments. (GO 1275; 1946 AR:313)

March 4. The Joint Committee on the Organization of Congress recommends "that the Legislative Reference Service be immediately increased in size and scope more adequately to serve the individual members of Congress and also to provide a pool of experts available for use by the committees of Congress." (79/2 SR 1011:15)

March 28. In a speech before the National Board of Review of Motion Pictures, Evans outlines his plans to develop a "national motion picture collection at the Library." (PR 327)

April 20. W. Somerset Maugham presents a manuscript of his novel *Of Human Bondage* to the United States and the Library to acknowledge "the kindness and generosity with which you received the women and children of my country when in fear of a German invasion they came to America." (1946 AR:250)

The strengthening of the Library's foreign acquisitions program was a major accomplishment of the Evans administration. In this January 1946 photograph, members of the Library of Congress Mission to Europe pose with Librarian Evans on the eve of their departure. Left to right, standing: David C. Clift, Harry M. Lydenberg, Richard S. Hill, Julius Allen, Don Carlos Travis, Daniel Schacter and Janet Emerson. Maj. James M. Horan, coordinator of libraries, U.S. War Department, is seated beside the Librarian. LC–USP6–412C

123

APRIL 22. Librarian Evans submits a lengthy budget justification to the House Subcommittee on Legislative Branch Appropriations. The budget estimates, which were "conceived in the light of what we believe to be the Congressional conception of the role and work of the Library," call for a rapid and comprehensive expansion of the Library and an increase in its appropriation from $5,104,568 in fiscal 1946 to $9,756,852 for fiscal 1947. (1947 HRA:1-3)

APRIL 30. Law Librarian Eldon R. James retires.

(1946 AR:294)

MAY. The inventory of the collections is terminated owing to lack of funds.

(LCA)

MAY 14. The House Committee on Appropriations recommends an appropriation of $5,859,900 for the Library, an increase of $755,332 above fiscal 1946. It explains that a principal reason for not approving the amount requested was to give attention to the need for a determination as to what the policy of the Library of Congress is going to be in the way of expansion and service to the public and to the Congress. The original purpose in establishing the Library was to serve Congress; however, it would seem that the Library has evolved not only into a Congressional Library but a national and international library as well. It is believed that the responsibility for determining Library policy rests with legislative committees of the Congress charged with the responsibility for operation of the Library and not with the Appropriations Committee whose responsibility it is to appropriate for projects and activities duly authorized by the Congress. If it is the desire to build and maintain the largest library in the world which, according to testimony, the Library of Congress is at present, that is one matter, and if it should be the policy to maintain a library primarily for the service of Congress, it is quite another matter from the standpoint of fiscal needs.

(79/2 HRR 2040:6)

JUNE 10. The Senate Committee on Appropriations recommends an appropriation of $6,172,437 for the Library for fiscal 1947.

(79/2 SR 1436:4)

JULY 1. President Truman approves the legislative branch appropriations act for fiscal 1947, which grants the Library $6,069,967—an increase of $965,399 above the previous year, but $3,686,885 less than the request.

(60 Stat. 386)

JULY 1. In cooperation with the American Library Association and the Association of Research Libraries, the Library creates a documents expediting project to acquire and distribute federal documents that are especially difficult to obtain.

(1946 AR:267-68)

AUGUST 2. President Truman approves the legislative branch reorganization act of 1946, which expands the responsibilities of the Library's Legislative Reference Service in assisting Congress and its committees and gives the service permanent statutory basis as a separate Library department. The act authorizes increased appropriations to enable the service to employ nationally eminent specialists in 19 broad subject fields. It also stipulates that the Joint Committee on the Library shall consist of the chairman and four members of the Committee on Rules and Administration of the Senate and the chairman and four members of the Committee on House Administration of the House of Representatives.

(60 Stat. 812)

AUGUST 8. The Librarian announces that Edith Bolling Wilson, widow of the former President, has given the Library the 9,000-volume personal library of Woodrow Wilson, which will be housed in a special room adjacent to the Rare Books Division.

(PR 357)

AUGUST 22. In recognition of "the development of folklore as a field of scholarly inquiry," the Library establishes a Folklore Section in the Music Division. The Archive of American Folk Song is incorporated into the section.

(GO 1295; 1946 AR:284-85)

characterizes as "the most important state paper to issue from the Library since the Report of the Committee on Library Reorganization in 1802," is also reprinted. Furthermore, the Librarian reports that he has recently appointed a Library of Congress Planning Committee, composed of eminent persons representing various categories of the Library's users. The committee plans "to produce a report by mid-January for me to forward to the Congress as a presentation of what is believed to be the best judgment of the country, short of the judgment of the Congress itself, as to what role the Library of Congress ought to play in the national life."
(1946 AR:13–227, 233–34)

NOVEMBER 26. The Conference on International Cultural, Educational, and Scientific Exchanges, being held at Princeton, N.J., under the auspices of the American Library Association, recommends that the Library of Congress "formulate and present to ALA, ARL, SLA, and other library associations in this country, for their comment and criticism, plans for editing and publishing a complete, current national bibliography of the United States."
(1947 AR:15, 112)

DECEMBER 20. In a letter to Association of Research Libraries Executive Secretary Paul North Rice, Librarian Evans urges that an ARL committee be formed to plan a nationally coordinated effort for the "microfilming of extensive runs of library materials."
(LCA)

DECEMBER 26. Actress Mary Pickford gives the Library her personal collection of motion pictures "for preservation and research use."
(LCA; 1947 AR:45)

FEBRUARY 5. Writing in the Library's *Information Bulletin*, Librarian Evans responds to a bill recently introduced by Representative Karl E. Mundt of South Dakota which would "transfer the administration of the Library of Congress from the Office of the President of the United States

SEPTEMBER. Secretary of State James F. Byrnes appoints Librarian Evans to the U.S. National Commission on Unesco.
(LCIB Sept. 24–30, 1946:8)

OCTOBER 1. The Librarian centralizes and expands the Library's services for the blind. The Division of Books for the Adult Blind absorbs the Loan Division's Service for the Blind Section as well as the functions, personnel, and collections of the National Library for the Blind, Inc.
(GO 1299; 1946 AR:285)

OCTOBER 3. The Library's motion picture project is designated as the Motion Picture Division.
(GO 1300; 1946 AR:285)

OCTOBER 16. The name of the Division of Books for the Adult Blind is changed to the Division for the Blind.
(GO 1302)

OCTOBER 16. Evans announces that regularly scheduled tours of the Library for the general public are now available.
(GO 1303)

OCTOBER 22. Librarian Evans consolidates the administrative structure of the Processing Department. Changes include the establishment of the Catalog Maintenance Division and the abolition of the Cooperative Cataloging Section in the Descriptive Cataloging Division.
(GO 1305; 1946 AR:284)

NOVEMBER 15. The Librarian submits his annual report for fiscal 1946 to Congress. In the introduction, he points to the May 14 report of the House Appropriations Committee as a glaring example of "how guilty the Library has been of failure to provide essential information on itself"; as one corrective, the annual report features a history of the Library—"The Story up to Now," by David C. Mearns, director of the Reference Department. The Library's budget justification for fiscal 1947, which Evans

... to the Congress of the United States." Under the heading "the relation of the Library to the Congress," Evans explains that "the Librarian of Congress, while appointed by the President (since 1897 by and with the advice of the Senate), is not a political appointee, does not go out of office with a change in the presidency or the party in power, does not appoint his subordinates on the basis of party affiliation or political activity, and does not accept direction from the President in the discharge of his responsibilities."

(LCIB Feb. 4–10, 1947:7–9)

FEBRUARY 24. Evans appoints the acting director of the Administrative Services Department, John C. L. Andreassen, to be director.

(1947 AR:7)

MARCH 5. The Librarian names Verner W. Clapp as Chief Assistant Librarian. The position is now that of "the principal staff and planning officer" of the Library and not the Library's executive officer, as in the past.

(PR 397; 1946 AR:284)

MARCH 12. The Library of Congress Planning Committee, chaired by Keyes D. Metcalf, director of libraries at Harvard University, submits its report. The committee strongly urges an expansion of the Library's national functions, maintaining that "if the Library fails to provide the services outlined in this report . . . it will be necessary to build elsewhere in the Government and throughout the nation the services which it is recommended that the Library of Congress should provide, and that these services, because of their lack of centralization and of connection with the greatest collection of books and other materials in the nation, will be less satisfactory and more expensive than if they were provided by the Library of Congress." The committee also recommends that "the actual status of the Library as a National Library should be officially recognized in its name and that it should be designated 'The Library of Congress, the National Library of the United States of America.'"

(1947 AR:102–8)

MARCH 14–15. The Association of Research Libraries holds a special conference at the Library to consider the implementation of the Farmington Plan.

(LCIB March 18–24, 1947:4–5)

APRIL 24. Librarian Evans announces that Processing Department director Herman H. Henkle will resign, effective August 31, to become librarian of the John Crerar Library in Chicago.

(1947 AR:86)

MAY 12–JUNE 6. Delegates from 22 nations attend the first Assembly of Librarians of the Americas, held at the Library with support from the Department of State.

(1947 AR:40)

MAY 15. The Librarian creates a Library of Congress Loyalty Board to administer an employee loyalty program.

(GO 1319; 1948 AR:28–29)

MAY 21. Librarian Evans issues a new general order "permitting the Legislative Reference Service a general supervision of the Library-wide services to Members without interfering with the execution of the services themselves."

(1947 AR:26, 116)

JUNE. The Library publishes its Rules for Descriptive Cataloging, Preliminary Edition.

(1948 AR:89–90)

JUNE 3. The Library establishes a Science and Technology Project "with divisional status" in the Reference Department. The project, which has been created by a transfer of funds from the Office of Naval Research, will provide certain bibliographic and library services for the same agency.

(GO 1323; 1948 AR:69–70)

JUNE 9. The Library announces a cooperative project with the General Education Board and the American Council of Learned Societies to locate and microfilm files of American Negro newspapers from their earliest dates to 1900.

(PR 418)

JUNE 20. Paul Vanderbilt, acting chief of the Prints and Photographs Division, submits a paper to the American Library Association that summarizes the Library's point of view on the subject of national bibliographic control. Included is a tentative plan for developing the Library's *Cumulative Catalog of Library of Congress Printed Cards* into a national bibliography.　(1947 AR:109–15)

JULY 26. The Library opens to the public the papers of Abraham Lincoln which his son Robert Todd Lincoln gave to the Library in 1923 with the provision that they not be opened until 21 years after the latter's death.
　(1948 AR:14–16)

JULY 31. Under the terms of the legislative appropriations act for fiscal 1948, the Motion Picture Division is liquidated.　(PR 446; 1947 AR:45–46)

AUGUST 6. Librarian Evans announces that the Processing and Acquisitions departments "are hereby merged," and that Herman H. Henkle, director of the Processing Department, will serve as director of the merged departments.　(GO 1329; 1948 AR:75, 100)

AUGUST 26. Acting Librarian of Congress Herman H. Henkle announces additional steps in the merger of the Processing and Acquisitions Departments. The position of director of the Acquisitions Department is abolished, and the duties of the position, with the exception of acquisitions policy planning, are assigned to the director of the Processing Department. The planning function is transferred to the Chief Assistant Librarian. The Processing Department will be responsible for carrying out all acquisition activities of the Library, including selection of materials for the collections.　(GO 1331)

SEPTEMBER 1. Librarian Evans appoints Frederick H. Wagman, assistant director of the Reference Department for public reference service, to be director of the Processing Department.　(1947 AR:5–6)

OCTOBER 7. Librarian Evans redefines the functions of the Prints and Photographs Division and transfers the Exhibits Office from the division to the Office of the Chief Assistant Librarian.　(GO 1334; 1948 AR:67)

NOVEMBER 3. The name of the Department of Administrative Services is changed to the Administrative Department.　(GO 1343)

NOVEMBER 15. In his annual report for 1948, Librarian Evans informs Congress that the merger of the Processing and Acquisitions departments took place only after "long and thorough consideration of the advisability of assigning to one officer responsibility for managing acquisitions and processing operations."　(1948 AR:100)

DECEMBER 15. The U.S. Library Mission to Japan, consisting of Chief Assistant Librarian Verner W. Clapp and Iowa State College Librarian Charles H. Brown, begins its work, in Tokyo, of planning a National Diet Library. At the request of the Japanese legislature, the new institution will be patterned after the Library of Congress.
　(LCIB Dec. 30, 1947–Jan. 5, 1948:7;
　July 27–Aug. 2, 1948:11–13)

JANUARY 8. Librarian Evans announces additional organizational changes. The Information Office and the Publications Section of the Secretary's Office are created to replace the Information and Publications Office. The duties of the Chief Assistant Librarian are redefined and that office is assigned general responsibility for the direction of the Information Office, the Exhibits Office, the Bibliographic Planning Project, and the consultant in motion pictures. The Division for the Blind and the Office of the Keeper of the Collections are transferred from the Office of the Chief Assistant Librarian to the Administrative Department.　(GO 1353; 1948 AR:100)

MARCH 4. Evans announces that a grant from the Bollingen Foundation has enabled the Library to establish the Bollingen Prize in Poetry, to be awarded each year "for the best book of verse by an American author to be published during the preceding calendar year." The selection jury will be the Fellows in American Letters of the Library of Congress, a group of 13 poets and writers serving the Library as honorary consultants.

(PR 467; 1948 AR:103)

MARCH 5. The Librarian announces that, effective at once, the Union Catalog is to be known as the National Union Catalog. The name of the Union Catalog Division is unchanged.

(GO 1357; 1948 AR:101)

MARCH 5. Using funds transferred from the U.S. Air Force, the Library establishes an Air Research Unit in the Aeronautics Division to provide "special research services to the USAF in connection with the collections of the Library."

(GO 1358)

MARCH 10. The name of the Indic Section of the Orientalia Division is changed to the South Asia Section, a title "better descriptive of its functions."

(GO 1359; 1948 AR:101)

JUNE 7. The Librarian reports that the administration has acted on most of the recommendations made by the Special Committee on Library Services to Area Studies, which was appointed earlier in the year. The committee's purpose is to "study and recommend policies and procedures for the Library of Congress in relation to scholarly studies in the government and outside the government regarding different areas of the world."

(LCIB June 8–14, 1948:12–13)

JULY 1. The Library establishes the Publications Board Section in the Photoduplication Service to administer new functions in acquiring and reproducing scientific and technical reports—functions previously performed by the library of the Department of Agriculture, the Army Medical Library, and the Office of Technical Services in the Department of Commerce.

(GO 1367; 1948 AR:46)

JULY 22. The Library's Air Research Unit is designated as the Air Research Division.

(GO 1375)

AUGUST. The Cooperative Acquisitions Project for European wartime publications, inaugurated in 1945, is completed.

(LCA; 1948 AR:17)

SEPTEMBER 1. The American Book Center for War-Devastated Libraries, Inc., sponsored by the Council of National Library Associations and housed in the Library of Congress, is succeeded by the U.S. Book Exchange, Inc. The new organization will promote "the distribution and interchange of books, periodicals, and other scholarly materials among libraries and other educational and scientific institutions in the United States."

(1948 AR:17–18)

SEPTEMBER 10. The Library establishes a European Affairs Division in the Reference Department. The new division has "acquisitions, reference, bibliographical, research, and liaison responsibilities similar to those of other area divisions, but no custodial responsibilities."

(GO 1382; 1949 AR:66–67)

NOVEMBER 5. The Librarian alters the organization of the Exchange and Gift Division, establishing new European, American and British, Orientalia, and Hispanic Exchange Sections.

(GO 1387)

DECEMBER. The first edition of *Newspapers on Microfilm: A Union List*, prepared by the Library of Congress, is published by the Association of Research Libraries. (LCA)

DECEMBER 8. The name of the Legislative Reference Section of the Legislative Reference Service is changed to the Senior Specialists Section.

(GO 1392)

DECEMBER 10. The first Juilliard String Quartet concert in the Coolidge Auditorium is also the first Library concert to be broadcast on FM radio. (PR 527; 1949 AR:181)

The Library of Congress Fellows in American Letters, in the Whittall Pavilion, February 29, 1948. Standing from left to right: Conrad Aiken, Cleanth Brooks, and Robert Penn Warren (consultant in poetry, 1944–45). Seated from left to right: W. H. Auden, Mrs. Frances Biddle, Librarian Evans, Leonie Adams (consultant in poetry, 1948–49), and Richard H. Blackmur. LC–USP6–2082–C

129

DECEMBER 20. Librarian Evans announces the Library's sponsorship, with support from the Rockefeller Foundation, of a 16-volume series of extended essays "dealing with various aspects of American civilization in the twentieth century." General editor of the Library of Congress Series in American Civilization will be Ralph H. Gabriel of Yale University.

(PR 528; 1949 AR:80–81)

JANUARY 8. In ceremonies attended by Mrs. Wilson, the Library's new Woodrow Wilson Room is formally dedicated.

(1949 AR:99)

JANUARY 17. Writing in the *New Republic*, former Representative Maury Maverick of Texas offers the following advice to new members of Congress: "Go over to the Library of Congress. It has the most beautiful interior in the world. Also, the greatest and richest treasury of knowledge. Work those people to death. They like it. They will do research for you over the phone, and deliver books to you, marked right where you want them."

JANUARY 17. Librarian Evans establishes the Air Studies Division, which consists of the former Air Research Division and a new Information Section. The entire division will be operated on funds transferred from the U.S. Air Force.

(GO 1393)

FEBRUARY 14. "To make provision to lighten the load of work which now falls upon the Librarian," Evans increases the responsibilities of the Chief Assistant Librarian and establishes the position of Assistant Librarian—which will have primary responsibility for the Library's external relations and its publications program. The Librarian appoints David C. Mearns, director of the Reference Department, as the new Assistant Librarian.

(GO 1396; 1949 AR:138)

FEBRUARY 18. Poetry recordings, prepared with funds from the Bollingen Foundation, are offered for purchase

for the first time. Of particular interest among the five-album series, titled Twentieth Century Poetry in English, is a five-record set recorded for the Library by T. S. Eliot, winner of the 1948 Nobel Prize for Literature.

(PR 543)

FEBRUARY 20. The Library announces that its Fellows in American Letters have awarded the first annual award of the Bollingen Prize in Poetry to Ezra Pound for his book *The Pisan Cantos*. The Fellows take cognizance of public knowledge that Pound is under indictment for treason and committed to an institution for the insane, stating that they "are aware that objections may be made to awarding a prize to a man situated as is Mr. Pound."

(PR 542; 1949 AR:88–94)

MARCH 21. Because "recruiting qualified librarians during the past few years has been a formidable task," Librarian Evans announces the inauguration of a "special recruiting program" to select and train outstanding library school graduates for the Library's staff.

(LCIB March 22–28, 1949:3)

APRIL. The Library publishes *Rules for Descriptive Cataloging in the Library of Congress* (adopted by the American Library Association). In the preface, Lucile M. Morsch, chief of the Descriptive Cataloging Division, emphasizes the need for this single set of rules "to achieve uniformity which will expedite cooperative cataloging and international bibliography."

(LCA)

JUNE 3. The Librarian establishes a Science Division in the Reference Department. The Science and Technology Project becomes a section in the new division and is designated the Navy Research Section.

(GO 1403)

JUNE 27. The Librarian reorganizes the Legislative Reference Service into the American Law, Senior Specialists, Economics, Foreign Affairs, Government, History and General Research, and Library Services Sections.

(GO 1407; 1949 AR:139)

1949

JUNE 30. President Truman approves the Federal Property and Administrative Services Act of 1949. Section 104 of the new law transfers the National Archives and its functions to the General Services Administration; the National Archives Council and the National Historical Publications Commission also are transferred. (63 Stat. 377)

JULY 5. In response to a request from the Association of Research Libraries, the Library of Congress establishes a Microfilming Clearing House to serve as a central source of information about "extensive microfilming projects involving newspapers, serials, and manuscript collections" (LCA)

AUGUST 19. Primarily because of the controversy resulting from the award of the Bollingen Prize to Ezra Pound by the Fellows in American Literature, the Joint Committee on the Library unanimously recommends that the Library cancel "all arrangements for the giving of prizes and the making of awards." Evans announces the Library's immediate compliance, stating that "the awards which, in the past, the Library has made, and which will not be made in the future, are the Elizabeth Sprague Coolidge Medal for 'eminent services to chamber music,' the Bollingen Prize in Poetry, and three awards made in connection with the annual national exhibition of prints." (PR 590, 592; 1949 AR:88–94)

SEPTEMBER. The Capitol Page School, established by the Legislative Reorganization Act of 1946, is moved to the Main Building of the Library. (LCA)

SEPTEMBER 2. Librarian Evans appoints W. Lawrence Keitt as Law Librarian. (1949 AR:6)

OCTOBER 15. President Truman approves an act of Congress increasing the salaries of high-level government officials; the annual salary of the Librarian of Congress is raised to $15,000. (63 Stat. 380)

1949

NOVEMBER 28. Librarian Evans promotes Burton W. Adkinson from acting director to director of the Reference Department. (1949 AR:5)

DECEMBER. The last issue of the State Law Index, prepared by the Library since 1927, is published. The appropriation for the Index was not continued by Congress because of the "development of comparable apparatus by private organizations which it regards as adequate to the purpose." (1950 AR:24–25)

DECEMBER 15. Librarian Evans announces the establishment, by the Library of Congress Trust Fund Board, of the Serge Koussevitzky Music Foundation. The initial endowment, in excess of $100,000, represents a continuation of the Koussevitzky Music Foundation, Inc., which the conductor created in 1942. The primary purpose of the foundation will be the commissioning of new works by distinguished composers. (1950 AR:45)

1950

APRIL 13. As the 150th anniversary of the founding of the Library approaches, President Harry S Truman sends Librarian Evans a congratulatory letter, noting that neither the Library's collections nor its services "could ever have been fashioned without the power of the principle of free inquiry and the support of that principle by the people and the Congress." (LCIB April 24, 1950:1)

MAY 17. President Truman delivers an address in the Coolidge Auditorium as part of a program marking the publication by Princeton University Press of the first volume of The Papers of Thomas Jefferson. (1950 AR:92)

JULY 10. The Library expands its interlibrary loan service to include positive microfilm, in order "to prevent wasteful expenditures by libraries for research materials ... for which they have only occasional need." (GO 1436)

On May 17, 1950, President Harry S. Truman delivered an address in the Coolidge Auditorium in a program marking the publication by Princeton University Press of the first volume of The Papers of Thomas Jefferson, edited by Julian P. Boyd. The program was part of the Library's commemoration of the 150th anniversary of its founding. Pictured in the Whittall Pavilion from left to right are Verner W. Clapp, Chief Assistant Librarian of Congress, President Truman, Gen. George C. Marshall, and Harold W. Dodds, president of Princeton University.

1950

JULY 24. The Library publishes a 107-page preliminary bibliography about Korea, a bibliography which is "suitable for the emergency requirements of the early stages of the Korean conflict." (PR 693, 717)

SEPTEMBER 5. President Truman approves the Federal Records Act of 1950, which places virtually all national archival and records management authority in the Office of the Administrator of General Services. The National Historical Publications Commission is reconstituted to include membership from all three branches of government, the American Historical Association, and the public at large; the Librarian of Congress is designated an ex officio member. The National Archives Council is abolished and replaced with the Federal Records Council. (64 Stat. 578)

OCTOBER 20. In order "to lighten the administrative load of the Librarian and the Chief Assistant Librarian," Librarian Evans establishes the new position of Deputy Chief Assistant Librarian and appoints Dan M. Lacy, assistant director for cataloging in the Processing Department, to the new post. (GO 1447; 1950 AR:5)

OCTOBER 29. The Library announces the completion of the state legislative journals microfilming project, begun in 1941 in cooperation with the University of North Carolina but delayed during the war years. Over 1,700 reels of microfilm were produced; the contents of those reels are described in an 800-page guide published by the Library. (PR 713; 1950 AR:105–6)

NOVEMBER 19. Chicago businessman Alfred Whital Stern donates "the most extensive collection of Lincoln literature ever assembled by a private individual" to the Library. (PR 726; 1951 AR:46–47)

DECEMBER 12. Librarian Emeritus Herbert Putnam receives a standing ovation at a banquet given by the American Library Association to honor the Library in its sesquicentennial year. In his remarks Putnam notes:

"Very few executives have had the fortune to live with their posterity and to be welcomed with a eulogy instead of an elegy. But if you are summoning shades of the past, you must not fail to summon one shade and keep *him* contemporary—the valiant, persistent (I was seeking for the other word) and it is 'forecasting,' 'foretelling,' 'prophesying' shade . . . Ainsworth Spofford." (HP)

DECEMBER 25. Librarian Evans announces that the Library has accepted, from Gertrude Clarke Whittall, a "generous gift for the development of a poetry center," in the Library. The Gertrude Clarke Whittall Poetry Fund will be used to "promote the appreciation and understanding of poetry," primarily through a series of lectures on poetry and poetry readings. (PR 741; LCA-T)

1951

JANUARY 15. Acting Librarian Clapp announces the establishment of the Slavic Division in the Reference Department. (GO 1462)

FEBRUARY 20. Librarian Evans announces the transfer of the Division for the Blind from the Administrative to the Reference Department. (GO 1468)

MARCH 19. The first issue of the *Microfilming Clearing House Bulletin* is published as an appendix to the Library's *Information Bulletin.* (LCIB 10:March 19, 1951)

APRIL 23. The Poetry Room, located in the northwest corner of the third floor of the Main Building, is formally opened—on the birthday of William Shakespeare. The guest of honor is Gertrude Clarke Whittall, who provided funds for the decoration and furnishing of the room. (LCIB 10:April 30, 1951:10)

MAY 1. Burgess Meredith and Cleanth Brooks present a program about Edward Arlington Robinson in the Coolidge Auditorium, the first public program held under the auspices of the Whittall Poetry Fund. (1951 AR:57)

On April 1, 1953, Librarian Evans presented Librarian Emeritus Herbert Putnam with a recording of remarks made at a ceremony a few years earlier marking the 59th anniversary of Putnam's association with the Library. A portrait of Putnam is in the background. LC-USP6-2411-C

134

1951

MAY 1. Librarian Evans reorganizes the Library's services to the Department of the Air Force, abolishing the Air Studies Division and creating the Air Research and Air Information Divisions.
(GO 1471; 1951 AR:92)

MAY 16. The Librarian redistributes responsibilities for the control and allocation of space between the keeper of the collections and the chief of the Buildings and Grounds Division.
(GO 1474)

MAY 28. Register of Copyrights Sam Bass Warner resigns.
(1951 AR:101)

MAY 28. Librarian Evans names Assistant Librarian David C. Mearns to be chief of the Manuscripts Division and Assistant Librarian for the American Collections. Manuscript Division Chief Solon J. Buck is appointed Assistant Librarian.
(1951 AR:5)

JUNE. The Map Division organizes its first special map processing project, which employs students and faculty members from college and university geography departments to process noncurrent maps and atlases.
(1951 AR:89–90)

AUGUST 1. An Information and Publications Office is established in the Office of the Assistant Librarian.
(1952 AR:96)

SEPTEMBER 12. The Librarian appoints acting register of copyrights Arthur Fisher to be register.
(1951 AR:8)

SEPTEMBER 17. Librarian Evans grants Deputy Chief Assistant Librarian Dan M. Lacy a leave of absence to serve as chief of the Division of Overseas Information Centers of the Department of State.
(1952 AR:100)

SEPTEMBER 21. President Truman and Chief Justice Frederick M. Vinson participate in a Constitution Day ceremony at the Library that marks the completion of certain new technical measures for the longterm preservation of the Declaration of Independence and the Constitution of the United States. (1952 AR:xv–xvii)

NOVEMBER 19–20. The Library sponsors the first National Conference on Library Services for the Blind. (PR 825; LCIB 10:Nov. 26, 1951:6–8)

NOVEMBER 20. Librarian Evans appoints Frederick H. Wagman, director of the Processing Department, to be Deputy Chief Assistant Librarian. (1952 AR 103)

DECEMBER. The Library publishes the first issue of its East European Accessions List, which is supported by grants from the National Committee for a Free Europe Inc., and the Rockefeller Foundation. (1952 AR:27)

JANUARY. The Library publishes the first issue of its Southern Asia Accessions List, sponsored jointly by the Social Science Research Council and the American Council of Learned Societies. (1952 AR:27)

JANUARY 10. A Cyrillic Union Catalog Section is established in the Office of the Director of the Processing Department for the purpose of preparing a subject union catalog of publications in Cyrillic alphabets. The new section assumes responsibility for preparation of the Monthly List of Russian Accessions. (GO 1486; 1952 AR:96)

JANUARY 12. Librarian Evans outlines new procedures and policies for the loan of materials. Generally speaking, materials in the collections of the Library of Congress "shall be available for loan in order to promote knowledge in the United States and abroad when such materials are not otherwise reasonably available." (GC 1483)

FEBRUARY 26. Librarian Evans transfers responsibility for editing the Library's Quarterly Journal of Current Acquisitions from the selection officer in the Processing Department to a new position to be established in the Information and Publications Office in the Office of the U.S. Assistant Librarian. Responsibility for editing the U.S. Quarterly Book Review is transferred from the Reference Department to the Office of the Assistant Librarian. (GO 1492; 1952 AR:96)

APRIL 1. Mrs. Frances Clarke Sayers of the New York Public Library begins a special assignment at the Library of Congress "to make a study looking toward the development of an effective children's literature program in the Library." The appointment is made possible by funds provided by a joint committee of the American Association of University Women and the Association for Childhood Education International. (PR 862; 1952 AR:16)

APRIL 4. Philanthropist and rare book collector Lessing J. Rosenwald formally presents to the Library, as a gift to the nation, the Giant Bible of Mainz—a magnificent illuminated manuscript Bible written in Mainz, Germany, between April 4, 1452, and July 9, 1453. (1952 AR:52)

APRIL 22. Librarian Evans establishes, in the Reference Department, a Technical Information Division "to provide special research and documentation services on contract for agencies of the Defense Department in connection with the science and technology collections of the Library of Congress." (GO 1502)

APRIL 30. The Joint Committee on the Library orders that two official documents of the U.S. government be transferred to the National Archives—the Declaration of Independence and the Constitution of the United States. Writing in the LC Information Bulletin, Librarian Evans explains that the decision "was in substance that the routine application of the statutes concerning the records of the U.S. Government and of its predecessors re-

1952

quired this action.... It is naturally an emotional wrench to surrender the custody of the principal documents of American liberty. Logic and law require it, however, and we can only join Dr. Wayne C. Grover, the Archivist of the United States, and his staff in celebrating the occasion."

MAY 23. Gertrude Clarke Whittall donates additional funds to the Library, which are to be used "to sponsor presentations of general literature." (LCA-T)

JULY 3. President Truman approves an act of Congress that extends the services of the Library's Division for the Blind to include children as well as adults. (66 Stat. 326)

JULY 23. The Library receives the first installment of a collection of materials relating to Sigmund Freud, collected and deposited by the Sigmund Freud Archives, Inc., of New York. (LCIB 11:31:2)

JULY 27. Librarian Evans announces policies for the administration of a new and comprehensive microfilming program within the Library, a program concerned with acquisitions, preservation, collection security, and reduction of storage and binding costs. (Go 1506)

AUGUST 6. In response to a request from the acting prime minister of Canada, the Library of Congress sends an advisor to Ottawa to assist in the salvaging of water-soaked materials from the Parliamentary Library, where over 200,000 volumes were damaged "when a fire in the Parliamentary building caused the automatic sprinkler system to turn on." (LCIB 11:33:9–10)

SEPTEMBER 12. The Library publishes the first of five volumes of a definitive catalog of Thomas Jefferson's personal library "as it was at the time of its sale to the Nation in 1815." The catalog, compiled by bibliographer E. Millicent Sowerby, is the culmination of the Thomas Jefferson catalog project begun in 1942. (LCA; 1943 AR:67)

1952

OCTOBER 1. Librarian Evans promotes John W. Cronin from acting director to director of the Processing Department. (1952 AR:vii)

OCTOBER 1. As part of his program of rotation assignments for top-level Library administrators, Librarian Evans appoints Administrative Department director John C. Andreassen to be chief of the Aeronautics Division. (1952 AR:v, 99)

OCTOBER 27. Evans names Deputy Chief Assistant Librarian Wagman to be director of the Administrative Department. (1953 AR:vii)

DECEMBER 13. Acting Librarian Verner W. Clapp and Senator Theodore F. Green of Rhode Island, chairman of the Joint Committee on the Library, place the Declaration of Independence and the Constitution of the United States in the custody of the Department of Defense for transfer to the National Archives. (LCIB 11:51:8–9)

DECEMBER 15. President Truman delivers the main address at ceremonies marking the enshrinement of the Declaration of Independence and the Constitution in the main exhibition hall of the National Archives. (LCIB 11:52:12)

1953

JANUARY. In accordance with a recommendation from professional library groups, the Library publishes the first issue of New Serial Titles—an expansion of Serial Titles Newly Received which includes reports of new serial titles acquired by other cooperating libraries. (1953 AR:23–24)

FEBRUARY. The Library initiates the "All-the-Books" plan, whereby publishers supply the Library with advance copies of their books and then print the card number preassigned by the Library in the volume itself. (1953 AR:27–28)

MARCH 22. Deputy Chief Assistant Librarian Dan M. Lacy resigns to become managing director of the American Book Publishers Council. (1953 AR:93)

MARCH 23. Librarian Evans announces a new pattern for the Library's catalogs in book form. Under a single title, the *Library of Congress Catalog*, the series will be published in five separate parts: *Books: Authors; Books: Subjects; Films; Maps and Atlases;* and *Music and Phonorecords.* (PR 995; 1953 AR:36)

MARCH 31. Librarian Evans outlines the functions of the Legislative Reference Service and redesignates its sections as divisions. (GO 1522)

MAY. The Library publishes *Cataloging Rules and Principles: A Critique of the ALA Rules for Entry and a Proposed Design for Their Revision*, by Seymour Lubetsky, consultant on bibliographic and cataloging policy. (1953 AR:29–30)

MAY 25. Librarian Evans appoints Lucile M. Morsch, chief of the Descriptive Cataloging Division, as Deputy Chief Assistant Librarian. (1953 AR:97)

MAY 25. The Librarian changes the name of the Slavic Division to the Slavic and East European Division. (GO 1527)

JUNE 15. The Executive Board of the United Nations Educational, Scientific and Cultural Organization (Unesco) nominates Librarian Evans to the post of director of Unesco. (1953 AR:1)

JULY. The Office of the Secretary of the Library begins assisting congressional offices "in solving problems relating to filing systems and classification schemes, paperwork management processes, and mailing lists." (1956 AR:49–50)

JULY 1. The Unesco General Council confirms the Executive Board's selection of Luther H. Evans to be the new director general. Evans submits his resignation as Librarian of Congress, effective July 5, 1953, to President Dwight D. Eisenhower. (1953 AR:1)

JULY 4. Verner W. Clapp, Chief Assistant Librarian, becomes Acting Librarian of Congress. (1954 AR:v, 85)

JULY 24. Frederick H. Wagman, director of the Administrative Department, resigns to become director of libraries at the University of Michigan. (1953 AR:98–99)

JULY 27. Acting Librarian Clapp names Robert C. Gooch, assistant director of the Reference Department, to be director of the Administrative Department. (1954 AR:vii)

JULY 29. Acting Librarian Clapp announces the administrative transfer of the Microfilm Reading Room from the Rare Books Division to the Stack and Reader Division. (GO 1533)

AUGUST 6. The Acting Librarian announces the transfer of the motion picture collection from the Reference Department Office to the Stack and Reader Division. (GO 1534)

SEPTEMBER 8–19. The Library of Congress and Princeton University cosponsor a conference, held on the Princeton campus and at the Library, known as the "Colloquium on Islamic Culture in Its Relation to the Contemporary World." (PR 54–8)

NOVEMBER. The Library and the Lake Placid Club Foundation, holder of the copyright for the *Dewey Decimal Classification*, agree that the Library will prepare a new edition, the 16th, of the *Classification*. (1954 AR:8)

1953

NOVEMBER. The Library and the American Academy of Motion Picture Arts and Sciences announces the successful completion of experiments to convert the Library's early paper prints of motion pictures to durable, modern film.
(LCIB 12:49:11–12)

NOVEMBER 10. Acting Librarian Clapp announces that, effective November 15, 1953, the Aeronautics Division will be abolished and an Aeronautics Section will be established in the Science Division.
(GO 1541)

1954

JANUARY 4. The Library establishes the Dewey Decimal Classification Editorial Office in the Processing Department.
(GO 1544; LCIB 13:28:2–3)

FEBRUARY 1. The Library establishes a Far Eastern Section in the Law Library.
(1954 AR:vi)

APRIL 22. President Dwight D. Eisenhower nominates L. Quincy Mumford, director of the Cleveland Public Library and president-elect of the American Library Association, to be Librarian of Congress.
(CR 100:5413)

MAY 19. In its report on the Library's appropriation for fiscal 1955, the House Committee on Appropriations states: "The new Librarian should be mindful that the Library is the instrument and the creature of Congress. Its duties historically have been to meet the needs of the Members of Congress first and to limit its service to others to that which can be furnished with the funds and staff available."
(83/2 HRR 1614:4)

JUNE 21. At the 73rd annual meeting of the American Library Association, held in Minneapolis, the ALA council approves a resolution enthusiastically endorsing President Eisenhower's nomination of L. Quincy Mumford to be Librarian of Congress.
(LCA; ALAB 48:448)

1954

JULY 26. The Senate Committee on Rules and Administration, chaired by Senator William E. Jenner of Indiana, holds hearings on the Mumford nomination. Three representatives of the American Library Association testify in favor of the nomination.
(83/2 SH:1–27)

JULY 28. Senator Jenner, on behalf of the Committee on Rules and Administration, submits an executive report to the Senate favoring the nomination of Mr. Mumford.
(CR 100:12323)

JULY 29. The U.S. Senate confirms, without objection, the nomination of L. Quincy Mumford to be Librarian of Congress.
(CR 100:12488)

AUGUST 31. Assistant Librarian Solon J. Buck retires.
(1955 AR:6)

AUGUST 31. President Eisenhower approves an act of Congress modifying aspects of the copyright law and ratifying the adherence of the United States to the Universal Copyright Convention, signed at Geneva, Switzerland, on September 6, 1952.
(68 Stat. 1030; 1954 AR 7–8)

SEPTEMBER 1. In a ceremony held in the Library's Whittall Pavilion, L. Quincy Mumford takes the oath of office as the 11th Librarian of Congress. The oath, taken on a Bible published in Philadelphia by Robert Aitken in 1782, is administered by Harold H. Burton, associate justice of the U. S. Supreme Court. The Library of Congress has a book collection of approximately 10 million volumes, a staff of 1,600, and in fiscal 1954 a total appropriation of $9.5 million.
(LCIB 13:36:2–4; 1954 AR:126)

SEPTEMBER 13. The Library receives the Brady-Handy photographic collection, containing over 3,000 negatives made by the famed Civil War photographer Mathew B. Brady and several thousand plates by his nephew, Levin C. Handy. The collection was donated by its owners,

1954

Mary H. Evans and Alice H. Cox, daughters of L. C. Handy.
(LCA; LCIB 13:41:1–2)

OCTOBER. The Librarian of Congress and the director of the Bureau of the Budget agree to terminate the Census Library Project, since it "has succeeded admirably in meeting the objectives which were set for it" when it was established in September 1940. (LCIB 13:46:10–11)

NOVEMBER 24. Librarian Mumford announces several organizational changes necessitated by a reduction in the Library's appropriation. The position of Assistant Librarian, vacant since August 31, 1954, is abolished, and the direction of the Exhibits Office and the Information and Publications Office is transferred to the Office of the Chief Assistant Librarian. The *United States Quarterly Book Review* office is transferred to the Reference Department, and the European Affairs Division in the Reference Department is abolished. (GO 1568; 1955 AR:35–37)

DECEMBER 17. The Library of Congress Trust Fund Board accepts additional gifts totaling $100,000 from Gertrude Clarke Whittall to support "activities of the Library in developing the appreciation and understanding of good literature." (LCA-T; 1955 AR:53)

1955

JUNE 6. The Joint Committee on the Library concurs with Librarian Mumford's recommendation that the Library's "Books for the Blind" activity remain in the Library of Congress and not be transferred to the Department of Health, Education, and Welfare. (LCIB 14:28:8)

AUGUST 5. The President approves an act of Congress establishing the Permanent Committee for the Oliver Wendell Holmes Devise, which will oversee the preparation of a history of the Supreme Court. The Librarian of Congress is designated ex officio chairman of the committee. (69 Stat. 533; 1956 AR:73–74)

L. Quincy Mumford, Librarian of Congress from 1954 to 1974, who greatly expanded services to both the U.S. Congress and the library community. During the Mumford administration the Library's staff expanded from approximately sixteen hundred to forty-two hundred employees and its annual appropriation from approximately nine million dollars to ninety-six million dollars. Photograph courtesy of Harris and Ewing, 1964.

AUGUST 12. President Eisenhower approves an act of Congress that authorizes the inclusion of presidential libraries as part of the National Archives system.
(69 Stat. 695)

AUGUST 14. Death of Herbert Putnam, Librarian Emeritus of Congress.
(1955 AR:v)

SEPTEMBER 16. The Universal Copyright Convention goes into effect.
(1955 AR:41, 42; 1956 AR:4)

OCTOBER. The Library announces that, beginning with the January 1956 issue, the *Library of Congress Catalog— Books: Authors* will be expanded to include titles and holdings of books of 1956 and of later imprints that were reported by other North American libraries, in addition to covering Library of Congress cards.
(1956 AR:11–12)

MARCH 6. Librarian Mumford changes the name of the Slavic and East European Division to the Slavic and Central European Division.
(60 1605)

MARCH 12. At the first meeting of the Permanent Committee for the Oliver Wendell Holmes Devise, the committee accepts chairman Mumford's invitation to establish its official headquarters at the Library of Congress.
(1956 AR:74)

MARCH 23. The Librarian announces the establishment of an interdepartmental binding committee.
(60 1607)

APRIL 5. The Library marks the 57th anniversary of the date on which Herbert Putnam became Librarian of Congress with an observance in his memory in the Coolidge Auditorium. David C. Mearns, chief of the Manuscripts Division and Assistant Librarian for the American Collections, delivers an address on "Herbert Putnam and His Responsible Eye."
(so 842)

JUNE. The *United States Quarterly Book Review* ceases publication with the June 1956 issue. After the withdrawal of State Department financial support in 1948, the publication was supported by the Library's appropriated funds, but a 1955 reader survey convinced Library officials that "continued requests for appropriations . . . could not be justified."
(1955 AR:34)

JUNE 13. Librarian Mumford reasserts the Library's position with regard to the acquisition of manuscripts. In response to an inquiry from the Council of the American Association for State and Local History, he explains that because the Library of Congress "has a duty to the nation . . . it cannot abdicate the collecting of manuscripts of national importance to scholarship in favor of any association or any other repository."
(LCA; *History News* 11:83)

JULY 31. President Eisenhower approves an act of Congress adjusting the salaries of heads of executive departments and other federal agencies. The annual salary of the Librarian of Congress is raised to $20,000.
(70 Stat. 736)

AUGUST 3. The President approves an act of Congress that expands the functions of the Armed Forces Medical Library and designates it as the National Library of Medicine. The Librarian of Congress is named an ex officio member of its Board of Regents.
(70 Stat. 960)

SEPTEMBER 19. Librarian Mumford announces the resignation, after a 33-year Library of Congress career, of Chief Assistant Librarian Verner W. Clapp, who has been elected president of the newly created Council on Library Resources, Inc. The council has been organized at the instance of the Ford Foundation with a five-year $5 million grant to be spent in assisting libraries generally—and research libraries especially—in finding solutions to specific problems.
(PR 57–9; LCB 15:501–5)

1956

SEPTEMBER 24. The Library announces the establishment of the Verner W. Clapp Publication Fund, a revolving fund which will be used to publish facsimiles of historic and rare materials in the Library's collections. (LCIB 15:518)

NOVEMBER 6. The Anglo-American, European Law, Far Eastern Law, and Hispanic Law Divisions are established in the Law Library. (GO 1624)

1957

JANUARY 8. Librarian Mumford announces that the names of the following divisions have been changed as designated: Rare Books Division to Rare Book Division, Manuscripts Division to Manuscript Division, and Serials Division to Serial Division. (GO 1626)

FEBRUARY 5. The Librarian establishes the Education and Public Welfare Division in the Legislative Reference Service. (GO 1629)

APRIL. Librarian Mumford submits a codification of the federal laws relating to the Library of Congress, prepared at the request of Congress, to the Joint Committee on the Library. (1957 AR:2)

MAY 21. Defending an increase in the Library's budget, Representative Clarence Cannon of Missouri, chairman of the House Committee on Appropriations, states: "The Library of Congress is the greatest library in the world. It is the visible, irrefutable evidence of the academic and intellectual achievement of the American people. It is convincing proof that we are . . . a people of culture, learning, and scientific progress equal if not superior to any on the globe. Let no action here on the floor today retard the continued growth and development of this national institution." (CR 103:7319)

MAY 29. Librarian Mumford establishes an interdepartmental music processing committee. (GO 1636)

141

The ninth and eleventh Librarians of Congress, Archibald MacLeish (right) and L. Quincy Mumford, on December 4, 1956. LC–USP6–3149C

JUNE 3. The Librarian establishes a facsimile program to "publish selected materials from the collections, especially those of research and educational value, for sale to the public." (GO 1637)

AUGUST 15. Librarian Mumford announces the appointment of Rutherford D. Rogers, chief of the Reference Department of the New York Public Library, to be Chief Assistant Librarian of the Library of Congress. Mr. Rogers will assume his duties in early December. (PR 58-2)

AUGUST 16. President Eisenhower approves an act of Congress that authorizes the Presidential Papers Program in the Library of Congress. Under the terms of the new law, the Library will arrange, index, and microfilm the papers of the Presidents in its collections "in order to preserve their contents against destruction by war or other calamity and for the purpose of making them more readily available for study and research." (71 Stat. 368)

SEPTEMBER 7. President Eisenhower approves an act of Congress creating the U.S. Civil War Centennial Commission. One of the commission's 25 members will be from the Library of Congress—the Librarian or his designated representative. (71 Stat. 626)

DECEMBER 1. Librarian Mumford announces that the Library has initiated a research project to study the preservation of sound recordings. The project is made possible by a $65,000 grant from the Rockefeller Foundation. (PR 58-18)

DECEMBER 1. Reference Department Director Burton W. Adkinson resigns to become director of the Office of Scientific Information at the National Science Foundation. (1958 AR:V; LCIB 16:44:585-86)

DECEMBER 2. Rutherford D. Rogers assumes his duties as Chief Assistant Librarian. (1957 AR:6)

DECEMBER 19. Librarian Mumford announces the appointment of six noted American writers to serve the Library of Congress for the next three years as honorary consultants and explains that, during the last two years, the Library has been converting its various titles for nonsalaried advisors—such as "consultant," "fellow," "honorary consultant," and "specialist"—to the uniform one of "honorary consultant." (PR 58-25)

JANUARY. Librarian Mumford establishes an interdepartmental committee on mechanical information retrieval to study "the problem of applying machine methods to the control of the Library's general collections." (1959 AR:36)

JANUARY 28. The Librarian changes the name of the Science Division to the Science and Technology Division. (GO 1646)

FEBRUARY 1. The Librarian transfers the Bibliography Section of the Technical Information Division to the Science and Technology Division. The other sections of the Technical Information Division are transferred to the Armed Services Technical Information Agency and consolidated with its Documents Service Center. (GO 1647)

MARCH 11. Librarian Mumford announces the reorganization of the Library's fiscal services and the establishment of a new Budget Office. (GO 1649)

APRIL 3. Librarian Mumford appoints Roy P. Basler, acting director of the Reference Department, to be department director. (1958 AR:V)

JUNE 26. The Library announces that it has received a $55,000 grant from the Council on Library Resources, Inc., for a one-year test of a "cataloging-in-source" program that will enable publishers "to print cataloging information in the books themselves." (PR 58-69; 1958 AR:4)

1958

JULY 23. Librarian Mumford forms an interdepartmental space planning committee "to consider the immediate and long-range space needs of the Library and to develop plans for meeting these needs." (GC 1662)

JULY 28. The position of coordinator for the development and organization of the collections is established in the Reference Department. (1959 AR:v)

AUGUST 13. Following an intensive study by Library officials, the Architect of the Capitol submits a detailed tabulation of requirements for a third Library building to the Joint Committee on the Library. (1959 AR:60)

AUGUST 19. The Library establishes a Natural Resources Division in the Legislative Reference Service to "handle inquiries in agriculture, conservation, and natural resources." (GO 1663)

AUGUST 25. With the concurrence of the Joint Committee on the Library, Librarian Mumford issues a statement regarding the use of the Library by high school students. Beginning on September 1, 1958, high school students must present a letter signed by the principal of their school and certifying the student's specific need to use the Library's research resources. Otherwise, such students should use their school or public libraries. (GO 1664)

AUGUST 27. President Eisenhower approves a supplemental appropriations act for fiscal 1959 which includes $60,000 to the Library of Congress for the preservation of early motion pictures in its collections. (72 Stat. 864; 1959 AE:38-39)

SEPTEMBER 2. The President approves the National Defense Education Act of 1958. One provision of the new law directs the National Science Foundation to establish a Science Information Council; the Librarian of Congress is named as an ex officio member. (72 Stat. 1580)

1958

SEPTEMBER 2. The President approves an act of Congress establishing a national cultural center as a bureau of the Smithsonian Institution. The center (later named the John F. Kennedy Center for the Performing Arts) will be administered by a board of trustees; the Librarian of Congress will serve as an ex officio member of the board. (72 Stat. 1698)

SEPTEMBER 6. The President approves an amendment to the Agricultural Trade Development and Assistance Act of 1954 (Public Law 83-480) which authorizes the Librarian of Congress to utilize U.S.-owned foreign currencies for "the acquisition of such books, periodicals, and other materials and the deposit thereof in libraries and research centers in the United States specializing in the areas to which they relate." (72 Stat. 1790)

SEPTEMBER 12. Ernest S. Griffith retires as director of the Legislative Reference Service to become dean of the new School of International Relations at American University. (1958 AR:vi, 6)

SEPTEMBER 15. Librarian Mumford appoints Hugh L. Elsbree, deputy director of the Legislative Reference Service, to be director. (1958 AR:vi, 6)

NOVEMBER 24. The Librarian announces the establishment of the Decimal Classification Office, which will have divisional status in the Processing Department. (GO 1676)

DECEMBER 28. The Library announces that it has received a $200,000 grant from the Council on Library Resources, Inc., to establish and publish a national inventory of important manuscript collections which will be known as the National Union Catalog of Manuscript Collections. (PR 59-28; 1959 AR:16)

1959

JUNE. The Library publishes the first issue of the *World List of Future International Meetings*, which attempts to meet "the growing need by officers of the Government and by scholars and research persons generally for an up-to-date comprehensive listing of international meetings." The *List*, to be published monthly, is supported by funds transferred from other federal agencies.

(1959 AR:47)

AUGUST. The Library establishes the Union List of Serials Project in the Processing Department. Created as a result of a $244,651 grant from the Council on Library Resources, Inc., to the Joint Committee on the Union List of Serials, Inc., the project will prepare a third and final edition of the *Union List of Serials*.

(1959 AR:16–18; 1960 AR:7)

SEPTEMBER. The Library publishes *Preservation and Storage of Sound Recordings*, the study initiated in December 1957 with a grant from the Rockefeller Foundation.

(PR 60–11)

OCTOBER 16. Librarian Mumford announces the establishment of the Near East and North African Law Division in the Law Library.

(GO 1693)

DECEMBER 7. The Carnegie Corporation announces a $200,000 grant to the Library of Congress to establish and operate, for a period of five years, an Africana section. In a press release, Librarian Mumford notes that the new unit is being created in response to "increasing interest in African studies" and will enable the Library "to exploit more fully its outstanding collections of Africana."

(PR 60–22)

JANUARY 19. The Africana Section is established in the General Reference and Bibliography Division of the Reference Department.

(1960 AR:22)

MARCH. In a report on the cataloging-in-source experiment, the Library concludes that a permanent, full-scale

program of cataloging-in-source cannot be justified in terms of financing, technical considerations, or utility.

(1960 AR:8)

MARCH 14. Librarian Mumford announces that the office of Chief Assistant Librarian, held by Rutherford D. Rogers, has been combined administratively with the office of Librarian, both "to achieve a more logical pattern of organization" and to reflect the status of the Chief Assistant Librarian as the deputy to the Librarian of Congress. The position of Deputy Chief Assistant Librarian, held by Lucile M. Morsch, "will continue to be essentially a staff position." The position of Assistant Librarian for Public Affairs is created, and Elizabeth E. Hamer, information and publications officer, is appointed to the post. New and separate positions of information officer and publications officer are established; both will report directly to the Assistant Librarian for Public Affairs, as will the exhibits officer.

(GO 1709)

APRIL 22. The Library announces that, with aid from a $5,525 grant from the Council on Library Resources, Inc., it is conducting a study of the use made of its book stacks "to help determine the future efficacy of shelving books according to a subject classification."

(PR 61–3)

MAY 9. Librarian Mumford announces that the branch bindery has been returned to the Government Printing Office after being located in the Library for almost 60 years; the move was necessary "because of the crowded space situation in the Library." However, small "repair stations" for manuscripts, maps, prints and photographs, rare books, newspapers, and books in the general collections have been retained in the Library.

(GO 1718)

MAY 14. President Eisenhower approves an act of Congress that authorizes the Architect of the Capitol to prepare preliminary plans and cost estimates for an additional Library of Congress building.

(74 Stat. 132)

Robert Frost, who served as the Library's poetry consultant in 1958–59, returned to the Library on May 2, 1960, to give a reading under the auspices of the Gertrude Clarke Whittall Poetry and Literature Fund. This photograph was taken at a luncheon in the Whittall Pavilion. Standing, left to right, are Oscar Williams, Richard Eberhart (poetry consultant for 1959–60), and Hy Sobiloff; seated, left to right, are Frost, Carl Sandburg, and Librarian Mumford. LC–USP6–3823–C

JUNE. The Library publishes *A Guide to the Study of the United States of America; Representative Books Reflecting the Development of American Life and Thought*, prepared by the General Reference and Bibliography Division of the Reference Department. The 1,193-page volume identifies and describes over 10,000 individual titles. (LCA; PR 60–52)

JULY 12. President Eisenhower approves the legislative branch appropriations act for fiscal 1961. The new law appropriates $75,000 to prepare preliminary plans and cost estimates for a third Library building and additional funds enabling the Library to rent 62,500 square feet of space for temporary use in the Washington, D.C., area. (74 Stat. 446)

OCTOBER. The Library publishes *Official Publications of British East Africa*, part 1, the first in a series of guides to the publications of African governments to be prepared by the Africana Section. (LCA)

NOVEMBER 12. Death of Arthur Fisher, the register of copyrights. (1961 AR:62)

DECEMBER. The expiration of the grant supporting the *Southern Asia Accessions List* forces the Library to cease its publication with the December issue. (1961 AR:39–40)

DECEMBER 24. Librarian Mumford appoints Acting Register of Copyrights Abraham L. Kaminstein to be register. (1961 AR:62)

MARCH. The Library publishes *Archive of Recorded Poetry and Literature: A Checklist*, the first detailed inventory of the holdings of the archive. (PR 61–45; 1961 AR:38)

MARCH 13. Librarian Mumford establishes the Office of the Information Systems Specialist to study the "automa-

tion of the bibliographic functions of the Library." (1964 AR:xxx)

APRIL 23. The Library announces that it has received a $100,000 grant from the Council on Library Resources, Inc., "for a survey of the possibilities of automating the organization, storage, and retrieval of information." The six-man survey team will be headed by Gilbert W. King, director of research for the International Business Machines Corporation. (PR 61–51; 1961 AR:XV)

JULY 10. Librarian Mumford sends Congress a comprehensive report from the register of copyrights on the proposed revision of the U.S. copyright law. The 227-page report contains the Copyright Office's recommendations for the revision and is a result of an extensive series of studies conducted by the Copyright Office during the past five years. (PR 62–1; 1961 AR:65–66)

JULY 31. President John F. Kennedy approves an act of Congress authorizing the Library to arrange, transliterate, index, and microfilm the vital statistics portions of its collection of the original records of the Russian Orthodox Greek Catholic Church in Alaska. (75 Stat. 241; 1963 AR:32)

AUGUST 10. President Kennedy approves the legislative branch appropriations act for fiscal 1962, which includes the first appropriation to the Library of Congress for the acquisition of foreign research materials under the provisions of Public Law 83–480, as amended on September 6, 1958. (75 Stat. 320)

OCTOBER 8. A Library survey team arrives in New Delhi "to establish a center for the operations of the P.L. 480 program." (LCIB 20:598–99)

OCTOBER 17. Librarian Mumford changes the name of the Air Information Division to the Aerospace Information Division. (GO 1748)

A 1961 photograph of the Main Reading Room. Edwin H. Blashfield's painting The Evolution of Civilization can be seen in the collar of the dome. Portrait statues of "illustrous figures in civilized life and thought" are visible along the balustrade of the upper gallery. Photograph by Peter C. Costas. LC–USZ62–36227

147

1961

NOVEMBER 1. The Librarian transfers the Motion Picture Section from the Stack and Reader Division to the Prints and Photographs Division, "thus placing in one division responsibility for the major pictorial collections and for reference service on them." (1962 AR:26)

NOVEMBER 2. A Library survey team arrives in Cairo to plan Public Law 480 operations. (1962 AR:2)

DECEMBER. The new Library of Congress Public Law 480 offices in New Delhi and Cairo begin functioning. (LCA)

DECEMBER. Because of the withdrawal of funds by the federal agencies supporting its publication, the Library terminates the *East European Accessions Index*. The last issue is dated November/December 1962. (1962 AR:7–8, 107)

1962

MARCH 23. Secretary of Agriculture Orville L. Freeman marks the 100th anniversary of the library of the Department of Agriculture by designating it as the National Agricultural Library. (LCIB 21:150–51)

APRIL 12. The Joint Committee on the Library approves the Librarian's request to change the title of the position of Chief Assistant Librarian to Deputy Librarian of Congress. (LCA)

MAY 24. Senator Claiborne Pell of Rhode Island, a member of the Joint Committee on the Library, introduces into the *Congressional Record* a memorandum prepared at his request "on the subject of the Library of Congress and connected library matters." Written by Douglas W. Bryant, associate director of the Harvard University Library, the memorandum addresses itself to "what the Library of Congress does and what it ought to do for the Government and the Nation generally." Speaking on the floor of the Senate, Senator Pell expresses his hope that Mr. Bryant's proposals will be discussed widely because "we have tended to take for granted our Library of Congress—our basic working tool which underlies all our useful scholarship, the responsible work of our Congress, and the very culture of our nation." In his memorandum, which is dated May 1, 1962, Bryant urges further expansion of the national role of the Library of Congress, concluding: "Though it would be desirable, it is not essential to transfer the Library of Congress to the Executive; but it is essential that legislation recognize officially what the Library is and what it ought to do, and that a National Library Advisory Board (if not a National Research Library Foundation) be established in the Executive Branch."

(CR 108:9158–60; 1962 AR:89–94)

JULY. The Library begins publication of Public Law 480 accessions lists from India and Pakistan.

(1963 AR:3)

JULY 2. The Library announces a $34,200 grant from the Council on Library Resources, Inc., to develop and publish a classification scheme for Anglo-American law.

(PR 62–58; 1962 AR:9–10)

JULY 3. President Kennedy approves an amendment to the Library of Congress Trust Fund Board Act that raises the limit on the sum the board can deposit with the Treasurer of the United States as a permanent loan to the U.S. Treasury. The new limit is $10 million. (76 Stat. 135)

AUGUST 13. Librarian Mumford announces the establishment, with funds from the National Science Foundation, of the National Science and Technology Referral Center— a clearinghouse designed to provide coordinated access to the nation's scientific and technical information.

(GO 1783; 1963 AR:xvii)

AUGUST 31. The Librarian announces that, effective immediately, the title of Chief Assistant Librarian is changed administratively to that of Deputy Librarian of Congress.

Furthermore, the title Deputy Chief Assistant Librarian is discontinued "although the position heretofore bearing that designation is being retained within the Office of the Librarian."

(GO 1784)

SEPTEMBER 3. Librarian Mumford names Lucile M. Morsch, formerly Deputy Chief Assistant Librarian, to be chief of the Descriptive Cataloging Division as well as the Library's representative on the ALA Catalog Code Revision Steering Committee. In both capacities she replaces C. Sumner Spalding, the newly appointed editor of the catalog code revision project.

(1962 AR:VII, 12)

SEPTEMBER 19. President Kennedy approves an act of Congress that extends the period of copyright protection for certain works pending the enactment of a general revision of the copyright law.

(76 Stat. 555)

SEPTEMBER 28. In his reply to the Bryant memorandum, Librarian Mumford strongly defends the Library's location in the legislative branch of the government. He also points out that "the Library of Congress today performs more national library functions than any other national library in the world."

(LCA; 1962 AR:94–111)

OCTOBER. The Library publishes the first volume of The National Union Catalog of Manuscript Collections.

(LCA; 1963 AR:XX)

OCTOBER 4. The Juilliard String Quartet presents its first concert as the Library's new "resident" chamber ensemble, replacing the Budapest String Quartet.

(LCB 24:317)

OCTOBER 9. President Kennedy approves an act of Congress establishing in the Library's Division for the Blind "a library of musical scores and other instructional materials to further educational, vocational, and cultural opportunities in the field of music for blind persons."

(76 Stat. 763)

1962

OCTOBER 22. Librarian Mumford establishes the Children's Book Section in the General Reference and Bibliography Division of the Reference Department.
(GO 1793; 1963 AR:26)

OCTOBER 22–24. Over 30 poets take part in the Library's first National Poetry Festival, which is supported by funds from the Bollingen Foundation. The general theme, "Fifty Years of American Poetry," marks the 50th anniversary of *Poetry* magazine.
(1963 AR:44)

1963

JANUARY 4. Librarian Mumford discontinues the position of Assistant Librarian for Public Affairs and transfers Mrs. Hamer to the newly created post of Assistant Librarian. The Assistant Librarian will "participate with the Librarian of Congress and the Deputy Librarian of Congress in the overall administration of the Library."
(GC 1803)

FEBRUARY 18. The Library announces that it has undertaken a comprehensive program to microfilm some 500 current foreign newspapers in lieu of binding. (LCIB 22:77)

APRIL 8. The Library announces the reorganization of the Office of the Keeper of the Collections and its designation as the Collections Maintenance and Preservation Office in the Administrative Department.
(GO 1809; 1963 AR:63)

MAY 26–30. The Library of Congress, the National Science Foundation, and the Council on Library Resources, Inc., sponsor the "Conference on Libraries and Automation," held at the Airlie Foundation in Warrenton, Va. The NSF and CLR provide the financial support for the meeting.
(1963 AR:xiv)

JUNE 6. The House Committee on Appropriations recommends an appropriation of $20,487,800 for the Library in fiscal 1964. In its report, the committee notes that "a third building is badly needed—now" and observes:

This is a great cultural and research institution and in the committee's view ought to be brought to a good state of accommodation and efficiency at an early date. Although originally conceived and established as the Library of Congress, it is in fact, by reason of many congressional actions over a long period of years, the national library of the United States and of inestimable value to the nation's library facilities at all levels. . . . There have been suggestions over the years, renewed recently, that the Library of Congress ought to be officially designated as the National Library of the United States and its administration shifted to the Executive Branch. There is a considerable reservoir of feeling in the committee against such a proposition of transfer and, very likely, that feeling would be shared by many Members of the Congress. . . . As to the matter of designation, it has been said that custom and tradition are stronger than the law. There would, likely, be considerable opposition to a change of the name although there would appear to be merit in a formal designation of the Library as the National Library. There are now two specialized libraries so designated formally—one in the field of agriculture, and the other in the field of medicine. But even so, it would be said to be a distinction without benefit of the substance of so much difference.
(88/1 HRR 369:15–16)

JUNE 22. The Brookings Institution holds a conference to review the findings of a recent survey of federal departmental libraries, conducted by the institution and funded by a grant from the Council on Library Resources, Inc. A major recommendation of the conference is that "the Library of Congress and the Bureau of the Budget jointly invite appropriate agencies to explore the desirability of establishing a continuing interagency group to advise on the problems of federal libraries."
(LCA)

AUGUST 13. Law Librarian William L. Keitt retires. (LCA)

AUGUST 21. Librarian Mumford establishes the Data Processing Office as a separate organizational unit in the Administrative Department.
(GO 1823)

SEPTEMBER 10. The Librarian changes the name of the Air Research Division to the Defense Research Division.
(LCA)

1963

NOVEMBER 1. The Library announces that, in cooperation with the Association of Research Libraries, it soon will initiate "a major new bibliographic tool for American and foreign libraries—a centralized register of all master negatives of microfilms, whether in process or already produced." (PR 64-16; 1964 AR:17)

DECEMBER 30. President Lyndon B. Johnson approves an act directing the Library of Congress to prepare compilations of research and bibliographic data relating to the annual national high school and college debate topics. The compilations will be published as Senate and House documents. (77 Stat. 802)

1964

JANUARY. With the January issue, the scope of the Library's *Quarterly Journal of Current Acquisitions* is broadened and its title is changed to the *Quarterly Journal of the Library of Congress*. (QJ 21:iii)

JANUARY 2. Librarian Mumford announces the appointment, effective January 6, 1964, of Lewis C. Coffin as the new Law Librarian. Mr. Coffin is the associate director of the Processing Department. (PR C-64-1)

JANUARY 15. Librarian Mumford announces the creation of the Arms Control and Disarmament Bibliography Section in the General Reference and Bibliography Division of the Reference Department. The new unit is funded by the U.S. Arms Control and Disarmament Agency. (GO 1847; PR 65-6)

JANUARY 15. The Library's first computer, a rented IBM 1401, is put into operation; it is used for payroll, budget, and related fiscal work. (LCIB 23:28-30; 1964 AR:63-64)

JANUARY 22. The Library releases *Automation and the Library of Congress*, the feasibility study sponsored by the Council on Library Resources, Inc. The survey team, headed by Gilbert W. King, concludes that the automation

1964

of bibliographic processing, catalog searching, and document retrieval is technically and economically feasible in large research libraries, urges the establishment of an automation program at the Library, and recommends that the Library of Congress, "because of its central role in the American library world as the national library," take the lead in automation efforts. (PR 64-8; 1963 AR:xiii-xiv)

MARCH. The Bibliographical Society of America publishes *Incunabula in American Libraries*, a census of 15th-century books in North American libraries compiled and edited by Frederick R. Goff, chief of the Rare Book Division. The census determines that the Library's collection of 5,616 incunabula is the largest in North America, followed by the Henry E. Huntington Library and Harvard University Library, with 5,314 and 2,910 incunabula, respectively. (LCA-R)

MARCH 26. Librarian Mumford announces that Deputy Librarian of Congress Rutherford D. Rogers will resign his post before September 1 to become director of libraries at Stanford University. (PR C-64-20)

MAY 4. The Main Reading Room is closed for cleaning and restoration and for the installation of a new heating, air-conditioning, and ventilating system and new lighting. (1964 AR:xxxv)

JUNE. Lessing J. Rosenwald donates an additional 700 rare books to the Library, increasing the size of the Rosenwald Collection to over 2,200 titles. (1964 AR:34-35)

JUNE. The General Services Administration makes warehouse facilities in Middle River, Md., several miles east of Baltimore, available to the Library "for the storage of equipment and material not frequently needed." (1965 AR:76)

JUNE. The American Library Association, after exploring the possibility of publishing the Library's pre-1956 Na-

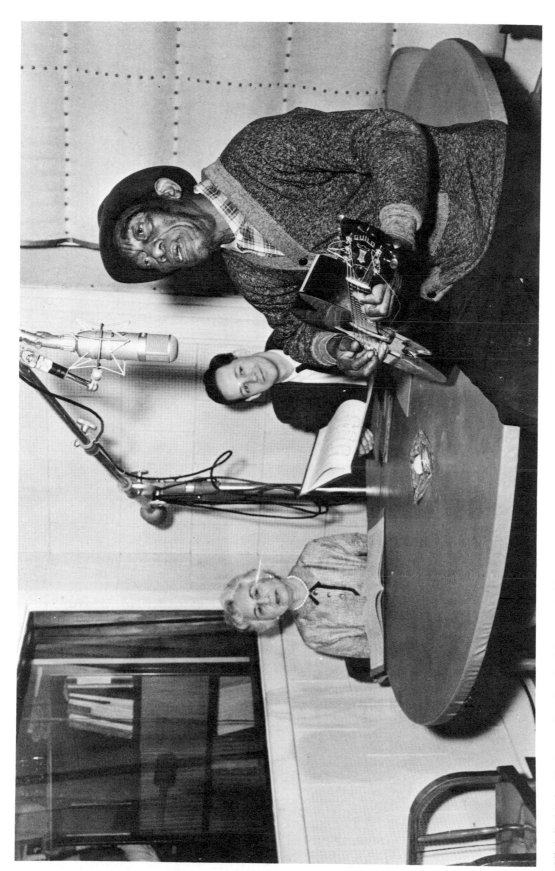

Mississippi John Hurt recording for the Library's Archive of Folk Song. March 1964. Rae Korson and Joe Hickerson of the Library's staff are in the background. LC–USP6–4376C

151

1964

tional Union Catalog, undertakes a project to secure funds for editing the catalog cards and to arrange for publication in book form. The Library agrees to perform the editorial work upon a transfer of funds from the A.L.A.

(LCA: 1967 AR:43–44)

JULY. The Library publishes *Specifications for Library of Congress Microfilming,* which was prepared by the Photoduplication Service in response to inquiries concerning the practices and recommendations of the Library of Congress in relation to microfilming. (LCIB 23:404–5)

JULY. Because of crowded conditions in the Library's principal buildings, the Card Division and the Catalog Maintenance and Publication Division are moved to buildings about a mile away in the Navy Yard Annex, part of the former Naval Weapons Plant.

JULY 8. Librarian Mumford changes the name of the Aerospace Information Division to the Aerospace Technology Division. (1965 AR:71)

JULY 20. A comprehensive bill for the general revision of the U.S. copyright law is introduced in Congress by Senator John L. McClellan of Arkansas and Representative Emanuel Celler of New York. The bill is the result of nine years' work by the Copyright Office.

(LCIB 23:367–68; 1964 AR:76–77)

JULY 31. Deputy Librarian of Congress Rutherford D. Rogers resigns.

(1965 AR:vii, 20–21)

AUGUST. Because of increasing congressional interest in scientific and technical issues, the Library establishes the Science Policy Research Division in the Legislative Reference Service.

(1965 AR:43–44)

AUGUST. Librarian Mumford establishes the Information Systems Office, which will "be responsible for the Library's

In 1964 the Library of Congress and the American Library Association agreed to make arrangements for the publication of the pre-1956 portion of the National Union Catalog. In 1967 Mansell Information/Publishing Ltd., under terms of a contract with the ALA, undertook the massive publishing project—which would result in the largest book catalog ever published. The first five volumes were published in late 1968, when this photograph was taken. Examining the volumes are (left to right): John Commander, of Mansell Information/Publishing Ltd.; Gordon Williams, director of the Center for Research Libraries in Chicago and chairman of the ALA subcommittee on the National Union Catalog; L. Quincy Mumford, Librarian of Congress; and Johannes L. Dewton, editor of the Pre-1956 Imprints catalog.

program to utilize mechanical and electronic equipment in library processes. (PR C-64-37; 1965 AR:15-17)

AUGUST 14. President Johnson approves the Government Employees Salary Act of 1964, which increases the annual salary of the Librarian of Congress to $27,000 and establishes the salary of the Deputy Librarian at $25,500 a year. (78 Stat 400)

NOVEMBER. The Library receives the first installment of the gift of the records of the National Association for the Advancement of Colored People (NAACP), a private archive of more than one million items. (LCA; QJ 22:333)

DECEMBER 1. Librarian Mumford establishes an interdepartmental committee on automation to advise the Librarian on matters concerned with the Library's automation program. (LCR 218-11)

JANUARY. The Library publishes the first issue of the new quarterly bibliography *Arms Control and Disarmament*. The issue is dated winter 1964-65. (PR 65-6; 1965 AR:9)

JANUARY. The Library publishes the first in a series of directories which will be prepared by the National Referral Center for Science and Technology: *A Directory of Information Resources in the United States: Physical Sciences, Biological Sciences, Engineering*. (1965 AR:60)

JANUARY 11. A conference on machine-readable catalog copy, sponsored by the Library of Congress, the automation committee of the Association of Research Libraries, and the Council on Library Resources, Inc., is held at the Library. The basis for discussion is a report or "The Recording of Library of Congress Bibliographic Data in Machine Form," prepared by Lawrence F. Buckland of Inforonics, Inc., for the CLR. (LCIB 24:33-34)

FEBRUARY 8. The Council on Library Resources, Inc., publishes the Buckland study. In the preface, CLR Presi-

dent Verner W. Clapp notes that Buckland's conversion method in general has been accepted by the library community. (LCA)

FEBRUARY 9. The Library announces that it has received a grant of $35,000 from the Council on Library Resources, Inc., to initiate work on a National Register of Microform Masters. (PR 65-16; 1965 AR:29-31)

MARCH 11. The Library and the Bureau of the Budget announce the establishment of the Federal Library Committee "to provide more effective planning, development, and operation of federal libraries." Its secretariat will be in the Library. (PR 65-21; 1965 AR:20)

APRIL 2-3. The Library sponsors the "Symposium on the Little Magazine and Contemporary Literature," financed by a grant from the Carnegie Corporation. (LCA; 1965 AR:50)

MAY 26. Subcommittee no. 3 of the House Committee on the Judiciary, with Representative Robert W. Kastenmeier of Wisconsin presiding as acting chairman, begins hearings on a bill to revise the U.S. copyright law. The first witness is Librarian Mumford. Other witnesses include officials from the Copyright Office, representatives of authors' organizations, attorneys and representatives from the publishing industry, and several writers—Elizabeth Janeway, John Hersey, Rex Stout, and Herman Wouk. (LCIB 24:251-52)

JUNE. Mr. and Mrs. Walter C. Louchheim, Jr., of Washington, D.C., donate funds to the Library for the distribution of tapes of the Library's music concerts to educational and commercial broadcasters throughout the country. (1965 AR:63; PR 65-70)

JULY 21. The Library announces that it has received a grant of $75,300 from the Council on Library Resources,

Inc., to establish a Center for the Coordination of Foreign Manuscript Copying. (PR 65–52; 1966 AR:9–10)

AUGUST 11. Librarian Mumford announces the appointment of John G. Lorenz, director of the Division of Library Services and Educational Facilities in the U.S. Office of Education, to be Deputy Librarian of Congress. (PR 65–56)

AUGUST 16. The Main Reading Room is reopened after major renovation and restoration. (1965 AR:19–20)

SEPTEMBER 2. The Map Division is renamed the Geography and Map Division. (LCA)

SEPTEMBER 29. President Johnson approves the National Foundation on the Arts and Humanities Act of 1965. The new law creates a Federal Council on the Arts and the Humanities; the Librarian of Congress is designated an ex officio member of the council. (79 Stat. 845)

OCTOBER 11. John G. Lorenz assumes his duties as Deputy Librarian of Congress. (1965 AR:vii, 21)

OCTOBER 19. President Johnson approves a supplemental appropriations act for fiscal 1965 which authorizes $75 million for the construction of a third Library of Congress building, "to be named the James Madison Memorial Building," and to contain a Madison Memorial Hall." The structure will be located directly south of the Main Library Building. (79 Stat. 986)

NOVEMBER 8. President Johnson approves the Higher Education Act of 1965. Title II-C of the act authorizes the Office of Education to transfer funds to the Library of Congress for the purpose of 1) acquiring, in so far as possible, all library materials currently published throughout the world that are of value to scholarship; and 2) provid-

ing catalog information for these materials promptly after receipt, distributing bibliographic information by printing catalog cards and other means, and enabling the Library of Congress to use for exchange and other purposes such of these materials as are not needed for its own collections. (79 Stat. 1219)

DECEMBER 22. Librarian Mumford appoints Lester S. Jayson, deputy director of the Legislative Reference Service, to be director of the service when Hugh L. Elsbree retires as director in February 1966. (PR 65–80)

JANUARY 13. A conference at the British Museum of national librarians and other library officials from six countries results in agreement on the shared cataloging procedures proposed by the Library of Congress for adapting the cataloging data of other nations as part of the new program authorized by Title II-C of the Higher Education Act of 1965. The new Library of Congress program will be known as the National Program for Acquisitions and Cataloging (NPAC). (1966 AR:29)

JANUARY 21. The Library announces that it has received a grant of $87,650 from the Council on Library Resources, Inc., to support the secretariat of the Federal Library Committee on a full-time basis for three years. A $10,000 grant from CLR has supported the secretariat until now. (PR 66–55; 1966 AR:23)

JANUARY 21. The Library announces that it has received a grant of $130,000 from the Council on Library Resources, Inc., for investigations which will lead to the inauguration of a pilot program for the distribution of cataloging information in machine-readable form. Under the terms of the grant, the Library will also study the feasibility and value of providing such service on a wider scale and on a continuing basis. The new project is christened MARC (MAchine-Readable Cataloging). (PR 66–10; 1966 AR:17–18)

FEBRUARY 1. The H. W. Wilson Company of New York publishes the third edition of the *Union List of Serials in Libraries of the United States and Canada.* The five-volume work, supported by a grant from the Council on Library Resources, Inc., was compiled under terms of a contract between the Library of Congress and the Joint Committee on the Union List of Serials, Inc. (1966 AR:11)

FEBRUARY 25. Hugh L. Elsbree, director of the Legislative Reference Service, retires. (1966 AR:vi)

FEBRUARY 28. Lester S. Jayson assumes his duties as the new director of the Legislative Reference Service. (1966 AR:vi)

APRIL. The Library establishes a Children's Literature Cataloging Office in the Processing Department to prepare annotated catalog cards for children's books. (1966 AR:39)

APRIL. The Library begins printing and distributing catalog cards prepared under a "shared cataloging" arrangement with the *British National Bibliography.* (1966 AR:32)

MAY 2. Mrs. Adrian Van Sinderen of Washington, Conn., places in the custody of the Library the last copy remaining in private hands of the famed "Bay Psalm Book" of 1640—the first extant book known to be published in English-speaking North America. Mrs. Van Sinderen will retain ownership of the book during her lifetime but will bequeath the book to the Library. (LCIB 25:231-32)

MAY 13. President Johnson approves the second supplemental appropriation act for fiscal 1966, which includes $300,000 for the acquisition and cataloging of library materials under the provision of Title II-C of the Higher Education Act of 1965. (80 Stat. 141)

JUNE 3-5. Library officials participate in an administrative conference at the Airlie Foundation, Warrenton, Va.,

to discuss current programs and long-range goals of the Library. (LCIB 25:297).

JUNE 24. The Library opens its London shared cataloging office, the first overseas office in the new National Program for Acquisitions and Cataloging. (1966 AR:32)

JUNE 28. The Library establishes the Shared Cataloging Division in the Processing Department to "handle the descriptive cataloging of books received under the Title II-C program." (1966 AR:viii, 33)

JULY 1. The Library inaugurates an automated control system for manuscript collection records in its Manuscript Division. (LCIB 25:389-90)

JULY 4. President Johnson approves an act establishing the American Revolution Bicentennial Commission; the legislation names the Librarian of Congress as an ex officio member of the commission. (80 Stat. 259)

JULY 11. Speaking at the annual ALA meeting, John W. Cronin, director of the Processing Department, points out that with passage of Title II-C of the Higher Education Act of 1965, "the Congress took two important steps to aid libraries of higher education in the United States: 1) it fully recognized for the first time the importance of granting Federal aid and assistance toward solving the problem of cataloging in this country; and 2) it gave the Library of Congress a clear mandate to provide new and unparalleled services for the benefit of academic and research libraries." (LRTS 11:35)

JULY 30. President Johnson approves an act of Congress extending national books-for-the-blind service to include all persons who are unable to read conventional printed materials because of physical or visual handicaps. (80 Stat. 330)

1966

SEPTEMBER 2. By executive order, President Johnson establishes the National Advisory Commission on Libraries. The Librarian of Congress is invited to serve on the commission. (1967 AR:23–24)

SEPTEMBER 6. In a letter to President Johnson, Librarian Mumford accepts the invitation to serve as a member of the National Advisory Commission on Libraries. (LCA)

OCTOBER. The Library opens a shared cataloging office in Rio de Janeiro, the first NPAC regional acquisitions center. (1967 AR:38)

OCTOBER. The Library establishes the Technical Processes Research Office in the Processing Department to develop, coordinate, and administer a comprehensive program of research in bibliographical control. (1967 AR:46)

OCTOBER 23. The Library announces that it has received a generous gift from the Martha Baird Rockefeller Fund for Music, Inc., which will enable it to transfer its earliest field recordings of American folk music to magnetic tape for their future preservation. (PR 66–51)

NOVEMBER. The Library begins its pilot project to test the feasibility of distributing machine-readable cataloging data to other libraries by sending weekly distributions of MARC tapes to 16 participating libraries. (1967 AR:17)

DECEMBER. To improve its service in providing "quick" answers for Congress, the Library establishes the Congressional Research Division in the Legislative Reference Service. (1967 AR:2)

DECEMBER 30. Robert C. Gooch, director of the Administrative Department, retires. (LCIB 26:6–7)

1967

JANUARY. The American Library Association publishes the *Anglo-American Cataloging Rules: North American Text*, prepared by the ALA, the Library of Congress, the Library Association, and the Canadian Library Association, with financial support from the Council on Library Resources, Inc. The general editor is C. Sumner Spalding, chief of the Library's Descriptive Cataloging Division, who succeeded the first editor, Seymour Lubetsky, in 1962. The editor of the rules for description is Lucile M. Morsch, who retired from the Library in 1965. (1967 AR:44–45)

JANUARY 31. The Library announces the inauguration of a pilot project, in cooperation with the Association of Research Libraries, to study techniques for the preservation of deteriorating or "brittle" books—those published since about 1870 on paper that disintegrates with age. The project is undertaken through a $26,800 grant which the Council on Library Resources, Inc., has made to the ARL. (PR 67–6; 1967 AR:4)

FEBRUARY. The American Library Association announces it has selected the Mansell Information/Publishing, Ltd., of London and Chicago to publish the pre-1956 National Union Catalog, "as the Library of Congress completes portions of the editorial work." Using funds transferred from ALA, the Library establishes the National Union Catalog Publication Project to begin editorial work on "the largest single bibliographical undertaking in the Library's 167-year history." (1967 AR:43–44)

FEBRUARY. The Library opens an office in Belgrade to serve its NPAC and Public Law 480 programs jointly. (1967 AR:36)

FEBRUARY. The Library moves the Division for the Blind and Physically Handicapped from its crowded quarters in the Main and Annex buildings to rental facilities at 1291 Taylor Street in northwest Washington. (LCIB 26:110–11)

FEBRUARY 2. Librarian Mumford announces the appointment of Paul L. Berry, associate director of the Administrative Department, to be department director. (PR 67–7)

The National Program for Acquisitions and Cataloging, a responsibility entrusted to the Library of Congress by Title II–C of the Higher Education Act of 1965, dramatically expanded the Library's overseas operations. In this 1966 photograph, Jerry R. James, field director in charge of acquisitions in East Africa, travels in a gharry to visit government offices in Asmara, Ethiopia.

157

1967

May 15. The Library reorganizes its preservation activities and changes the name of the Office of Collections Maintenance and Preservation to the Preservation Office.

(1967 AR:4, 92–93)

May 19. Mrs. Charles William Engelhard, Jr., of Far Hills, N.J., presents a gift of $10,000 to the Library for the establishment of a revolving fund. The new Jane Engelhard Fund will be used to expand the Library's facsimile publications program and to support other publications which describe the Library's collections and services.

(PR 67-29; 1967 AR:127)

June 5. At the request of the Library, the Bureau of the Budget instructs federal agencies to furnish the Library of Congress with four copies of each publication "produced by agency printing plants or procured through commercial contract." The Library's request was an effort to formalize and increase its receipt of U.S. government publications.

(1967 AR:42)

June 26. At the 86th annual conference of the American Library Association, the Library of Congress, the National Library of Medicine, and the National Agricultural Library announce the establishment of the U.S. National Libraries Task Force on Automation and Other Cooperative Services. The goal of the combined effort will be to "achieve systems compatibility at the national level."

(PR 67-33; 1967 AR:21-22)

July. Staff members of the Library of Congress, the National Library of Medicine, and the National Agricultural Library begin work on the first phase of the National Serials Data Program. Its broad objective is the creation of a national data base of machine-readable information identifying the content and location of serial titles in the national libraries. The project is sponsored by the Joint Committee on the Union List of Serials, Inc., with funds contributed by the Council on Library Resources, Inc., and the National Science Foundation.

(1967 AR:22-3; 1968 AR:5)

1967

August 25. At a press conference in the Library's Wilson Room, Senator B. Everett Jordan of North Carolina and Representative Omar Burleson of Texas, chairman and vice-chairman of the Joint Committee on the Library, make public the model and the plans for the future Library of Congress James Madison Memorial Building. Senator Jordan and Representative Burleson are joined by Librarian Mumford and architect Alfred Easton Poor in discussing the building. It is announced that, according to present plans, the following administrative units will occupy the Madison Building: the Office of the Librarian, the Administrative Department, the Copyright Office, the Law Library, the Legislative Reference Service, the Processing Department, and six divisions of the Reference Department (the Geography and Map, Manuscript, Music, Prints and Photographs, Rare Book, and Serial Divisions).

(PR 67-38)

September. The Library moves the Defense Research Division into rental quarters in a building on Massachusetts Avenue in northeast Washington, the first of several units to be moved into the building.

(LCIB 26:641; 1968 AR:63–64)

October 23. The Library organizes the Preservation Office into the following units: binding, collections maintenance, preservation research and testing, restoration, and the preservation microfilming (brittle books) project.

(1968 AR:60)

November 1. The Library installs in the Legislative Reference Service two leased computer terminals to be used in the preparation of the *Digest of Public General Bills and Resolutions*, the first use of computer terminals in the Library.

(1968 AR:6)

APRIL 30. John W. Cronin, director of the Processing Department, retires. (LCIB 27:235–36)

MAY 6. Librarian Mumford appoints William J. Welsh, associate director of the Processing Department, to be director. (LCIB 27:253–54)

JUNE 6–8. Senior Library officials meet at the Belmont conference center in Elkridge, Md., to discuss the Library's services and how they might be improved. (LCA)

JUNE 20. Librarian Mumford establishes an interdepartmental preservation committee. (LCR 218–3)

JULY 1. In accordance with the terms of an agreement with the Library, the Government Printing Office places the restoration shops it operates in the Library's buildings under the Library's direct supervision. (LCIB 27:342–43)

AUGUST 8. The Librarian announces four new administrative appointments which will become effective on October 1, 1968. Roy P. Basler, director of the Reference Department, is appointed chief of the Manuscript Division and occupant of the Library's chair of American history. John Lester Nolan, associate director of the Reference Department, will become the department's new director. Paul L. Berry, director of the Administrative Department, will succeed Mr. Nolan as associate director of the Reference Department and will become director of the department upon Mr. Nolan's retirement in April 1969. Robert H. Rohlf, coordinator of building planning in the office of the Librarian, will succeed Mr. Berry as director of the Administrative Department. (PR 68–49; LCIB 27:478–80)

SEPTEMBER. The Library completes a reorganization of its Administrative Department into three major functional areas: management services, personnel services, and preservation of library materials. (LCIB 27:563–65)

DECEMBER 16. President Johnson approves the Postal Revenue and Federal Salary Act of 1967, which raises the annual salary of the Librarian of Congress to $28,750. (81 Stat. 613)

DECEMBER 16. David C. Mearns retires after 49 years' service as a member of the Library of Congress staff—the last 16 years as chief of the Manuscript Division and Assistant Librarian for the American Collections. (LCIB 26:840–42)

JANUARY. The Library publishes The MARC II Format: A Communications Format for Bibliographic Data, prepared by Henriette D. Avram, John F. Knapp, and Lucia J. Rather of the Information Systems Office. (LCA)

JANUARY. The Library's MARC format is adopted as a standard for use by the National Library of Medicine, the National Agricultural Library, and three divisions of the American Library Association. (1968 AR:5–6)

FEBRUARY. The Processing Department is realigned administratively into three major functional areas: acquisitions and overseas operations, cataloging, and processing services. (1968 AR:12)

MARCH. The Legislative Reference Service begins issuing a monthly Legislative Status Report, which is intended to inform members of Congress and congressional committees about the details and the status of pending legislation. (1968 AR:33)

MARCH 21. The Library announces that it has received a grant of $33,500 from the Council on Library Resources, Inc., to develop machine-readable cataloging data for single-sheet maps. (PR 68–30; 1968 AR:7)

APRIL 19. Librarian Mumford establishes an interdepartmental committee on motion pictures. (LCR 218–8)

1968

SEPTEMBER. The Library and the American Film Institute conclude a cooperative agreement for the further development of the Library's national motion picture collection. The institute gives the Library an initial grant of $125,000 toward acquisition of American film classics not in the collection, with priority acquisitions to be films made between 1912 and 1942. The Library will house the films, make preservation copies, and provide its usual reference services for scholars studying motion pictures.

(1969 AR:9–10)

SEPTEMBER 19. The Library holds its first seminar in a new doctoral program in American civilization, sponsored jointly with George Washington University. A principal purpose of the program, which emphasizes library research and collections, is to help meet the need for scholarly administrators in the nation's libraries.

(LCIB 27:579–81)

OCTOBER 2. The Library inaugurates Phase 1 of the Card Automated Reproduction and Distribution System (CARDS), which enables the Card Division to process order slips for LC catalog cards automatically.

(LCIB 27:614–15)

OCTOBER 3. In its report to President Johnson, the National Advisory Commission on Libraries recommends the "recognition and strengthening of the role of the Library of Congress as the National Library of the United States and the establishment of a Board of Advisors for the Library."

(LCA; 1969 AR:2)

OCTOBER 9. Mr. and Mrs. Walter C. Louchheim, Jr., of Washington, D.C., present the Library of Congress Trust Fund Board with a gift to establish the Katie and Walter Louchheim Fund. The fund will provide support for musical performances and poetry readings, for the preparation of audio and video tapes for broadcasting the Library's chamber music concerts and literary presentations, and for the production of sound recordings and video tapes for dissemination to the general public and to educational institutions.

(LCA; 1969 AR:41)

1968

OCTOBER 24. President Johnson approves an act of Congress establishing the Woodrow Wilson International Center for Scholars; the Librarian of Congress is named an ex officio member of the center's board of trustees.

(82 Stat. 1356)

NOVEMBER. As part of the effort to alleviate crowded conditions in the Library's stacks, the Library begins the move of its foreign newspaper collection of over 50,000 bound volumes to a warehouse on Duke Street in Alexandria, Va. The newspapers are the first collection to occupy the newly renovated warehouse, which contains 53,000 square feet of storage space.

(LCIB 27:704; 1968 AR:64)

NOVEMBER 13. The Library announces that it has received a $25,000 grant from the Council on Library Resources, Inc., to support a three-month project to determine the feasibility of converting LC retrospective cataloging records to machine-readable form.

(PR 68–58; 1969 AR:4)

DECEMBER. Mansell Information/Publishing, Ltd., publishes the first five of the projected 610 volumes in the *National Union Catalog: Pre-1956 Imprints.* (LCIB 28:8–9)

DECEMBER 3. The Council on Library Resources, Inc., gives the Library a grant of $58,376 to continue the work of the Center for the Coordination of Foreign Manuscript Copying for two more years.

(LCA)

1969

FEBRUARY 14. In accordance with section 225 of the Postal Revenue and Federal Salary Act of 1967, and upon the recommendation of the President of the United States, the annual salary of the Librarian of Congress is raised to $38,000.

(81 Stat. 613; LCA)

MARCH 27. With the mailing of the first computer tapes containing cataloging data, the MARC Distribution Service is inaugurated.

(1969 AR:3)

160

MARCH 29–31. The Library moves the Copyright Office from its crowded quarters on Capitol Hill to a temporary location in Crystal Mall in Arlington, Va.
(PR 69–14; 1969 AR:72)

APRIL 7. The Library transfers the MARC Production Group from the Information Systems Office to the Processing Department, where it is renamed the MARC Editorial Office.
(LCA; LCIB 33:A219–A221)

APRIL 21. Reference Department Director John Lester Nolan retires and Associate Director Paul L. Berry becomes director.
(LCA; LCIB 28:203–4)

MAY. A projected reduction in the funds which the Department of Health, Education, and Welfare had previously transferred to the Library to support the *Monthly Index of Russian Accessions* forces the Library to discontinue its publication. The last issue of the *Monthly Index*, published by the Library since 1948, is dated May 1969.
(1969 AR:5)

MAY 23. In its report on the pending legislative reorganization bill, the Senate Committee on Government Operations stresses that the Legislative Reference Service "must be modernized and expanded if it is to keep pace with congressional requirements." The committee observes that "sound congressional decisionmaking is rooted in the availability of accurate information and expert analysis; that each succeeding session confronts the Congress with an increased number of complex programs and policy decisions; and that the Congress must maintain a research capability that will keep pace with both the growing amount of business and its multiplying intricacies."
(91/1 SE. 202:18)

MAY 23. At the opening of its exhibition commemorating the 150th anniversary of the poet's birth, the Library announces that it will acquire the Charles Feinberg collection

of Walt Whitman materials. This important collection, which includes over 20,000 items, will be purchased for the Library by benefactors who prefer to remain anonymous.
(PR 69–26; 1969 AR:8–9)

AUGUST 3. Robert H. Rohlf, director of the Administrative Department, resigns to become director of the Hennepin County (Minn.) Library System.
(LCIB:28:399; 1970 AR:71)

AUGUST 28. Librarian Mumford reorganizes the Office of the Secretary of the Library in the Administrative Department into the Central Services Division. The title of secretary of the Library is discontinued.
(LCR 212–11; LCIB 28:424)

SEPTEMBER. The Library establishes an Environmental Policy Division which replaces the Natural Resources Division in the Legislative Reference Service.
(1970 AR:34)

SEPTEMBER. Because of the loss of financial support from other federal agencies, the Library ceases publishing the *World List of Future International Meetings* with the September–October 1969 issue.
(1969 AR:6)

SEPTEMBER 3. After a substantial reduction in support from other government agencies, the Aerospace Technology Division is reorganized into the Aerospace Reference Project in the Reference Department Office.
(LCR 214–1; LCR 214–2; 1970 AR:39)

OCTOBER 17. The Library completes a four-week move of the Geography and Map Division to rental quarters on Pickett Street in Alexandria, Va. Approximately three and one half million maps were transported in some 4,000 five-drawer steel map cases.
(LCIB 28:600)

OCTOBER 28. The Library establishes the American Revolution Bicentennial Office in the Office of the Assistant

1969

Librarian. The new office will be staffed by professional historians specializing in the revolutionary era who will compile guides to the collections and plan special events using the Library's collections of 18th-century source materials.

OCTOBER 31. The Aerospace Technology Project in the Reference Department Office is abolished. (1970 AR:39)

NOVEMBER 3. The Library establishes a motion picture preservation laboratory in the cellar of the Main Building. (LCA; LCIB 28:630)

DECEMBER 29. Antiquarian bookdealer Hans P. Kraus of New York City donates to the Library a notable collection of manuscripts relating to the history and culture of Spanish America in the colonial period. (LCA; 1970 AR:43)

1970

FEBRUARY 5. The Library announces plans to establish a preservation research laboratory which, in addition to basic research, will also seek to develop solutions to preservation problems for libraries and archives throughout the United States. A grant of $70,000 from the Council on Library Resources, Inc., will be used to purchase scientific equipment for the new laboratory.
(LCA; PR 70-10; LCIB 29:56-57)

FEBRUARY 13. The Library announces that it has received a grant of $200,959 from the Council on Library Resources, Inc., to continue the RECON (Retrospective Conversion) pilot project, which will ascertain the problems and the costs of providing cataloging data in machine-readable format for retrospective publications. The project is expected to continue through August 1971.
(PR 70-13; LCIB 29:83-84)

FEBRUARY 16. Librarian Mumford announces that Fred E. Croxton, executive vice-president of Informatics Tisco, Inc., has been appointed director of the Administrative Department. He will assume his new duties on April 1,

1970

1970. Simultaneously, the Information Systems Office, which has been part of the Office of the Librarian, will be assigned to the Administrative Department.
(PR 70-14; LCIB 29:80-81)

MARCH. The size of the Defense Research Division is sharply reduced in accordance with a reduction in funds received for its support from the Department of Defense.
(LCA)

MARCH 16. President Richard M. Nixon approves an act of Congress increasing the authorization for appropriations for the James Madison Memorial Building to $90 million, with an added proviso: "Nothing contained in the Act of October 19, 1965 (79 Stat. 986) shall be construed to authorize the use of the third Library of Congress building authorized by such Act for general office building purposes." (84 Stat. 69)

MARCH 26. The Library announces the establishment of the McKim Fund, an endowment received under a bequest of the late Mrs. W. Duncan McKim, to be used to support the composition and performance of chamber music for violin and piano.
(PR 70-27; LCIB 29:147-48)

APRIL 8. Librarian Mumford changes the name of the Defense Research Division to the Federal Research Division.
(LCA)

APRIL 13-15. The Library sponsors an International Poetry Festival, featuring readings by prominent foreign poets from eight different countries. The festival is supported by the Gertrude Clarke Whittall Poetry and Literature Fund.
(1970 AR:41)

JUNE 12. The Library is authorized to purchase office equipment and furniture directly; heretofore appropriations were made to the Architect of the Capitol for this purpose.
(84 Stat. 309)

1970

Publication Division, which replace the single Catalog Maintenance and Catalog Publication Division.

(LCR 213–2, 213–4; 1971 AR:28)

AUGUST 3. The Johns Hopkins University Press publishes, for the Library of Congress, *American Prints in the Library of Congress*, a 568-page volume which contains entries for about 12,000 prints by 1,250 artists. Publication of the volume is made possible by a grant received in 1964 from the Ford Foundation.

(PR 70–52; LCIB 29–387–88)

AUGUST 8. The Library announces that it has concluded its five-year program to gather and disseminate information about photocopying of manuscript and archival material in foreign repositories, a program supported by grants from the Council on Library Resources, Inc. The Center for the Coordination of Foreign Manuscript Copying will cease to exist as an organizational unit at the end of the calendar year.

(Library of Congress *News Note* 70–5)

OCTOBER 26. President Nixon approves the Legislative Reorganization Act of 1970. The new law changes the name of the Legislative Reference Service to the Congressional Research Service (CRS), effective January 3, 1971. The duties of the service are expanded, with increased emphasis to be placed on policy research and analysis and on direct services to the committees and to the individual members of Congress. To assist CRS in performing its new functions, the act authorizes the appointment of senior specialists and specialists in fields other than those specifically listed in the statute, as well as the use of the services of other experts, consultants, and research organizations. In addition, CRS is required to prepare and file a separate annual report with the Congress. The act gives the CRS maximum administrative and fiscal autonomy within the Library's organizational structure, stipulating that the Librarian of Congress shall "in every possible way,

1970

JUNE 17. In its report on the pending legislative reorganization bill, the House Committee on Rules recommends increased autonomy for the Legislative Reference Service, which should be renamed the Congressional Research Service (CRS), and a closer relationship between CRS and the Congress. A considerable expansion of the CRS is recommended; the committee notes: "We would expect the CRS, for example, to triple its staff by 1975." The committee also observes: "As did the Joint Committee on the Organization of the Congress, we considered and rejected a complete divorcement of the Service from the Library. In our judgment, the Library serves as a useful mantle for protecting the Service from partisan pressures. Furthermore, the effectiveness of the CRS will be enhanced by its continued instant access to the Library's collections and administrative support services." (91/2 HRR 1215:18–20)

JUNE 29. Librarian Mumford establishes the MARC Development Office in the Processing Department. It will be responsible for the development and implementation of systems for recording data in machine-readable form, as well as for the uses of those records. The Information Systems Office will continue to be responsible for coordinating the overall automation program of the Library.

(LCA; LCIB 29:331–32)

JULY 20. President Nixon approves an act of Congress creating a permanent National Commission on Libraries and Information Science; the Librarian of Congress is designated as an ex officio member of the commission.

(84 Stat. 440)

JULY 21. Librarian Mumford dissolves the Union Catalog Division. The pre-1956 imprints section of the division is transferred to the Reference Department. Other functions formerly performed by the Union Catalog Division are absorbed by two divisions in the Processing Department: the Catalog Maintenance Division and the Catalog

The Legislative Reorganization Act of 1970 greatly expanded the role and responsibilities of the Congressional Research Service. To provide better service CRS established reference centers in House of Representatives and Senate office buildings. This photograph shows a Senate staff member using CRS computer services in the Senate Reference Center.

1970

encourage, assist, and promote the Congressional Research Service," according it "complete research independence and the maximum practicable administrative independence." The pay level of the director of the CRS is raised above that of other Library departmental heads. The act also states that the director of the Congressional Research Service shall be appointed by the Librarian of Congress "after consultation with the Joint Committee on the Library."

(84 Stat. 1140; 1971 AR:3, 33–35)

DECEMBER 30. The Ford Foundation announces a $500,000 eight-year grant to the Library to support an extensive revision and enlargement of the Edmund C. Burnett edition of *Letters of Members of the Continental Congress*, to be edited in the Library's American Revolution Bicentennial Office.

(LCIB 29:699–700)

1971

JANUARY 8. The Library announces that it has received a $25,000 grant from the Kulas Foundation of Cleveland, Ohio, which will be used to study the application of computer technology to the transcription of music notation into braille.

(PR 71–2; LCIB 30:22–23)

JANUARY 11. The Library establishes the first branch of the Congressional Research Service in a congressional office building. The new Reference Information Center is located in the Rayburn House Office Building.

(1971 AR:38–39, 44)

JANUARY 14. The Library announces that it has received a grant of $96,700 from the U.S. Office of Education for the RECON Pilot Project for fiscal 1971.

(LCIB 30:23)

APRIL 22. The Architect of the Capitol awards the contract for the first phase of the construction of the James Madison Memorial Building.

(1971 AR:1, 71)

MAY 27. The House Office Building Commission, chaired by Representative Carl Albert of Oklahoma, the Speaker of the House, recommends that no further action be taken on the appropriation of funds for a third Library of Congress building until the location of a fourth House office building has been determined. (1971 AR:1)

MAY 28. Law Librarian Lewis C. Coffin retires. (LCIB 30:331)

JUNE 1. Excavation work for the Library of Congress James Madison Memorial Building begins. (1971 AR:1)

JUNE 1. The House Committee on Appropriations, chaired by Representative George Andrews of Alabama, recommends an appropriation of $67,391,250 for operating expenses to the Library of Congress during fiscal 1972, and $71,090,000 to the Architect of the Capitol for construction of the superstructure of the James Madison Memorial Building. (92/1 HRR 236:10–11)

JUNE 4. In debate in the House of Representatives on the legislative branch appropriation bill for fiscal 1972, by a vote of 69–48 the House rejects an amendment which would delete the recommended appropriation for the James Madison Memorial Building. (CR 117:18C40–45)

JUNE 14. Librarian Mumford announces the appointment of Associate Law Librarian Carleton W. Kenyon as Law Librarian. (PR 71–33)

JUNE 20. The Library announces that it has received matching grants of $200,000 each from the National Endowment for the Humanities and the Council on Library Resources, Inc., to support a new program of providing cataloging data to be printed in the books themselves. The project, to be directed by the Processing Department, will be known as the Cataloging in Publication (CIP) program. The grants will support CIP in its experimental phase, which will extend from July 1, 1971, through June 30, 1973. (PR 71–34; 1971 AR:2–3, 21–23)

JUNE 23–28. A four-day work stoppage among approximately 25 staff members who work as Library deck attendants results in the dismissal of 11 of the employees. (1971 AR:9–10; LCIB 30:A103–A106)

JUNE 25. At its 90th annual conference, held in Dallas, Tex., the council of the American Library Association approves a membership resolution calling on the council to inquire into and report on the allegations by a personal member that the Library of Congress "discriminates on racial grounds in recruitment, training, and promotion practices." (LCIB 30:A148–A154)

JULY 9. President Nixon approves the legislative branch appropriations act for fiscal 1972, which includes $68,053,250 for the Library of Congress and $71,090,000 for the Architect of the Capitol for construction of the superstructure of the James Madison Memorial Building. (85 Stat. 125)

JULY 13. The Cataloging in Publication program is launched with the selection by lot of the first 27 participating publishers. (LCIB 30: 426–27)

AUGUST 27. Librarian Mumford announces the appointment of George D. Cary, deputy register of copyrights, to be register of copyrights following the retirement of Abraham L. Kaminstein. (SA 425)

AUGUST 31. Register of Copyrights Abraham L. Kaminstein retires. (LCIB 30:499–501)

SEPTEMBER. Phase II of cards commences, enabling the Library to reproduce selected catalog cards from photocomposed MARC records. (1972 AR:22)

SEPTEMBER 7. The Library institutes a new Equal Opportunity Program, which replaces the Fair Employment

Practices Program. The revised program provides the Library with four equal opportunity officers.

(LCR 2010–3; LCIB 30:442–43)

SEPTEMBER 29. Judge William B. Jones of the U.S. District Court for the District of Columbia grants a motion for summary judgment on behalf of Barbara A. Ringer, assistant register of copyrights, thereby ruling that the appointment of George D. Cary as register of copyrights was defective because of the Library's failure to follow its own procedures.

OCTOBER 15. President Richard M. Nixon approves an amendment to the copyright law that will make it possible, for the first time, to register claims to U.S. copyright for sound recordings. After the law becomes effective on February 15, 1972, two copies of each registered recording will be sent to the Library.

(85 Stat. 391; 1972 AR:65–66)

OCTOBER 29. Librarian Mumford announces that, having followed all the procedures outlined in Library of Congress regulations, he is naming George D. Cary, acting register of copyrights, to be register of copyrights effective November 1, 1971.

(SA 440)

NOVEMBER 9. On the instructions of Representative Wayne L. Hays of Ohio, chairman of the Joint Committee on the Library, Librarian Mumford informs the American Library Association that the Library will not present testimony before the ALA inquiry team which is investigating the charges of racial discrimination in the Library. In the opinion of Representative Hays, "the American Library Association is infringing on and usurping the oversight responsibilities of Congress in making an investigation of an Agency under the exclusive jurisdiction of Congress."

(1972 AR:7–8)

NOVEMBER 16. A reception in the Great Hall of the Library marks the publication of the first volumes in *The History of the Supreme Court of the United States.* The series is sponsored by the Oliver Wendell Holmes Devise Fund, which is administered by a permanent committee appointed by the President of the United States; the Librarian of Congress serves as ex officio chairman of the committee.

(LCIB 30:672–77)

JANUARY 25. The ALA Inquiry Team investigating the personnel policies and procedures of the Library releases its report. The team concludes that, based on the evidence it heard, there was "a pattern of actions for which it could conceive no other motivation than racial discrimination."

(AL 3:277–79)

JANUARY 27. In a telegram to ALA President Keith Doms, Librarian Mumford protests the conclusions of the ALA Inquiry Team, which reflect "on the integrity of over 600 Library of Congress supervisors." Mumford is particularly concerned about "an obvious lack of specifics contained in the serious charges made against the Library," adding that the report "fails to recognize the Library of Congress' accomplishments in the area of race relations."

(SA 462; PR 72–7)

MARCH 24. President Nixon approves the Equal Employment Opportunity Act of 1972. Section 717, which relates to nondiscrimination in federal government employment, includes the Library of Congress. The Library was included through an amendment offered in the Senate by Senators Alan Cranston of California and Peter H. Dominick of Colorado. The amendment had the support of Librarian Mumford and Senator B. Everett Jordan of North Carolina, chairman of the Joint Committee on the Library.

(86 Stat. 103; LCIB 31:138–39)

APRIL 17. A headquarters office for the National Serials Data Program, a cooperative effort of the Library of

Congress, the National Agricultural Library, and the National Library of Medicine, is established at the Library of Congress.

(LCIB 31:124–25)

APRIL 26. Librarian Mumford redefines the scope of the work of the Hispanic Foundation and changes its name to the Latin American, Portuguese, and Spanish Division.

(LCR 214–6; LCIB 31:185)

APRIL 27. Pursuant to the Legislative Reorganization Act of 1970, the Joint Committee on the Library publishes the annual report of the Congressional Research Service for fiscal 1971. This 186-page joint committee print is the first separate annual report of the service.

(LCA)

MAY 5–6. The Library holds the first in a series of five symposia on the American Revolution, a series supported by the Morris and Gwendolyn Cafritz Foundation of Washington. Professor Richard B. Morris of Columbia University, a member of the Library's Advisory Committee on the American Revolution Bicentennial Program, serves as chairman. Five papers and four commentaries are presented on the theme "The Development of a Revolutionary Mentality."

(PR 72–28; LCIB 31:209)

MAY 29. In accordance with the recommendations of the Foreign Newspaper Microfilm Committee of the Association of Research Libraries, the Library assumes responsibility for coordinating a national program for the microfilming of foreign newspapers.

(LCA; LCIB 31:253)

JUNE. In an attempt to relieve the overcrowded conditions in the stacks, the Library undertakes a massive relocation project. During the next three years, "nearly 9 million volumes occupying over 600,000 linear feet" will be shifted.

(LCIB 31:280–81)

JUNE 15. Death of Verner W. Clapp, consultant to the Council on Library Resources, Inc, president of the coun-

cil from 1956–67, and Library of Congress staff member.

(LCIB 31:275–79)

JUNE 20. Librarian Mumford presides over a memorial program for Verner W. Clapp in the Coolidge Auditorium. In addition to the Librarian, William S. Dix, librarian of Princeton University; Frederick H. Wagman, director of libraries at the University of Michigan; and David C. Mearns, the Library's honorary consultant in the humanities, offer tributes.

(LCIB 31:293–94)

JUNE 21. "In order to provide additional opportunities for effective communication between staff members and management," Librarian Mumford asks the six departments to form ad hoc human relations committees and a Library-wide Human Relations Council.

(SA 487; LCIB 31:279)

JULY. The Library transfers its collection of 50,000 volumes of United States newspapers to the Library's warehouse on Duke Street in Alexandria, Va. The volumes can now be serviced only on 48-hour notice.

(LCA; 1972 AR:36)

AUGUST 1. In cooperation with the Brookings Institution, the Congressional Research Service begins a series of seminars on public policy issues for members of Congress. The first seminar, held in the Whittall Pavilion, concerns U.S. relations with China.

(LCIB 31:367)

AUGUST 31. The National Serials Data Program announces that it has received a $20,000 grant from the Council on Library Resources, Inc., to supplement the budgetary support provided by the three national libraries, thus enabling the program to enter its third and operational phase.

(PR 72–57)

OCTOBER 6. President Nixon approves the Federal Advisory Committee Act, which stipulates that the director of the Office of Management and Budget shall provide for the collections of the Library of Congress at least eight copies of each report made by every advisory committee, as well as appropriate background reports. The Librarian of Congress shall establish a depository for such reports and papers where they shall be available for public instruction and use.

OCTOBER 13. President Nixon approves an act of Congress creating an Office of Technology Assessment in the legislative branch. The director of the Congressional Research Service is designated an ex officio member of its Advisory Council.

(86 Stat. 797; LCIB 31:523–24)

NOVEMBER. The National Serials Data Program begins assigning International Standard Serial Numbers (ISSN) to American publications.

(LCA; 1973 AR:13)

JANUARY 29–30. The Library sponsors a "Conference on the Teaching of Creative Writing," which is supported by the Gertrude Clarke Whittall Poetry and Literature Fund.

(1973 AR:146–47)

FEBRUARY 23. Librarian Mumford approves a new employment opportunity plan for fiscal 1973, inaugurating a comprehensive affirmative action program for the Library under the provisions of the Equal Employment Opportunity Act of 1972.

(1973 AR:8–9)

FEBRUARY 23. The Librarian announces that he has designated the newly established Special Services Division of the District of Columbia Public Library as the D.C. Regional Library for the Blind and Physically Handicapped. In the past this function had been performed by the Division for the Blind and Physically Handicapped of the Library of Congress.

(PR 73–8; 1973 AR:7)

FEBRUARY 28. Judge William B. Jones of the U.S. District Court for the District of Columbia rules in favor of the plaintiff in a suit brought against the Librarian of Congress by Barbara A. Ringer, former assistant register of copyrights. Ms. Ringer had charged the Librarian with discriminating on the grounds of both sex and race in failing to appoint her register of copyrights. (86 Stat. 770)

MARCH 9. Register of Copyrights George D. Cary retires.

(LCIB 32:88–89)

APRIL 13. The Librarian announces the appointment of a Federal Women's Program Coordinator, who will be responsible for advising the Library administration on special concerns regarding the employment and advancement of women on the Library's staff.

(PR 73–19; LCIB 32:133, 135–36)

JUNE 5–7. Five members of the American Library Association, accompanied by ALA Executive Director Robert Wedgeworth, visit the Library and confer with the Librarian and other officials regarding the Library's affirmative action program.

(LCIB 32:206)

JUNE 25. The Library distributes the first MARC tapes containing cataloging information for serials.

(LCIB 32:280; LCIB 33:A81–A84)

JULY 27. The Librarian appoints an ad hoc committee for labor-management relations. The committee will develop a proposal for a labor-management system for the Library.

(LCIB 32:371, 425, 429–30)

AUGUST. The editing of *The National Union Catalog: Pre-1956 Imprints* reaches the halfway point after over five years' work and the editing of approximately 10 million cards.

(LCIB 32:314)

SEPTEMBER 7. Librarian Mumford announces the appointment of Barbara A. Ringer, director of the copyright division in the office of international standards and legal affairs of Unesco and former assistant register of copyrights, to be register of copyrights.

(PR 73–74; LCIB 32:319, 325)

SEPTEMBER 21. Officials from the Library meet in Toronto with representatives from other institutions to plan a concentrated effort to create, as rapidly as possible, a comprehensive national serials data base in machine-readable form. Funds for this meeting of the "Ad Hoc Discussion Group on Serials" are provided by the Council on Library Resources, Inc.   (LCA; LCIB 33:A35–A38)

SEPTEMBER 21. In order to create more office space for staff, the Library undertakes several major space shifts in the Annex, including the removal of the Annex Card Catalog to storage and the relocation of several reading rooms.

(LCIB 32:328)

DECEMBER 11. President Nixon approves an act of Congress establishing the American Revolution Bicentennial Administration, successor to the American Revolution Bicentennial Commission, of which the Librarian of Congress was a member. The new law "authorizes and requests" the Librarian of Congress, the secretary of the Smithsonian Institution, and the Archivist of the United States to cooperate with the Administration "especially in development and display of exhibits and collections and in the development of bibliographies, catalogs, and other materials relevant to the period of the Revolutionary War."

(87 Stat. 697)

DECEMBER 30. President Nixon issues an executive order exempting Librarian Mumford from mandatory retirement until December 31, 1974.

(LCIB 33:7)

1974

JANUARY 23. The council of the American Library Association accepts without dissent the report of the ALA membership team which visited the Library in June 1973. The report notes the extensive efforts being made

1974

by the Library to combat racial discrimination but recommends further efforts and the monitoring of the Library's progress by the ALA and other organizations.

(LCIB 33:A70–71)

FEBRUARY. The Library announces the availability of a new information retrieval system called SCORPIO (Subject-Content-Oriented Retriever for Processing Information On-line). Developed by the Computer Applications Office, SCORPIO is part of a program of developing and implementing information-processing tools for the Congressional Research Service that can also be used in the Library as a whole.   (1974 AR:66, LCIB 34:175–76)

MARCH 8. Librarian Mumford, Senator Howard W. Cannon of Nevada, chairman of the Joint Committee on the Library, and Architect of the Capitol George M. White participate in an informal ceremony for the laying of the cornerstone of the Library of Congress James Madison Memorial Building.   (LCIB 33:81)

APRIL 24. The Library establishes an interdepartmental Federal Women's Program Committee.

(SA 638; LCIB 33:206–7)

MAY. The Library publishes Films and Other Materials for Projection (formerly Library of Congress Catalog—Motion Pictures and Filmstrips), which is the first Library of Congress book catalog produced by computer-aided composition techniques.   (1974 AR:27; LCIB 33:198–99)

MAY 24. The Library announces that its Cataloging in Publication (CIP) program is absorbing the LC preassigned number program, which itself began in 1956 as part of the Library's All-the-Books program.

(PR 74–21; 1974 AR:20)

JUNE 3. Librarian Mumford transfers the National Serials Data Program from the office of the Librarian to the

1974

Processing Department "to provide more effective coordination of the processing functions of the Serial Record Division, the automation functions of the MARC Development Office, and the functions that are the responsibility of the NSDP through its participation in the Unesco-sponsored International Serials Data System (ISDS)."

(LCA; 1974 AR:27–28)

JULY. The Library's National Serials Data Program receives a grant of $150,000 from the National Science Foundation for the development of an automated national data base of serials in science and technology. With the concurrence of the NSF, the Library postpones work on the project until initiation of the CONSER (Conversion of Serials) project, which will provide the systems capability for the new effort. The CONSER project, to be supported and managed by the Council on Library Resources, Inc., will attempt to develop a large scale machine-readable data base for serials through the contributions of several institutions sharing bibliographic data via the Ohio College Library Center (OCLC) system.

(LCA; LCIB 33:A245–48; LCIB 34:A10)

DECEMBER 16. The Library announces that it has received a grant of $106,132 from the Council on Library Resources, Inc., for the expansion of the automated bibliographic services provided by the Library through its MARC system. The grant will support an 18-month pilot project (COMARC) concerned with the certification by the Library of Congress of LC source records converted to machine-readable form by other organizations, along with two additional studies at the Library.

(PR 74-44; LCIB 33:416–18)

DECEMBER 17. The Council on Library Resources, Inc., and the Ohio College Library Center sign an agreement providing for the use of OCLC's computer network in the CLR-managed CONSER project for the next two years. The machine-readable file of serials produced by CONSER will

170

1974

be available to libraries through the National Library of Canada and the Library of Congress.

(LCIB 34:18, A38–A42)

DECEMBER 19. President Gerald R. Ford approves the Presidential Recordings and Materials Preservation Act. The new law provides for the creation of a Public Documents Commission to study the control, disposition, and preservation of records and documents of federal officials; the Librarian of Congress is named as a member of the commission.

(88 Stat. 1695; LCIB 34:A1–A2)

DECEMBER 31. After a 20-year career as Librarian of Congress, L. Quincy Mumford retires. In accordance with LCR 211–1, Deputy Librarian John G. Lorenz becomes Acting Librarian of Congress.

(SA 668; LCIB 34:1, 3–5)

DECEMBER 31. Roy P. Basler, chief of the Manuscript Division and former director of the Reference Department, retires.

(LCIB 34:9–11)

1975

DECEMBER 31. President Ford approves an act of Congress which establishes, as part of the Library of Congress, a National Commission on New Technological Uses of Copyrighted Works (CONTU).

(88 Stat. 1873)

JANUARY. In order to coordinate more effectively the serials processing functions of the Library with the international responsibilities of the National Serials Data Program, the NSDP is incorporated into the Library's Serial Record Division.

(LCIB 34:A105)

JANUARY 18. At a meeting of the Association of Research Libraries held in Chicago, Processing Department Director William J. Welsh and John C. Rather, chief of the Technical Processes Research Office, discuss the future of catalog control at the Library of Congress. They express the hope that an automated system of cataloging control using the MARC data base will be available by 1979. At the

Congress authorized the construction of the third major Library building, the James Madison Memorial Building, in 1965. Construction work on the massive structure, which will contain over two million square feet, commenced in 1971. This August 1974 photograph shows construction workers on the unfinished top floor. The Library of Congress Main Building is directly across Independence Avenue and the dome of the U.S. Capitol can be seen at the far left.

This August 1974 photograph of the Madison Building was taken from the roof of the Library's Thomas Jefferson Building. The southeast corner of the Main Building is seen at the right and the Cannon House Office Building in the right background. The Madison Building is connected by tunnels to the other Library buildings and to the Cannon Building. Photograph courtesy the Office of the Architect of the Capitol.

171

172

A November 1975 photograph of the Madison Building, which will be ready for occupancy in 1979. Photograph courtesy the Office of the Architect of the Capitol.

same meeting, the ARL formally expresses its appreciation to L. Quincy Mumford for his two decades of service as Librarian of Congress, a job that requires "astute participation in many levels of governmental relationships, a perception of national, public, and professional needs, and a cordial and mutually productive interaction with many professional and business communities." (LCIB 34:A35–A37)

FEBRUARY. The Library publishes *Procedures for Salvage of Water-Damaged Library Materials*, prepared by the Preservation Office. The booklet inaugurates a new series, LC Publications on Conservation of Library Materials. (LCA)

FEBRUARY 1. The Library changes the name of the Card Division to reflect the division's role as the Cataloging Distribution Service. The division distributes Library of Congress cataloging data in its various physical forms—MARC tapes, microforms, printed catalog cards, proofsheets, book catalogs, and technical publications. (LCIB 34:27–28)

APRIL 16. The National Science Foundation, the National Commission on Libraries and Information Science, and the Council on Library Resources, Inc., announce the establishment of an Advisory Group on National Bibliographic Control. William J. Welsh, director of the Library's Processing Department, is named to the six-member advisory group. (LCA; LCIB 34:186)

APRIL 24. The 175th anniversary of the founding of the Library is marked by the opening of the Library's American Revolution Bicentennial exhibit "To Set a Country Free." Also on view are two commemorative exhibits concerning the history of the Library. (LCIB 34:162–64)

APRIL 24. Acting Librarian of Congress John G. Lorenz establishes a formal labor-management program in the Library of Congress, to become effective on October 24,

1975

1975

1975. He explains that the program was developed after careful study and has the endorsement of the chairman and vice-chairman of the Joint Committee on the Library. (LCR 2026; LCIB 34:219, 221–22)

JUNE 2. In ceremonies held in the Library's Whittall Pavilion, the heirs of Alexander Graham Bell donate the distinguished inventor's manuscripts to the Library. The collection of approximately 130,000 items is presented by Melville Bell Grosvenor, grandson of the scientist and chairman of the board of the National Geographic Society. (LCIB 34:239, 241)

JUNE 9. At a meeting of the Council for Computerized Networks (CCLN), held in the Whittall Pavilion, Processing Department Director William J. Welsh presents a paper entitled "The Library of Congress as the National Bibliographic Center: A Current View From the Processing Department." According to Welsh, the Library's proper function "is to develop and maintain standard bibliographic devices that will promote consistency in decentralized input to a comprehensive national data base." (LCIB 34:265, 267–68)

JUNE 20. President Gerald R. Ford nominates historian and author Daniel J. Boorstin, senior historian at the Smithsonian Institution, to be Librarian of Congress. (CR 121:S11250; LCIB 34:265)

JUNE 28. The Library announces that it has received a contract award of $52,000 from the National Commission on Libraries and Information Science for a study to define the role of the Library of Congress in the evolving national network for library and information science. (PR 75–60; LCIB 34:317, 319)

JULY. The National Commission on Libraries and Information Science releases its report *Toward a National*

REPORT OF THE LIBRARIAN OF CONGRESS, 1945.

CHART I
REFERENCE DEPARTMENT, PRE-REORGANIZATION

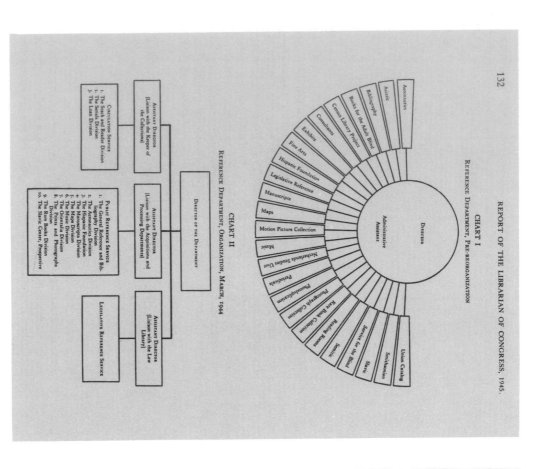

CHART II
REFERENCE DEPARTMENT, ORGANIZATION, MARCH, 1944

Organizing the Reference Department in the most effective manner has been a difficult problem for 20th-century Librarians of Congress. This page from Librarian MacLeish's 1945 annual report illustrates the changes made during his administration. In 1946 the Legislative Reference Service was established as a separate Library Department.

ORGANIZATION CHART

As of November 1, 1975

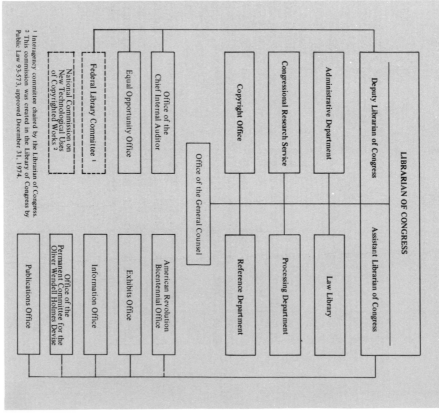

The organization of the Library of Congress in November 1975.

Program for Library and Information Services: Goals for Action. The commission emphasizes that the participation of the Library of Congress is crucial to the development of its proposed national program and notes that "new legislation may be needed to designate the Library of Congress as having responsibility for integral aspects of the National Program." Moreover, the commission states its belief that the Library of Congress should be designated as the National Library. Finally, the commission lists nine areas in which it believes the Library of Congress, as the national library, should accept responsibility in the proposed national program: 1) expansion of its lending and lending-management function to that of a national lending library of last resort; 2) expansion of the National Program for Acquisitions and Cataloging (NPAC); 3) expansion of the Machine-Readable Cataloging (MARC) program; 4) distribution of bibliographic data through on-line communication; 5) development of an expanded general reference program to support the national system for bibliographic services; 6) operation of a comprehensive national serials service; 7) establishment of a technical services center to provide training in, and information about, Library of Congress techniques and processes, with emphasis on automation; 8) development of improved access to state and local publications; and 9) further implementation of the national preservation program.

(LCA)

JULY 3. The Rare Book Division is renamed the Rare Book and Special Collections Division. (LCA; LCIB 34:334)

JULY 4. At its 94th annual conference, held in San Francisco, Calif., the American Library Association adopts a resolution opposing the nomination of Daniel J. Boorstin to be Librarian of Congress because "Dr. Boorstin's background, however distinguished it may be, does not include demonstrated leadership and administrative qualities which constitute basic and essential characteristics necessary in the Librarian of Congress." (94/1 SH:142)

JULY 30. The Senate Committee on Rules and Administration, chaired by Howard W. Cannon of Nevada, begins hearings on the Boorstin nomination. Witnesses testifying in favor of the nomination are: Representative Carl Albert of Oklahoma, Speaker of the House of Representatives; John J. Rhodes, minority leader of the U.S. House of Representatives; Herman Wouk, representing the Author's League of America; and S. Dillon Ripley, secretary of the Smithsonian Institution. The nomination is opposed by representatives of the American Library Association.

(94/1 SH:1–64)

JULY 31. The committee continues its hearings. The nomination is opposed by representatives from the Capitol Area Council of Federal Employees, No. 26, AFSCME, AFL-CIO, the Black Employees of the Library of Congress, and the Ethnic Employees of the Library of Congress. Chairman Cannon recesses the hearings until September 10, 1975, after the congressional recess. (94/1 SH:165–206)

AUGUST 9. President Ford approves the Executive Salary Cost-of-Living Adjustment Act, which authorizes an increase in the salary of the Librarian of Congress. Effective October 1, 1975, the annual salary will be $39,900.

(89 Stat. 419; LCA)

AUGUST 15. The Library announces that it has received a grant of $237,200 for fiscal 1976 from the National Endowment for the Humanities and the Council on Library Resources, Inc., to accelerate the development of a national serials data base in the humanities in machine-readable form. The grant will be used by the Library's National Serials Data Project as part of the CONSER (Conversion of Serials) Project. (PR 75–63; LCIB 34:342–43)

AUGUST 15. The National Endowment for the Humanities announces that it has awarded a grant of up to $110,000 to the Library for the preparation of a computer-based catalog of two significant collections of early motion

On November 12, 1975, Daniel J. Boorstin took the oath of office as the 12th Librarian of Congress. The oath is administered by Carl Albert, Speaker of the House of Representatives. President Gerald R. Ford observes.

1975

pictures—the George Kleine and Theodore Roosevelt collections.

(LCA; LCIB 34:341)

SEPTEMBER 10. After hearing additional testimony from the nominee, the Senate Committee on Rules and Administration concludes its hearings on the nomination of Daniel J. Boorstin to be Librarian.

(94/1 SH:207–389)

SEPTEMBER 25. The Senate Committee on Rules and Administration, chaired by Senator Howard W. Cannon of Nevada, reports in favor of the Boorstin nomination. The vote is unanimous.

(94/1 SER 94–6)

SEPTEMBER 26. The U.S. Senate confirms, without debate, the nomination of Daniel J. Boorstin to be Librarian of Congress.

(CR 121:S16984)

SEPTEMBER 30. Lester S. Jayson, director of the Congressional Research Service, resigns to accept a teaching post.

(SA 714; LCIB 34:390)

OCTOBER 20–21. The Library sponsors a "Conference on the Publication of Poetry and Fiction." The conference is held under the auspices of the Gertrude Clarke Whittall Poetry and Literature Fund, with additional support from the National Endowment for the Arts.

(LCA; LCIB 34:435, 437–38)

NOVEMBER 12. In a ceremony held in the Library's Great Hall and attended by President Gerald R. Ford and Vice President Nelson A. Rockefeller, Daniel J. Boorstin takes the oath of office as the 12th Librarian of Congress. Presiding officer for the ceremony is Representative Lucien N. Nedzi of Michigan, chairman of the Joint Committee on the Library. The oath, taken on the Thomson Bible from the Jefferson collection, is administered by the Speaker of the House of Representatives, Carl Albert. The Library of Congress has a book collection of nearly 17 million volumes, a staff of 4,500, and an appropriation in fiscal 1976 of over $116 million.

(LCA; LCIB 34:445–49)

Sources for Further Study

General

David C. Mearns once described the Library of Congress as perhaps "the most completely fenestrated institution of its kind in the world" (*Library Trends* 4 [July 1955]:105). The Library's extensive documentation of its own activities, principally in the *Annual Report of the Librarian of Congress* (1866–), the weekly *Library of Congress Information Bulletin* (1942–), and the *Quarterly Journal of the Library of Congress* (1943–), furnishes the student with an almost overwhelming amount of information. Furthermore, since 1897 the Library has published several thousand specialized bibliographies, pamphlets, catalogs, indexes, and descriptive guides which contain detailed information about the Library and its collections. The older publications can be located through the Library's card catalog; information about the availability of recent publications is in the annual *Library of Congress Publications in Print*. The 1975 edition of this booklet lists 395 publications, 43 folk recordings, and 28 literary recordings.

The most informative and liveliest general book about the Library is Charles A. Goodrum's account, *The Library of Congress* (New York: Praeger Publishers, 1974). This volume includes an extensive bibliography of secondary readings about the Library and its activities. Mary C. Lethbridge and James W. McClung have presented an interesting overview in their article "The Library of Congress," *Encyclopedia of Library and Information Science*, vol. 15 (New York: Marcel Dekker, 1975), pp. 19–93. "The Library of Congress: The Nation's Bookcase," *National Geographic Magazine* 148 (November 1975): 671–87, is a recent, popular account by Fred Kline.

Historical Development

Documentation of the Library's activities has not always been as abundant as it is today. In fact, the Library's own records were not systematically preserved until the advent of Herbert Putnam's librarianship in April 1899. For this reason the Library's archives for the 19th century are generously described as being miscellaneous in nature. Nonetheless, there are two series of early records that are especially important: the Librarians' Letterbooks, 19 volumes containing correspondence—letters sent—from 1843 to 1886 and from 1897 to 1899; and 13 volumes of incoming correspondence received during the administration of John Russell Young, July 1897–January 1899. Other items of special interest include a volume of extracts from the minutes of the Joint Committee on the Library, 1861–98; unpublished annual reports of the Librarian of Congress for 1861 and 1862; and a group of ledgers, receipts, and correspondence relating to the construction of the Main Building of the Library, 1889–97.

Until the librarianship of Ainsworth Rand Spofford (1865–97), there was comparatively little communication between the Library of Congress and other libraries. After 1870, however, Spofford's administration was increasingly dominated by copyright matters—which is why so little official correspondence can be found on any other topic. Most of the incoming copyright correspondence, applications, and receipts have been preserved in the Copyright Office archives.

A thorough record of the Library's official activities has been maintained since the beginning of Putnam's administration. The major record groups of the official Putnam archives describe subsequent records as well. They include Librarian's letterbooks, general orders and special orders issued by the Librarian, correspondence and financial records relating to the Library's budget, appropriation hearings and reports, acquisitions correspondence and files, interlibrary loan records, correspondence and records kept by individual administrative units, and miscellaneous scrapbooks, ledgers, and memorandum books.

Special note should be taken of the annual appropriation hearings, which have been published since the 1890s. These documents contain information available nowhere else and provide an important perspective on the hopes and plans of the various Librarians. In addition, the 1896 hearings on the reorganization of the Library (*Condition of the Library of Congress*, U.S. Senate Report 1573) are a landmark in the history of the Library and in the history of American librarianship. Other congressional documents on topics concerning the Library, such as the construction of the Main Building (1888) and the creation of the Legislative Reference Service (1913), should not be overlooked, nor should the published hearings on the confirmation of Librarian L. Quincy Mumford (1954) and the confirmation of Librarian Daniel J. Boorstin (1975).

The Prints and Photographs Division is the custodian of the Library's photographic archives. Of special interest is an extensive series of photographs taken during the construction of the Main Building, 1886–97. Herbert Small's *Handbook of the New Library of Congress* (Boston: Curtis & Cameron, 1897) is still the best guidebook to the Main Building. Those interested in the history of this magnificent structure should consult the October 1972 issue of the Library's *Quarterly Journal*.

The Librarian of Congress has a remarkable degree of autonomy in administering and shaping the Library. The personal papers of the various Librarians both supplement and illuminate the official records. The Library's Manuscript Division holds the papers of George Watterston, Ainsworth Rand Spofford, John Russell Young, Herbert Putnam, Archibald MacLeish, Luther H. Evans, and L. Quincy Mumford. In addition, correspondence from John Silva Meehan can be found in the George Watterston Papers. Access to the Evans Papers is restricted. Between April 1975 and July 1976, the Library of Congress *Quarterly Journal* is publishing a series of biographical articles about the 11 men who occupied the office from 1802 until 1974.

The best published source for the history of the Library of Congress is, not surprisingly, the *Annual Report of the Librarian of Congress* (1866–). The reports for the years 1897 through 1946 are especially rich in historical materials. Three volumes are of particular interest: Herbert Putnam's 1901 report, the most comprehensive in the Library's history; Archibald MacLeish's 1940 report, which describes MacLeish's formulation of a set of objectives for the Library and his impending reorganization; and Luther Evans' 1946 report, which includes the Librarian's sweeping budget request and justification for fiscal 1947 and David C. Mearns' brief but delightful history, *The Story up to Now; the Library of Congress, 1800–1946*.

In addition to Mearns' history, which the Library published as a monograph, the student should consult William Dawson Johnston's *History of the Library of Congress, 1800–1864* (Washington: Library of Congress, 1904). Johnston's comprehensive volume reproduces many documents and reports concerning the Library; certain items used by Johnston have since disappeared, making this work a truly unique source.

The personal papers of both Mearns and Johnston, located in the Manuscript Division, contain material relating to their histories. Johnston's projected second volume never was completed, but several manuscript chapters are in his papers. Among the many other collections of personal papers of Library officials in the Manuscript Division, two are of particular value: the papers of Chief Assistant Librarian Frederick William Ashley and those of Verner W. Clapp. Clapp's special contributions to the Library are outlined in *Verner W. Clapp, 1901–1972: A Memorial Tribute* (Washington: Library of Congress, 1973).

Archibald MacLeish's article "The Reorganization of the Library of Congress, 1939–1944," *Library Quarterly* 14 (October 1944): 277–315, is a fascinating account of the Library's administrative history and structure. "The Library of Congress: A Sesquicentennial Review," *Library Quarterly* 20 (July–October 1950): 157–79, 235–58, is a trenchant historical analysis by Dan M. Lacy of the Library's acquisitions and reference functions. Almost every week of the sesquicentennial year of 1950, the Library of Congress *Information Bulletin* featured informative and amusing historical anecdotes compiled by the indefatigable David C. Mearns. The April 1971 issue of the Library's *Quarterly Journal* focuses on the history and the significance of the copyright function.

Finally, an interesting perspective on the Library's history can be gained from numerous recordings made by the Library. All are available in the Recorded Sound Section. An especially fertile period was the administration of Luther H. Evans, who took a personal interest in oral history and in the interpretation of the Library's past. Many recordings of the proceedings of meetings and orientations during the Evans years are available. Perhaps the most interesting, however, is a series of recordings made in late 1949 as the Library approached its sesquicentennial year. Librarian Evans, aided by his assistants Verner W. Clapp and David C. Mearns, undertook a recorded survey of the Library's functions through interviews with various specialists and division chiefs. In addition, Evans, Clapp, and Mearns interviewed each other about the Library's history and functions. The result is a unique group of recordings that combine historical facts with the personal opinions of the Library's principal officers. The interviews were broadcast during the 15-minute intermissions of the Library's chamber music concerts in the Coolidge Auditorium. A partial list of these recordings is found in the January 9, 1950, issue of the Library's *Information Bulletin*.

The Legislative and the National Roles

The question of the legislative and national responsibilities of the Library of Congress is perhaps the principal theme in most studies of the institution, including this one. In 1814 Thomas Jefferson asserted that the legislative and national roles of the Library were complementary, but that assertion has been debated from Jefferson's time until our own. The effect of the debate on the growth of the institution is outlined in my article "For Congress and the Nation: the Dual Nature of the Library of Congress," *QJ* 32 (April 1975): 118–38. There are dozens of documents and articles that provide important perspectives on this subject. Here is a list of those that I

have found to be most useful: Ainsworth Rand Spofford's plan for a separate Library building, *Annual Report of the Librarian of Congress for 1872*, pp. 6–11; Ainsworth Rand Spofford, "The Function of a National Library," in *Handbook of the New Library of Congress*, comp. by Herbert Small (Boston: Curtis & Cameron, 1897), pp. 123–28; the 1896 congressional hearings on the condition and future organization of the Library of Congress (U.S. Senate Report 1573), especially pp. 139–228; Richard R. Bowker, "The American National Library," *Library Journal* (August 1896): 357–58; "A Congressional or a National Library?" *Library Journal* (January 1897): 7–9; Herbert Putnam, "What May Be Done for Libraries by the Nation," *Library Journal* 26 (August 1901): C9–15; Herbert Putnam, "The Library of Congress as a National Library," *Library Journal* 30 (September 1905): C27–34; the establishment of the Legislative Reference Bureau, in the *Annual Report of the Librarian of Congress for 1914*, pp. 10–14; Librarian Archibald MacLeish's statement of objectives in the *Annual Report of the Librarian of Congress for 1940*, pp. 20–29; the response of Librarian Luther H. Evans to congressional questions about the Library's functions, *Annual Report of the Librarian of Congress for 1946*, pp. 11–12, 307; the report of the Library of Congress Planning Committee, *Annual Report of the Librarian of Congress for 1947*, pp. 101–8; the Douglas W. Bryant memorandum on the Library of Congress and the response of Librarian L. Quincy Mumford, *Annual Report of the Librarian of Congress for 1962*, pp. 89–111; a statement prepared by the staff of the Library for the National Advisory Commission on Libraries, "The Library of Congress as the National Library: Potentialities for Service," in *Libraries at Large: Tradition, Innovation, and the National Interest*, ed. by Douglas M. Knight and E. Shepley Nourse (New York: R. R. Bowker, 1969), pp. 435–65; and the remarks of Congressman Lucien N. Nedzi, President Gerald Ford, and Librarian of Congress Daniel J. Boorstin at Librarian Boorstin's swearing-in ceremony, which are in the *Library of Congress Information Bulletin* of November 21, 1975 (34:458–61).

Index

Subentries in this index are arranged chronologically according to the order of their first appearance in the text.

☆ U.S. GOVERNMENT PRINTING OFFICE: 1978 O–588–010

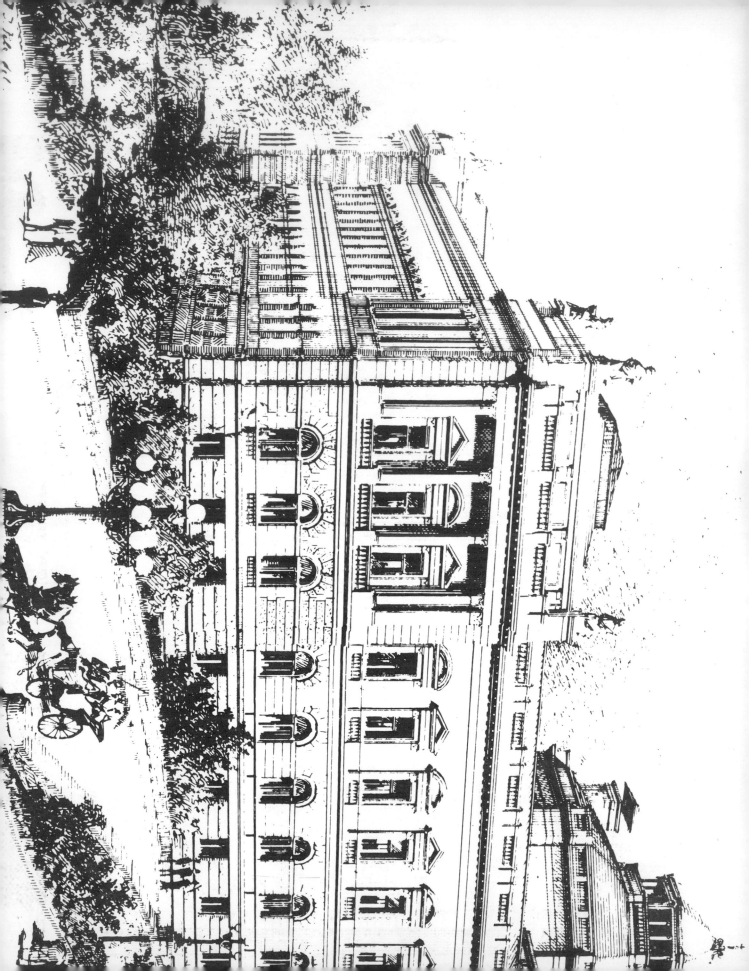

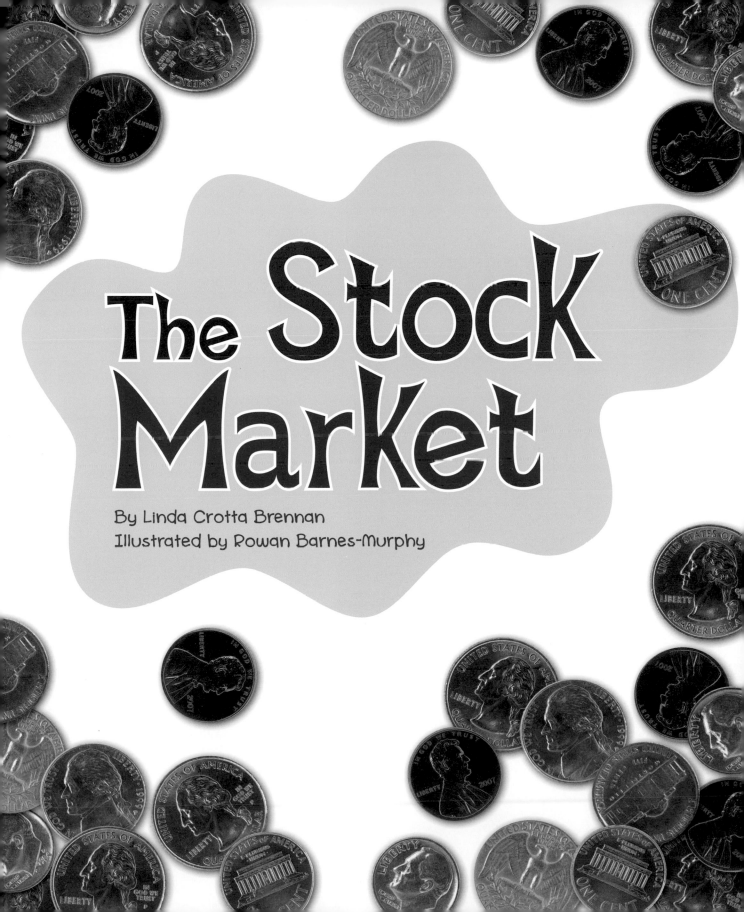

The Stock Market

By Linda Crotta Brennan

Illustrated by Rowan Barnes-Murphy

The Child's World®

Published by The Child's World®
1980 Lookout Drive • Mankato, MN 56003-1705
800-599-READ • www.childsworld.com

Acknowledgments
The Child's World®: Mary Berendes, Publishing Director
The Design Lab: Design and production
Red Line Editorial: Editorial direction

Design elements: Eric Krouse/Dreamstime

ISBN 9781614732464
LCCN 2012932828

Printed in the United States of America
Mankato, MN
July 2012
PA02122

About the Author

Linda Crotta Brennan has a master's degree in early childhood education. She has taught elementary school and worked in a library. Now, she is a full-time writer. She enjoys learning new things and writing about them. She lives with her husband and goofy golden retriever in Rhode Island. She has three grown daughters.

About the Illustrator

Rowan Barnes-Murphy has created images and characters for children's and adults' books. His drawings have appeared in magazines and newspapers all over the world. He's even drawn for greeting cards and board games. He lives and works in Dorset, in southwest England, and spends time in rural France, where he works in an ancient farmhouse.

Mia checked the cash box. "Wow, we made a lot of money from our lemonade stand!"

"Great! Maybe we should open another one," Tomás said.

Mia tapped her chin. "Hmm . . . we could. We'll need wood to make another stand. We'll need more signs, too. And we may have to pay someone to work at the new stand."

Tomás wrinkled his nose. "We don't have enough money for all that."

What might Tomás and Mia do to get money? They could borrow money. But then they'd have to pay it back. Is there another way they could raise money?

There is! They could sell **stocks**. A stock gives someone a **share**, or part ownership, in a business. Sharing ownership also means Mia and Tomás could share expenses.

Mia and Tomás decided to sell ten shares in their business. They each bought three shares. They sold the other four shares. Tomás's Uncle Tito bought two shares. Jack, their friend and classmate, bought one share. Molly, Mia's older sister, also bought one share. These people **invested**, or gave money, to help Mia and Tomás's business grow.

Mia and Tomás sold ten shares. They each bought three. That gives each of them 30% of the company: $3/10 = .3 = 30\%$. Uncle Tito bought two shares, so he has 20% ownership: $2/10 = .2 = 20\%$. Jack and Molly each own 10% because they bought 1 share: $1/10 = .1 = 10\%$.

Tomás hammered in the last nail on their new stand. "Don't we have to pay our **investors** back?" he asked.

"No, we don't. Instead, they get part ownership of the business. They get to vote on who runs our business," said Mia as she tacked on their sign. "And investors get part of our earnings. Those are called **dividends**."

After a few weeks, Mia and Tomás's new lemonade stand started to earn money. They put part of their earnings back into the business. After buying lemons and sugar, they had $10 left over to pay dividends.

Mia and Tomás each earned $3 in dividends—$1 for each share they own. Uncle Tito earned $2, and Jack and Molly each earned $1.

CHECKOUT

The size of an investor's dividend depends on how many shares the person owns.

12

Mia and Tomás couldn't pay dividends every month. Sometimes, they needed all their earnings to help the business grow. At the end of each month, Mia and Tomás reported their earnings to their investors. They let investors know if there were dividends.

"We know you won't always make a **profit**," said Uncle Tito. "We want your business to do well."

"That's right," said Molly. "That will give us another way to make money. We bought our shares at a low price. If you're successful, we'll be able to sell the shares for a higher price."

Molly had paid $6 for her share in the lemonade stand. After a few months, she sold her share to Mr. Smith, her neighbor and softball coach, for $10. Buying her share for $6 and selling it for $10 earned Molly $4.

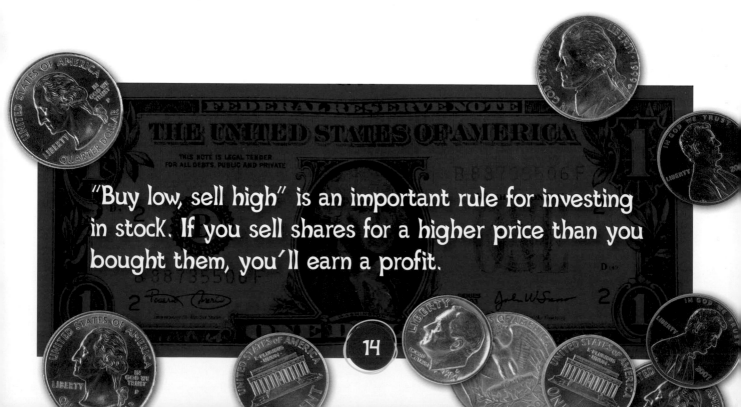

"Buy low, sell high" is an important rule for investing in stock. If you sell shares for a higher price than you bought them, you'll earn a profit.

Mr. Smith attended the next investor meeting instead of Molly. He explained that he had bought Molly's share.

"So, the price of a share can go up or down?" Tomás asked.

"That's right," said Mr. Smith. "The price is higher if a business is making lots of money. The price of a share also depends on how many people want to buy them. If many people want to buy shares, the price will be higher. If only a few people want to buy them, the price will be lower."

"Our new lemonade stand is making lots of money. We should open more," said Mia. "I wish there were a place where we could sell shares to thousands and thousands of people."

"There is a place like that," said Uncle Tito. "It's the stock market. It's where people can buy and sell shares in different companies."

"Where is it? How can we get there?" asked Tomás.

You don't have to travel anywhere," Uncle Tito said. "You can buy stocks online. You can also use a stockbroker. This person buys and sells stocks for others."

"So, they spend other people's money?" said Tomás. "That could be fun."

"It isn't a game," Uncle Tito replied. "There are risks. You can make money if the price of your stocks goes up. But you can lose money if the price goes down."

"Yes!" Mr. Smith added. "I invested in the High Style Sneakers Company. After a while, their sneakers went out of style. I lost a lot of money."

Stockbrokers have to know a lot about the stock market. They have to pass a special test and get a license. That's because they need to help their customers make wise choices.

19

The Dow Jones Industrial Average reports whether most stock prices are going up or down. A plus sign before the number means prices went up. A minus sign means they went down. Find today's Dow Jones Industrial Average. You can look for it in the newspaper. Is today's stock market bullish or bearish?

Later that day, Mia and Tomás were at Mia's house watching television. Mia shook her head as she watched the news. "That big earthquake may cause trouble with the stock market."

"Why?" Tomás asked.

"Dad told me that when good things happen, investors are happy. They buy more stocks and prices rise. That's a bull market." Mia made bull horns, pointing up, with her fingers. "When bad things happen, investors get worried. They sell their stocks and prices go down. That's a bear market."

Tomás pretended to be a bull and charged at Mia. "Let's hope for a bull market!" he cried.

Mia dodged Tomás on the way to the kitchen. There, she got a pitcher from the cupboard. "Good thing people always want lemonade!"

Tomás measured in the sugar. "We're making lots of money now, and we'll make even more when we open the stand by the baseball field."

"Our business is a good **investment**," Mia said as she stirred.

Tomás nodded. "I bet we'd be a big success on the stock market."

Imagine you want to invest in a company. What kind of company would you look for? What things do you, your family, and your friends like to buy? Do you think people will want to buy those things in the future? What company makes those products? Make a list of those companies. Maybe you'd like to invest in some of them.

Glossary

dividend (DIV-i-dend): A portion of money earned by an investment is a dividend. When the lemonade stand is successful, its investors earn dividends based on the number of shares they own.

invest (in-VEST): To invest is to give money to a company with the hope of getting more money back in the future. Uncle Tito invested in the lemonade stand when he bought shares of stock.

investment (in-VEST-mint): Something a person can or has given money to, such as a business from which they hope to get more money later is an investment. Mia and Tomás think their lemonade stand is a good investment.

investor (in-VEST-er): Someone who gives money to a company is an investor. Uncle Tito, Molly, and Jack are investors in Mia and Tomás's lemonade stand.

profit (PRAH-fit): The profit is the money left over after expenses have been paid or when something is sold for more than it was purchased. Molly sold her share of stock in the lemonade stand for more than she paid for it and made a profit.

share (shair): A share is a single piece of ownership in a company. Uncle Tito, Molly, and Jack bought shares of stock in Mia and Tomás's lemonade stand.

stock (stahk): Owning stock in a company gives you part ownership of the company. Uncle Tito bought stock in Mia and Tomás's lemonade stand.

Books

McGowan, Eileen Nixon, and Nancy Lagow Dumas. *Stock Market Smart*. Brookfield, CT: Millbrook, 2002.

Orr, Tamra. *A Kid's Guide to Stock Market Investing*. Hockessin, DE: Mitchell Lane, 2008.

Roman, Rick. *I'm a Shareholder Kit: The Basics about Stocks for Kids and Teens*. 3rd ed. Gilbert, AZ: Leading Edge Gifts, 2009.

Web Sites

Visit our Web site for links about the stock market:
childsworld.com/links

Note to Parents, Teachers, and Librarians: We routinely verify our Web links to make sure they are safe and active sites. So encourage your readers to check them out!

Index

PLANETS, STARS, AND
GALAXIES

A VISUAL ENCYCLOPEDIA OF OUR UNIVERSE

WRITTEN AND ILLUSTRATED BY
DAVID A. AGUILAR

CONTRIBUTING WRITERS CHRISTINE PULLIAM & PATRICIA DANIELS

**NATIONAL
GEOGRAPHIC**

WASHINGTON, D.C.

TABLE OF CONTENTS

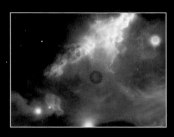

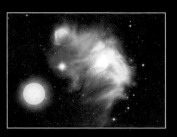
*Art preceding pages: Page 1, A decorative composite of a planet, star, and galaxy;
Pages 2–3, An alien world and its moon in the heart of the Milky Way*

ARE WE ALONE? 148

DREAMS OF TOMORROW 162

ABOUT THE ILLUSTRATIONS

The art for this book was created by David Aguilar on his computer. He began by gathering the best scientific information available. Using that information, he sketched images that were as realistic as possible in his notebook. Then he transferred those sketches to his computer and painted with his mouse, using Adobe PhotoShop and building up layer on layer, until his vision of space appeared. Sometimes he built models of spaceships out of junk plastic found around his house (again using the latest data to guide his hand). Or he made planetary landscapes out of torn pieces of paper towels dipped into watered-down plaster of Paris, then photographed them and colored them in Photoshop. In some cases he also incorporated images taken by telescopes and satellites into the art. Why do we even need artwork in a book about the real world? Sometime we don't. For example, we have very good photographs of Mars, but there are many other places (such as extra-solar planets) and many perspectives (such as gazing at Jupiter from the surface of Europa) and possible future events (such as astronauts visiting Uranus's moon Miranda) that we can only visualize by turning scientific data into art. Some of these imaginary images will never actually be seen, because no telescope is capable of photographing them.

The photographs in this book were taken by satellites and telescopes, as well as by cameras here on Earth. Most came from NASA, the National Aeronautics and Space Administration.

In the "To The Stars & Beyond" chapter, when a picture of a constellation, galaxy, or nebula has the binocular symbol beside it, that means you can use your own binoculars to look for the object in the night sky.

As you read *Planets, Stars, and Galaxies,* I expect you'll begin to imagine what it would be like to soar high above Earth, to explore faraway planets or even the vast reaches of our galaxy, the Milky Way.

In April 2001, I was fortunate enough to realize a dream I had been pursuing since I was a teenager—to fly in space. As a crew member of the Russian Soyuz TM-32 spacecraft, I traveled to the International Space Station, where I spent one of the most amazing weeks of my life. Not even my months of training could prepare me for the awe and wonder I felt at seeing our beautiful Earth, the fragile atmosphere at its horizon, and the vast blackness of space against which it is set.

Unlike my generation, people your age will have much greater access to space travel. In the future, it won't be something that just trained astronauts and scientists get to do. With the commercialization of space travel, many more individuals will have an opportunity to experience what I did— weightlessness and the freedom of effortless movement you feel as you soar above Earth.

We humans are essentially explorers, so we'll always be interested in what lies just beyond the next hill or sea— or star. At some point, we'll exhaust Earth's resources, and we'll need to expand the reaches of our civilization to survive. In other words, we won't just visit the moon and other planets, we'll live in space.

I hope you'll be inspired to explore as you read *Planets, Stars, and Galaxies,* and that one day you'll join the ranks of those who can say they have traveled beyond the bonds of Earth. Safe travels.

DENNIS A. TITO
First Space Tourist

The Horsehead Nebula seen from the moon of a nearby planet (art left)

Growing up in the Santa Clara Valley in California, I lived in a dreamland for anyone in love with nature. Orchards full of quail and pheasant stretched as far as a young person could hike in a day. The white, pink, and blue blossoms of fruit trees filled the air when gentle breezes blew in from the Pacific Ocean. Half an hour away, tide pools and clear cold waters awaited the young underwater explorer. It was a nature lover's paradise.

My bedroom was filled with insect collections, pressed wildflowers, fossils, terrariums, and model airplanes. On the walls were posters and drawings of planets and galaxies, and in the corner stood my trusty three-inch reflecting telescope, which I constructed all by myself (photo-illustration at right).

To make my telescope, I had used two glass casters "borrowed" from my grandmother's four-poster bed for the mirror. The casters were like small glass cups that people used to put beneath the legs of their beds so that the legs wouldn't scratch the floor. I had ground the casters together with abrasives purchased from a rock shop, then polished them using a mixture of water and jeweler's rouge on top of sticky pitch collected from our cherry tree.

My eyepiece was constructed from two slightly chipped lenses salvaged from the pirate spyglass my brother bought at the county fair. I glued the lenses inside the plastic top of a mouthwash bottle. My cardboard telescope tube came from the trash bin behind a carpet store, and my mount was made from scrap lumber and a few inexpensive plumbers pipe fittings. A little paint here and there, and I was in business exploring the universe.

My telescope worked better than anything Galileo used to make his discoveries. I named it Mable, after my grandmother.

The first thing I looked at was the moon. I saw craters, flat valleys, and mountains everywhere! Seeing the moons of Jupiter and the rings of Saturn opened my eyes and imagination in ways I had never experienced before. Little did I know that my hobby would someday become my career.

Besides telescopes, there was something else that drew me to astronomy. It was the mystery of UFOs. In my young mind the same question kept popping up: What if they are real? What if they really are out there?

Today, I am part of one of the largest astronomical research organizations in the world—the Harvard-Smithsonian Center for Astrophysics. Our observatories are located on mountaintops in Chile, Arizona, and Hawaii and in orbit above our heads in space. When I come to work each morning, I never know what great discovery may await me.

The discoveries astronomers make sometimes change the way we think about ourselves and our place in the universe. In the next 25 years we may know the answers to these really big questions: What caused the big bang? What invisible force is speeding up the expansion of the universe? Are there other universes out there besides our own? What type of life exists on other planets? Are there other "Earth-worlds" out there? And maybe, once and for all, what is this phenomenon we call UFOs all about?

This is why I love astronomy so much. The biggest questions regarding our universe are waiting to be answered. Somewhere out there in the world today are the future scientists who will find the answers to these great questions. Maybe one of them will be you.

DAVID A. AGUILAR

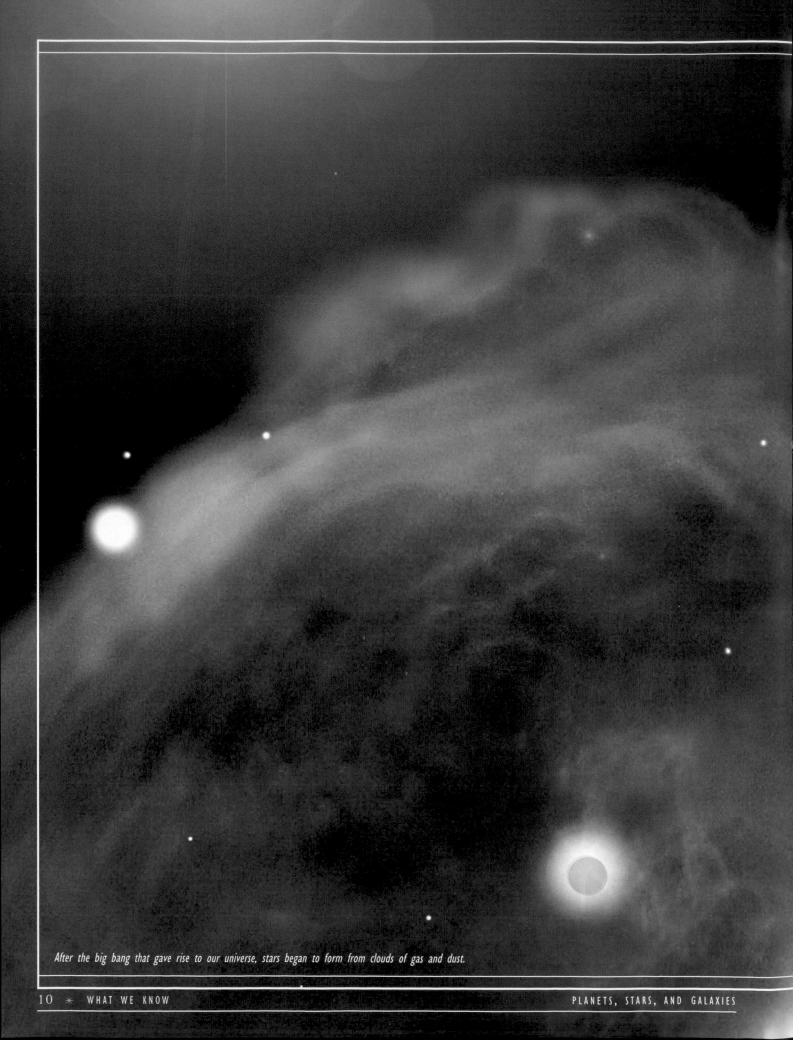

After the big bang that gave rise to our universe, stars began to form from clouds of gas and dust.

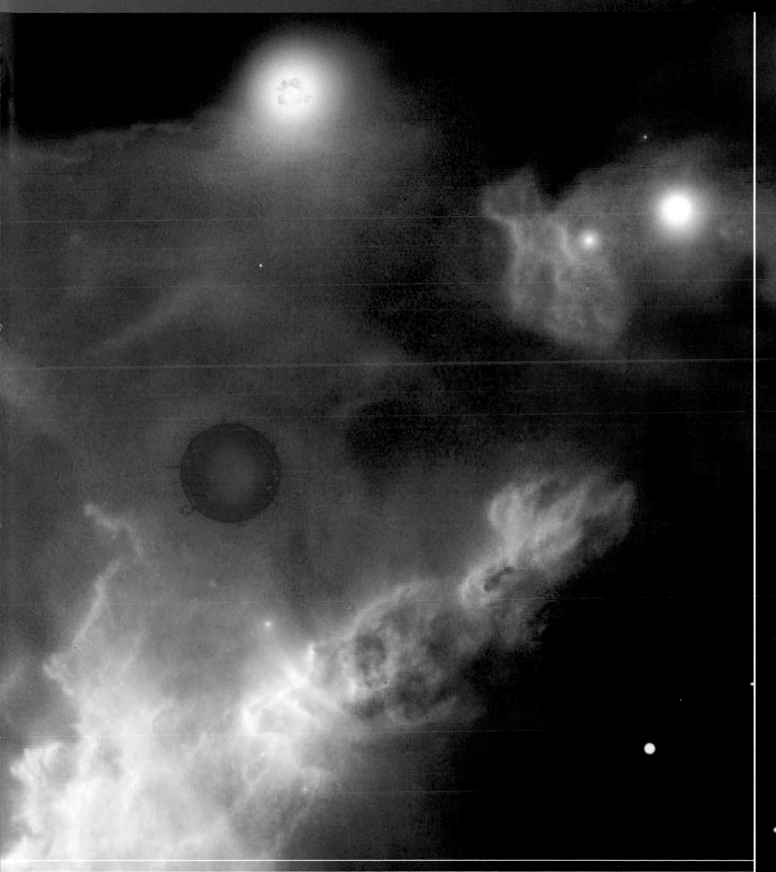

Clear your mind for a minute and try to imagine this: All the things you see in the universe today—all the stars, galaxies, and planets floating around out there—do not exist. Everything that now exists is concentrated in a single, incredibly dense point scientists call a singularity. Then, suddenly, the elements that make the material universe flash into existence. That actually happened about 13.7 billion years ago, in the moment we call the big bang.

For centuries scientists, religious scholars, poets, and philosophers wondered how the universe came to be. Was it always there? Will it always be the same, or will it change? If it had a beginning, will it someday end or will it go on forever?

These were huge questions. But today, because of our recent observations of space and what it's made of, we think we may have answers to some of them. We know the big bang created not only matter but space itself. And we think in the very distant future stars will run out of fuel and blink out. Once again the universe will become dark.

Everything we can see or detect around us in the universe began with the big bang. It wasn't a violent explosion like a stick of dynamite blowing up. Instead, it was like a giant balloon inflating.

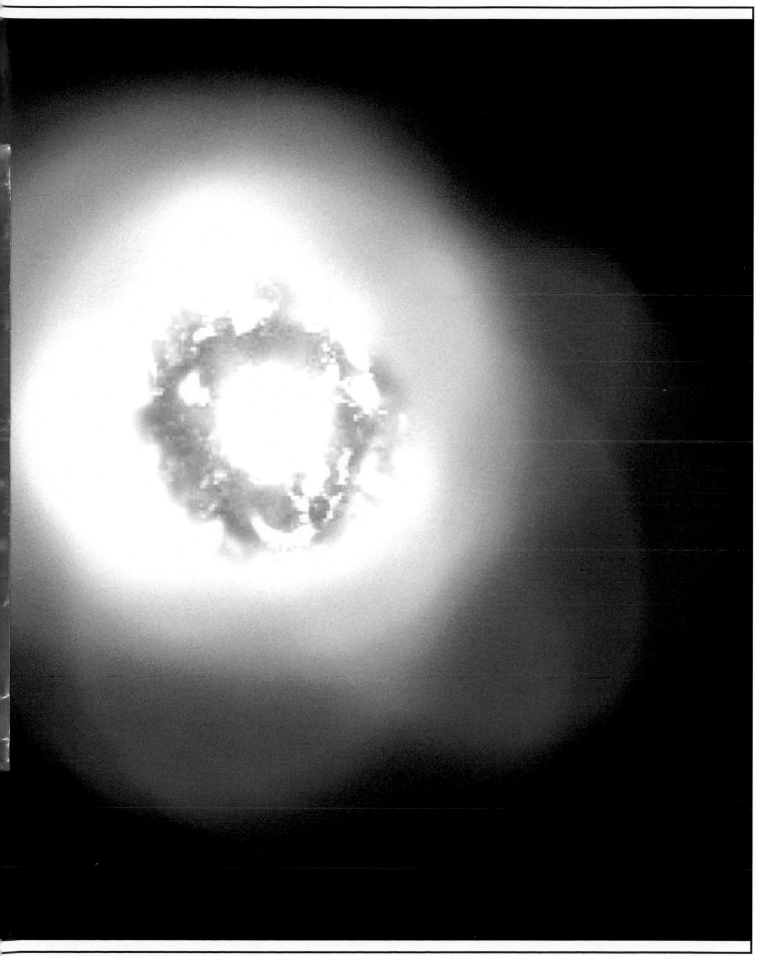

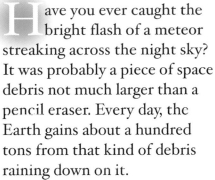
Have you ever caught the bright flash of a meteor streaking across the night sky? It was probably a piece of space debris not much larger than a pencil eraser. Every day, the Earth gains about a hundred tons from that kind of debris raining down on it.

Most of it is no bigger than a lemon, but not all. About 150 impact craters have been identified on Earth, created by falling objects larger than a house.

In 1908, in the air above a forest in the Tunguska region of Siberia, something exploded, flattening 80 million trees over an area of 830 square miles (2,150 sq km). Some 50,000 years ago, a meteor hit the desert in what is now southern Arizona, creating the Barringer Crater. It's three-quarters of a mile (1.2 km) in diameter and almost 600 feet (183 m) deep.

But the most dazzling collision came 65 million years ago, when a very large asteroid struck off the eastern coast of Mexico. That spectacular event changed global weather. Some scientists think the change in climate eventually led to the extinction of the dinosaurs.

A 5000°F (2760°C) fireball four miles (6.5 km) in diameter slams through our atmosphere (art left), its blinding light a hundred times brighter than the Sun. Could Earth get hit by an asteroid? Yes. More than 250 near-Earth asteroids cross our orbital path. Many have the potential to collide with us in the future.

Since the invention of the telescope in the 1600s, telescopes have shown that there is more to the universe than meets the eye. By magnifying the light of distant objects, telescopes can reveal previously unseen planets, stars, and galaxies.

The first telescopes collected visible light, or light we can see with our eyes. Even though astronomers could see more things with a telescope than without, all they could measure was how bright a star was and where it was located in the sky.

Then astronomers learned to split a beam of light into a rainbow of colors, called a spectrum. Different chemical elements leave different signatures on that spectrum, so astronomers could figure out what exactly celestial objects were made of. Helium was discovered when astronomers saw its signature in a spectrum of the Sun.

BEYOND THE VISIBLE

In the 1800s, scientists realized there was much more to see than just visible light. We call this invisible light "radiation," short for electromagnetic radiation. Beyond the red end of the visible spectrum, astronomers observed radiation they called infrared. Infrared light is less energetic, or "cooler," than visible light. At the opposite end of the spectrum, beyond

the violet, is ultraviolet radiation — the kind of light that causes sunburn. Ultraviolet light is more energetic than visible light.

Radio waves, x-rays, and gamma rays are all different kinds of radiation. By studying these different kinds of cosmic radiation, astronomers can learn how hot a star is, how fast it is moving, and how far away it is.

To collect different types of radiation, astronomers build different telescopes. Radio telescopes use dish-shaped antennas to listen to cosmic beeps and static hisses of radio waves. Earth's atmosphere blocks dangerous x-rays (lucky for us), so orbiting satellites are used to gather cosmic x-rays.

By observing all forms of radiation, astronomers learn more about the universe than they could from visible light alone.

Scheduled to launch in 2013, the James Webb Space Telescope (main art, left) will explore the infrared universe, orbiting a million miles from Earth. The Kepler Telescope (art above) launches in 2009 and will search for Earth-size planets circling distant stars.

Humans long believed that there were other planets out there in space, circling around distant stars. Scientists just never knew where to look for them. In the past five years, though, all that has changed. Today astronomers have identified almost 300 different stars with orbiting planets. Yet none of these solar systems looks like ours. Instead of small rocky worlds with orbits close to their stars, most of the planets in these other systems are frozen giants like Jupiter and Saturn. They migrated in from deeper space and pushed any smaller planets, like Mars, Earth, and Venus, into their suns. So the smaller planets in these systems have been vaporized.

In the next ten years scientists will probably begin finding the first Earthlike worlds out there, but don't be surprised if they're not copies of our own planet. Some will be much larger in size, maybe even five or six times larger than Earth. Some will be completely cloaked in ice, and others will be covered with global oceans. Will there be life on them? That may be known within the next ten years, too!

This art imagines an icy planet with a kind of life (bottom left) that has a very different way of sensing its surroundings than the way life does on Earth. There may be millions of Earthlike planets just in our own Milky Way Galaxy, with all kinds of life we've never dreamed of.

As our spaceship passes Neptune, the sunlight is bright, even though the Sun is nearly three billion miles away.

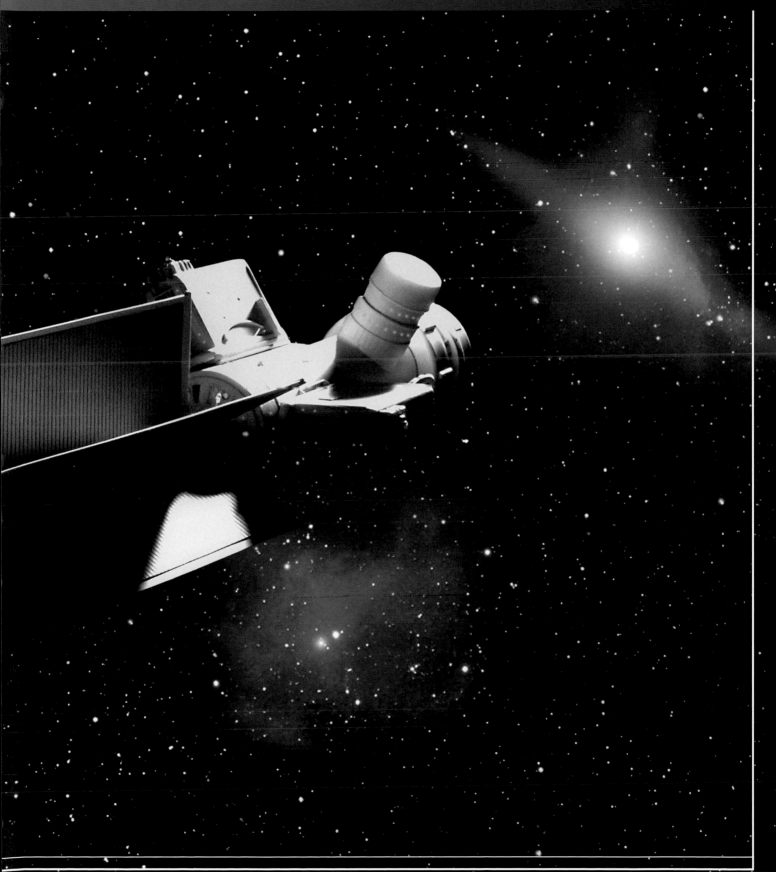

Sun

Mercury

Venus

Earth

Mars

Ceres

Jupiter

The solar system is made up of planets, asteroids, and comets orbiting around a star we call the Sun. Our star system formed 4.6 billion years ago from a nebular cloud, a large, spinning cloud of gas and dust. Today, astronomers divide the solar system into three different categories of planets,

based on their size and density. Orbiting closest to the Sun are the small, dense, rocky worlds of Mercury, Venus, Earth, and Mars. If they were dropped into a gigantic tub of water, they would sink. We call them the terrestrial planets—a word taken from the Latin word *terra,* which means land.

Beyond the terrestrial planets lies the asteroid belt, filled with small rocky asteroids and our fifth planet, Ceres. It's a dwarf planet, a category established in 2006 by the International Astronomical Union.

Next come the gas giants— Jupiter, Saturn, Uranus, and Neptune. They're large,

Saturn

Uranus

Neptune

Pluto

Eris

surrounded by rings and multiple moons, and made out of gases. Astronomers call them the Jovian planets, after the Roman god Jove, which is another name for Jupiter.

Past the gas giant planets, extending far out into space, is the Kuiper belt, an area filled with comets and other galactic

debris. Also orbiting the Sun in the Kuiper belt are Pluto; its moon, Charon; and our 11th planet, Eris. Like Ceres in the asteroid belt, these are now classified as dwarf planets. They're made of a mixture of ice and rock.

This artwork shows the 11 planets that astronomers now recognize in our solar system. The relative sizes of the planets are also shown but not the relative distances between them or their true placements as they orbit the Sun. Many of the planets, except the ones far from the Sun, can be seen without a telescope in the night sky.

THE GRAND TOUR

Longer than most luxury cruise ships traveling Earth's oceans, our imaginary voyager, *Stella Nova*, which means new star, will take us to the dwarf planet Eris in the farthest reaches of the solar system. Our crew consists of a captain, a chief pilot and navigator, a flight engineer, a medical doctor, two scientists, a payload specialist, and two lucky guests. The total number of crew members isn't much more than what's usually on board the space shuttle today.

This will be mostly a sight-seeing and reconnaissance tour, so we'll spend a lot of time simply observing. Much of what needs to be done will be done by the computers on board the ship. Even the flight plan is locked in, so *Stella Nova* will more or less fly itself. That's good, because

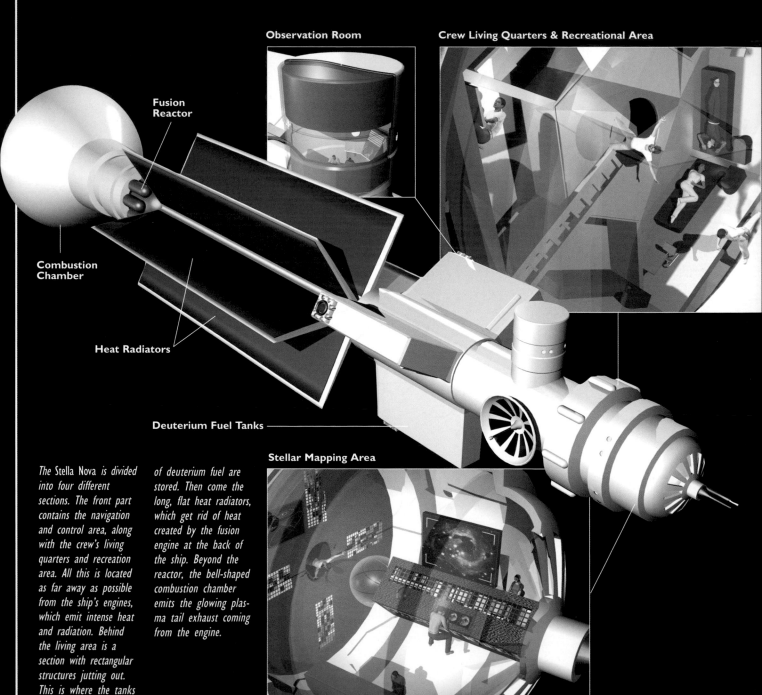

Observation Room

Crew Living Quarters & Recreational Area

Fusion Reactor

Combustion Chamber

Heat Radiators

Deuterium Fuel Tanks

Stellar Mapping Area

The Stella Nova is divided into four different sections. The front part contains the navigation and control area, along with the crew's living quarters and recreation area. All this is located as far away as possible from the ship's engines, which emit intense heat and radiation. Behind the living area is a section with rectangular structures jutting out. This is where the tanks of deuterium fuel are stored. Then come the long, flat heat radiators, which get rid of heat created by the fusion engine at the back of the ship. Beyond the reactor, the bell-shaped combustion chamber emits the glowing plasma tail exhaust coming from the engine.

whatever we try to do, from work to exercise, we'll have to do in zero gravity, which means we'll be floating through *Stella Nova* as we speed through space.

MOVING FAST

Our journey to the most distant planet now known will take only months instead of years, because our spaceship is powered by nuclear fusion. The nuclear reactor on board fuses deuterium, also called heavy hydrogen, and helium -3. This allows us to travel incredibly fast—at one percent the speed of light. Light travels at about 186,380 miles per second, so we'll be zooming along at six million miles per hour. At that speed we can complete a round-trip journey out to Eris and be back on Earth in just 60 days. By comparison, the space shuttle pokes along at 17,000 miles per hour, so the same trip now, without any stops, would take more than 70 years to complete.

Although the idea of a fusion-powered ship is already scientifically possible, building one isn't practical yet. We still need to develop the technology to contain the heat and radiation that fusion would generate. Scientists are working on this problem right now.

Our flight will take us in toward the Sun before we zoom out to the planets beyond Earth. We planned it that way to take advantage of something called "gravitational assist." This is how it works: We aim the ship at a particular angle when approaching a planet or the Sun. Gravity pulls us into that object's orbit, so we both accelerate and save on fuel. Passing the planet, we spin out of its orbit and shoot into space as if hurled by a giant slingshot. Many satellites already use this method to speed them along.

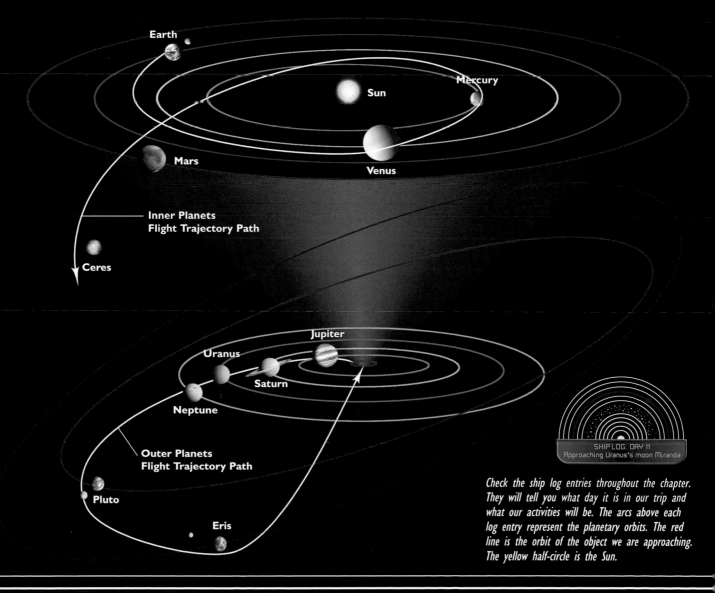

Earth

Sun   Mercury

Mars

Venus

Inner Planets
Flight Trajectory Path

Ceres

Jupiter

Uranus

Saturn

Neptune

Outer Planets
Flight Trajectory Path

Pluto

Eris

SHIP LOG: DAY 11
Approaching Uranus's moon Miranda

Check the ship log entries throughout the chapter. They will tell you what day it is in our trip and what our activities will be. The arcs above each log entry represent the planetary orbits. The red line is the orbit of the object we are approaching. The yellow half-circle is the Sun.

VENUS

S hining like a brilliant jewel in space, Venus has been called Earth's sister planet. Despite the fact that humans like to associate it with things of beauty, Venus has an eerie red landscape with thick clouds that choke out the sunlight.

Slightly smaller than Earth, Venus has a chemical composition similar to Earth's. In the past it may have been covered by oceans and may have had a moon. But today Venus is one of the most inhospitable planets in the solar system.

Blanketed in a cloud layer of carbon dioxide 40 miles thick, Venus has the densest atmosphere of any planet in the solar system, 90 times denser than Earth's atmosphere. Anyone venturing out onto the surface would be crushed like a paper cup—or toasted.

Venus's surface temperatures reach 872°F (467°C)— hot enough to melt lead. At the top of its clouds, winds roar at more than 200 miles (320 km) per hour. On the surface, though, the wind hardly blows. But the air has so much density that even a gentle breeze would push you along like a large ocean wave.

SHIP LOG 8 HOURS: Approaching Venus, radar reconnaissance of volcanism

FACTS ABOUT VENUS	
AVERAGE DISTANCE FROM THE SUN	67,230,000 miles (108,200,000 km)
POSITION FROM THE SUN IN ORBIT	SECOND
EQUATORIAL DIAMETER	7,520 miles (12,100 km)
MASS (EARTH = 1)	0.815
DENSITY (WATER = 1)	5.25
LENGTH OF DAY	243 Earth days
LENGTH OF YEAR	225 Earth days
AVERAGE SURFACE TEMPERATURE	864°F (462°C)
KNOWN MOONS	0

Earth

Venus

As our spaceship approaches it (art right), the golden crescent of Venus shines brilliantly because the planet's clouds reflect sunlight back into space. Beyond Venus, the stars of the Pleiades constellation, also called the Seven Sisters, sparkle in the sky.

U ntil the late 1950s, scientists believed Venus was a world covered by swamps and lush tropical jungles. Today, we know it doesn't look like that at all. Venus is one of the driest places in the solar system, with no trace of water. No need for weather predicting here. As far as astronomers can tell, rain never occurs. Falling droplets of sulfuric acid evaporate before they ever reach the ground. The temperature doesn't change between day and night. It is the same forecast all the time.

Venus's surface is pocked by large meteor craters ranging in size from 1.5 miles to 170 miles (2.4 to 270 km) across. There are no small craters because the thick atmosphere causes smaller meteorites to burn up before hitting the ground. Two large, flat highland areas may have been left behind from an earlier time, when there were ancient oceans on Venus. One in the northern hemisphere, Ishtar Terra, is about the size of Australia. Along the equator, Aphrodite Terra is about the size of South America.

A VOLCANIC WORLD

Volcanoes of every size and type rise from the planet's vast plains, and much of Venus is covered by lava. Almost 170 of these volcanoes are more

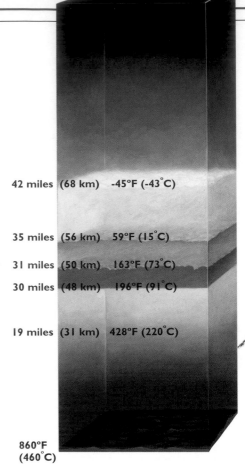

42 miles (68 km) -45°F (-43°C)

35 miles (56 km) 59°F (15°C)

31 miles (50 km) 163°F (73°C)

30 miles (48 km) 196°F (91°C)

19 miles (31 km) 428°F (220°C)

860°F (460°C)

Core: nickel-iron

Mantle: silicates

Crust: silicates

Like Earth, Venus has a nickel-iron core surrounded by a molten-rock mantle and crust. As this mantle of molten rock pushed up, it flowed out of volcanoes in the form of lava. The oldest surface features on Venus are less than 800 million years old.

Clouds form a thick blanket around Venus (art above), reflecting sunlight back into space and keeping the planet much cooler than it would be without them. But the high concentration of carbon dioxide in the atmosphere also traps heat, causing the greenhouse effect. Scientists are now concerned about the growing concentration of carbon dioxide in our own atmosphere.

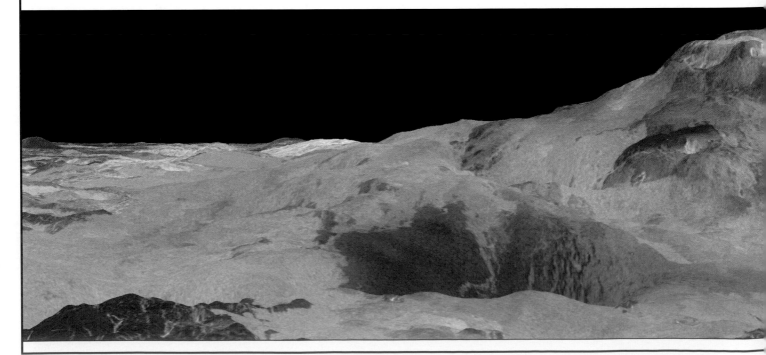

than 60 miles (97 km) wide.

The tremendous heat on Venus was the result of volcanic eruptions that released carbon dioxide into the atmosphere, creating the greenhouse effect. Scientists think rising temperatures caused Venus's ancient oceans to evaporate.

Some day, hundreds of millions of years from now, when the volcanic eruptions are far in the past, Venus will begin to cool, and oceans may form. They will help speed up the removal of carbon dioxide from the atmosphere by naturally dissolving it into the seawater, just as oceans do here on Earth. Venus may then be more Earthlike and become our true twin sister.

The landscape of Venus is 80 percent volcanic plains covered by strange dome-like structures that are the result of molten rock bulging out, then hardening. The shield volcano known as Gula Mons (art below) stands about 2.4 miles (4 km) high.

PHASES OF VENUS

Venus is the third brightest object in our sky, after the Sun and Moon. In fact, if you have a star chart and know where to look in the sky, you can spot Venus even in the daytime. The ancient Greeks believed it was two separate objects: Hesperos, the evening star, and Phosphoros, the morning star. Because its orbit is inside the Earth's, Venus can appear in both the early evening sky and the early morning sky.

Viewed from Earth, Venus goes through phase changes (art above), just like the Moon. When it is farthest away from us in its orbit, it looks smallest in size but fully illuminated by the Sun. In shape it resembles a full Moon. As it draws nearer to Earth, its size grows larger but its phase now resembles a thin crescent, so it looks dimmer to us.

When the astronomer Galileo first observed Venus in 1610, it was added proof that not everything in the heavens circled around Earth, as many believed. Galileo's observation was important evidence for the theory that Earth—and all the other planets—circled around the Sun.

You can easily watch Venus change phases over a period of weeks with a small telescope at 40x. It may appear slightly distorted with rings of yellow and purple around it because our thick atmosphere distorts light from Venus.

MERCURY

SHIP LOG 17 HOURS: Landing on Mercury, replace seismic monitors

The next planet on our tour is Mercury, the innermost and smallest of the rocky planets. Because it orbits so close to the Sun, this planet is usually lost in the Sun's glare and difficult to see from Earth. Traveling across the surface of Mercury will be a nightmare. The terrain is scarred with craters, high ragged walls, and old mountainous volcanoes.

Mercury's axis doesn't tilt, so the Sun shines directly on the equator, making it sizzling hot during the day and freezing cold at night. Temperatures can range from 800°F (427°C) in the sunlight to –300°F (–183°C) on the night side.

Mercury speeds around the Sun once every 88 Earth days, but it takes about 25 Earth weeks to go from sunrise to sunset. One day on Mercury is almost 176 Earth days long! Rotating three times on its axis for every two orbits around the Sun, Mercury also has bizarre sunrises and sunsets. If you were standing on Mercury's equator, you would see the Sun rise and set in different ways, depending on where you were. At some places, the Sun would rise toward its high point in the sky, then stop and reverse direction, seeming to set. Then it would stop and rise again, eventually getting smaller as it finally set in the west.

FACTS ABOUT MERCURY	
AVERAGE DISTANCE FROM THE SUN	35,980,000 miles (57,900,000 km)
POSITION FROM THE SUN IN ORBIT	FIRST
EQUATORIAL DIAMETER	3,030 miles (4,878 km)
MASS (EARTH = 1)	0.055
DENSITY (WATER = 1)	5.43
LENGTH OF DAY	176 Earth days
LENGTH OF YEAR	88 Earth days
SURFACE TEMPERATURES	-300°F (-183°C) to 800°F (427°C)
KNOWN MOONS	0

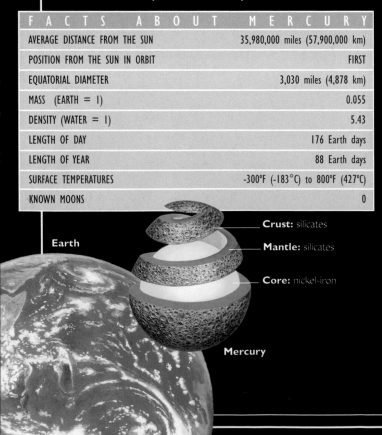

Earth

Crust: silicates

Mantle: silicates

Core: nickel-iron

Mercury

One day, as imagined here, astronauts may explore Mercury's Caloris Basin (art right), one of the largest craters in the solar system. Its diameter stretches 800 miles (1,287 km). It was created 400 million years ago, when a giant asteroid, with the impact of a trillion hydrogen bombs, slammed into the planet.

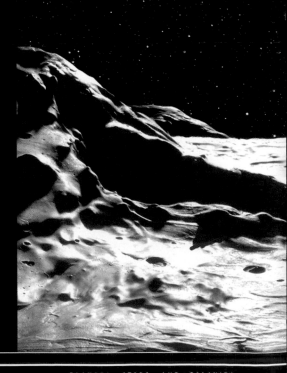

THE SUN

The Sun is a middle-age star about 4.6 billion years old. As the anchor that holds our solar system together, it provides the energy necessary for life to flourish on Earth. It accounts for 99 percent of the matter in the solar system. The rest of the planets, moons, asteroids, and comets added together amount to the remaining one percent.

Even though a million Earths could fit inside it, the Sun is still considered an average-size star. Betelgeuse (say BET-el-jooz), the star on the shoulder of Orion in that constellation, is almost 400 times larger. Like other stars, the Sun is a giant ball of hydrogen gas radiating heat and light

SHIP LOG DAY 2: Flyby of Sun, use gravitational assist to accelerate

through the process of nuclear fusion. Unlike nuclear fission, where atoms are split apart and create deadly radiation, fusion rams atoms together, producing cleaner and hotter reactions. Through fusion, the Sun converts about four million tons of matter to energy every second.

Also like other stars, the Sun revolves around its galaxy. Located halfway out in one of the arms of our Milky Way galaxy, the Sun takes 225 to 250 million years to complete one revolution around the galaxy.

FACTS ABOUT THE SUN	
DIAMETER	870,000 miles (1,390,000 km)
AVERAGE TEMPERATURE	9932°F (5500°C)
KIND OF STAR	Yellow G2
AGE	4.6 billion years

As our ship passes within a safe distance of the Sun, a giant solar flare erupts (art right). Traveling away from us millions of miles across space (art left), a solar flare unleashes more energy than all the atomic bombs ever exploded on Earth combined.

Earth

Sun

The Sun is composed of about 74 percent hydrogen, 25 percent helium, and one percent trace elements like iron, carbon, lead, and uranium. These trace elements provide us with an amazing insight into the history of our star. They're the heavier elements that are produced when stars explode. Since these elements are relatively abundant in the Sun, scientists know they were forged from the materials that came together in two previous star explosions. The Sun and all the elements that are found in it and on Earth and in our bodies were recycled from those two exploding stars.

When viewed in space by astronauts, our Sun burns white in color. But when we see it from Earth, through our atmosphere, it looks like a yellow star. When astronomers study the Sun's surface

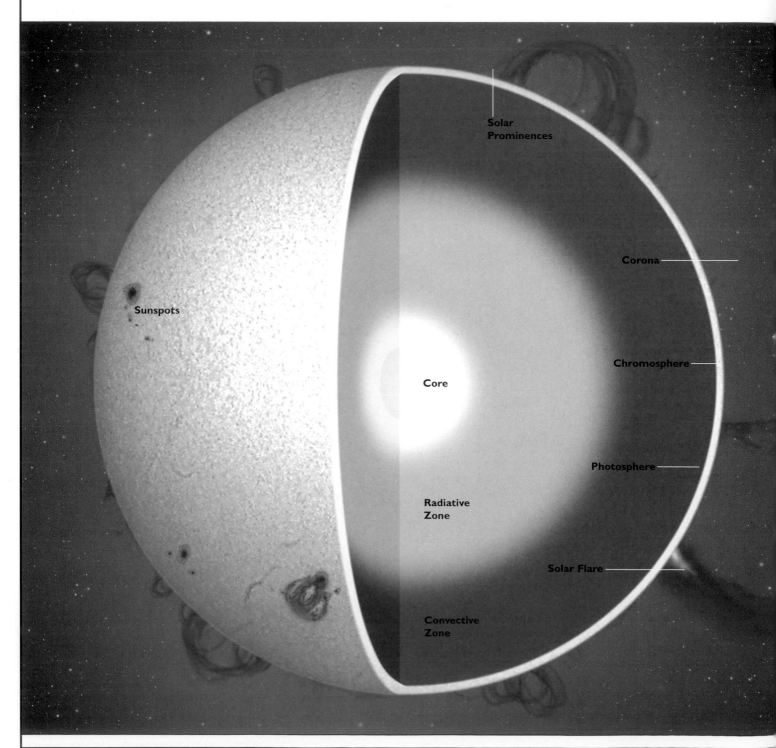

Solar Prominences

Corona

Chromosphere

Sunspots

Core

Photosphere

Radiative Zone

Solar Flare

Convective Zone

features, they see a much more complex structure than just a big bright ball of gas. Most obvious are the sunspots. These dark blotches are slightly cooler areas that appear darker against the hotter background. The surface of the Sun averages about 10,000°F (5000°C), while the sunspots average about 6000°F (3000°C). Out of these sunspots shoot loops, or prominences, of super-hot gas. They follow invisible magnetic lines that connect the sunspots together. Loops extend for hundreds of miles above the photosphere, or visible surface of the Sun. Solar flares, explosions of charged particles, sometimes erupt from the Sun's surface into the farthest reaches of space. They create beautiful aurora displays on Earth, Jupiter, Saturn, and even distant Uranus and Neptune.

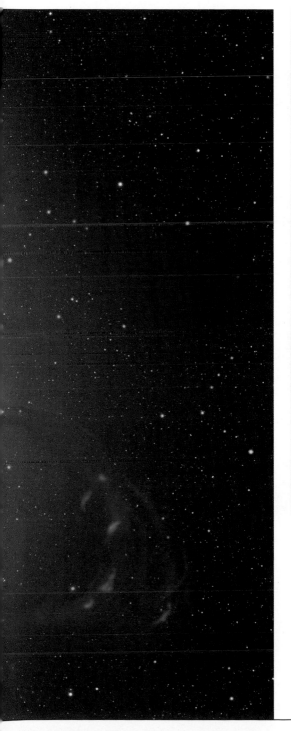

Above the Sun's visible surface, or photosphere, is the chromosphere (art left)—a layer about a thousand miles thick. Surrounding this is the corona, or crown. One of the big mysteries today is how the Sun's corona can be thousands of times hotter than its surface. Astronomers are still guessing.

In the satellite photograph above, the wispy streamers of gas in the Sun's corona are visible, extending millions of miles into space. On Earth, the corona is only visible during a total eclipse of the Sun.

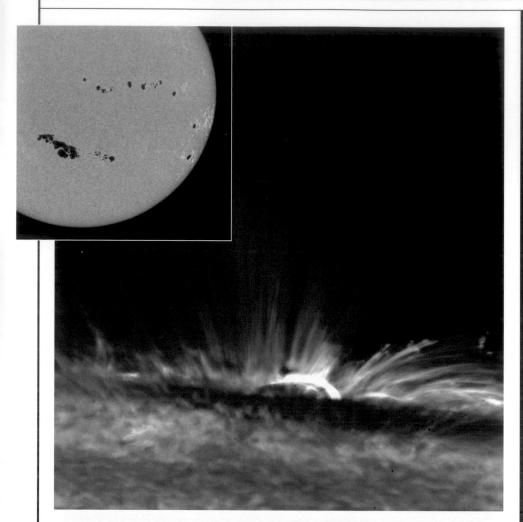

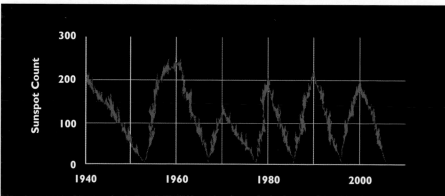

The Sun has a huge magnetic field that reverses direction every 11 years (graph above). Sunspots, slightly cooler areas on the photosphere (photo top left), respond to these cycle changes. The largest ones are almost twice the size of Earth. Their frequency varies on an 11-year cycle, too.

The photo at the top right shows a solar flare erupting near the edge of the Sun.

We know the Sun makes life possible here on Earth. We couldn't survive without it. But it causes problems, too.

On Oct 28, 2003, we found out just how serious those problems can be. A huge solar flare, pointed directly at Earth, shot highly charged energetic particles right at us, like bullets. Airplanes had to stop flying over the poles because passengers would have been exposed to increased radiation. A power blackout occurred in Sweden, and some satellites were damaged. Many others,

including the Hubble Space Telescope, had to be shut down and put into "safe" mode, to protect their delicate electronics.

As humans depend more and more on new technologies, they also face the prospect of overloaded power grids, a shutdown of electronic communications, and massive power blackouts caused by solar flares. Space travelers especially need to take extra precautions when one of these solar events occurs.

On dark winter nights, the northern sky (photo above) lights up with green and red waves of auroral displays shimmering overhead. Called aurora borealis, they're caused by charged particles in the solar winds colliding with atmospheric particles high above Earth.

MARS

SHIP LOG DAY 3: Approaching Mars, landing on its moon Phobos

Now we're coming to the planet nearest to Earth. Mars is also the size of Earth, and it has some of the most spectacular scenery in the solar system. Its soaring canyons would stretch across North America, and its skyscraping volcanoes overlook jumbled plains that may once have been shallow seas.

Mars also boasts polar ice caps, majestic sand dunes, impact craters formed millions of years ago, and dust devils that whirl around like small tornadoes. In the 19th century, astronomers began to think Martian engineers might have designed canals to crisscross the planet and bring water from the poles to Martian cities. That idea vanished when spacecraft reached Mars, but could it be capable of supporting microscopic life?

Liquid water is necessary for life on Earth. The atmosphere on Mars is so thin and the temperatures so cold that liquid water can't exist on the surface. It would quickly freeze or evaporate. That's why there are no oceans. But there are signs that underground water does occasionally flow onto the surface. Mars could well have hidden wet habitats that are capable of supporting life.

FACTS ABOUT MARS	
AVERAGE DISTANCE FROM THE SUN	141,633,000 miles (227,936,000 km)
POSITION FROM THE SUN IN ORBIT	FOURTH
EQUATORIAL DIAMETER	4,333 miles (6,794 km)
MASS (EARTH = 1)	0.107
DENSITY (WATER = 1)	3.93
LENGTH OF DAY	26 Earth hours
LENGTH OF YEAR	1.88 Earth years
SURFACE TEMPERATURES	-270°F (-133°C) TO 80°F (27°C)
KNOWN MOONS	2

Mars

Earth

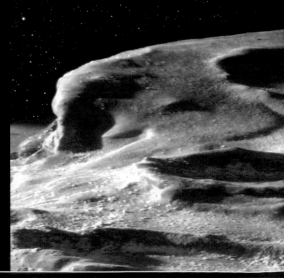

Mars looms like a great red sphere over the barren terrain of its largest moon, Phobos (art right), which orbits very close to the planet. Astronauts like those imagined here would have to be prepared for frigid nights.

An orange beacon in the night skies, Mars grows brighter and dimmer on a two-year cycle, as it moves closer to then farther away from Earth. Its distinctive color is due to iron oxide in the soil. Like a piece of metal left outside, Mars has rusted. Although there are no thunderstorms here, weather is extremely unpredictable. Out of nowhere, blinding dust storms can blow up and blanket the landscape for months. Temperature swings are also enormous. Noontime highs can reach 80°F (13°C) around the equator, then at night dip to –150°F

Mantle: silicates

Core: iron sulfide

Crust: silicates

Mars's rocky interior (art above) doesn't contain much metal, so the planet has only a tenth the mass of Earth and weak surface gravity, about a third what we experience on Earth.

(–101°C). Mars's two moons, Phobos and Deimos, appear to be captured asteroids. Unlike our Moon, these two tiny space rocks zip across the night sky.

STRANGE VOLCANOES
Martian volcanoes are not restricted in size by earthquakes and shifting ground the way Earth volanoes are, because

Besides gigantic volcanoes, Mars has the longest canyon in the solar system, the Valles Marinaris, seen as a dark slash around the planet's middle in the photo above. Measuring over 3,100 miles long (4,990 km), this huge system of valleys is some 120 miles (193 km) wide and 4 miles (6 km) deep. It was not carved by water but by the cooling and wrinkling of the landscape over time.

The photograph below was taken by one of the NASA rovers that landed on Mars in January 2004. They've sent back images of the rusty Martian terrain for a few years, far longer than NASA had expected.

Mars has no shifting subsurface plates. On Mars volcanoes can grow to a hundred times larger than they can on Earth. Soaring 15 miles (24 km) high, Olympus Mons is the largest of four enormous volcanoes located near Mars's equator. If we were to place the Rocky Mountains on top of the Himalaya and stack the Alps on top, it would almost equal the height of this one massive volcano!

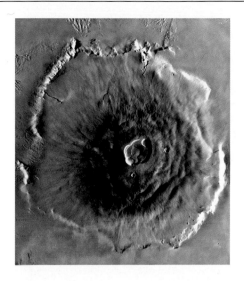

Olympus Mons (photo left) is a shield volcano, meaning it rises from the surface of the planet. The crater measures 57 miles (98 km) across, and the total area of the volcano is about the same as the state of New Mexico.

The photographs below were taken inside a crater in the southern hemisphere of Mars. Scientists think that the white streak in the one on the right, taken in 2005, is where flowing water from underground broke through to the surface, then quickly froze into a long piece of ice. The first image, taken in 1999, shows no ice markings.

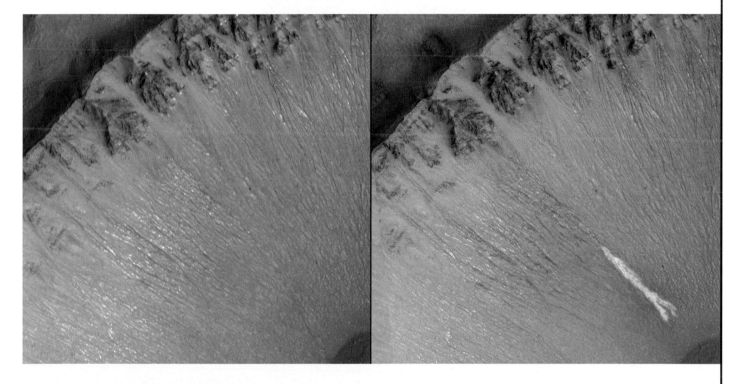

CERES & THE ASTEROID BELT

Ceres is one of our newly named dwarf planets, a classification established in 2006. Astronomers have known about Ceres since 1801. When it was first discovered, they thought it might be the "missing planet" that many astronomers believed orbited between Mars and Jupiter. For the next half a century it was called a planet. But then more and more large rocks, called asteroids, were discovered in that region of space. So Ceres was reclassified as an asteroid, and there it remained until its status changed to dwarf planet.

About 585 miles in diameter, roughly equal to the size of our moon, it's in the heart of

SHIP LOG DAY 4: Passing through asteroid belt, flyby of Ceres

the asteroid belt. Its mass is almost a third of the entire mass of the millions of asteroids in the belt.

Asteroids come in all shapes and sizes, but all of them orbit the Sun. Collisions between them happen a lot, but these relics of the early solar system aren't crammed together as they're sometimes shown in science fiction movies. Occasionally, the influence of Jupiter's gravity can nudge an asteroid out of orbit, sending it in toward the Sun. When that happens, the asteroid can strike one of the terrestrial planets.

FACTS ABOUT CERES	
AVERAGE DISTANCE FROM THE SUN	248,771,000 miles (400,358,000 km)
POSITION FROM THE SUN IN ORBIT	FIFTH
EQUATORIAL DIAMETER	585 miles (940 km)
MASS (EARTH = 1)	0.016
DENSITY (WATER = 1)	2.08
LENGTH OF DAY	9 Earth hours
LENGTH OF YEAR	4.60 Earth years
AVERAGE SURFACE TEMPERATURE	-159°F (-106°C)
KNOWN MOONS	0

Ceres

Earth

Ceres (top right in artwork, right) lies deep inside the asteroid belt between the planets Mars and Jupiter, by far the largest object found here. Ceres and more than 100,000 other rocky objects called asteroids are the debris left over from the formation of the solar system.

JUPITER

Can you imagine a planet with no ground to walk on? Or a world where a red hurricane three times the size of Earth has been raging for centuries? What about a planet where ferocious winds rip through the skies at 225 miles per hour (362 kph), brilliant bolts of lightning blast across the sky, and auroras dance around the poles?

That planet, Jupiter, is coming up next on our tour. The largest planet in the solar system, Jupiter is so big that all the other planets, including Saturn, could easily fit inside it and still have room to spare. With at least 63 moons circling around it, Jupiter is almost a

SHIP LOG DAY 5: Approaching Jupiter, landing on its moon Europa

miniature solar system by itself.

No matter what instruments we use to view Jupiter, we can only see the tops of its clouds. In essence, we're looking at the outside of a gigantic slushy snowball.

Some people have called Jupiter a failed star. They say that if Jupiter had been just a little bit bigger when it formed, nuclear fires would have ignited deep inside it, radiating heat and light just like our Sun. If that had happened, we would have had two suns in our sky instead of one.

FACTS ABOUT JUPITER	
AVERAGE DISTANCE FROM THE SUN	483,682,000 miles (778,412,000 km)
POSITION FROM THE SUN IN ORBIT	SIXTH
EQUATORIAL DIAMETER	86,880 miles (139,800 km)
MASS (EARTH = 1)	318
DENSITY (WATER = 1)	1.3
LENGTH OF DAY	9.9 Earth hours
LENGTH OF YEAR	11.9 Earth years
AVERAGE SURFACE TEMPERATURE	-235°F (-150°C)
KNOWN MOONS	at least 63

Jupiter

Earth

Standing on the frozen surface of Jupiter's moon Europa, space travelers (imagined in art, right) could peer into the Great Red Spot. This churning hurricane, almost three times the size of Earth, looks like a cosmic eye staring from the candy-striped world of Jupiter.

Days are very short on Jupiter. It spins so quickly on its axis that it makes one complete rotation every ten hours. Because it rotates so fast, it's not perfectly round. Egg-shaped, it bulges out around its equator like a spinning water balloon.

Composed of 90 percent hydrogen and almost 10 percent helium, its atmosphere would be poisonous for us to breathe. Here, little has changed since the planet formed 4.5 billion years ago.

Looking at Jupiter through a small telescope, we can easily see the two main features — the colored bands of clouds and the Great Red Spot.

The Great Red Spot (art below) is at least 300 years old, maybe older. Cyclonic storms like this are common on the gas giant planets and appear in a variety of colors. As we fly toward the Great Red Spot, we can see the moons Io (foreground) and Callisto (background).

Because of Jupiter's rapid rotation and solid metallic core, it generates the strongest planetary magnetic field in the solar system. The magnetic field, in turn, causes magnificent auroral displays that illuminate the northern and southern poles (art above).

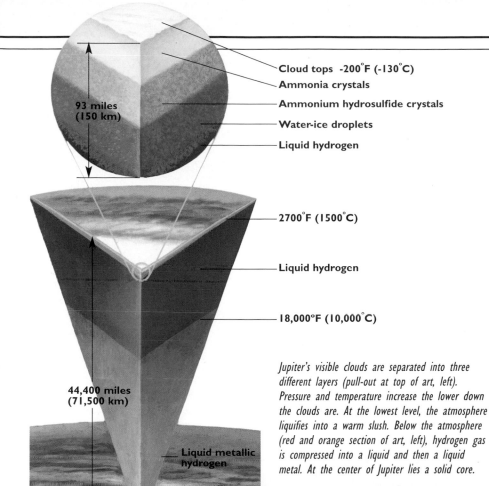

Cloud tops -200°F (-130°C)
Ammonia crystals
Ammonium hydrosulfide crystals
Water-ice droplets
Liquid hydrogen

93 miles (150 km)

2700°F (1500°C)

Liquid hydrogen

18,000°F (10,000°C)

44,400 miles (71,500 km)

Liquid metallic hydrogen

34,000°F (19,000°C)

Water & ammonia

Metallic Core   Molten rock

Jupiter's visible clouds are separated into three different layers (pull-out at top of art, left). Pressure and temperature increase the lower down the clouds are. At the lowest level, the atmosphere liquifies into a warm slush. Below the atmosphere (red and orange section of art, left), hydrogen gas is compressed into a liquid and then a liquid metal. At the center of Jupiter lies a solid core.

The white clouds are made of smelly frozen ammonia ice. The darker colored layers of brown, orange, and red are made of ammonium hydrosulfide. They would smell really bad, too, like rotten eggs. As Jupiter spins on its axis, the clouds are pulled into stripes and bands by fast-moving jet streams. The white bands around the equator rotate faster than the darker ones. Where their edges meet, they tear and pull at each other.

Jupiter has rings like Saturn, but they're too thin and faint to be seen from Earth. The rings are made of rocky material ejected from smaller moons.

Jupiter has at least 63 moons. The four largest can be seen through a pair of binoculars. They're called the Galilean moons because they were discovered by Galileo in 1610.

The first Galilean moon, Io, is located closest to Jupiter.

Almost the size of our Moon, it's the most geologically active body in the solar system. Jupiter's gravitational pull bends and stretches Io like taffy, causing intense heating inside. That causes volcanoes to erupt constantly on the surface.

Callisto is the most heavily cratered moon in the solar system. Its icy surface may be covering a salty ocean. If that ocean is liquid, Callisto would be a potential candidate for life in our solar system, but scientists suspect it is frozen solid.

ORBITS OF GALILEAN MOONS

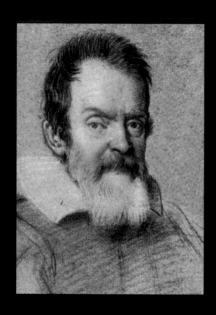

When medieval astronomer Galileo (art left) discovered Jupiter's moons Io, Europa, Ganymede, and Callisto in 1610, he called the four together the Medicean stars, in honor of his patron, Cosimo II de Medici, the Grand Duke of Tuscany. Galileo was hoping that, by conferring this honor on his patron, the grand duke would give him more money, so that his future research could be funded in style.

Galileo gave each moon a number instead of a name. But as more and more moons were discovered, the numbering system became a cumbersome way to refer to them. Finally, in the mid-1800s, the numbers were dropped, and the four Galilean moons were named after the girlfriends of the Greek god Zeus (Jupiter to the Romans).

All four moons (art below) are easily spotted with a pair of binoculars

because they form a straight line on either side of Jupiter. Io is the closest of the four Galilean moons, Europa, the second. Ganymede, the third, is the largest moon in the entire solar system. Callisto, the last of the four, is one of the most heavily cratered moons in the solar system.

If you have a pair of binoculars or a small telescope, go out on a clear night and look for the Galilean moons.

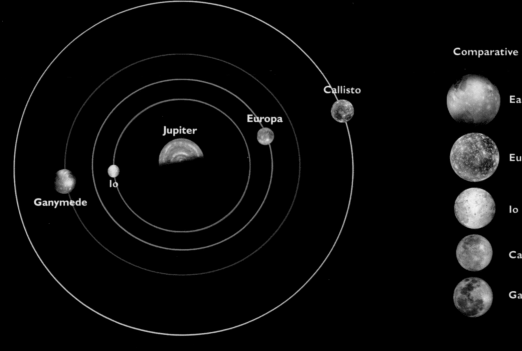

The surface of Io (photos above and right) looks like a pizza. The colors are layers of sulfur and lava that are constantly being sprayed out from very active volcanoes, like the one in the photograph on the right.

The heavily cratered surface of Callisto (photos above and right) was formed a long time ago—maybe four billion years in the past. Unlike Europa, Callisto seems to be frozen solid, with no liquid oceans hidden underneath its surface of thick ice.

Ganymede (photos below and left) is bigger than our Moon and the planets Pluto, Eris, and Mercury, and Ceres.

The Galilean moon Ganymede is the largest moon in the solar system. If it circled around the Sun, it would be considered a planet and would be the eighth largest in the solar system.

The darker regions of Ganymede are the original icy surfaces that have been covered with meteorites and dust. This Jovian moon appears to be frozen solid, but it could have liquid oceans under the ice. Astronomers don't know yet.

Europa is slightly smaller than Io. It has an icy surface that covers a saltwater ocean hidden below. Water was important for life to begin here on Earth, and Europa may have

The face of Europa (photos above and left) is deceptive. Its icy surface looks like a mosaic of giant cracks. However, there is much more to this moon than meets the eye. Underneath all the ice is a saltwater ocean that may be more than 60 miles deep.

even more water than Earth. This means that Europa is an excellent place to look for life in the solar system. But drilling through the 16 miles of solid ice that cover these oceans will be a real challenge.

When Galileo discovered these moons, most people still believed that Earth was the center of the solar system. They thought that all the heavenly bodies revolved around Earth. These four moons of Jupiter provided the first real evidence that there was something in outer space that did not rotate around Earth.

Monitoring a drilling rig, future astronauts (imagined in art, left) bore down through the half-mile thick sheets of ice covering the surface of Europa. The challenge is keeping the freshly drilled hole from immediately freezing over, so that a robotic probe can be inserted through the hole to explore the mysterious dark waters below.

SATURN

SHIP LOG DAY 8: Approaching
Saturn, orbit its moon Mimas

When people first see Saturn through a telescope, they usually gasp in wonder. As our spaceship gets close to the seventh planet, we can see its beauty close up. No other planet in the solar system has the visual splendor of Saturn.

When Galileo pointed his own crude telescope toward it in 1610, the telescope was not good enough to separate the rings from the rest of the disk. So he thought he'd found a "triple-bodied" planet.

Today, we know all four gas giant planets have rings, but Saturn's are the only ones visible by telescope from Earth. Surrounded by a brilliant halo of ice and dust, Saturn seems to mimic the formation of the early solar system. The diameters of its rings together measure 120,000 miles (200,000 km), almost the distance between the Earth and Moon. Traveling at the speed of a jet, it would take ten days and nights to cross Saturn's rings. As amazing as this is, even more astounding is the fact that the rings are less than 20 feet in thickness. If we could shrink them down to just two miles in diameter, at that scale the rings would be less than the thickness of a piece of paper.

FACTS ABOUT SATURN	
AVERAGE DISTANCE FROM THE SUN	886,526,000 miles (1,426,725,000 km)
POSITION FROM THE SUN IN ORBIT	SEVENTH
EQUATORIAL DIAMETER	72,370 miles (116,460 km)
MASS (EARTH = 1)	95
DENSITY (WATER = 1)	0.71
LENGTH OF DAY	10 Earth hours
LENGTH OF YEAR	29.46 Earth years
AVERAGE SURFACE TEMPERATURE	-218°F (-170°C)
KNOWN MOONS	AT LEAST 60

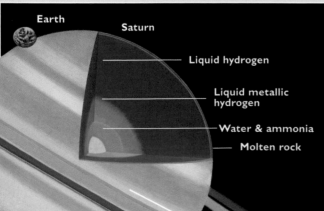

Earth

Saturn

Liquid hydrogen

Liquid metallic hydrogen

Water & ammonia

Molten rock

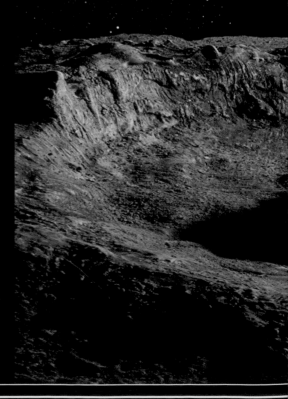

If you were standing in the giant Herschel crater on Saturn's moon Mimas (art right), the planet would fill the sky. From this viewpoint, it's easy to see how thin the planet's rings actually are.

Like Jupiter, Saturn has no surface to walk on. Its slushy atmosphere is mostly liquid hydrogen and helium, driven by gale-force winds into pale, colored bands and stripes. Occasionally, large white, oval-shaped storms appear, similar to the Great Red Spot on Jupiter.

Saturn spins very quickly on its axis, completing a rotation every 10 hours 14 minutes. But it takes thirty years to make one orbit around the Sun. Its magnetic field is 500 to 600 times stronger than Earth's, producing aurora fireworks that change hourly.

Saturn's rings reflect back 70 percent of the light from the Sun and are sometimes even brighter than the planet.

Ring names are assigned letters alphabetically in order of their discovery. Right now, they have names that go from A through G. The rings may have formed within the past 50 to 100 million years, either from the break-up of an icy moon or a captured asteroid. Astronomers think the object would have been about 240 miles in diameter.

The particles from this captured body are still gravitationally attracted to one another, as if the body were trying to reassemble itself.

The rings consist of thousands of closely spaced bands, called ringlets, with gaps in between them. The largest gap, the Cassini Division, is about 3,000 miles (4,700 km) wide and visible from Earth through a telescope. The rings change over time, and every 15 years, when they face Earth edge-on, they disappear from our view. Early astronomers questioned their own reasoning when they noticed that the rings vanished, only to reappear a few years later. The next time the rings disappear will be in 2009.

This remarkable photograph of Saturn was taken by the Cassini spacecraft as it passed along the shadowed back side of the ringed planet. From this angle, with the Sun hidden, a wonder never before seen came into view—the E ring, the faint one farthest out in the photograph. It's invisible to telescopes on Earth.

The largest and most intriguing of Saturn's moons, Titan (photo above) is nearly half the size of Earth. A photograph (right), taken by the Huygens spacecraft, shows Titan cloaked in thick orange atmospheric haze; the small rocks in the foreground are only a few inches in size.

Like Jupiter, Saturn has a fascinating array of moons—at least 60 of them. The precise number is uncertain, and most are quite small and oddly shaped. Still, seven are massive enough to have formed into spheres under the influence of their own gravity.

Titan, the second largest moon in the solar system after Jupiter's Ganymede, is bigger in diameter than Mercury and any of the known dwarf planets. It's the only moon in the solar system with a substantial atmosphere. Underneath Titan's dense orange blanket of clouds is a primordial world brimming with mysteries. Because the atmosphere is so thick and the gravity so low, humans could fly through it by attaching wings to their arms and flapping them up and down like butterflies. The moon's surface holds dark lakes of liquid methane with drainage channels rimming the shore-lines. Scientists believe the early atmosphere on Earth was very similar to the atmosphere on Titan today.

If that is so, Titan is one of the objects in the solar system, along with Earth, Mars, Jupiter's Europa, and possibly Saturn's Callisto, that may harbor life.

Mimas, about 240 miles (385 km) in diameter, is composed mostly of frozen ice and some rock. It sports one of the biggest black eyes in the solar system—a crater that is almost 80 miles (130 km) in diameter. The crater is named Herschel for Sir William Herschel, who discovered Mimas in 1789.

The huge crater on Mimas (photo above) was caused by a collision with a giant piece of space debris that almost destroyed the moon sometime in the distant past.

Dione's surface markings (photo above) resemble the dark marks on our Moon and were probably caused by water flooding the surface and quickly freezing.

Enceladus (photo left) reflects 100 percent of the sunlight reaching it back into space. The surface of this moon (photo below) is coated with fine crystals of pure water that spread from erupting water volcanoes.

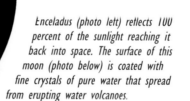

URANUS

A s we approach it, Uranus glows like an aquamarine gem in the outer reaches of our solar system.

Like Neptune, this planet is an icy giant. Neither has a solid surface. Uranus's blue-green color is caused by the absorption of red wavelengths of distant sunlight entering its frosty atmosphere. Methane gas reflects the blue and green wavelengths back into space.

Unlike any other planet, Uranus has a 98-degree tilt to its axis. Hit by something gigantic long ago, it almost lies on its side! Right now, its north pole faces the Sun, while the south pole faces away into space. This brings 42 years of

SHIP LOG DAY 11: Approaching Uranus, landing on its moon Miranda

constant sunlight to one side of the planet, followed by 42 years of complete darkness.

Since Uranus is tipped over on its side, its 13 thin, wispy rings do not circle it the way Saturn's rings do.

Of all the planets, Uranus may boast the greatest literary roots. Its 27 known moons are mostly named after characters from the works of William Shakespeare, the great English playwright. Two of its largest moons, Oberon and Titania, are named for the king and queen of the fairies.

FACTS ABOUT URANUS

AVERAGE DISTANCE FROM THE SUN	1,784,000,000 miles (2,870,970,000 km)
POSITION FROM THE SUN IN ORBIT	EIGHTH
EQUATORIAL DIAMETER	31,500 miles (50,724 km)
MASS (EARTH = 1)	15
DENSITY (WATER = 1)	1.24
LENGTH OF DAY	17.9 Earth hours
LENGTH OF YEAR	84 Earth years
AVERAGE SURFACE TEMPERATURE	-323°F (-200°C)
KNOWN MOONS	27

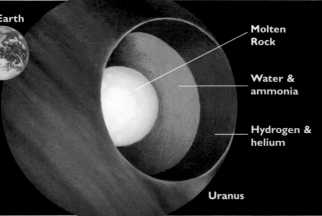

Earth

Molten Rock

Water & ammonia

Hydrogen & helium

Uranus

Astronauts visiting Uranus's moon Miranda (imagined in art, right) would clearly see the way the planet spins tipped over on its axis. The surface of Miranda would probably be slippery to walk on because of the ice and snow that scientists think erupt from its water volcanoes.

NEPTUNE

Ye're nearing the pale blue, icy world of Neptune. It has the wildest weather of any planet in the solar system, with winds that blow at speeds over 1,200 miles per hour (2,000 kph).

Like the other Jovian planets, Neptune doesn't have a surface to walk on. Although the clouds surrounding it are very cold, -350°F, its rocky iron core is hotter than the Sun's surface. This internal heat causes the planet's violent winds and hurricanes. Dark spots or storms similar to Jupiter's Great Red Spot dot its surface. The largest, called the Great Dark Spot, is bigger than Earth. Astronomers call one of the

SHIPLOG DAY 17: Approaching Neptune, close flyby of its moon Triton

lighter colored spots Scooter because this small, fast-moving storm seems to chase other storms around. Four rings, two thick and two thin, surround the planet.

Neptune was detected by mathematical calculation rather than observation in 1846. Astronomers realized something very large was affecting the orbit of Uranus. That something was Neptune, even though it lies a billion miles farther out in space.

Since its discovery more than 160 years ago, Neptune hasn't completed even one full orbit of the Sun!

FACTS ABOUT NEPTUNE	
AVERAGE DISTANCE FROM THE SUN	2,795,000,000 miles (4,498,250,000 km)
POSITION FROM THE SUN IN ORBIT	NINTH
EQUATORIAL DIAMETER	30,775 miles (49,528 km)
MASS (EARTH = 1)	17
DENSITY (WATER = 1)	1.67
LENGTH OF DAY	19 Earth hours
LENGTH OF YEAR	164.8 Earth years
AVERAGE SURFACE TEMPERATURE	-353°F (-210°C)
KNOWN MOONS	13

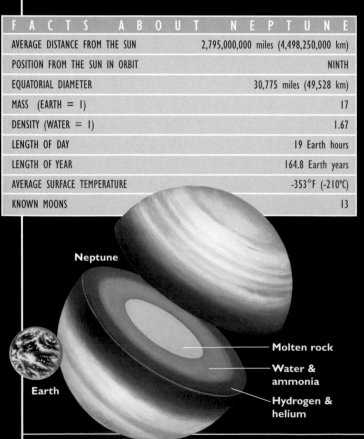

Neptune

Earth

Molten rock

Water & ammonia

Hydrogen & helium

Neptune's blue methane clouds help illuminate the frozen surface of its large moon, Triton (art right). Astronauts here would have to be careful of the surface gashes, craters, and large frozen-water lakes caused by erupting water volcanoes.

A huge concentration of galactic debris and assorted planetary leftovers make up a faraway region known as the Kuiper (rhymes with viper) belt. It extends from the orbit of Neptune to hundreds of millions of miles beyond the dwarf planet Pluto.

Astronomers believe that after the gas giant planets had taken shape during the formation of the solar system, gravitational interactions between Jupiter and Saturn may have ejected this galactic debris far out in space.

Today, the dwarf planets Pluto and Eris and their moons are all considered members of the Kuiper belt. So are Halley's comet and the other "short-period" comets that make regular trips around the Sun every 200 years or more. So far, more than 700 KBOs (Kuiper belt objects) have been identified and numbered. But there may be more than 100,000 of these icy objects, each with the potential of becoming a new comet in Earth's nighttime skies.

Orbit of Neptune   **Kuiper Belt**

Shaped like an egg, 2003 EL61 (art right) is one of the oddest known objects in the solar system. It's as big across as Pluto, and every four hours it spins end over end, like a kicked football. Mostly rock, this Kuiper Belt object appears to have an icy covering that makes it shine as it travels through space.

PLUTO

SHIP LOG DAY 25: Approaching Pluto, sightseeing flyby

For 76 years, Pluto reigned as the ninth planet in our solar system. But in 2006, everything changed. Like a popular sports star who gets demoted to second string, Pluto has been reclassified as a dwarf planet.

Originally, astronomers thought Pluto might be about the size of Earth. Its true size was difficult to tell because it was so far away. No matter what telescope was used to look at it, no details could be seen. It simply appeared as a speck of light. The best the Hubble Space Telescope could do was capture an image of a small ball with patches of dark and light. We now know Pluto is smaller than our own Moon.

Pluto is located in the Kuiper belt, where comets that return again and again originate. Made of rock and ice, it's very cometlike in composition. If this dwarf planet could somehow be relocated near the Sun, it would have a tail and look a lot like a comet.

Pluto also has a large moon named Charon (SHAR-on). Because of their sizes, Pluto and Charon together are considered a dwarf double-planet by many astronomers.

FACTS ABOUT PLUTO	
AVERAGE DISTANCE FROM THE SUN	3,670,000,000 miles (5,906,300,000 km)
POSITION FROM THE SUN IN ORBIT	TENTH
EQUATORIAL DIAMETER	1,485 miles (2,400 km)
MASS (EARTH = 1)	0.002
DENSITY (WATER = 1)	2.03
LENGTH OF DAY	6.38 Earth hours
LENGTH OF YEAR	248 Earth years
AVERAGE SURFACE TEMPERATURE	-369°F (-220°C)
KNOWN MOONS	3

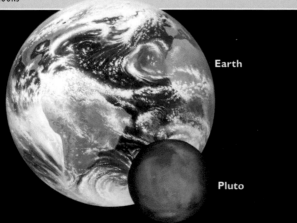

Earth

Pluto

The Milky Way stretches behind the dwarf planet Pluto and its large moon, Charon (art right). In the distance, Pluto's two smaller moons, Nix and Hydra, can be seen silhouetted against the starlit sky.

Pluto's story begins with the discovery of Neptune. Realizing there was something odd about the orbit of Uranus, early astronomers theorized there might be another planet pulling on it. After searching for many years, they discovered Neptune in 1846.

After that, observations of Neptune indicated something was disturbing its orbit, too. Was there another undiscovered planet out there? In 1905, Percival Lowell began searching for this Planet X from his observatory in Flagstaff, Arizona.

Today we know that Pluto is too small to have had any influence on Neptune, but Lowell spent the rest of his life searching for the undiscovered planet. He never found it, but a night assistant at the Lowell Observatory named Clyde Tombaugh did.

At 22 years old, Clyde (photo right) built his own six-inch reflecting telescope and sent drawings of Mars and Jupiter to the Lowell Observatory. Scientists there offered him a job, and he began taking pictures of the same area of the sky a week apart. If an object changed position on one of the photographic plates, it might be Planet X. On February 18, 1930, something showed up on one of Clyde's plates. Everyone was amazed. This object became the ninth planet in the solar system.

The right to name it belonged to Lowell Observatory. The observatory scientists asked for name submissions, and an 11-year-old English girl came up with Pluto! Shortly after that, Disney Studios named Mickey Mouse's dog Pluto in honor of this new planet. Pluto's astronomical symbol, PL, stands for the first two letters in its name and honors the initials of Percival Lowell.

In 2006, everything changed. After three new planet-like objects about Pluto's size were discovered in the Kuiper belt, astronomers began wondering just how many more might be out there. At a meeting, the International Astronomical Union considered whether other dwarf planets should be upgraded to full planet status or whether Pluto should be downgraded. Debate among the astronomers turned into arguments that went on for days, but in the end, Pluto was downgraded.

But Pluto's demotion created more problems.

The new definition for a planet says it must be round, it must orbit the Sun, and it must have cleared out smaller debris from its orbit. Pluto hasn't cleared out debris from its orbit, but neither have Earth, Mars, Jupiter, and Neptune. In other words, by this definition, they aren't planets, either.

The debate about Pluto is probably not over yet.

Pluto and Charon's very peculiar orbit around the Sun is egg-shaped instead of more circular. They orbit so far out on the edge of the solar system that from the surface of Pluto, the Sun would look like just another bright star in the sky. Besides Charon, Pluto has two smaller moons named Nix and Hydra.

In a few years we should know a lot more about the distant world of Pluto. On July 14, 2015, the New Horizon spacecraft will fly by Pluto, showing us this little world up close for the first time. New Horizon's trip is no small feat. The spacecraft will take nine years to reach the dwarf planet.

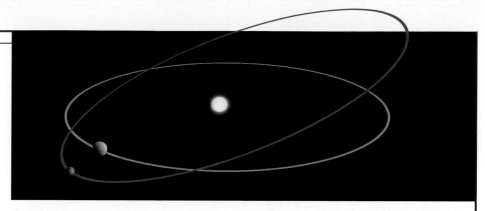

All the other planets, except Eris, orbit in a flat plane in nearly circular orbits, but Pluto's orbit (art above) is inclined 17 degrees above the plane in an elliptical (oval) instead of circular orbit.

Pluto (art below) is one of the coldest objects in the solar system. In fact, when it is at its farthest from the Sun, its atmosphere freezes, like a thin ice frosting on the ground.

ERIS

The coldest, most distant object ever found in our solar system is now looming before us. Eris was just discovered in 2005. It has an orbit that goes through the Kuiper belt but also extends out beyond it—ten billion miles from the Sun. Eris orbits the Sun every 560 Earth years! It's bigger than Pluto and has a moon named Dysnomia.

Eris's discoverer, Mike Brown, was amazed to find something so far out in the solar system. When it became classified as a new planet, some astronomers weren't too happy. If Pluto remained a planet, and Ceres and Eris were added to the list too, the solar system might keep expanding until we

SHIP LOG DAY 33: Approaching Eris, initiate return journey to Earth

had more planets than anyone could name. Instead, at the 2006 meeting of the International Astronomical Union, scientists came up with the new classification of dwarf planet, which included Pluto.

Pluto, Ceres, and Eris are different from the other eight planets. They're smaller than some of the moons of Jupiter, they're a combination of rock and ice, and their orbits are different from the others.

Right now, our solar system has 11 planets. But there are probably more out in space we haven't discovered yet.

FACTS	ABOUT	ERIS
AVERAGE DISTANCE FROM THE SUN		6,200,000,000 miles (10,000,000,000 km)
POSITION FROM THE SUN IN ORBIT		TH
EQUATORIAL DIAMETER		1,678 miles (2700 km)
MASS (EARTH = 1)		0.0028
DENSITY (WATER = 1)		2.1
LENGTH OF DAY		less than 8 Earth hours
LENGTH OF YEAR		557 Earth years
AVERAGE SURFACE TEMPERATURE		-406°F (-243°C)
KNOWN MOONS		1

Earth

Eris

The new dwarf planet Eris and its moon Dysnomia (art right) are as far as our expedition through the solar system takes us. This icy distant rock is the largest of the new dwarf planets and the most distant from the Sun.

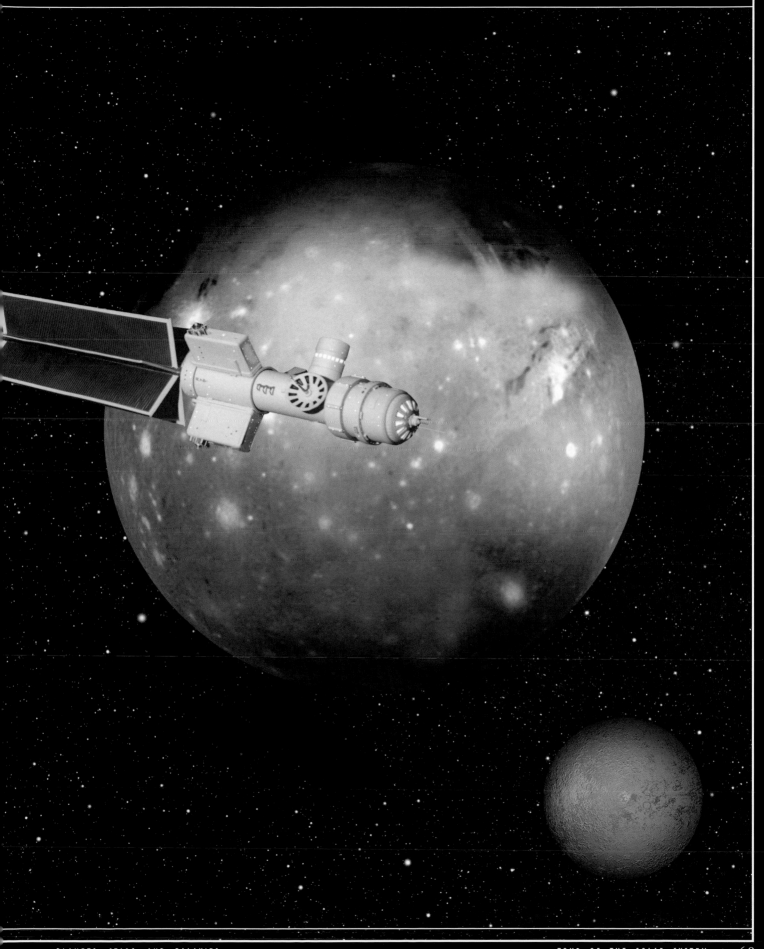

If we could travel 18 trillion miles (30 trillion km) from the Sun, out past the extreme edges of the solar system, astronomers think that we would encounter an enormous cloud known as the Oort cloud. They also think this is the remains of the original nebula that coalesced to form our solar system nearly 4.6 billion years ago. The cloud marks the outer boundaries of the Sun's gravitational field.

In 1950, Dutch astronomer Jan Oort set out to determine the origin of comets. He proposed that a vast and remote reservoir existed one to two light-years from the Sun, far beyond Pluto's orbit. Although no one has actually observed the Oort cloud, astronomers believe it's the base camp for most comets. These icy fragments probably orbit the Sun here until a passing star's gravity nudges one of them, sending it on a new journey in toward the Sun. Since comets zoom in from all directions, astronomers think the Oort cloud wraps around the solar system.

Other stars may also have Oort-like clouds around them. The icy comets in these clouds could help future space travelers on their way. Water ice from the comets could provide hydrogen to power their ships, water to drink, and oxygen to breathe.

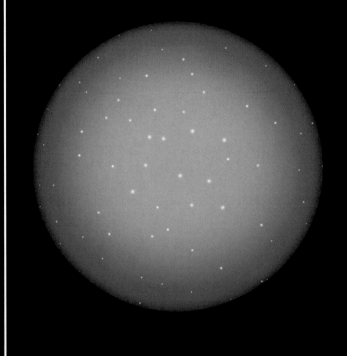

Though the Oort cloud (art left) has not yet been detected by astronomical instruments, scientists believe that not only our solar system but other star systems may have Oort clouds. The art at right shows a cloud around our solar system (middle), Alpha Centauri (lower right), and other more distant stars.

COMETS

Of all the objects in the night sky, comets are the most spectacular. Most of these unexpected visitors originate far out in the Oort cloud where they take hundreds, even millions, of years to complete one orbit around the Sun. A second major group comes from the Kuiper belt. They're called short-period comets because their orbital periods are less than 200 years. Comet Halley, one of the most famous short-period comets of all time, comes from this area.

The word comet comes from the Greek word *kometes,* which means long-haired. Today, we know that these objects are leftovers from the formation of the solar system 4.6 billion years ago. Made of sand, water ice, and carbon dioxide, comets have been called big, dirty snowballs.

As they pass by Jupiter on their way toward the Sun, comets begin to defrost. Solar heating vaporizes ice, which forms a halo of gas and dust, or coma, around the comet's nucleus. As they near the orbit of Mars, they may start to form long spectacular tails, sometimes hundreds of millions of miles long. Blown by the solar wind, the tails of comets always point away from the Sun.

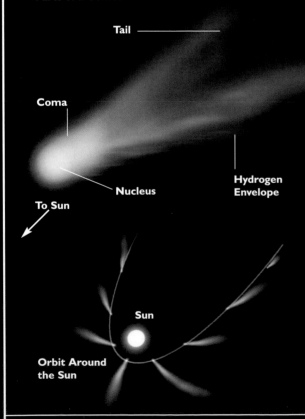

Parts of a Comet

Tail

Coma

Nucleus

Hydrogen Envelope

To Sun

Sun

Orbit Around the Sun

Low in the west, just after sunset, the tail of a brilliant comet lights up the evening sky (art right). Short-period comets, such as Halley's Comet, return every 200 years or sooner in their journeys around the Sun. The comet pictured here is a long-period comet that will not return again for thousands of years.

EARTH

Our tour of the solar system is coming to an end, and we're heading home. Now that we've visited other planets, we can appreciate better than ever what a Garden of Eden our Earth is.

From space, Earth appears deep blue because of the nitrogen in the atmosphere and the oceans that cover 71 percent of its surface. Since Earth spins on its axis more than 1,000 miles per hour (1,600 kph) and travels around the Sun at 66,700 miles per hour (107,300 kph), all of us who live on Earth are actually traveling through space all the time!

Located at just the right distance from the Sun, Earth is

SHIP LOG DAY 61: Reenter Earth orbit, stop for a moon landing

warm enough for water to exist as a liquid, which is an essential element for most life. Its atmosphere is oxygen rich and swirled by white clouds. And Earth has the most diverse terrain of any planet. The polar caps are covered with sheets of ice. Along the Equator vast deserts border grasslands that give way to lush tropical jungles. In temperate zones, green forests surround mountains thrust up by volcanoes or the movements of tectonic plates.

So far, our planet is the only place in the universe we know of that has life on it.

FACTS ABOUT EARTH	
AVERAGE DISTANCE FROM THE SUN	93,000,000 miles (149,600,000 km)
POSITION FROM THE SUN IN ORBIT	THIRD
EQUATORIAL DIAMETER	7,900 miles (12,750 km)
MASS (EARTH = 1)	1
DENSITY (WATER = 1)	5.52
LENGTH OF DAY	24 hours
LENGTH OF YEAR	365 days
SURFACE TEMPERATURES	-126°F (-88°C) to 136°F (58°C)
KNOWN MOONS	1

Moon

Earth

Earth (art right) is the crown jewel of our solar system, at least from a human perspective. Returning to this blue world, we can see that it is daytime in India (center), the Middle East (slightly to the left), and Africa (far left). On the opposite side of the world, it's nighttime.

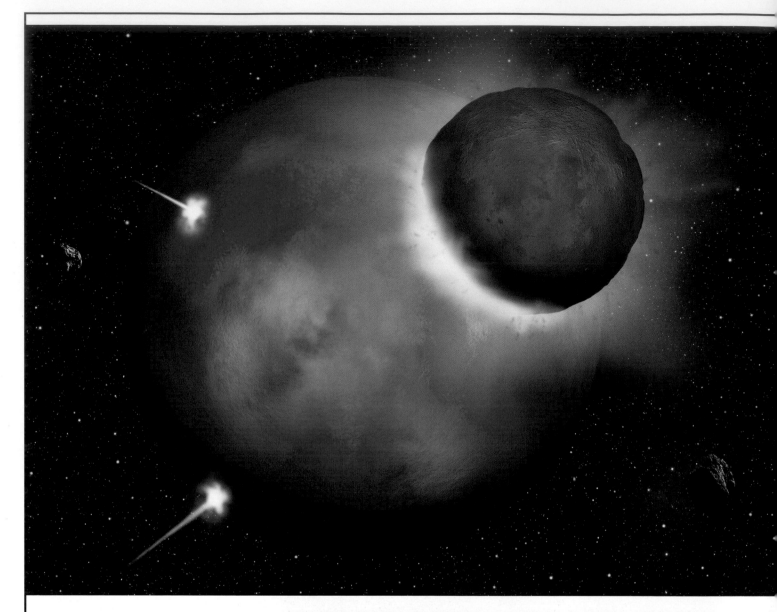

Using computer simulations and samples of lunar rocks, astronomers have figured out that the Moon formed out of the material left behind by a collision (just beginning in art above) between Earth and a Mars-size object some 4.5 billion years ago.

Earth formed about 4.6 billion years ago out of a gigantic star explosion that gave birth to the Sun and the rest of the solar system. As rocky debris rained down on the planet's young molten surface, an unexpected cosmic collision suddenly changed everything. Around 4.5 billion years ago, an object about the

When the object hit the molten Earth (art above), the material knocked off first stabilized into a ring of molten rock, then fused back together, and eventually re-formed into the Moon we see today. In the early solar system, collisions like this happened all the time.

size of Mars slammed into Earth, tilting it 23.5 degrees on its axis. This collision knocked off a big chunk of the planet. The chunk broke into pieces and formed a gigantic ring around Earth. The pieces, still hot and molten, quickly came back together and formed the Moon. This may explain why the Moon's composition is nearly identical to that of the Earth's crust.

Once formed, the Moon helped to stabilize the rotation of Earth. That's one of the lucky events that made it possible for life to survive here. If Earth were spinning upright on its axis, the Equator would heat up much more than it does today. We would have no change of seasons, and the weather on our planet would be much more severe.

A WET WORLD

As the Earth and Moon began the long process of cooling down, new changes took place on the planet. Erupting volcanoes released water vapor that formed into clouds. The clouds quickly returned water to the surface as rain. Comets still raining down on the surface also brought in staggering amounts of water that slowly filled basins. Gradually, Earth's surface was completely covered with one global salty ocean averaging two miles deep. It was in these warm salty oceans that biologists believe life first began.

ABOUT 3.5 BILLION YEARS AGO Earth was covered by one gigantic reddish ocean, whose color came from hydrocarbons. The first life on Earth were simple bacteria that could live without oxygen. These bacteria released large amounts of methane gas into an atmosphere that would have been poisonous to us.

ABOUT THREE BILLION YEARS AGO something new appeared in the global ocean. Erupting volcanoes linked together to form larger landmasses. And a new form of life appeared—blue-green algae, the first living thing that used energy from the Sun.

TWO BILLION YEARS AGO these algae filled the air with oxygen, killing off the methane-producing bacteria. Colored pools of greenish-brown plant life floated on the ocean waters. The oxygen revolution that would someday make human life possible was now underway.

600 TO 550 MILLION YEARS AGO, the Cambrian explosion occurred. It's called an explosion because it's the time when most major animal groups first appeared in our fossil records. Back then, Earth was a place of swamps, seas, a few active volcanoes, and oceans teeming with strange life.

MORE THAN 450 MILLION YEARS AGO, life began moving from the oceans onto dry land. About 200 million years later, along came the dinosaurs. For almost 250 million years, they would dominate life on Earth.

Over time, land-masses thrust up by volcanic activity began to rise out of Earth's oceans. These landmasses began to drift and collide, growing larger and larger until they formed a giant supercontinent called Rodinia about 1.1 billion years ago. Rodinia eventually broke apart into smaller continents. About 225 million years ago the smaller continents pushed together again to form Pangaea. Slowly, after another 70 million years, that supercontinent separated into the continents we see today.

Even today, the continents are drifting. Scientists predict that 250 million years from now North America will collide with Africa, and South America will wrap around the southern tip of Africa. By then, the Pacific Ocean will cover half of Earth.

The idea that the solid ground we are standing on may be slowly moving is difficult to believe. But even more amazing is that the interior structure of Earth is still pretty much a big mystery to us. Scientists believe the structure of Earth consists of four separate layers. Covering the outer surface, the part where we build houses and plant trees, is the rocky crust. It averages three to six miles (six to eleven km) thick under the oceans and up to 25 miles (42 km) thick under the conti-nents. If Earth were the size

Rodinia
425 million years ago

Pangaea
225 million years ago

94 million years ago

Today

The surface of the Earth is always changing. The crust is made up of plates that move slowly, carrying the oceans and continents with them.

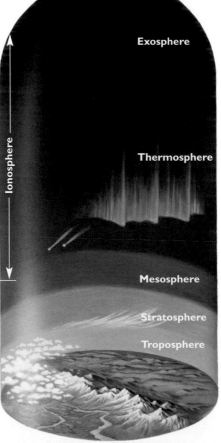

Exosphere

Thermosphere

Ionosphere

Mesosphere

Stratosphere

Troposphere

Our layered atmosphere (art above) is composed mostly of nitrogen and oxygen, with small amounts of carbon dioxide and other gases mixed with water vapor. All weather occurs in the lowest level, the troposphere.

of an apple, the crust would be about the thickness of the apple peel.

In 1970, Russian scientists began trying to drill through the crust. They only succeeded in digging a hole about a third of the way through it before they gave up. It took them 19 years to drill down 7.6 miles (12 km). Even though they did not make it beyond the crust, what they found surprised them. First, the temperatures down there were hot enough to cook a turkey or bake a pie! And, the rock at that depth was saturated with water—something nobody believed was possible.

Below the crust is the mantle, a layer of dense, semisolid rock. It flows out through cracks onto the surface as lava when volcanoes erupt. Beneath the mantle is a liquid outer core that spins like a motor, generating a magnetic field around Earth that repels damaging solar radiation. At the center of our planet is a solid core where the temperatures may reach 9000°F (5000°C)—about as hot as the surface of the Sun.

EARTH'S ATMOSPHERE

Today, Earth's atmosphere is 77 percent nitrogen and 21 percent oxygen, with traces of carbon dioxide, water, and argon. The small amount of carbon dioxide in the atmosphere helps moderate the temperatures of our planet. If there were too little carbon dioxide, Earth would become too cold, too much and it would grow unbearably hot.

Unlike any other place that we know of in our solar system, the oxygen in our atmosphere is provided and replenished by living organisms. Plant life on

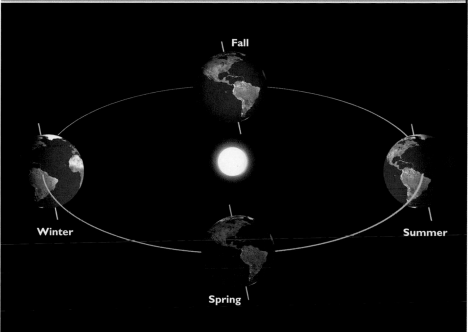

Fall

Winter

Summer

Spring

The reason we have seasons can be confusing. Some people think summer occurs in the hemisphere closest to the Sun, and that the hemisphere farthest away experiences winter. This sounds like a great explanation, but unfortunately it's wrong. Seasons occur because Earth tilts 23.5 degrees on its axis. That tilt affects the intensity of the sunlight hitting the surface, and that in turn causes the seasons. When North America, Europe, and northern Asia are having summer (above), it's because they're tilted directly toward the Sun and receiving the most concentrated sunlight. During the same time, in the Southern Hemisphere, South America, Africa, and Australia are tilted away from the Sun, so sunlight is less concentrated and there's less heat. Six months later, when Earth has circled around to the other side of the Sun, everything reverses. The Northern Hemisphere has winter and the Southern Hemisphere has summer. In January, when people in Vermont are out skiing down snowy slopes, Australians down under are waxing their surfboards and sunbathing on the beach.

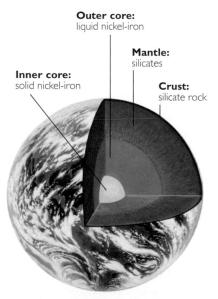

Outer core:
liquid nickel-iron

Mantle:
silicates

Inner core:
solid nickel-iron

Crust:
silicate rock

A thin layer of cooled rock, Earth's crust supports the oceans and the continental plates. Just beneath the crust lies the molten rock of the mantle, the origin of lava, and beneath that two layers of core.

Earth "exhales" oxygen that animals need. Without plants, there would be no animal life. In turn, animals exhale carbon dioxide that plants use in photosynthesis.

Earth's atmosphere has no definite boundary. It just becomes thinner as it fades into outer space. The atmosphere is divided into layers. The layer closest to the ground is called the troposphere. It extends about eight miles (13 km) into the sky. This is the layer where all weather occurs and where most planes fly. Above the troposphere is the stratosphere, which continues out to about 30 miles (50 km) above the surface. In the lower stratosphere is the very important ozone layer. A special form of oxygen, ozone blocks deadly ultraviolet radiation from the Sun. Without it, plants and animals wouldn't survive.

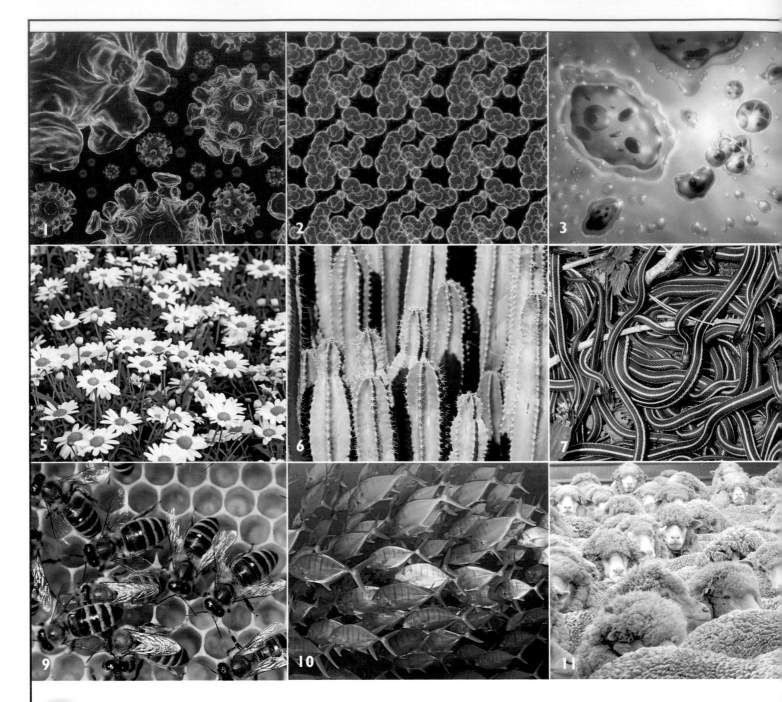

Living things are found everywhere on Earth, from the tropical Equator to the frozen poles, from the bottom of the ocean to the tops of mountains, inside other organisms (including us) and inside scalding volcanic sulfur pools. The diversity and distribution of life on Earth is staggering. From amoebas to elephants, electric eels to butterflies, scientists have yet to catalogue all of the species of life existing here on our planet. Taxonomists, the scientists who try to group life forms into similar categories, have identified close to two million distinct groups, mostly mammals and birds. But it's estimated that the number of undiscovered species— mostly fish, fungi, insects, and microbes—ranges from ten million to more than a hundred million. Scientists say that if you want to discover a new animal, all you have to do is spend a day in a tropical rain forest in South America, looking under a log or a rock.

Scientists are not quite sure how life began on Earth, but they're fairly certain where it began—in the sea. Most living creatures, including human

Life on Earth is as beautiful as it is diverse. The photographs above are just a sampling (the first four are tiny organisms seen in a microscope).

1 an influenza virus
2 bacteria cells
3 amoeba
4 phytoplankton
5 a field of daisies
6 desert cactuses
7 garter snakes
8 a flock of geese
9 honeybees inside their hive
10 a school of pilot fish
11 a herd of sheep
12 different kinds of coral
13 people gathered for a football game

beings, carry the fossil record of this past inside them. Since 71 percent of Earth is covered by water, and our bodies are about 60 percent water, in a way we are walking containers of ocean.

The earliest life on Earth probably looked like the bacteria we find everywhere on the planet today. Over the past 3.7 billion years, organisms on Earth have diversified and adapted to almost every environment imaginable. How they did this is still unknown. Has this same process occurred elsewhere in our solar system or on other planets circling distant stars?

Within the next 25 years we may well have an answer to this question.

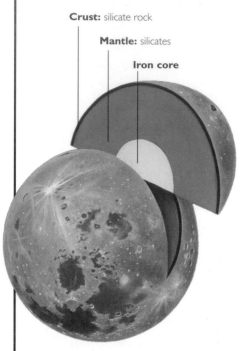

Crust: silicate rock

Mantle: silicates

Iron core

The Moon has far less iron than Earth, which helps explain why its density is only one-sixth that of Earth's.

The Moon is our closest companion in space. Only three days away by spacecraft, it's a dramatic reminder of how violent and chaotic the early solar system was. With just a pair of binoculars, we can see how the Moon's terrain was smoothed by the lava flows of ancient volcanoes or scarred with impact craters a hundred miles in diameter.

Earth's atmosphere causes most space objects to burn up before impact, but the Moon has no atmosphere. Everything heading for it hits its surface. None of these impact scars is erased over time by the actions of weather. The footprints left by the Apollo astronauts in 1969 will remain on the Moon's surface for at least another ten million years.

There are two types of terrain on the Moon: the deeply cratered highlands and the relatively smooth lowlands called "maria," from *mare,* the Latin word for sea. Maria are found mostly on the near side that faces Earth. They formed four billion years ago, when asteroids smashed into the Moon, causing lava to flow out and resurface vast areas. The far side of the Moon either missed being hit or the crust there is thicker and kept lava from reaching the surface.

SOLAR AND LUNAR ECLIPSES

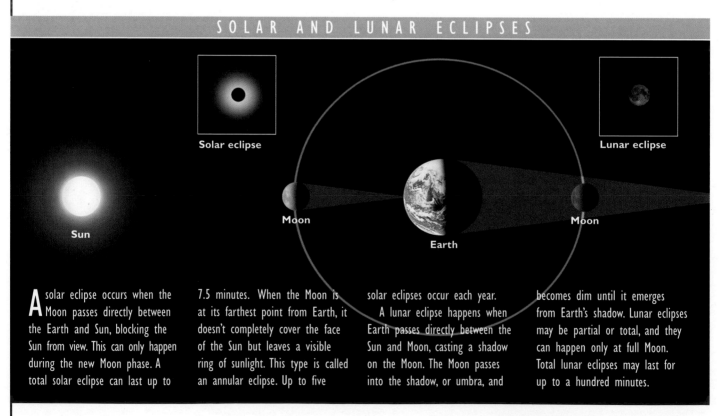

Solar eclipse

Lunar eclipse

Sun

Moon

Earth

Moon

A solar eclipse occurs when the Moon passes directly between the Earth and Sun, blocking the Sun from view. This can only happen during the new Moon phase. A total solar eclipse can last up to 7.5 minutes. When the Moon is at its farthest point from Earth, it doesn't completely cover the face of the Sun but leaves a visible ring of sunlight. This type is called an annular eclipse. Up to five solar eclipses occur each year.

A lunar eclipse happens when Earth passes directly between the Sun and Moon, casting a shadow on the Moon. The Moon passes into the shadow, or umbra, and becomes dim until it emerges from Earth's shadow. Lunar eclipses may be partial or total, and they can happen only at full Moon. Total lunar eclipses may last for up to a hundred minutes.

If you were standing on the Moon (like the imagined astronauts in art, right), a lunar eclipse (diagram above) would cast a golden orange glow over the landscape, reflecting sunlight passing through the thin red ring of Earth's atmosphere.

Like Earth, the Moon has mountain ranges. Many are found along the edges of large craters where the impacts of asteroids suddenly thrust them up. One of the biggest surprises for the Apollo astronauts was that the mountains of the Moon are not sharp and jagged but soft and rounded. Since the Moon doesn't have an atmosphere, there are only dark black shadows on the surface, not the soft gray ones we have on Earth. Because of this, and because there are no familiar objects like telephone poles, it's impossible for astronauts standing on the Moon to tell whether a mountain is large and distant or small and close by.

The gravitational forces of the Earth and Moon pull on each other. This causes some interesting results, including the tides along our shorelines. When the Moon formed over four billion years ago, it was six times closer to us than it is today. Over time, it has edged away in its orbit. Now it takes the same amount of time—28 days—for the Moon to rotate once on its axis and to revolve around Earth. This is called tidal lock, and it's the reason we only see one side of the Moon. Most of the larger moons in the solar system are in tidal lock with their planets, too.

About five billion years from now, Earth will gain a ring system as the Moon breaks apart. Earth and Moon will be reunited when lunar debris rains down from the burning heavens (art left).

HUMANS ON THE MOON

NASA plans to return to the Moon within the next 20 years. Since the Moon's gravitational force is only a sixth of the Earth's, astronauts visiting the Moon weigh less there. A 100-pound person would weigh only 16.6 pounds, and a solidly hit baseball could speed along at 10 miles per hour.

Astronaut Buzz Aldrin described the Moon as a world of "magnificent desolation." It offers no oxygen to breathe and no global magnetic field to protect it from deadly solar radiation.

THE MOON'S FUTURE

The Moon was created out of an ancient collision, and scientists believe it is headed for further catastrophe. In about five billion years, the Sun will enter its red giant phase and begin to expand in diameter. As it reaches the orbit of the Moon, it will push the Moon's orbital path back in toward Earth. Eventually, this will tear the Moon apart. At first, the lunar pieces will create a rather lumpy ring system around our planet, then they will crash onto Earth's surface.

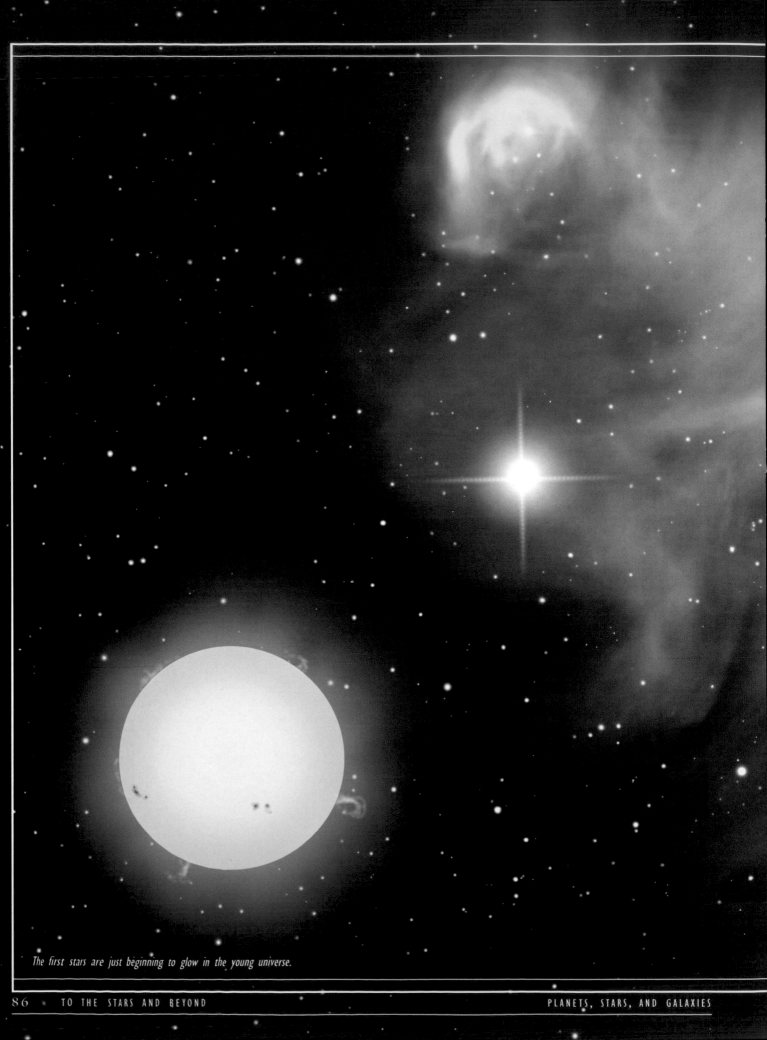

The first stars are just beginning to glow in the young universe.

TO THE STARS AND BEYOND

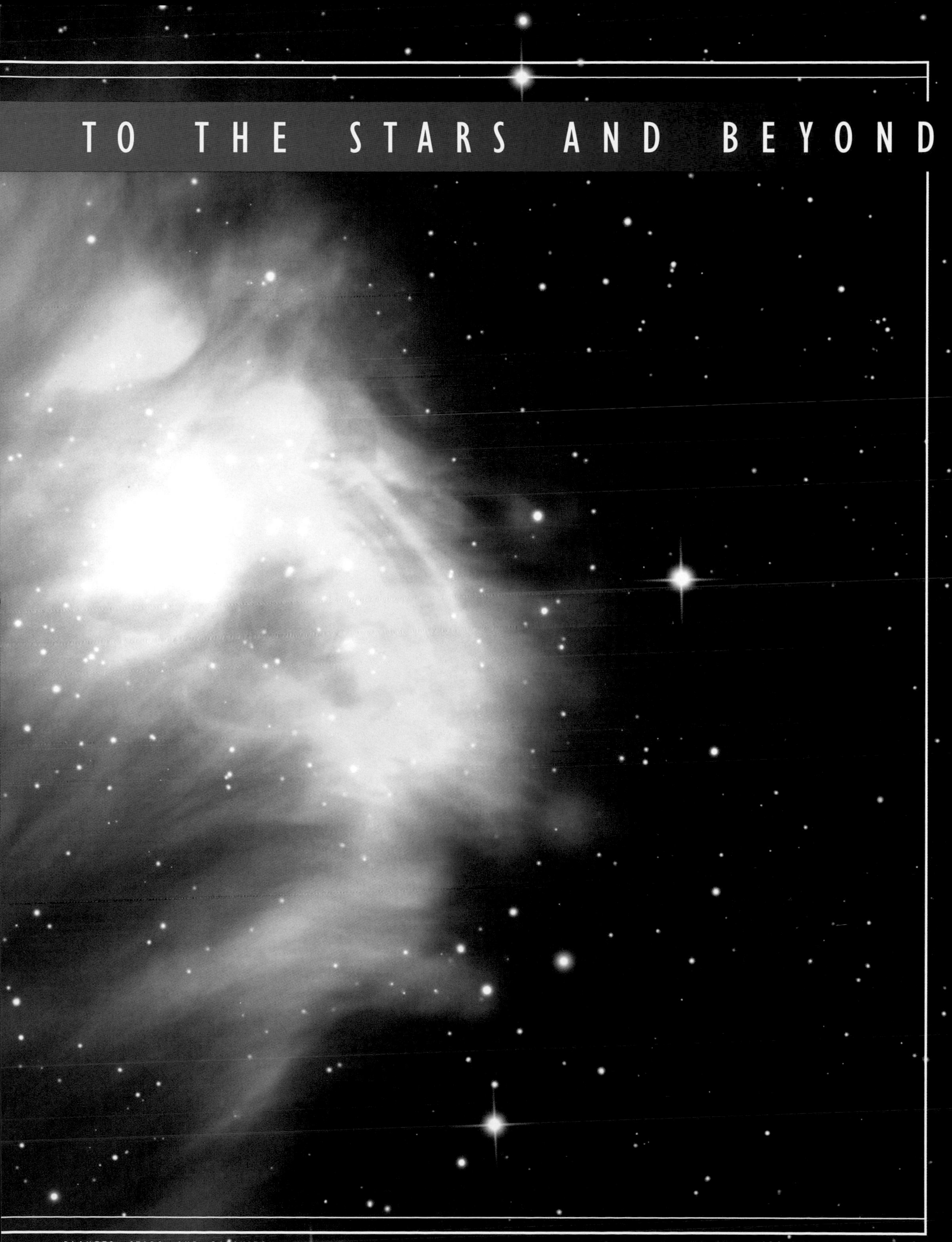

If you're on a dark country-side hill some night, look up at the heavens. Arcing overhead, you may see a faint band of light that looks like milk spilled across the sky. The ancient Romans called that band the *via lactea,* which means the "milky road" or "milky way." The name has stuck for 2,000 years.

A lot of people around the world use the term Milky Way, but some cultures have different names for the band of light. In China, it's called the silver river, and people of the Kalahari Desert in southern Africa call it the backbone of the night.

In 1610, Galileo and his telescope finally revealed that this band was actually made up of thousands and thousands of stars. The Milky Way also has dark patches sprinkled through it. Those patches aren't areas without stars. They're clouds of interstellar dust that block the light from the stars behind them.

This photograph looks toward the center of the Milky Way, which lies in the direction of the constellation Sagittarius. Dark dust clouds obscure the galactic center. The starlight there is actually a million times brighter than it looks to us here on Earth.

Long ago, people looking at the sky noticed that some stars made shapes and patterns. By playing connect-the-dots, they imagined people and animals in the sky. Their legendary heroes and monsters were pictured in the stars.

Today, we call these star patterns constellations. There are 88 constellations in all. Some are only visible when you're north of the Equator, and some only south of it.

The ones visible in the Southern Hemisphere, such as the Southern Cross, have names given them by European ocean voyagers. In the 16th-century Age of Exploration, their ships began visiting southern lands. Astronomers used the star observations of these navigators to fill in the blank spots on their celestial maps.

Constellations aren't fixed in the sky. The star arrangement that makes up each one would look different from another location in the universe. Constellations also change over time because every star we see is moving through space. Over thousands of years, the stars in the Big Dipper, which is part of the larger constellation Ursa Major (the Great Bear), will move so far apart that the dipper pattern will disappear.

Centered on Polaris, the North Star, the time-lapse photograph at the top shows how stars seem to spin around the sky as the Earth spins on its axis. Our ancestors imagined people and animals in star patterns, as in the constellation wheel above.

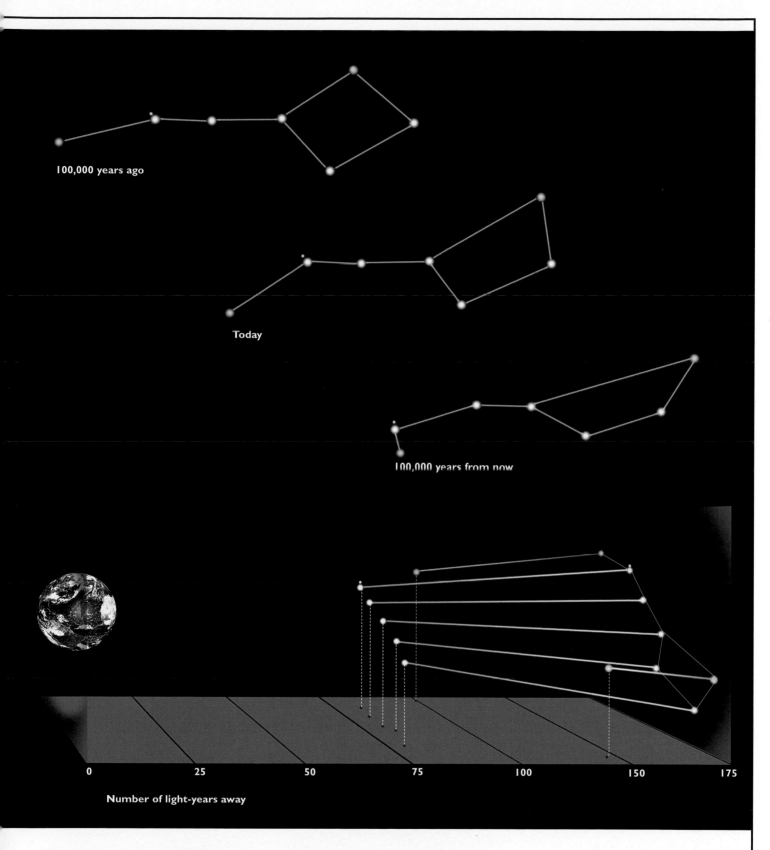

100,000 years ago

Today

100,000 years from now

Number of light-years away

0   25   50   75   100   150   175

Constellations are always changing because stars move through space. The Big Dipper looked more like a square in the past. In the future it will flatten (art top).

When we look up at the sky, the stars that seem to form patterns along a flat plane and to be close together may actually be in very different locations in space. Some stars in the Big Dipper are twice as far away from us as others (art bottom).

A telescope is a time machine, but a time machine that only takes you into the past. That's because a telescope shows things in the sky not as they are now but as they were.

To understand this, remember that a telescope collects light from the heavens. It takes time for that light to reach us, even moving at 186,000 miles (300,000 km) per second—the speed of light. Light from the Sun reaches Earth in eight minutes, so we see the Sun as it looked eight minutes ago. Light from Pluto takes about four hours to reach us because it has to cross three billion miles (five billion km) of space.

BIG DISTANCES

Once you move beyond the solar system, the distances get unbelievably big. In one Earth year, light travels six trillion miles. The closest star to the Sun, Alpha Centauri, is 24 trillion miles (41 trillion km) away. The center of the Milky Way is 125 thousand trillion miles away.

The numbers get so big that astronomers have created a word to describe cosmic distances: the light-year. One light-year is the distance light travels in an Earth year, so a light-year equals six trillion miles (10 trillion km). Since light from Alpha Centauri takes four years to reach us,

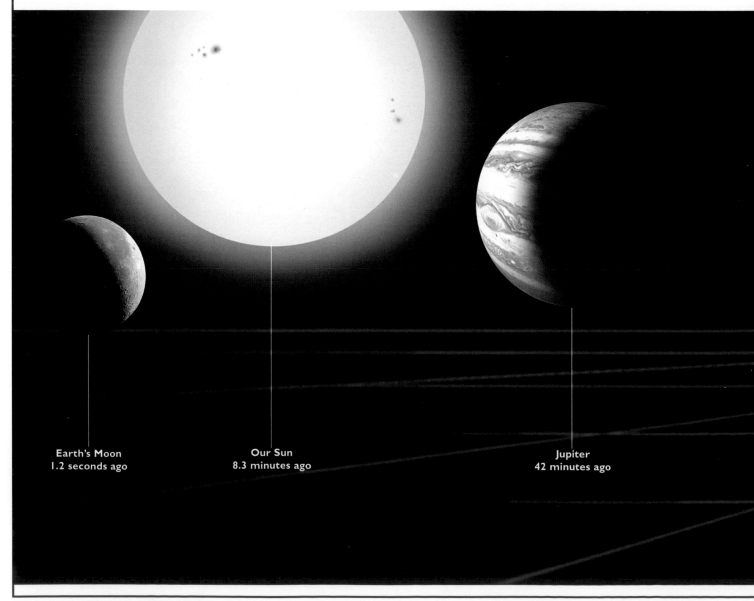

Earth's Moon
1.2 seconds ago

Our Sun
8.3 minutes ago

Jupiter
42 minutes ago

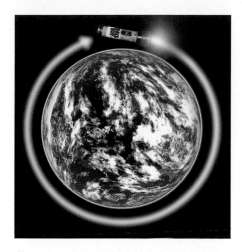

If you could shine a flashlight around the Earth, its light beam would circle the planet more than seven times in one second because that's the speed light travels. The much slower space shuttle circles the Earth once every hour and a half.

we say that Alpha Centauri lies four light-years away.

LOOK-BACK TIME

Look-back time is how far back in time we are seeing something in the sky. The look-back time for Alpha Centauri is four years. The red star Aldebaran in the constellation Taurus is about 65 light-years away, so it has a look-back time of 65 years. Looking at Aldebaran, we see that star as it was 65 years ago. It's like looking at pictures of your grandparents

when they were just children.

The travel time of light gets even longer when you look outside the Milky Way galaxy. For example, the closest large galaxy to us is the Andromeda spiral galaxy, two million light-years away. The light we see from Andromeda left there when the earliest ancestors of man first appeared on Earth.

A telescope is like a time machine because it allows us to see things as they were in the past. Light from the Sun takes about 8 minutes and 20 seconds to arrive at Earth, so we see the Sun as it was 8.3 minutes ago.

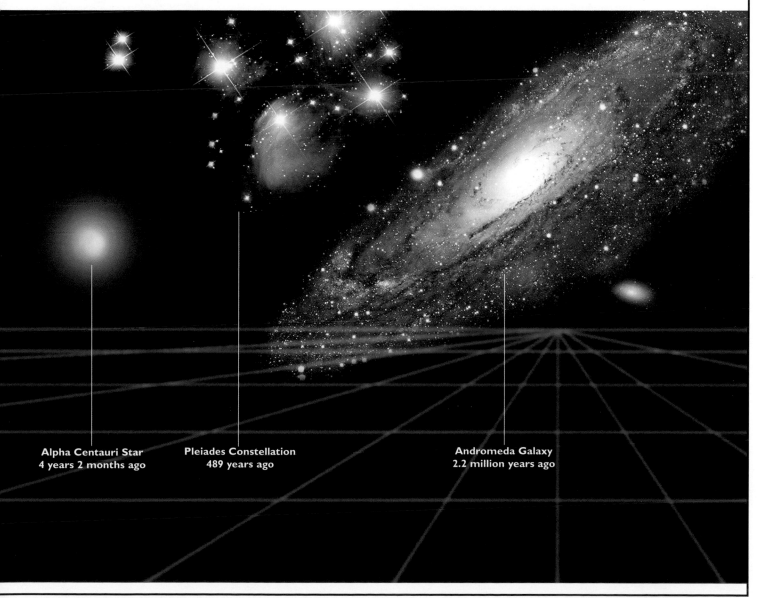

Alpha Centauri Star
4 years 2 months ago

Pleiades Constellation
489 years ago

Andromeda Galaxy
2.2 million years ago

Our Solar System

Globular Clusters

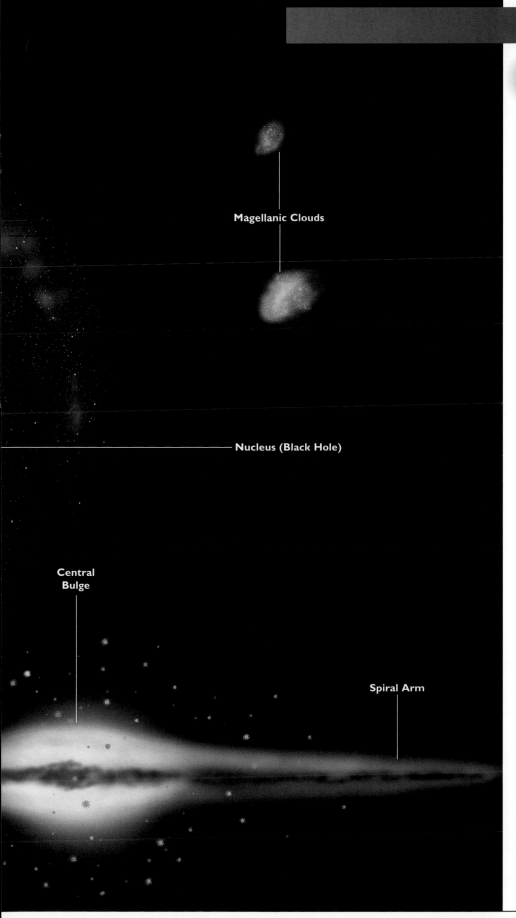

Magellanic Clouds

Nucleus (Black Hole)

Central
Bulge

Spiral Arm

Our galaxy, the Milky Way, appears to be a band of stars in the sky, but it's actually a disk. Its 400 billion stars are clumped into lines called spiral arms because they spiral outward. When we look up at the night sky, we're seeing the edge of the disk, like the side of a Frisbee.

Earth is located about halfway between the center of the Milky Way and its outer edge, in one of the spiral arms. Light from the galaxy's center takes 25,000 years to reach us.

Our solar system orbits the galactic center once every 250 million years. The last time we were on this side of the Milky Way, the earliest dinosaurs were just starting to emerge.

At the galaxy's center, frequent star explosions fry huge sections of space. Those explosions would wipe out any life on nearby planets. We're lucky that Earth is located where it is, far away from the center.

Our Milky Way galaxy (art left) has a bulge in its middle that surrounds the galactic center, or nucleus. In the nucleus is a giant black hole. The central bulge is surrounded by a flat disk. Within the disk, spiral arms of stars and gas wrap the center. Outside the disk, globular star clusters orbit like swarms of bees. Companion galaxies called the Magellanic Clouds also pass by the Milky Way.

The Milky Way may look like a peaceful, static arrangement of sparkling lights in our night sky, but it's really like a bustling restaurant kitchen, always cooking up something new. And stars are its main dish.

New stars form continually. In our galaxy, most of the action takes place in the spiral arms, which contain plenty of hydrogen gas to make stars. On average a new star is born every year in the Milky Way.

The births and deaths of stars are linked. When stars die, their remains mix with the remains of other stars over time to create new stars—or new solar systems.

Stars aren't the only things that are changing. Galaxies are moving through space, sometimes bumping into each other and re-forming. Scientists even think new universes might be forming and re-forming.

The red clouds in the larger photograph, taken by the Spitzer Space Telescope, are evidence that a huge star exploded near a famous gas and dust formation scientists call the Pillars of Creation (inset photo). Astronomers know that the explosion destroyed the pillars, but the light from their destruction hasn't reached Earth yet.

Poets might say that the stars are forever, but scientists know that's not true. All stars eventually die when they run out of fuel.

You might think a more massive star would live longer because it has more fuel to burn. But the heavier a star is, the faster it burns through its fuel, and the shorter its lifetime is. The most massive stars will live for only a few million years, while the least massive can live for trillions of years.

All stars spend most of their lives fusing hydrogen and turning it into helium in their cores. This nuclear fusion creates the energy we see as starlight. Eventually, the star's core runs out of hydrogen. This is the end for low-mass stars like the Sun.

When higher mass stars run out of hydrogen, they can start fusing the helium in their cores, creating carbon and oxygen. The most massive stars can keep fusing heavier and heavier elements until their core is full of hot, dense iron. That's the end of the road, because no energy comes from fusing iron.

All stars come from nebulas (top left in art, right), but then their lives take different courses to their final end. Smaller stars (top row) end as tiny, dead white dwarfs. But the more massive stars (bottom row) explode as supernovas and leave behind crushing black holes or neutron stars.

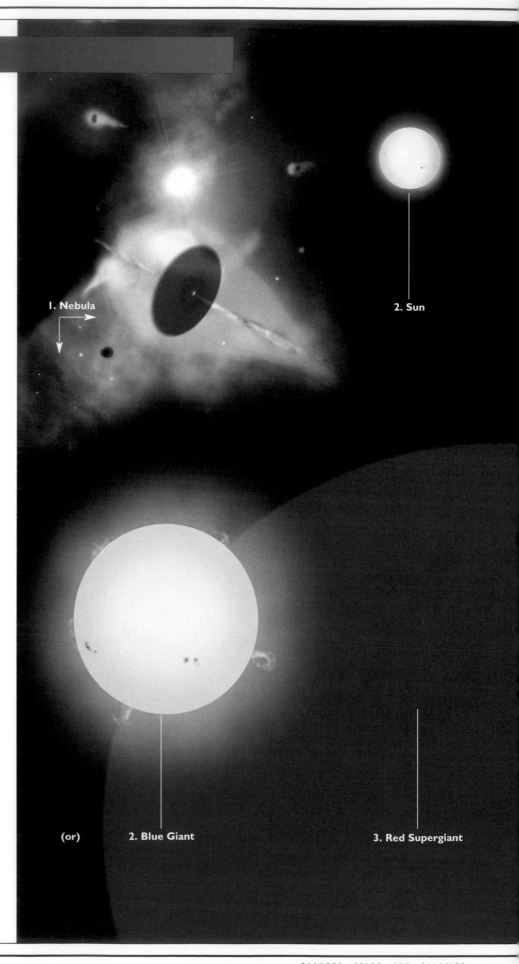

1. Nebula

2. Sun

(or)   2. Blue Giant

3. Red Supergiant

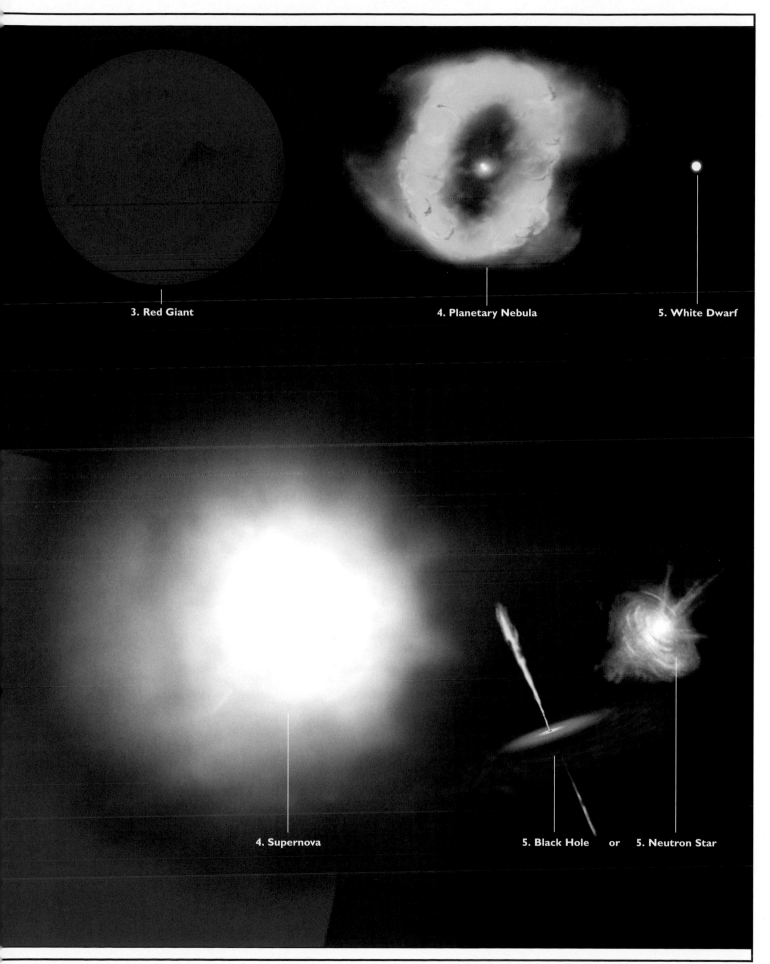

3. Red Giant

4. Planetary Nebula

5. White Dwarf

4. Supernova

5. Black Hole   or   5. Neutron Star

NEBULAS—STAR NURSERIES

A star is born inside an enormous cloud of hydrogen gas called a nebula. As clumps in a nebula attract more gas, they grow larger and hotter until they ignite and become stars.

Newborn stars light up the surrounding nebula the way car headlights light up a fog. A long-exposure photograph reveals a nebula's true colors, but in a telescope, it glows an eerie grayish-green. Many backyard astronomers look for nebulas, using a list made by Charles Messier.

These photographs show three nebulas in the Messier catalogue. In each photo the nebula is the glowing reddish formation near the center.

M42 (photo right) The Orion Nebula is the most well-known and easy-to-find nebula on Messier's list. It's visible to the unaided eye as the middle point of light in the sword of the constellation Orion, hanging below his belt, where the red X is in the circled diagram. The Orion Nebula contains hundreds of young stars, including a famous grouping of four bright stars called the Trapezium.

M17 (photo right) The Swan, or Omega Nebula, is located 5,000 light-years from Earth in the constellation Sagittarius. The nebula contains enough hydrogen to make hundreds of stars like our Sun.

Many nebulas that are easy to find with telescopes have several names. For example, the Orion Nebula is also called Messier 42, abbreviated M42. The Orion Nebula was the 42nd object on a list compiled by legendary astronomer Charles Messier.

Born in 1730, Charles Messier (top left) was a comet hunter in France. At the age of 14, the teenager became hooked on astronomy when an amazing, six-tailed comet appeared in the sky. When he was in his early 20s, he got his first job as an astronomer.

The only telescopes available to Messier were fairly small, and lots of different objects looked similar in them. It was easy to confuse a comet with a nebula or a galaxy. They all looked like faint fuzz balls in the telescope eyepiece.

To help clear up the confusion, Messier began keeping track of objects that looked like comets but didn't move across the sky the way comets do. He worked from his observatory in Paris (bottom left) and published his first catalogue of 45 objects in 1771. Messier continued to add to the list throughout his lifetime. Eventually, his catalogue grew to 110 objects.

Messier also tracked 20 comets. Although 7 of them were first spotted by others, 13 were seen by Messier before anyone else, and he still gets the credit for them.

Since Messier used telescopes similar to those available to anyone today, backyard astronomers often look for the so-called "Messier objects." Some of these enthusiasts even challenge themselves to a "Messier marathon" and try to observe all 110 objects in a single night.

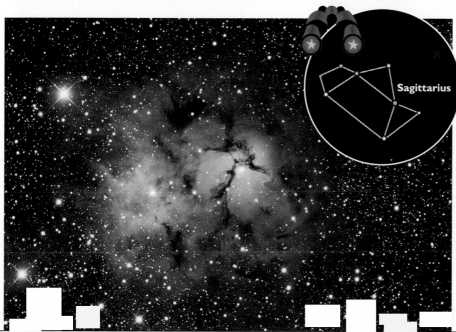

Sagittarius

M20 (photo left) The Trifid Nebula gets its name from its three-part appearance. Filaments of dark dust seem to divide it into sections. The red color comes from hot hydrogen gas heated by young stars, while the blue is the usual color of massive young stars.

STAR SIZES, TYPES OF STARS

Astronomers classify stars based on their size, temperature, and color. When astronomers talk about the size of a star, they usually mean the

Stars come in a variety of sizes and masses. When they're on the main sequence, they range from hefty, hot O stars to lightweight, cool M stars (art below). As smaller stars like our Sun age, they swell in physical size to become red giants, then fade away into dying embers called white dwarfs.

star's mass, or how much "stuff" it contains. This classification system is for young and middle-age stars. The rule changes when stars get old.

A STAR'S PRIME OF LIFE

Scientists say that when a star is in the prime of its life, it is on the "main sequence." That means it's producing energy

by converting hydrogen to helium (sidebar below right).

The mass of a star determines everything else about it: how hot it is, what color it is, and how long it will live. Massive stars are hot and blue, while small stars are cool and red.

To identify main sequence stars more easily, astronomers assign letters to the different star types. For historical reasons, some of the letters are skipped, so the labels

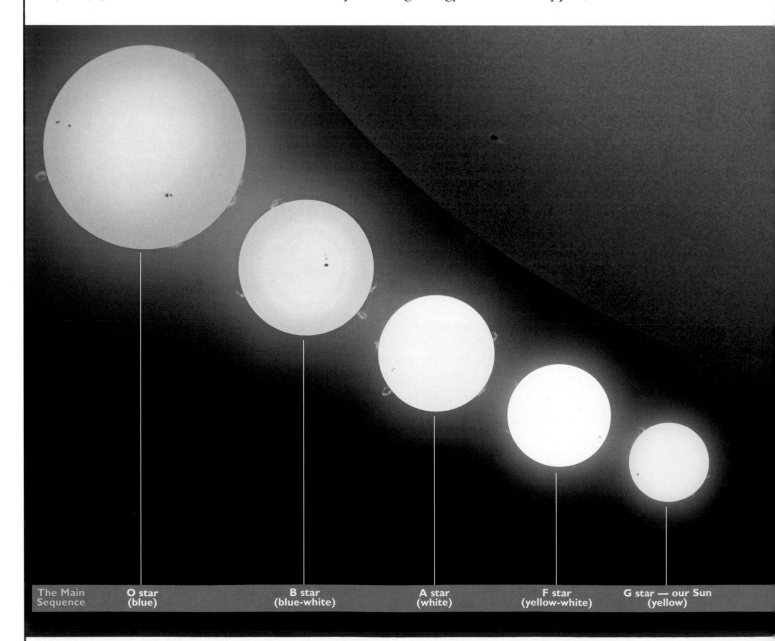

| The Main Sequence | O star (blue) | B star (blue-white) | A star (white) | F star (yellow-white) | G star — our Sun (yellow) |

are not in alphabetical order. Instead they're O, B, A, F, G, K, and M. The hottest stars are type O, while the coolest are type M.

The smallest stars are about one-tenth the mass of the Sun. They're cool, dim, and red. They can live for hundreds of billions of years, burning slowly and steadily. The largest stars are about a hundred times the mass of the Sun. They're hot, bright, and blue. They live fast and die young, burning out in only a few million years.

OLD STARS

A star's size changes as it stops fusing hydrogen and leaves the main sequence. It begins burning hydrogen in a thin shell-like area surrounding its core. Fusion energy from this shell heats the star and makes it swell up, expanding to many times its previous size. Small and medium-size stars, like our Sun, expand to be much, much bigger than an O star, but with far less mass. At this stage, they're called red giants. In the end, they fade into white dwarfs.

Large stars become red supergiants. One famous supergiant is the star Betelgeuse in the constellation Orion.

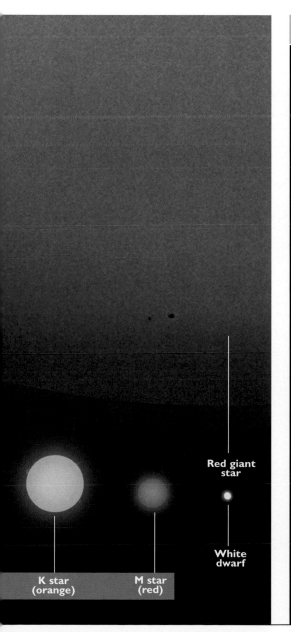

Red giant star

White dwarf

K star (orange)

M star (red)

HOW A STAR BURNS

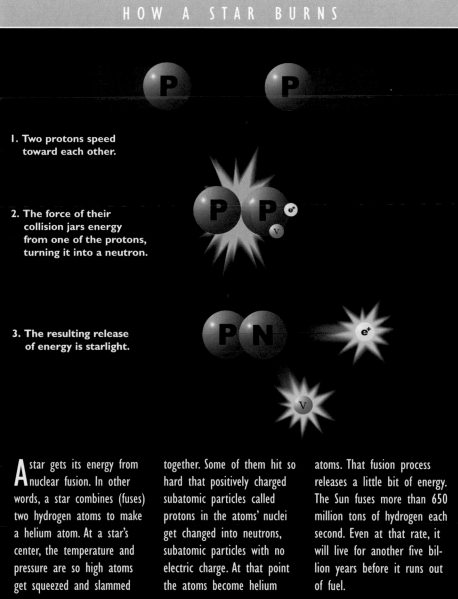

1. Two protons speed toward each other.

2. The force of their collision jars energy from one of the protons, turning it into a neutron.

3. The resulting release of energy is starlight.

A star gets its energy from nuclear fusion. In other words, a star combines (fuses) two hydrogen atoms to make a helium atom. At a star's center, the temperature and pressure are so high atoms get squeezed and slammed together. Some of them hit so hard that positively charged subatomic particles called protons in the atoms' nuclei get changed into neutrons, subatomic particles with no electric charge. At that point the atoms become helium atoms. That fusion process releases a little bit of energy. The Sun fuses more than 650 million tons of hydrogen each second. Even at that rate, it will live for another five billion years before it runs out of fuel.

DEATH OF STARS LIKE THE SUN

The end of a star like our Sun is both beautiful and peaceful. For a short time, it creates a brilliantly glowing, gaseous nebula.

When this kind of star runs out of hydrogen in its core, it begins fusing hydrogen in a shell-like layer that surrounds the core, the way an eggshell surrounds a yolk. Energy from the hydrogen-burning shell heats the star's outer layers, puffing them up. The star becomes a red giant.

These outer layers swell more and more until they blow off completely, leaving behind the star's hot, dead core. That core is called a white dwarf. It lights up the surrounding gas, creating a glowing nebula, a birthplace for new stars.

Over the course of about 10,000 years, the gas slowly spreads out until there is not enough left for us to see. The white dwarf gradually cools and fades away as well. All that remains is a cold black dwarf.

Our five-billion-year-old Sun (photo below) is a middle-age star. In another five billion years, it will reach its end, puffing off its outer gas layers to form a shining nebula, like those shown at right.

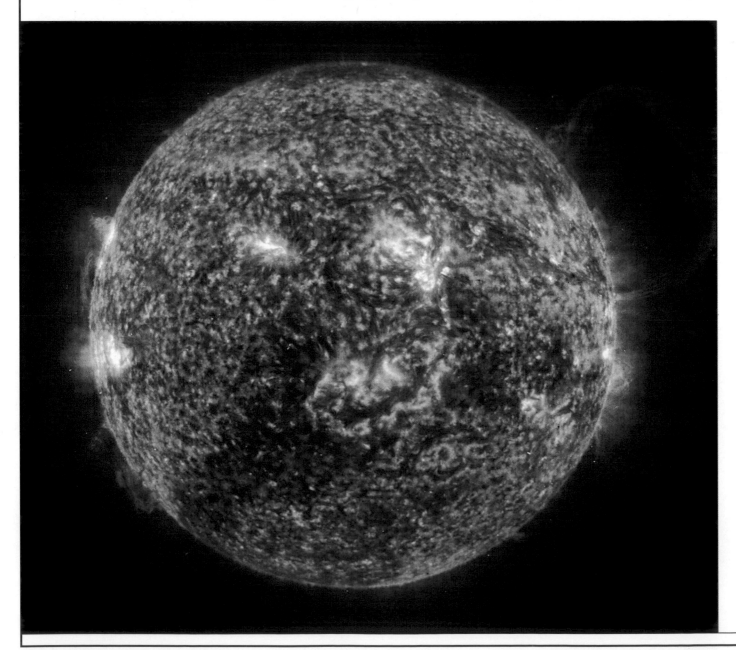

The Dumbbell Nebula, or M27, (photo left) was the first nebula from a dying, Sunlike star ever discovered. It's one of the brightest such nebulas in the night sky. The star at the center ejected gas in two cones that we see from the side, giving the nebula its unique shape.

Cygnus

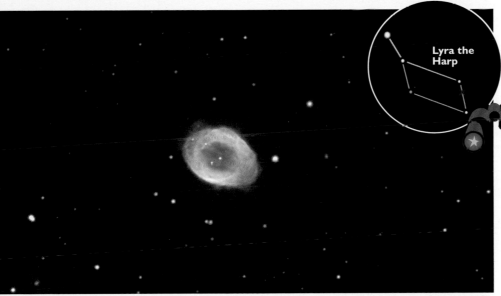

The Ring Nebula, or M57, (photo left) is shaped like the Dumbbell Nebula, with two cones of gas. But from Earth we see the ends of the cones, so the nebula appears ring-shaped. The ring is more than five trillion miles across. It's easy to locate in the constellation of Lyra the Harp.

Lyra the Harp

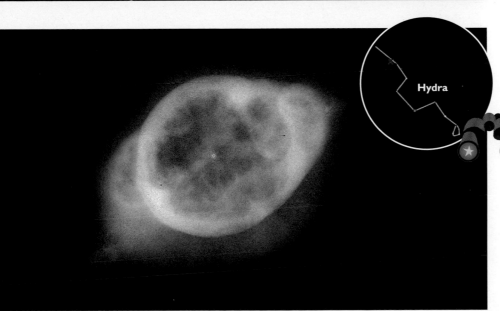

Found in the constellation Hydra, NGC 3242 (photo left) is nicknamed the Ghost of Jupiter because it looks similar to that planet in small telescopes. But NGC 3242 is about 1,400 light-years from Earth, much farther away than Jupiter. The NGC in its name stands for New General Catalog, a list of thousands of objects first compiled in 1888. The latest version of the NGC was published in 2000.

Hydra

Compared to a medium-size star like our Sun, the death of a giant star is dramatic and violent. It actually destroys itself.

Once a massive star runs out of hydrogen in its core, gravity pulls the core inward, making it dense enough and hot enough for its helium to fuse, making carbon and oxygen. That's when it becomes a red supergiant. Then the carbon and oxygen fuse to make sodium, magnesium, silicon, and heavier elements. The final stage of fusion creates iron.

Fusing iron removes energy rather than releasing it. With no energy source left to push outward against the force of gravity pulling inward, the star's core suddenly collapses. The star's outer layers rush inward, collide, then blast outward again with immense energy. The star explodes into a supernova.

Many of the elements, from helium to iron, that were created in the star's interior are scattered into space, where they can be used by the next generation. The calcium in our bones and the iron in our blood come from ancient supernovas.

In this artwork, a massive star has just exploded as a supernova. The explosion and radiation given off from such an explosion would sterilize any planet orbiting the star, leaving behind a dead world.

When a massive star explodes as a supernova, it scatters itself across space. Gas ejected by a supernova rushes out at a speed of millions of miles per hour.

The supernova also creates a shock wave, which slams into surrounding gas ejected by the star before the explosion. That blast wave heats the gas to a temperature of millions of degrees—hot enough to glow. We call that glowing gas cloud a supernova remnant.

A supernova remnant is so hot that it emits high-energy x-ray radiation. Special telescopes are needed to detect and study those x-rays.

A supernova remnant may also emit visible light that we can see with our eyes, or radio waves that can be detected by radio telescopes.

CREATORS AND DESTROYERS

The blast wave of a supernova can rip apart nebulas, but a supernova shock wave can also help new stars form. Interstellar gas compacted by the shock wave may clump together and gather more gas until it ignites as a star.

Taurus

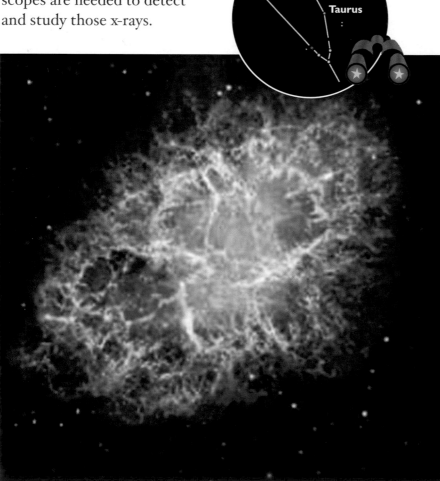

The Crab Nebula, or M1, (photo left) in the constellation Taurus is the only supernova remnant in Messier's catalogue. A star that exploded in the year A.D. 1054 created M1. Sightings of the supernova were recorded in China and possibly in the Americas.

No supernova has been observed in the Milky Way since the invention of the telescope. The next star to go might be Betelgeuse. In the art above, it's shown as a massive red glow consuming the moon (seen faintly toward the top of the art) of a nearby planet (the sphere in the foreground).

Orion

A supernova remnant can become either a black hole (see page 114) or a neutron star.

A neutron star isn't really a star. It's more like a giant atomic nucleus 5-10 miles (8-16 km) across, made entirely of neutrons. Normal atoms are made of three particles— protons, electrons, and neutrons. But the atoms in a supernova core have been squeezed so tightly together that protons and electrons have combined to form neutrons.

Since so much mass is stuffed into such a small sphere, a neutron star is very dense. A sugar cube-size lump would weigh about a billion tons, more than 10,000 aircraft carriers.

PULSARS

Some spinning neutron stars emit beams of radio energy that sweep across space like the beam of a lighthouse or searchlight. If the beam happens to pass over the Earth, we detect a pulsing radio signal every time the beam hits. The neutron stars that create these signals are called pulsars.

As shown in this artwork, the center of the Crab Nebula is a region of powerful energy. Hot gas swirls around a compact pulsar. That pulsar is all that remains of a once-mighty star.

Astronomers didn't always know that pulsars existed. In 1967, astronomer Jocelyn Bell, then at Cambridge University in England, discovered a strange radio signal coming from outer space that blinked on and off about once every second. She labeled it LGM-1 for "little green men," a joke about possible alien life.

No one really thought that the signal was from aliens, but astronomers weren't sure what was causing it. No steady radio pulses had ever been spotted in the Milky Way before.

Not long after the discovery, a scientist calculated that a spinning neutron star could make radio pulses. The strong magnetic field of a pulsar traps electrons that escaped when the star's core collapsed. Those electrons generate radio waves that are funneled outward by the star's magnetic field into beams of radiation. As the pulsar spins, the beam sweeps across the sky.

Since the discovery of the first pulsar, more than a thousand others have been found. Some spin so fast that they flicker on and off hundreds of times every second.

Astronomers have even found one pulsar that is orbited by three planets. Those planets are cold, barren, and bathed in harsh radiation, so we can be pretty sure no "little green men" live there.

The most powerful supernovas do more than announce the death of a star. They create huge blasts of high-energy radiation called gamma rays. Gamma ray bursts are the brightest explosions in the universe. They would destroy any life that existed on nearby planets.

A gamma ray burst has been called the birth cry of a black hole. When a massive star's core collapses, it can form a black hole. If the star was rotating very quickly, a fast-spinning disk of gas will surround the new black hole, and some material from the disk will shoot out in cone-shaped jets. Those jets, coming from deep in the interior of the dying star, will punch through it and rip the rest of the star apart.

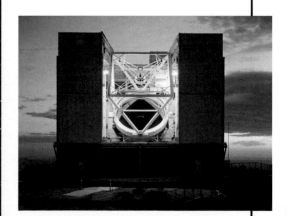

A gamma ray burst (art left) is the most powerful explosion in the universe. Only massive stars die this way. Observations using the Multiple Mirror Telescope, or MMT, in Arizona (photo above) proved the link between gamma ray bursts and supernovas.

A black hole really seems like a hole in space. Most black holes form when the core of a massive star collapses, crushing itself into oblivion.

A black hole has a stronger gravitational pull than anything else in the universe. It's like a bottomless pit, swallowing anything that gets near enough to it to be pulled in.

Black holes come in different sizes. The smallest has a mass about three times that of the Sun. The biggest one scientists have found so far has a mass about three billion times the Sun's. Really big black holes at the centers of galaxies probably form by swallowing enormous amounts of gas over time.

One of NASA's spacecraft has found thousands of black hole candidates in the Milky Way, but there are probably many more. The nearest one to Earth is about 1,600 light-years away.

The main artwork here shows hydrogen gas from a yellow star (at right in the art) falling into a black hole and forming a disk around it. The two bright white cones are gas that got close to the hole but escaped, thanks to a push from the hole's magnetic fields.

FALLING INTO A BLACK HOLE

Imagine falling into a black hole. As you move closer to it, the black hole's forces pull at your body, stretching it.

As the pull grows stronger, the atoms in your body are pulled apart. Those atoms are stretched and torn into smaller and smaller bits until nothing recognizable is left. You have just been "spaghetti-fied" by the might of a black hole.

Not every clump in a star-forming nebula will become a star. Sometimes, there's not enough gas nearby. Without that fuel, the object never gets dense enough and hot enough to maintain nuclear fusion. Instead, it fizzles.

Our Sun contains about a thousand times as much mass as Jupiter. The least massive stars are about 75 times the mass of Jupiter. Anything less massive than that is a failed star. Astronomers call them brown dwarfs, even though they're not really brown and they're not dwarf stars. They start out at their brightest, then become dimmer and redder than the dimmest star.

BROWN DWARF OR PLANET?

Astronomers are still debating what the difference is between planets and brown dwarfs. Most astronomers think that any-thing less massive than 13 Jupiters is a planet, while any-thing between 13 and 75 times the mass of Jupiter is a brown dwarf. The lower limit is the mass at which a brown dwarf can briefly fuse a form of hydro-gen called deuterium. Planets do not fuse hydrogen at all.

Looking like a glowing red coal, a brown dwarf (art right) is a stellar wannabe without enough mass to sustain nuclear fusion. It is destined to cool off slowly over billions of years, leaving any planets orbiting it in a never-ending deep freeze.

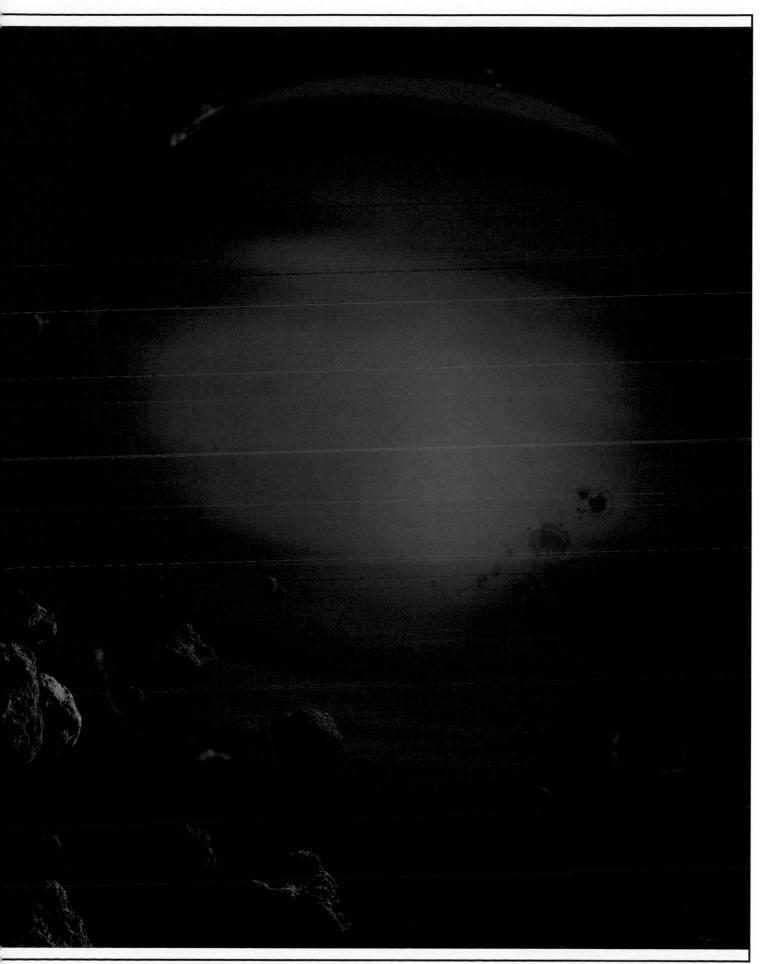

HOW PLANETS FORM

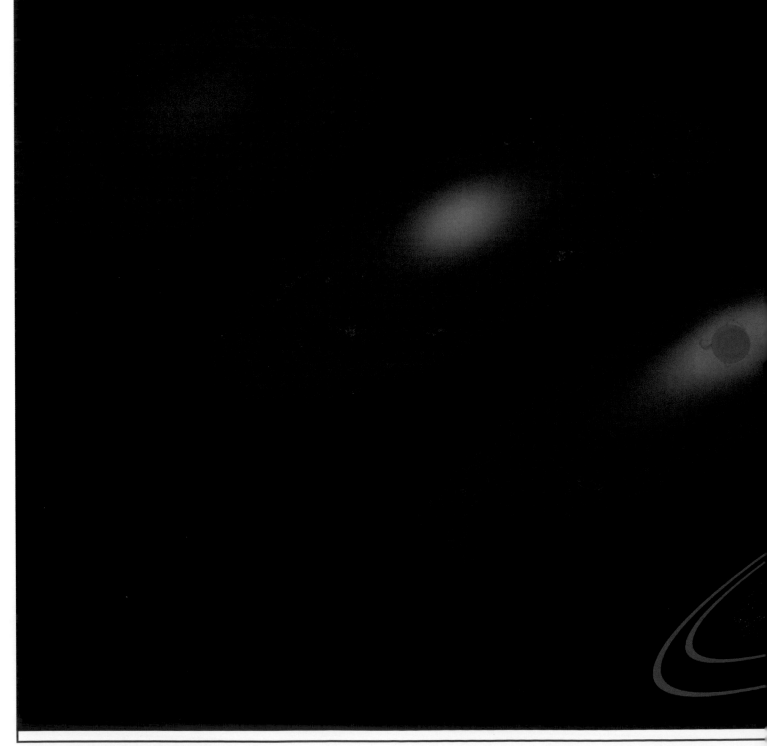

P lanets arise as a natural result of the star-formation process. Stars are born from large clouds of gas and dust. That gas and dust spins in space, flattening into a disk the way pizza dough does when a baker tosses it. The center of the disk becomes a star, while the rest of the disk may form planets.

Within the disk, dusty bits of carbon and silicon begin to clump together. Those clumps eventually get bigger and become rocky objects called protoplanets. Protoplanets smack into each other and stick together to make planets.

The asteroids in our solar system are leftover planetesimals, or small planets from the early solar system. Jupiter's gravity stirred them up and prevented them from sticking together. Astronomers have found evidence of asteroids in other star systems.

If a rocky planet grows large enough, it can collect and hold onto surrounding hydrogen gas. That's how the gas giants of our outer solar system grew so big.

Follow the artwork below from top left to bottom right to see how a star and its planets form from a single disk of gas and dust. As the infant star gathers hydrogen gas, leftover rocky bits stick together like giant dust bunnies. Eventually, those cosmic clumps grow to become full-size planets. Here a comet is streaking toward them.

Astronomers didn't discover planets outside our solar system until 1992. Then, three Earth-size planets were detected about 900 light-years away. Instead of orbiting a normal star, they were orbiting a dead star known as a pulsar.

Scientists think the three planets formed from atoms of iron and silicon that were ejected by the dying star. Most of the star's material was blasted into space, but enough stuck around to collect together again and make small worlds.

In 1995, Swiss astronomers found the first planet orbiting a normal star. That planet is named 51 Pegasi b. It is about the same mass as Jupiter, but unlike Jupiter it orbits very close to its star and has a year that is only four days long.

Since the discovery of 51 Pegasi b, astronomers have spotted more than 200 planets orbiting distant stars. Many of them are weird worlds very different from anything in our solar system.

This art shows what a beautiful sunset on a moon in a distant star system might look like. The moon's planet, a gas giant, hovers in the sky above it. If the moon were at the right distance from the star in this system, it could have oceans and maybe even life.

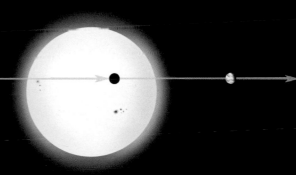

1. Wobbling Star

Look for a star that wobbles when a planet's gravity tugs at it.

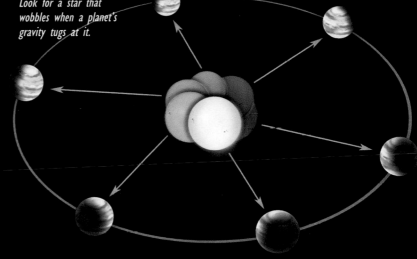

2. Eclipsing Star's Dimming Light

Look for a star that dims when a planet crosses in front of it.

It's hard to find planets around other stars. The stars are very far away, and planets are so small and dim that seeing one next to a star is like trying to see a firefly sitting next to a spotlight. Only in the past decade have astronomers gained the tools they need to find alien worlds.

Since a star is much easier to see than a planet, astronomers hunt planets by looking for their effect on their host star. Most of the 200 known alien worlds were found by looking for wobbling stars. Just as the star's gravity tugs on the planet, the planet's gravity tugs on the star. In this gravitational dance, the star wobbles back and forth. If it wobbles toward and away from us, we can use a spectrograph (an instrument similar to a prism that splits the light of the star into a spectrum of colors) to look for a slight shift in the star's movement. That is the way 51 Pegasi b was found. We can also look for stars that wobble left and right or up and down across the sky, but those searches are much harder because the wobble in the star's apparent position is so tiny.

Recently, planet hunters have had great success by looking for planets that eclipse their stars, making the star's light dim ever so slightly. (Since we are so far away, the planet appears to cover only a fraction of the star's disk.) Eclipse searches can find smaller planets than the search for "wobblers"— even planets as small as Earth.

The distant planet HD 189733 b (art left), located 60 light-years from Earth, is covered by a dark layer of clouds that hides all its surface features, making it one of the blackest planets ever found in the universe.

The gas giant planet Epsilon Eridani b, seen from one of its moons in this artwork, orbits a star a little cooler than our sun. Since the planet is more than 300 million miles from its star, it and its moons would be too cold to support life.

The Milky Way and other large galaxies are home to a special kind of star cluster: a globular cluster. These round balls hold up to a million stars crammed into a space only a few dozen light-years across. If you think of the sun as living in a quiet suburb, then the stars in a globular cluster are living in a crowded city center.

If you were to visit a planet inside a globular cluster, the night sky would be spectacular! From Earth we see only a few thousand stars with the unaided eye. The sky of a globular-cluster planet would be filled with a hundred thousand stars or more.

These clusters contain the oldest stars in our galaxy— almost as old as the universe itself. Many aging red giants and dead white dwarfs live in globular clusters.

Globular clusters orbit the center of the Milky Way in all directions, some looping high above or below our galaxy. Astronomer Harlow Shapley mapped globular clusters as a way to figure out the size and shape of our galaxy. He argued that since we see more globular clusters in one direction than the other, we must be off to the side of the Milky Way.

This art shows the night sky as seen from a cave opening on a rocky planet orbiting a star in a globular cluster. Thousands of nearby stars would make clear nights much lighter than they are on Earth.

Since so many stars are packed so close together in globular clusters, they're very bright and visible across great distances of space. That makes them favorite targets for a lot of backyard astronomers. Through a large telescope, a globular cluster looks like a large ball of stars filling the eyepiece with a spectacular display.

In small telescopes, globular clusters look more like fuzzy cotton balls. In fact, they look a lot like comets, which is why Charles Messier's catalogue of objects lists a lot of globular clusters.

Globular clusters are so crowded that sometimes two stars will collide to form a more massive star that burns hot and blue, appearing younger than it really is. Since those stars look like they've aged more slowly, lagging behind their neighbors, astronomers have named them blue stragglers.

Omega Centauri (photo below) is the largest and brightest globular cluster in the Milky Way. It contains millions of stars in a sphere 150 light-years across. Omega Centauri is best viewed from locations near Earth's Equator.

Centaurus

All spiral galaxies are surrounded by a halo of globular clusters (art left). The stars in the globular clusters were the first to form as the galaxy structures grew.

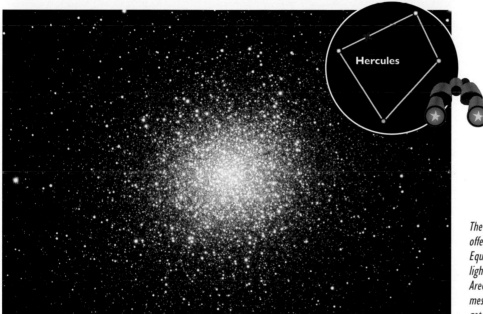

The Hercules Globular Cluster, or M13, (photo left) offers a spectacular view to observers north of the Equator. M13 is bright even though it's 25,000 light-years away. In 1974, astronomers used the Arecibo radio telescope in Puerto Rico to send a message toward it. If aliens live there, they won't get the message for 25,000 years.

The globular cluster M2 (photo left) is compact, which makes it more easily visible in small backyard telescopes. It's located on the opposite side of the galactic center from Earth, more than 37,000 light-years away.

THE GALACTIC ZOO

Billions of galaxies with hundreds of billions of stars populate our universe. Galaxies come in many varieties. Our home, the Milky Way, is a spiral galaxy. All spiral galaxies have a disk of stars. The stars gather into curlicues called spiral arms that extend from the galaxy's center to its edges. Some galaxies have tightly wound spiral arms; others have loosely wound spiral arms.

Some spiral galaxies are just a disk and as flat as a pancake. Others, including the Milky Way, have a big, central ball of stars called a bulge. The bulge often contains older stars, while the flat disk holds younger stars.

A barred spiral galaxy has a central bar, or rectangular

The galactic zoo is shown in the art above. An elliptical galaxy has a distinctly orange-yellow color because it contains mostly old, redder stars. Unlike spiral galaxies, ellipticals like this one typically hold little or no dust.

A spiral galaxy has older stars in its central bulge and young, blue stars in its disk and spiral arms. Dark patches show where large clumps of interstellar dust block starlight.

This unusual galaxy is in between a spiral and an elliptical, sharing characteristics of both. It has the flattened shape of a spiral, but its yellowish color and lack of dust are more like an elliptical.

clump, of stars that lies across the middle of the galaxy. The spiral arms extend from the ends of the bar, instead of from the center of the galaxy. Astronomers think that a galactic bar might form when a galaxy is disturbed by the gravity of another galaxy that passes nearby, or even collides with it.

The Milky Way is a barred spiral, but from Earth we're looking almost directly at one end of the bar, so it's hard to see from our location.

Another common type of galaxy is the elliptical galaxy. Elliptical galaxies are all bulge and no disk. They can be round, football-shaped, or anything in between. They tend to be made up of only old stars.

Another type of galaxy has no definite shape. Because of that, it's called an irregular galaxy. The nearby Magellanic Clouds are irregular galaxies, and in the beginning of the universe, the first galaxies that formed were irregulars.

A face-on view is the best way to enjoy the dramatic sweep of a galaxy's spiral arms. This spiral has a very small bulge compared to its disk.

This barred spiral galaxy appears tightly wound up. Sometime in its past, another galaxy probably passed nearby, ripping away some of its stars and gases and spinning the rest into a flattened S shape.

Irregular galaxies don't have the well-defined shapes of spirals or ellipticals. In this composite photograph, green shows where stars are, while blue and red highlight hot gas ejected from the galaxy into intergalactic space.

The closest large galaxy to the Milky Way is the Andromeda galaxy, also called M31. Andromeda is like the Milky Way's big sister, since it's twice as large as our galaxy. The Milky Way is 100,000 light-years across and holds about 400 billion stars. By comparison, Andromeda is about 200,000 light-years across and holds a trillion stars.

Another close neighbor of the Milky Way is the Triangulum galaxy, or M33. M33 is the runt of the litter. It is only 50,000 light-years across with about 100 billion stars. Unlike many galaxies, M33 has no giant black hole at its center.

Until the 1920s, astronomers thought M31 and M33 were nearby gaseous nebulas and part of the Milky Way. Then Edwin Hubble discovered that M31 and M33 were separate galaxies. Since both are moving toward the Milky Way, the three galaxies eventually will collide, and their stars will become part of one big galaxy. Astronomers have nicknamed that future galaxy Milkomeda.

The Andromeda galaxy is visible to your unaided eye if you're in a dark location. This long-exposure photograph taken with a small telescope shows Andromeda's full glory.

Stars don't collide too often because they're very far apart, relative to their size. Galaxies are much closer to each other relative to their size, so they collide frequently. Galactic collisions were even more common in the past, when the universe was smaller and galaxies were closer together.

When galaxies collide, strange things can happen. Sometimes a small galaxy punches through the center of a larger galaxy, leaving a hole and a surrounding ring of stars and creating a ring galaxy. Sometimes a large galaxy consumes a small one, destroying all signs that the smaller one ever existed.

Right now, the Milky Way is swallowing at least one "dwarf" galaxy. On the far side of the galactic center from Earth, the Sagittarius dwarf elliptical galaxy is plunging through the disk of the Milky Way. The Milky Way's stronger gravity is ripping apart the dwarf. Eventually its stars will become part of the Milky Way.

About 200 million years ago, M32, a smaller galaxy, punched through the disk of Andromeda. Ripples of interstellar dust spread out through

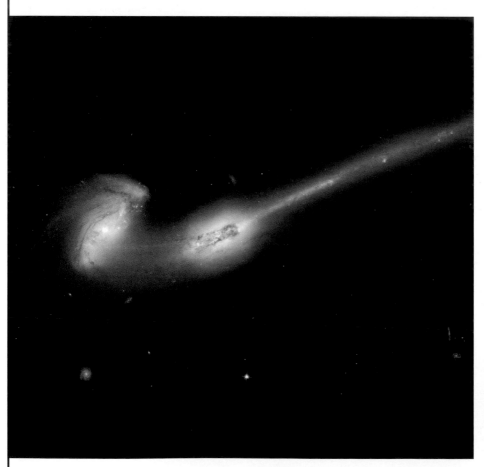

The Hubble Space Telescope captured this view of two galaxies playing a game of cat and mouse or, in this case, mouse and mouse. These colliding galaxies were nicknamed "the mice" because of the long tails of stars and gas that were thrown off them during the collision. They're located 300 million light-years from Earth.

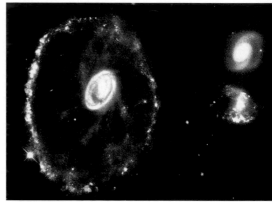

The Cartwheel Galaxy (photo top), 500 million light-years from Earth, suffered a head-on collision with another galaxy. Gravitational forces from the collision formed the two stunning rings of gas and newborn stars. The Whirlpool Galaxy (photo above) has a small companion known as NGC 5195. As the two galaxies brush past each other, gravity from NGC 5195 may be molding the dramatic spiral structure seen in the Whirlpool Galaxy.

Andromeda like water ripples in a pond. M32 survived the encounter, but one day it will be devoured by Andromeda.

When two galaxies close to the same size interact, the results are even more dramatic. Gravity can fling off streams of stars as the galaxies whip around each other. Gas clouds in the two galaxies may merge, fueling bursts of star formation.

In some colliding galaxies, stars form a hundred times faster than in calm galaxies like the Milky Way. Those stars live fast and die quickly. A star explodes as a supernova every couple of years there, compared to an average of once every hundred years in the Milky Way. Astronomers call colliding, starburst galaxies "supernova factories," since they produce supernovas so quickly.

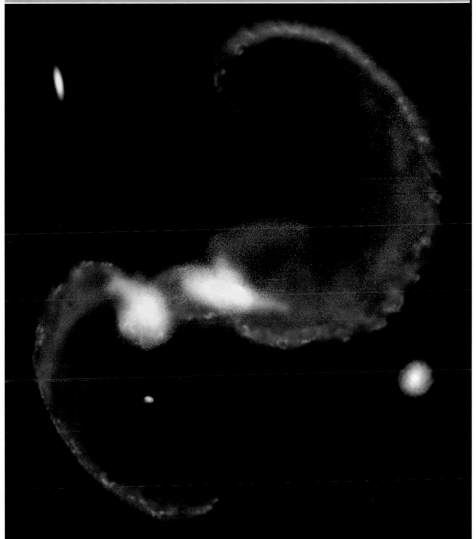

Like the Cartwheel Galaxy, Centaurus A (photo above) had a collision in the distant past. The obvious dark markings across the face of this galaxy are dust lanes from a long-gone spiral galaxy. Centaurus A swallowed the spiral, which left only a band of cosmic dust to mark its passing.

The Milky Way and Andromeda are on a collision course, approaching each other at a speed of about 300,000 miles per hour (483,000 kph). In a few billion years, these two galaxies will ram together (art above) to become a football-shaped, elliptical galaxy.

Since the Milky Way and Andromeda are both large, their collision will be particularly dramatic. The "damage" will be greater, just as the collision of two dump trucks would bend a lot more metal than if a small vehicle were to smack into a truck.

As the two galaxies interact gravitationally, some stars will be tossed outward, escaping into intergalactic space. Others will be flung from a galaxy's outskirts into the core (art above). Stars that once orbited in an orderly disk may be sent into new orbits that zoom outward before plunging back down, looping around and out again.

By the time the Milky Way and Andromeda collide, our star, the Sun, will be no more than a white dwarf.

Both the Milky Way and Andromeda hold plenty of gas that could form new stars. Most likely, a burst of star formation will take place when the collision happens. Thousands of new stars and planetary systems will be born. Older stars will be lost, ejected from both galaxies. Many new stars will quickly die off and explode as supernovas. The new galaxy will be an energetic place for millions of years after the collision.

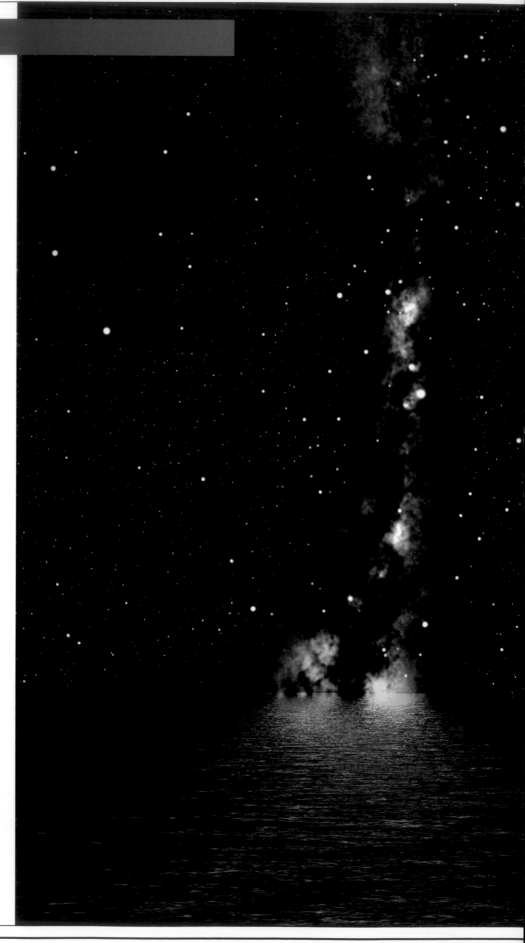

The twin Magellanic Clouds, or Clouds of Magellan, are not really clouds at all. They're galaxies visible deep in the southern half of the sky. North of the Equator you can't see them. Because of this, they remained unknown to most of the Western world until the voyage of Ferdinand Magellan.

In 1519, he sailed from Spain with a crew of more than 200 men, hoping to travel around the world. Magellan died along the way, but 18 members of his crew returned safely in 1522. With them, they brought their observations of the southern sky. When European astronomers used the mariners' records to make sky charts, they named two objects after Magellan, calling those objects the Large and Small Magellanic Clouds.

ABOUT THE CLOUDS

Although they may look like glowing clouds fixed to the sky, the Magellanic Clouds are both irregular galaxies that have been twisted and warped by the Milky Way's gravity.

Astronomers used to think that the Magellanic Clouds were permanent companions of the Milky Way, orbiting around our galaxy. But scientists now think these travelers may be "just passing through."

The Large Magellanic Cloud is located about 160,000

light-years from Earth. It's about one-twentieth as large as our galaxy in diameter and holds about one-tenth as many stars. The Small Magellanic Cloud is located about 200,000 light-years from Earth. It's about ten times smaller than its companion and a hundred times smaller than the Milky Way.

SUPERNOVA 1987A

In February 1987, astronomers spotted an exploding star in the Large Magellanic Cloud. Since it was the first supernova observed that year, it was named Supernova 1987A. This was the closest supernova to Earth seen since the invention of the telescope.

At its brightest, Supernova 1987A shone with the energy of a billion Suns and could be seen with the unaided eye, despite how far away it was. It slowly faded over time and now is visible only in telescopes.

Debris from Supernova 1987A formed a supernova remnant. Astronomers have searched the remnant looking for a neutron star that might have been created by the explosion, but they haven't found it. The explosion may have created a black hole instead.

When Magellan sailed into the Southern Hemisphere, his crew spotted two objects (top right in art) that no European had seen before. He used them as markers to navigate, not realizing they were actually companions to the Milky Way (middle, reflected on the sea).

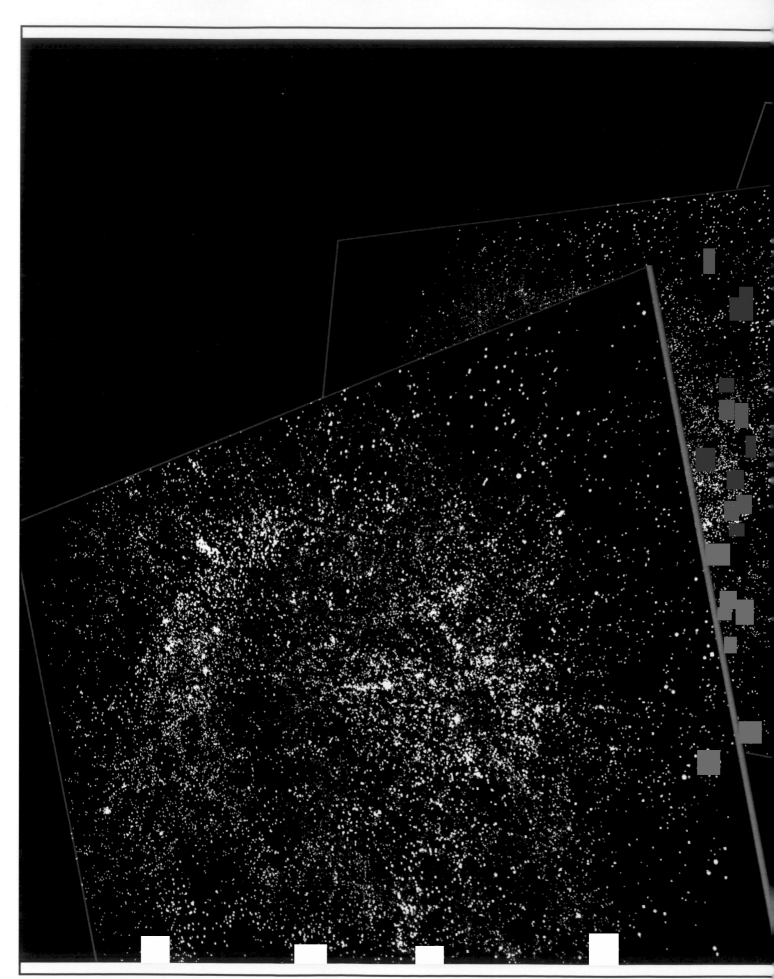

A stronomers used to think that galaxies were scattered randomly throughout the universe. But when they began mapping galaxies carefully, they were in for a surprise.

In 1989, astronomers Margaret Geller and John Huchra announced that, rather than being random, galaxies are clustered into gigantic structures. Dozens of galaxies they measured were lined up at about the same distance, forming a "great wall." Scientists have found many more walls of galaxies since then.

The universe started out very smooth, with matter spread out almost evenly through space. Over the past 13.7 billion years, gravity has pulled that matter together. Now, the universe close to us is very clumpy.

The Milky Way is part of a galaxy cluster called the Local Group. The Andromeda spiral galaxy, M33, the Magellanic Clouds, and about 30 dwarf galaxies all currently belong to the Local Group. The Milky Way and Andromeda are two of its largest members.

Most galaxies cluster into huge cosmic walls and filaments (art left), pulled together by their mutual gravity. More distant galaxies are redder than nearby galaxies, a fact that helps astronomers to measure distances across the visible universe.

In 2004, astronomers unveiled the longest time-length photograph of the sky ever made. The Hubble Ultra Deep Field shows an area (field) of the sky one-fiftieth the size of the full Moon, or smaller than a grain of sand held at arm's length. It required a total exposure time of a million seconds, or almost 700 days, and it reveals objects ten billion times fainter than what can be seen with the human eye.

"Deep" refers to areas of space outside our solar system. Some galaxies in this photograph are very faint because they're almost 13 billion light-years away. That means we're seeing them 13 billion years ago, when the universe was young.

The Hubble Ultra Deep Field shows about 10,000 galaxies. Some are spirals and ellipticals similar to nearby galaxies, but many others are oddballs—galactic toddlers still growing and developing. The Ultra Deep Field will remain our best view of the early universe until Hubble's successor, the James Webb Space Telescope, is launched in 2013.

Eight hundred photos taken over four months by the Hubble Space Telescope (just above) were processed and assembled to make this stunning view (left). It encompasses 10,000 galaxies, each containing about 200 billion stars.

There's a lot more to the universe than what we can see directly. It's like an iceberg. The part of the iceberg that's visible floating above the surface is only one-tenth of all the ice. The other nine-tenths lurks underwater, unseen.

In our universe, the gas, stars, and galaxies we can see make up only one-sixth of what is out there. We know there's more we can't see because the unseen "stuff" has gravity. It pulls on the stuff we can see. But gravity provides our only clue. The unseen stuff doesn't emit radiation that we can detect, so astronomers call it dark matter.

Trying to solve the puzzle of dark matter is one of the most important problems in modern astronomy. No one knows what dark matter really is.

Most scientists think that dark matter probably consists of huge numbers of tiny sub-atomic particles. They are hunting for those particles using large, sophisticated detectors. But for now, the true nature of dark matter is a mystery.

Astronomers found hints of dark matter when they studied rotating spiral galaxies, including the Milky Way. All of the galaxies they examined were rotating faster than expected—so fast that they should fly apart, scattering stars like dandelion seeds. Strong gravity had to be holding the galaxies together. That gravity came from unseen dark matter.

There are many other clues that dark matter exists. For one, galaxy clusters hold hot intergalactic gas. The gas is so hot that it should escape like steam from a teapot. The gravity of dark matter holds onto it.

In 2006, scientists got the strongest evidence yet that dark matter is real. They studied a pair of colliding galaxies and found that gas and stars were clustered in one spot, while the strongest gravity was concentrated in a different spot. The collision had dragged visible matter and dark matter in opposite directions.

Even the clumpiness of the universe shows that dark matter exists. Without the extra gravity of dark matter, visible matter wouldn't have had time to pull itself together to form galaxies and galaxy clusters. In that sense, we owe our very existence to something we've never seen.

We thought we knew what the universe was, but we didn't. Almost five-sixths of all matter is unseen and unknown. Astronomers hope to find the door (symbolized in the art left) that opens onto the answer to the mystery of dark matter.

To understand the accelerating universe, you first have to understand the birth of the universe—the big bang. This was not an explosion that tossed a bunch of atoms and energy into empty space. The big bang was an explosion of space itself. It created space where none existed before. And space is still being created right now.

When we say the universe is expanding, we mean that space itself is expanding. Galaxies rush away from each other not because they are speeding through space, but because the space between them is growing. A galaxy is like a person standing on a moving walkway. The person moves because the walkway moves.

SURPRISE!

Astronomers thought that the expansion of the universe had been slowing down ever since the big bang. The pull of gravity from all the matter in the universe, both normal matter and dark matter, should see to that. The only debate was whether the universe would slow to a stop and reverse, collapsing into a "big crunch," or whether the universe would just keep slowing down without ever really stopping.

In 1998, astronomers got a big surprise. Two teams studying distant supernovas found that those star explosions were dimmer than expected. Since light grows dimmer the farther away the light source is, the supernovas were more distant than expected. So the universe must be expanding faster than scientists had expected.

DARK ENERGY

In fact, calculations showed that the universe wasn't just growing faster than we thought; it was actually speeding up. Something must be providing a cosmic push. Astronomers named that mysterious something dark energy. The reverse of gravity, dark energy is pushing things away from each other.

No one knows what dark energy is, but many scientists are trying to answer that question. So far, it seems that dark energy is a property of space itself. The more space grows due to cosmic expansion, the more dark energy grows, and the more "push" there is to speed up the universe.

Whatever dark energy may be, its influence will decide the fate of our universe.

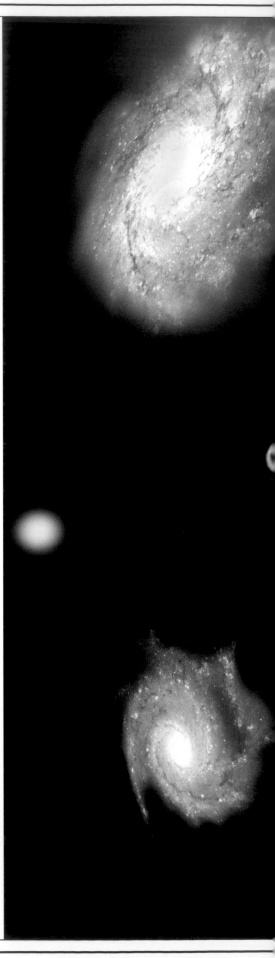

A mysterious force that astronomers call dark energy is speeding up the expansion of the universe. Galaxies are flying away from each other faster and faster (art right).

HOW THE UNIVERSE WILL END

We are on a one-way trip. Since the universe is expanding faster and faster, everything is getting farther and farther apart. At some point even our closest neighbors will have moved on. But before that happens, the Milky Way and Andromeda will collide. In a few billion years, they'll form a new combined galaxy that will pull in all the smaller galaxies in our neighborhood and swallow them up. More distant galaxies will escape and move beyond our sight, leaving only one visible galaxy: our own.

Our galaxy will suffer a slow

and steady decline. It will run out of the raw materials to form stars. All the gas needed to create stars will become locked into dead stellar remnants, like neutron stars, or will spread out so much that it can't clump together and ignite.

No new stars will be born. Those that already exist will live their lives and burn out.

Many trillions of years from now, all that will be left is a galaxy of black holes, neutron stars, and cold, black dwarfs that gradually fade away.

Tens of billions of years in the future, stars like our Sun will have died. Only faint, red stars that live for a long time will remain. Those fading embers will shed little warmth on worlds grown cold and quiet (art below).

OTHER UNIVERSES

When astronomers speak of the universe, they mean the observable universe—everything that we can see or detect with instruments. But what if there is more out there that we can't observe?

Astronomers have several ideas about how our universe formed. Some believe that a universe can pop into existence from a black hole (art below). If that's true, there could be thousands of other universes that we can't detect.

Using mathematics, scientists not only can imagine but also can describe in detail other possible universes, with different laws of physics. This is more than idle speculation. Other universes may actually exist.

To understand this mind-bending idea, consider what the word dimension means. In our everyday experience, a dimension is a direction in space.

We live in a three-dimensional world because we can move forward and backward, left and right, up and down.

Einstein showed that time also is a dimension, linked permanently to the other three. Past-future is the fourth dimension. So physicists have described the fabric of the cosmos as being four-dimensional space-time.

A FIFTH DIMENSION?
Recently, physicists have begun to think there may be more

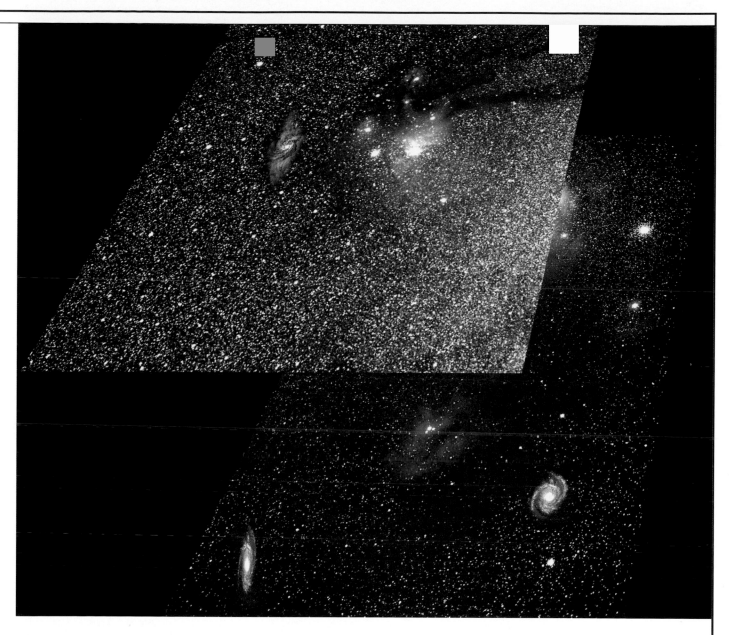

The most recent theory for the birth of our universe suggests that colliding branes (art above) may be the power source behind the big bang. If such collisions happen over and over, then universes may have been formed and re-formed many times in the past.

than the four familiar dimensions. The true nature of everything may involve many dimensions, but we can't perceive other dimensions with our senses.

We're like ants crawling on the surface of a giant hot-air balloon. The ants perceive only the flat, two-dimensional fabric stretching off in all directions as far as they can see. We perceive four-dimensional space-time stretching in all directions, when actually other dimensions may exist.

Scientists speculate that the visible universe may be a four-dimensional membrane, or brane for short, moving through unseen dimensions. Other branes, or parallel universes, may also exist. We would never be able to communicate with those other universes, much less travel among them.

COLLIDING BRANES

New research suggests that the event we call the big bang actually occurred when our brane collided with a neighboring brane. The collision generated the heat energy and push of expansion that we call the big bang. A lot of work lies ahead to determine if the colliding-brane theory is true.

In this imagined, alien world, creatures don't see the colors that we do. Instead they detect infrared heat like an infrared camera does.

Earth is the perfect world for life. But what makes it so special? Actually, there are a number of things.

To begin with, Earth is in the right orbit circling around the Sun. Not too hot and not too cold, it has just the right temperature range to support life and keep the water in our oceans from freezing or boiling.

Next, we orbit the right kind of star. Some stars have much shorter lifetimes than ours, leaving little time for life to evolve on the planets orbiting them. Some stars send out lethal amounts of radiation, which fry the surrounding planets and their moons. Our Sun is a long-lived, stable star—perfect for supporting life.

Earth is also the right size. It's large enough to generate the gravity needed to hold an atmosphere and not let it float away. We have a stabilizing moon as well, and a tilted axis that moderates weather cycles.

Finally, Earth is located out in an arm of the Milky Way where there aren't devastating explosions. All of these things put together mean we live on a perfect world.

Light from the Sun (peeking over the edge of Earth in the art) gives Earth just the right temperatures for life. The Moon helps stabilize its rotation. Jupiter protects us from asteroids; its gravity pulls them in before they reach us.

This seems like such an easy question to answer. Everybody knows singing birds are alive and rocks are not. But when we start studying plants, bacteria, and other odd microscopic creatures, things get more complicated. So what exactly is life?

Most scientists agree that if something can move on its own, reproduces to make more copies of itself, grows in size to become more complex in structure over time, takes in nutrients to survive, gives off waste products, and responds to external stimuli such as increased sunlight, changes in temperature, or somebody poking it with a stick, it's alive!

On Earth there are two basic types of life. The one we're most familiar with utilizes sunlight as an energy source and includes all the animals and green plants that inhabit land, sea, and air. However, deep beneath the oceans and embedded in rocks miles below the Earth's crust lives another form of life that does not use sunlight as a form of energy. It draws directly upon the chemicals surrounding it to provide energy. This is a very different form of life than what we're used to, but it's alive just the same. If there is life on Mars, Titan, or somewhere else in the solar system, it could be more like that, and if we find it, we want to be sure to recognize it as life.

To try and understand how a living organism works, it helps to look at one example of its simplest form—the single-cell bacteria called streptococcus. There are many kinds of these tiny organisms, and some are responsible for

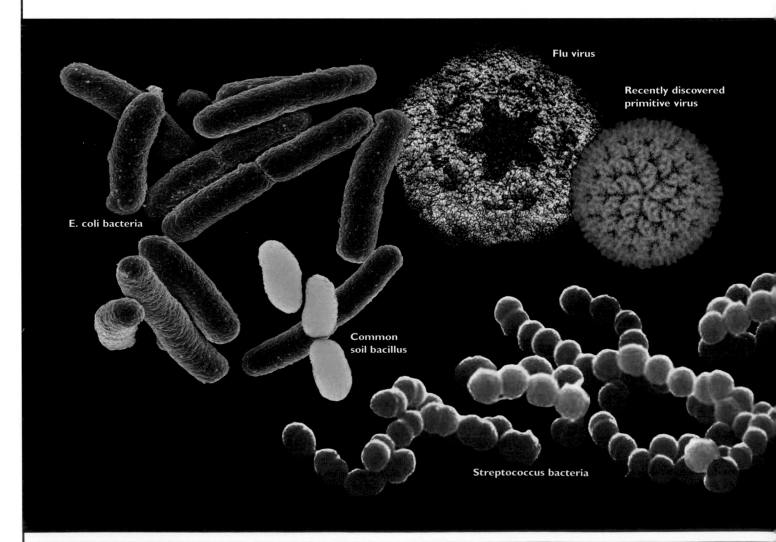

Flu virus

Recently discovered primitive virus

E. coli bacteria

Common soil bacillus

Streptococcus bacteria

human illnesses. What makes us sick or uncomfortable are the waste products the bacteria give off in our bodies.

A single streptococcus bacterium is so small that at least 500 of them could fit on the dot above the letter "i" in this sentence. Under a microscope, magnified to a thousand times their true size, they look like little round water balloons joined in long strings. Like a water balloon, they have an outside covering. Sort of like the skin on our bodies, this cell membrane separates the outside world from the inside, working parts of the bacterium.

Inside the membrane, thousands of molecules in different shapes and structures float in a gel.

These bacteria are one of the simplest forms of life we know. They have no moving parts, no lungs, no brain, no heart, no liver, no leaves or fruit. And yet, this life form reproduces and makes more of itself, grows in size by producing long chain structures, takes in nutrients, and gives off waste products. Also, heat kills it. That's why your body runs a temperature when it detects a strep infection. It's defending itself from an invader!

But what part of this tiny life form is alive? Even more baffling, how did a random collection of nonliving molecules come together, get organized, and become alive? We're not sure, but these are questions scientists are trying to answer.

Scientists think life began on Earth some 4.1 to 3.9 billion years ago, but no fossils exist from that time. The earliest fossils ever found are from the primitive life that existed 3.6 billion years ago. Other life forms soon followed, and some of these are shown in the images below. One big question is whether life was transported to Earth aboard meteorites that were actually broken-off chunks of Mars or Venus.

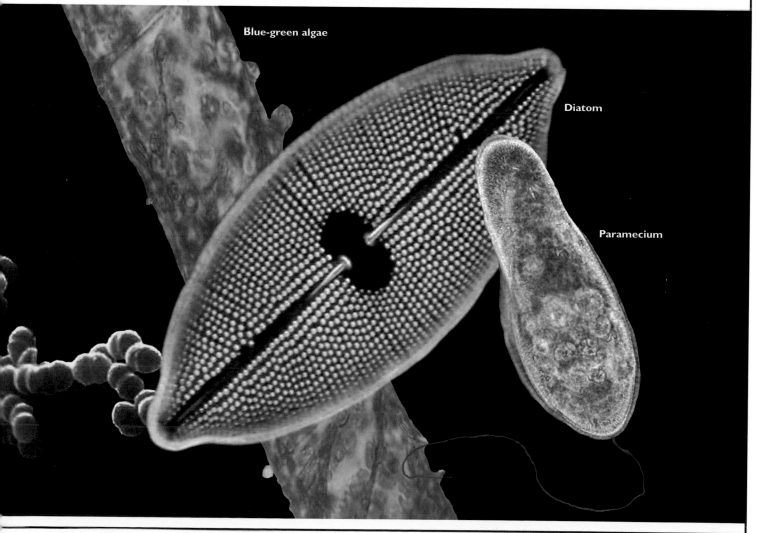

Blue-green algae

Diatom

Paramecium

In 1976, when the Viking Lander set down on the surface of Mars, no Martians were there to greet it. In one moment, the hope of finding intelligent life on Mars vanished. Now, more than 30 years later, no traces of life, not even microbes, have been discovered on Mars. The planet appears to be a vast desert wasteland. The surface water it used to have is locked up in the frozen polar ice caps. Life-supporting liquid water doesn't exist on the surface anymore.

On Venus, life might have existed billions of years ago, but today the planet's extreme atmospheric pressure and heat would crush or cook life.

A few scientists still hold out hope that alien forms of life may be found bobbing along like cosmic jellyfish in the upper cloud layers of Venus or Jupiter, but this is very unlikely. So where do we search for life elsewhere in our solar system? The answer is two distant moons—one circling Jupiter and the other orbiting Saturn.

Jupiter's moon Europa has something found only there and on Earth. Underneath the thick shell of ice that wraps the moon are dark, salty oceans— the only remaining water world aside from ours known to exist in the solar system today.

There are two conditions on Europa, though, that may bump it off the list for harboring life. First, its oceans are not just dark—they're pitch black. No sunlight penetrates through the ice. Life could form without sunlight, but it would be much more difficult for that to happen. Second, Europa is bathed in lethal radiation emitted by Jupiter. Anything on or near the surface of Europa's icy world would be killed. If there is life on this moon, it will surely be small and very hardy. And if there are warm, hydrothermal vents on the ocean floor, it will probably be living in the thick ooze next to them.

Hidden beneath an orange blanket of dense atmospheric haze, Saturn's moon Titan may be the final place to look for life in our solar system. Eons ago, on primitive Earth, living organisms put methane gas into our atmosphere. There's a good chance Titan's methane-rich atmosphere may be the result of primitive living organisms. Underneath its frozen methane lakes, there may be layers of liquid ammonia. Even though it's poisonous to life on our planet today, the ammonia wasn't harmful to the first inhabitants of Earth. So if there is life on Titan, it could be similar to early life on Earth, but not like any kind of life here now.

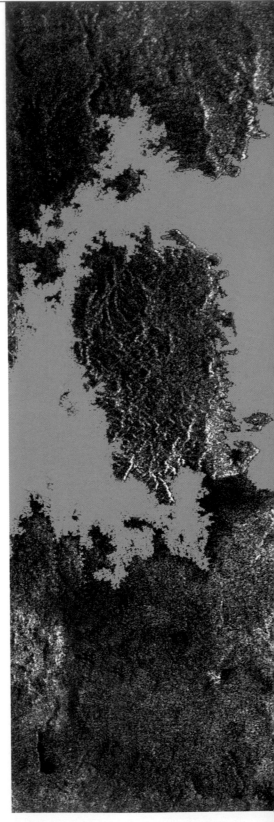

On Saturn's moon Titan there are whole lakes of liquid methane. In this image of Titan's surface, taken on the Cassini flyby mission in 2006, the lakes look lavender, but that's because the color has been changed in the photograph.

After drilling through almost half a mile of ice, a
futuristic hydrobot (art above) probes Europa's dark
waters. Surface temperatures are frigid here, but the
gravitational pull of Jupiter and possible volcanic
activity on the ocean floor may keep the deeper
water from freezing.

The possibility that intelligent beings exist out there on other worlds is something humans have imagined for a long, long time. Though there may be some slime, sludge, or bacteria living on Titan or Europa, there's probably no other intelligent life in the solar system.

To find intelligent life we have to look elsewhere. So far, astronomers have discovered more than 200 planets—all gas giants like Jupiter—circling around nearby stars. Scientists are pretty certain we won't find intelligent life on those worlds.

There are two theories about the source of intelligent life beyond Earth. Many scientists believe intelligent life is a natural part of evolution and is common throughout the universe. Another group believes intelligent life is rarer than we think. Intelligent life begins in one place, then spreads to other worlds. In other words, the second theory holds that one species ends up colonizing many other worlds.

For almost 50 years, humans have been listening for radio messages sent by other intelligent civilizations. So far, no ETs have left a text message or return address. But there are billions of cosmic bodies out there to try and listen to. NASA hopes to narrow the list of those bodies in the next few years. The Kepler Mission is scheduled to launch in 2008. The spacecraft's telescope will look at an area in outer space for four years, identifying stars with potential Earthlike planets circling them. With this new treasure map, it should be easier to narrow the search for planets that may have intelligent life and civilizations. In the next ten years, we could find our first intelligent, alien civilization.

On this imagined distant world (art right), alien technology is advanced and similar to our own. But the aliens, shown in the foreground, don't resemble us at all.

THE DRAKE EQUATION

$$N = R^* \times FP \times NE \times FL \times FL \times FC \times L$$

Almost 50 years ago, astronomer Frank Drake came up with this equation to figure out how many intelligent civilizations might exist in our galaxy. He considered the possible number of civilizations that might be capable of communicating, fractions of stars with planets, average number of planets and how many could support life, how many would have intelligent beings who wanted to communicate, and how long those civilizations might last. Based on his assumptions and today's knowledge, there could be between 4,000 and 5,000 alien civilizations somewhere out there among the 200 billion stars in our galaxy.

ALIEN LIFE—NOT WHAT WE'RE USED TO

The aliens in Hollywood are created so people will buy movie tickets, not to be examples of the weirdness of biology. What really lives out there may be beyond anything we can imagine, let alone deal with. There could be two-foot-long, green garden slugs that communicate using odors and see only in x-ray wavelengths of light. There have been some rather strange creatures here on our own world, too. If Earth hadn't had a run-in with an asteroid 65 million years ago, there might be some even stranger ones walking around today—and we wouldn't be one of them.

Before the asteroid hit, there was an Earth creature with two arms, two legs, and a head with two eyes. It stood upright and was about six feet (2 m) tall. Its name was *Stenonychosaurus*, and it was a dinosaur. After the asteroid hit

This artwork imagines a planet that was mostly covered by oceans until very late in its history. The intelligent creatures here quickly moved from the sea to the emerging volcanoes. There, they rapidly discovered the use of fire, electricity, and nuclear fusion, and they made fast advances in technology.

and the climate changed, this contender was knocked out of the race. Earth didn't become a planet of Dinopeople.

On other worlds, alien senses and anatomies may be so different that we won't even begin to be able to relate to them. They certainly won't look and talk like the aliens on *Star Trek*. If there were just slight changes in some of the physical conditions we take for granted here on Earth, life might follow some very odd pathways. If a planet had less gravity than Earth, life would grow taller and thinner. On a high-gravity world, body shapes would be shorter and more muscular. On a world with a thinner atmosphere, lungs might be larger and ears much bigger to pick up faint sound. On freezing worlds or ocean planets, new shapes and adaptations would certainly appear. And what about life that looks nothing like anything we've ever seen? The creatures imagined in Hollywood may not look nearly as strange as the ones designed by nature.

This hot, humid imaginary world (art above) is a little too near its own sun. Its odd creatures stand almost 9 feet (3 meters) tall and move slowly away when approached. The upper, baggy part of their bodies is filled with helium, like a party balloon. They pose no threat to visitors, and they seem to communicate by using electrical impulses.

Imagine driving home with your family late one night and encountering a large dome-shaped object hovering over the road in front of you. Silently, it glides over the trees, then flashes up and disappears into the starlit sky. You're not alone in this experience. Every year people from around the world report these sightings. Like them, you've witnessed a UFO— an unidentified flying object.

To the scientific community, UFOs are like untreated poison ivy. They're a nuisance that results in a lot of irritation, and they just won't go away.

Most astronomers will tell you that UFO sightings are the result of people misinterpreting natural phenomenon in the skies. The idea of traveling back and forth across the vast reaches of outer space does not compute with what we know about the physics of interstellar travel. A one-way journey to Earth's nearest star, Alpha Centauri, would take centuries for us humans. Obviously, then, UFOs are not visiting interstellar ships, unless there are aliens out there who can live thousands of years or who've discovered a method of time and space travel our scientists can't yet imagine.

Some psychologists believe that we humans have a deep subconscious desire to believe there are intelligent beings in

the vast reaches of space besides just ourselves. The idea makes us feel less alone in the universe. But the desire for company may play tricks on our eyes and our minds. Are UFOs, then, just our misinterpretations of objects seen in the sky, maybe the planet Venus or a weather balloon? Maybe some are, but air traffic controllers and military radar operators also report that they've watched UFOs zip back and forth across their screens at thousands of miles per hour.

For at least 60 years, UFOs have been part of our lives, and sightings continue to be reported. Every major world power has at one time or another established a government organization to investigate them, and the French government has put all of its official investigation files on the Internet for the world to see.

If there's one thing scientists from around the world agree on, it's that UFOs remain global phenomena that just don't seem to go away.

This photograph, taken in David Aguilar's backyard, re-creates what a "flying saucer" might look like. The first modern sighting of one happened in 1947, when a private pilot named Kenneth Arnold spotted nine "boomerang-shaped" silver objects fluttering along the snow-covered peaks of the Cascade Mountains in Washington. They looked like the flat saucers under a teacup.

In the future small supply ships and spaceships made from hollowed-out asteroids could service space stations.

Our close neighbors in space—the Moon and nearby asteroids—could give us new resources and new homes for our engineering projects. These resources will help us continue our exploration of the stars. Here are a few ways we might use the Moon and asteroids in the future.

A TELESCOPE ON THE MOON

Airless, cold, and dead quiet, the Moon is not a garden spot. But it could be the ideal place for gazing into space. Radio telescopes might be the first to go up, to capture radio waves from distant stars and planets. Placing the telescopes on the far side of the Moon would shield them from interfering radio waves from Earth.

Next to be built might be a liquid mirror telescope. The light-collecting surface of an LMT is usually made of the shiny liquid metal, mercury. Astronomers say that an LMT could be built at the Moon's south pole. Since the Moon has no air, clouds, or city lights to get in the way, an LMT there might allow us to see farther than ever before.

ASTEROID TREASURES

As people begin to colonize the inner solar system, they'll need to build homes and labs, space stations and hotels. The raw materials for those buildings

Two radio telescopes (art above), part of a larger group, could look toward space from the Moon's surface. These telescopes would pick up radio waves, not visible light, from all kinds of objects: stars, nebulas, galaxies, even planets. Signals picked up by a group of telescopes can be combined into one big image.

Asteroid miners, both humans and robots, could carry metals and ice from an asteroid to a space freighter (art right). Scientists on the spacecraft would break down the ice into oxygen and hydrogen for fuel, and the asteroid's metal would be flown where it was needed.

may well come from asteroids. Thousands of these chunks of rock, ice, and metal orbit close to Earth. Many are rich in iron and nickel; some contain platinum and gold. The ice in asteroids could be used for water, oxygen, and rocket fuel. Asteroid miners could be humans or robots. They would dig the metal and ice out of the asteroid and ship it out on space freighters.

The space taxi is waiting. Mars-bound astronauts climb into the little craft, buckle up, and lift off from Earth. Soon they see their next stop: a huge spaceship soaring past in the dark. Their pilot pulls alongside, carefully bringing the taxi's speed to 13,000 miles per hour (21,000 kph) to match the big craft's. With a few more delicate maneuvers, the pilot docks the taxi, and the astronauts enter their new home away from home: the moving Mars hotel.

Traveling to Mars on a regular spacecraft has some serious problems· The journey would require a huge amount of expensive fuel, and being weightless for a long time can badly weaken human bones and muscles. But "space hotels," also called cyclers, that ride the solar system's gravitational forces in a never ending loop between Mars and Earth wouldn't require much fuel, and each one would spin to create a kind of artificial gravity for the travelers inside. Cycler hotels could be the healthiest, cheapest, and most comfortable way to visit our planetary neighbor.

Although it's not luxurious, this imagined space hotel (far left in art) has comfortable little cabins, exercise machines, and games to play. After six months aboard, travelers would see the red planet looming in the hotel's windows. A space taxi would take the astronauts to the Martian surface to start their work.

Mars is a frigid desert with thin, poisonous air. But some scientists believe the planet could be transformed into a warm, green, Earthlike home by "terraforming" it.

Terraforming means to change something to make it like Earth. Terraforming Mars would be a huge project, taking hundreds or even thousands of years. The first step would be to make the Martian atmosphere warmer and thicker. This might be done by putting huge mirrors in orbit around the planet. The mirrors would focus the Sun's rays on Mars's south pole and turn the carbon dioxide trapped in the polar ice into gas. Once in the atmosphere, the carbon dioxide would help hold heat next to the planet's surface.

This warmer atmosphere would melt the water ice now frozen in the soil, creating oceans and rivers. Then green plants could be grown to take in carbon dioxide and give off oxygen, which humans need to breathe. In time—quite a long time—people might be able to stroll around on Mars and listen to the wind blowing through the trees.

1. Mars today (photo right): A cold and rocky desert, the red planet can't support human life. Its red tint comes from the iron in its soil. The planet chills under an average temperature of -85°F (-65°C). The atmosphere is 95 percent carbon dioxide and 200 times thinner than Earth's.

3. A green Mars: Under a thicker, warmer atmosphere fed by green plants, ice at Mars's poles and under the planet's surface would melt. Rivers would flow again on the surface and fill in ancient basins, creating oceans (art right).

2. *Mars begins to green (art left): After creating a thicker atmosphere by melting ice from Mars's poles, scientists could bring in specially engineered plants from Earth. Grown in the warmest regions of Mars, the plants would take in carbon dioxide and give off breathable oxygen.*

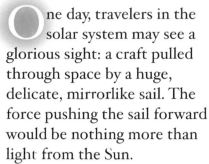

One day, travelers in the solar system may see a glorious sight: a craft pulled through space by a huge, delicate, mirrorlike sail. The force pushing the sail forward would be nothing more than light from the Sun.

The idea behind solar sailing is pretty simple. Light is made of extremely tiny particles called photons. When photons bounce off objects, they push on those objects just a little bit. On Earth we don't notice this because other forces, like friction in the air, are so much stronger. But in space, where there is no air to get in the way, the gentle pressure of photons from the Sun is enough to move a lightweight object.

Sunlight bouncing off a solar sail would move it—and the spacecraft attached to it— very slowly at first. Over time, the solar sailer would pick up speed, moving faster and faster. By the time the sailer passed the outer planets, it could be traveling at 200,000 miles per hour (324,000 kph), ten times as fast as today's space shuttle.

A solar sail probably would be made of shiny metallic cloth thinner than a butterfly's wing. It would also be huge, maybe as big as a football field.

We humans are not the fastest creatures on this planet. We do not have the keenest eyesight, the sharpest hearing, or the biggest brain, yet there is something very different about us.

Is it our ability to make things like houses, cars, bridges, and space stations? Or is it our unique desire to explore dangerous places? Whether it's the deep underwater world or a frozen ice sheet in Antarctica, humans are driven to investigate and explore. Why should outer space be any different?

In the coming decades astronauts will return to the Moon and venture onto Mars. Eventually, they may well reach the outer limits of our solar system. This will only be the start. Will it be the discovery of alien life on another planet circling a distant star or serious environmental problems that spur us on to explore the stars?

That future remains to be seen. Whether it is in our genes or part of our spirit, we'll no doubt keep going. Some day humans will leave on a journey to the stars. It will be the first step as we continue to explore our universe.

An imagined spacecraft (art right) races toward a distant star at nearly the speed of light. Future astronauts will not confine themselves to the solar system. New stars—and new planets—await us.

JANUARY

1

SATURDAY

SUNDA

MO

IF THE AGE OF THE SOLAR SYSTEM WAS COMPARED
TO THE LENGTH OF TIME IN A YEAR, HERE'S HOW LONG
THINGS WOULD TAKE TO FORM AND DEVELOP.

JANUARY 1
On New Year's Day, the solar system begins
condensing out of a swirling cloud of stardust.

JANUARY 7
The nuclear fires of our Sun ignite.

JANUARY 28
A truly memorable day—Earth forms.

FEBRUARY
Through the month of February, Earth
continues to shrink and cool.

MARCH 10
Escaped water vapor returns to Earth as rain,
and oceans form.

APRIL 15
Somewhere within Earth's warm blue-green
waters life begins.

MAY 22
Oxygen starts to form in the atmosphere.

JULY TO AUGUST
Life continues to develop.

SEPTEMBER 14
Somewhere in the oceanic depths, single-cell
plants begin sexual reproduction.

OCTOBER
Multicell creatures and plants burst
onto the scene.

DECEMBER 2
Some animals and plants begin to
live on land.

DECEMBER 13
Dinosaurs appear.

DECEMBER 25
Dinosaurs disappear.

DECEMBER 31
At 5:00 in the evening, "Lucy," the oldest recognizable
ancestor of the human tree, is born in Africa.

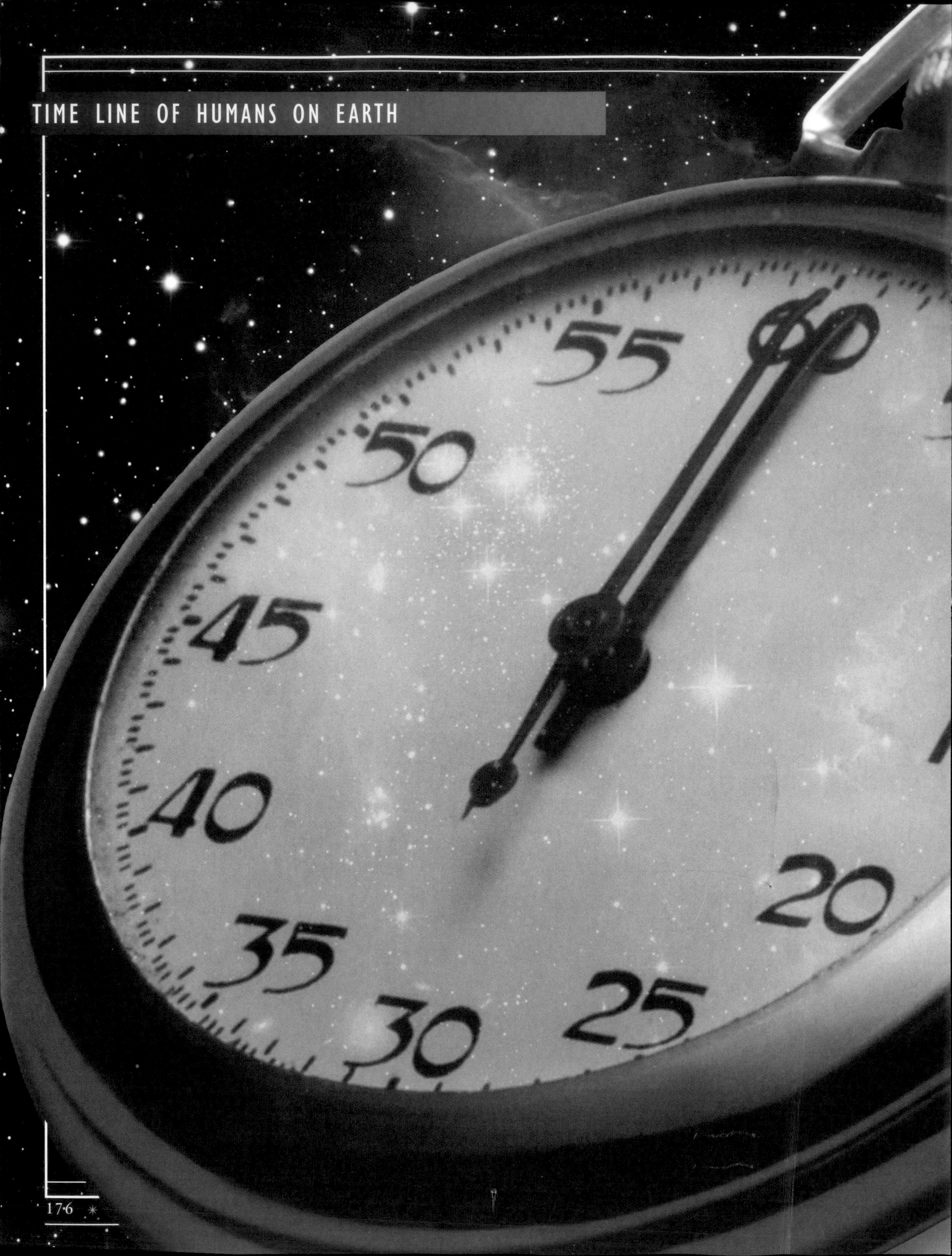
55
60
50
45
40
35
30
25
20

THE AMOUNT OF TIME WE HUMANS HAVE BEEN ON
EARTH RELATIVE TO THE AGE OF THE SOLAR SYSTEM IS SO
BRIEF THAT WE HAVE TO SWITCH NOW TO A STOPWATCH.

52 SECONDS BEFORE MIDNIGHT
On the last day of the year, Cro-Magnon humans,
anatomically like modern humans, appear in Europe.
Their cave paintings indicate they have an appreciation of culture.

40 SECONDS BEFORE MIDNIGHT
The pyramids are built.

33 SECONDS BEFORE MIDNIGHT
A succession of tribal peoples in what is now
Britain assembles Stonehenge.

23 SECONDS BEFORE MIDNIGHT
The golden age of Greece is celebrated.

17 SECONDS BEFORE MIDNIGHT
Jesus is born in Bethlehem.

8 SECONDS BEFORE MIDNIGHT
The Middle Ages begin.

5 SECONDS BEFORE MIDNIGHT
The Middle Ages end.

3 SECONDS BEFORE MIDNIGHT
The Pilgrims land in the New World.

1.5 SECONDS BEFORE MIDNIGHT
The Industrial Age begins.

1 SECOND BEFORE MIDNIGHT
The U.S. Civil War begins.

1/2 SECOND BEFORE MIDNIGHT
WWI breaks out.

3/8 SECOND BEFORE MIDNIGHT
WWII begins, ushering in the atomic age.

1/8 SECOND BEFORE MIDNIGHT
Neil Armstrong walks on the Moon.

1/16 SECOND BEFORE MIDNIGHT
The computer age begins.

1/32 SECOND BEFORE MIDNIGHT
The age of artificial intelligence and virtual reality follow.

1/64 SECOND BEFORE MIDNIGHT
Humans begin to realize that their activities, begun less than one
second ago on the cosmic timetable, have dramatically altered
the ecological balance of the planet. At no time in Earth's
history has a species had such an impact. What could that
mean for the future of Earth?

30,000 B.C. MOON PHASES
Early people carve lines on animal bones to track the phases of the Moon.

2500 B.C. STONEHENGE
Stonehenge is built in Britain. The circle of stones marks the rising and setting points of the Sun at the summer and winter solstice.

1300 B.C. CONSTELLATIONS AND PLANETS
Egyptians keep track of 43 constellations and the 5 visible planets—Mars, Venus, Mercury, Jupiter, and Saturn.

350 B.C. SPHERICAL EARTH
Greek scientist Aristotle argues that Earth is a sphere—not flat as believed before—because its shadow on the Moon during a lunar eclipse is always a circle.

250 B.C. EARTH'S CIRCUMFERENCE
Greek mathematician Eratosthenes uses geometry to calculate the circumference of Earth—almost 25,000 miles.

150 B.C. EARTH-CENTERED UNIVERSE
Greek astronomer Ptolemy publishes the *Almagest,* an astronomy book that says the universe is centered on Earth.

A.D. 1054 SUPERNOVA
Chinese astronomers record a supernova that is visible in the daytime; the remains of this explosion can now be seen as the Crab Nebula.

1543 SUN-CENTERED SYSTEM
Polish astronomer Nicolaus Copernicus publishes *De Revolutionibus,* which states that the Earth and other planets orbit the Sun.

1609 TELESCOPE
Italian astronomer Galileo Galilei uses a telescope to make important observations of the Sun, Moon, planets, and stars.

1610 PLANETARY MOTION
German mathematician Johannes Kepler discovers the laws of planetary motion, which describe the shape and speed of planetary orbits

1665-7 GRAVITY
British scientist Isaac Newton discovers the law of universal gravitation.

The Space Shuttle Atlantis *lifts off in April 2002.*

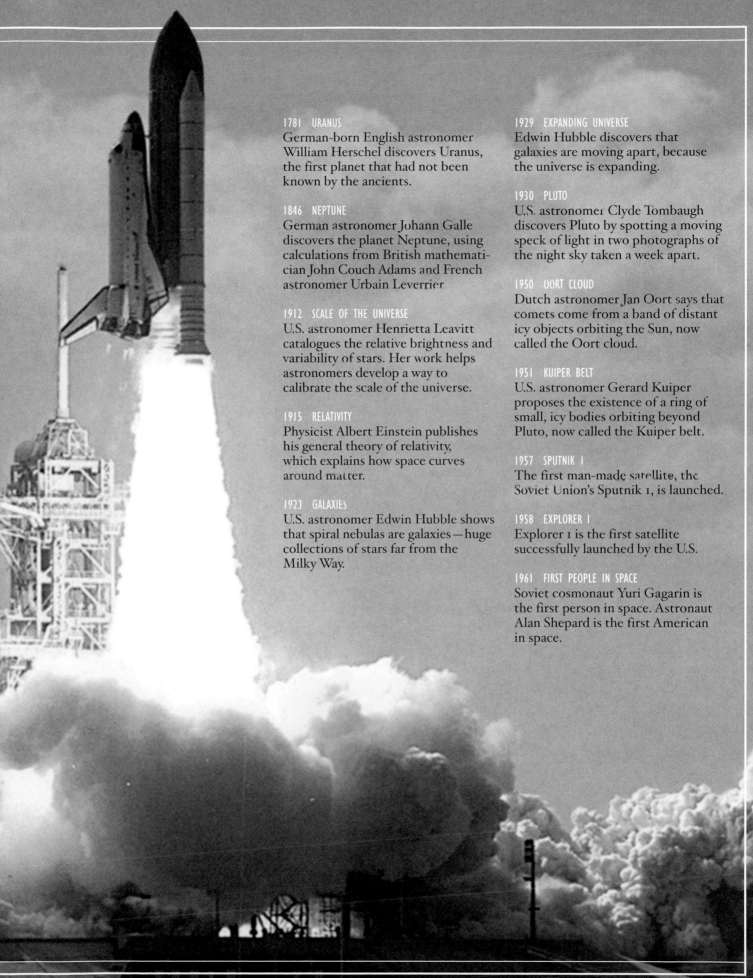

1781 URANUS
German-born English astronomer William Herschel discovers Uranus, the first planet that had not been known by the ancients.

1846 NEPTUNE
German astronomer Johann Galle discovers the planet Neptune, using calculations from British mathematician John Couch Adams and French astronomer Urbain Leverrier.

1912 SCALE OF THE UNIVERSE
U.S. astronomer Henrietta Leavitt catalogues the relative brightness and variability of stars. Her work helps astronomers develop a way to calibrate the scale of the universe.

1915 RELATIVITY
Physicist Albert Einstein publishes his general theory of relativity, which explains how space curves around matter.

1923 GALAXIES
U.S. astronomer Edwin Hubble shows that spiral nebulas are galaxies—huge collections of stars far from the Milky Way.

1929 EXPANDING UNIVERSE
Edwin Hubble discovers that galaxies are moving apart, because the universe is expanding.

1930 PLUTO
U.S. astronomer Clyde Tombaugh discovers Pluto by spotting a moving speck of light in two photographs of the night sky taken a week apart.

1950 OORT CLOUD
Dutch astronomer Jan Oort says that comets come from a band of distant icy objects orbiting the Sun, now called the Oort cloud.

1951 KUIPER BELT
U.S. astronomer Gerard Kuiper proposes the existence of a ring of small, icy bodies orbiting beyond Pluto, now called the Kuiper belt.

1957 SPUTNIK 1
The first man-made satellite, the Soviet Union's Sputnik 1, is launched.

1958 EXPLORER 1
Explorer 1 is the first satellite successfully launched by the U.S.

1961 FIRST PEOPLE IN SPACE
Soviet cosmonaut Yuri Gagarin is the first person in space. Astronaut Alan Shepard is the first American in space.

1963 FIRST WOMAN IN SPACE; QUASARS

Soviet cosmonaut Valentina Teresh-kova is the first woman in space. Dutch-born U.S. astronomer Maarten Schmidt discovers the first quasar, an extremely bright, distant galaxy.

1965 BIG BANG; MARINER 4

U.S. astronomers Arno Penzias and Robert Wilson use a radio telescope to detect very faint radiation coming from all directions in space. They realize this is radiation left over from the big bang, which helps prove that theory for the formation of the universe. Mariner 4 flies past Mars, sending back pictures of a dry, cratered surface.

1967 PULSARS

British astronomers Jocelyn Bell and Antony Hewish discover pulsars, later shown to be spinning neutron stars sending out beams of radiation.

1969 FIRST PEOPLE ON THE MOON; SOYUZ SPACE STATION

U.S. astronauts Edwin Aldrin and Neil Armstrong become the first people to land on the Moon. Soviet spacecraft Soyuz 5 docks with Soyuz 4 to form the first experimental space station.

1972 LAST MOON LANDING

Apollo 17 is the last Apollo mission to the Moon.

1973 VOYAGERS 1 AND 2

U.S. spacecraft Voyagers 1 and 2 reach Jupiter, then use gravitational assists from their swing past Jupiter to speed toward the more distant planets.

1976 VIKING LANDERS

U.S. Viking landers safely touch down on the surface of Mars and send back images and information from the planet's surface for several years.

1981 SPACE SHUTTLE LAUNCHED

U.S. space shuttle *Columbia* is launched, successfully making the first flight of a reusable shuttle.

1986 *CHALLENGER* DISASTER; MIR 1

The space shuttle *Challenger* explodes 73 seconds after launch, killing the crew. Soviets launch the long-lasting space station Mir 1.

1989 COBE

The Cosmic Background Explorer (COBE) satellite is launched. It detects microwave radiation in the universe that confirms modern theories about the big bang.

In French filmmaker Georges Méliès's 1902 fantasy movie A Trip to the Moon, *a canister carrying six astronomers hits the "Man in the Moon" in the eye.*

1990 MAGELLAN; HUBBLE SPACE TELESCOPE
U.S. spacecraft Magellan begins radar mapping of Venus. The Hubble Space Telescope is launched. In the years to come, it produces stunning images of distant stars and galaxies.

1992 KUIPER BELT OBJECT
Astronomers discover a reddish, planetlike object circling the Sun beyond the orbit of Pluto, confirming the existence of the Kuiper belt.

1995 PLANETS ORBITING OTHER STARS
Jupiter-size planets are discovered orbiting sunlike stars near our solar system in the Milky Way.

2003 *COLUMBIA* DISASTER
After 27 missions, the space shuttle *Columbia* explodes during reentry into Earth's atmosphere, killing all aboard.

2004 MARS ROVERS; CASSINI
U.S. rovers Spirit and Opportunity reach Mars and begin collecting information about the existence of water. The U.S. Cassini spacecraft goes into orbit around Saturn, sending back the best images ever of the planet, its rings, and its large moon Titan.

2005 ERIS
Eris, a planetlike object bigger than Pluto, is discovered orbiting the Sun almost 10 billion miles away, far past Pluto.

2006 PLUTO DEMOTED
Members of the International Astronomical Union vote to change the way planets are classified. Pluto is no longer considered a planet but officially becomes a dwarf planet, along with Eris and Ceres (formerly the solar system's biggest asteroid).

2015 PLUTO FLYBY
The U.S. New Horizons spacecraft will fly past Pluto on its way to the farthest reaches of the solar system.

2020 NEW FOOTSTEPS ON THE MOON
Spacecraft in the Constellation program are scheduled to return human explorers to the Moon.

ASTEROID
A rocky body, measuring from less than one mile to 600 miles in diameter, in orbit around a sun. Most asteroids in our solar system are found between the orbits of Mars and Jupiter.

ATMOSPHERE
The gases surrounding a planet, star, or satellite

BIG BANG
An enormous explosion that scientists believe was the initial event in the formation of the universe

BLACK DWARF
The cooling remains of a dwarf star that has used up its nuclear fuel

BLACK HOLE
Thought to form when a massive star collapses. Black holes are extremely dense objects of such strong gravitational force that nothing passing within a certain distance can escape them, not even light.

BROWN DWARF
A faintly glowing body too small to sustain a nuclear fusion reaction and become a star

COMET
A body of rock, dust, and gaseous ice in an elongated orbit around the Sun. Near the Sun, heat diffuses gas and dust to form a streaming "tail" around the comet's nucleus.

CONSTELLATION
A pattern of stars identified with an ancient god, goddess, or animal; also an area of sky with one of these star patterns

CORONA
The outermost layer of gases in the Sun's atmosphere

CRATER
A circular depression in the surface of a planet, caused by a meteorite impact or by volcanic action

DARK MATTER
An unknown substance that is only detected by the gravity it exerts. It makes up five-sixths of the universe.

DWARF PLANET
A spherical or nearly spherical rocky body, in orbit around the Sun and not the satellite of another body; smaller than most of the other planets in our solar system.

ECLIPSE
An event caused by the passage of one astronomical body between an observer and another astronomical body, briefly blocking light from the farther astronomical body

FISSION
The breakdown of atomic nuclei into the nuclei of lighter elements, releasing energy

FUSION
The combining of the nuclei of two atoms to form one heavier nucleus, a process that releases energy

GALAXY
A grouping of stars, gas, and dust bound together by gravity. Galaxies sometimes have many billions of stars.

GAMMA RAY BURST
A brief, intense burst of gamma radiation. These are the brightest explosions in the universe and come from unknown sources outside our galaxy.

KUIPER BELT
A reservoir of comets encircling an area just beyond the orbit of Neptune

LIGHT-YEAR
Equals 5.9 trillion miles, the distance light can travel in one Earth year

MAGNITUDE
A number measuring an astronomical body's brightness in relation to other luminous objects

MASS
The total quantity of material in an object, determining its gravity and resistance to movement

METEOR
A small object from space that appears as a streak of light when it passes through Earth's atmosphere. A meteorite is the remains of a meteor found on Earth. A meteoroid is a rocky or metallic object in orbit around the Sun that has the potential to become a meteor.

NEBULA
A glowing interstellar cloud of gas and dust

NEUTRON STAR
A body of densely packed neutrons, formed after the explosion of a supernova. A neutron star only ten miles in diameter could have more mass than three sun-size stars.

OORT CLOUD
A reservoir of comets surrounding our solar system

ORBIT
The regular path a celestial body follows as it revolves around another body

PLANET
A spherical object larger than 600 miles in diameter that orbits a star and has cleared its neighborhood of other like-size objects.

PLANETARY NEBULA
The glowing cloud of gas resulting from a supernova explosion

PLANETESIMAL
A small rocky body in orbit around a star, which may become a planet by drawing in more material

PULSAR
Thought to be a spinning neutron star that sends out bursts of electromagnetic radiation with clockwork regularity

RED GIANT
A cool, aging low-mass star that has fused most of its core hydrogen and expanded greatly from its previous size

RING
A band of material around a planet, formed of dust-to-boulder-size pieces

SATELLITE
A natural or man-made object orbiting a planet

SOLAR (STELLAR) WIND
A stream of charged particles radiating outward from the Sun or another star

SPECTRUM
The range of radiation wavelengths from long radio waves to short gamma rays. The visible portion can be seen as colors when the radiation (light) is passed through a prism.

SUPERGIANT
A very massive, luminous star with a relatively short life span

SUPERNOVA
The violent, luminous explosion at the end of a massive star's life

WHITE DWARF
The small, dense core of a once larger star that has fused all the helium in its core

INDEX

Boldface indicates illustrations.

corona 34–35, 182
death of **104**
images 32–33, 35, **36**
interior structure 34–35
life cycle **98**
look-back time **92**, 93
magnetic field 36
sizc **102–103**
solstice 178
Sunspots 35, **36**
Supernova 1987A 135
Supernovas
   ancient sightings 178
   definition 183
   elements 107
   expanding universe 142
   formation 133
   life cycle of stars **98–99**
   nebulas **108**
   remnants **108–109**

T

Taurus (constellation) 93
Telescopes
   Arecibo radio telescope 127
   distances 92, 93
   globular clusters 126
   Hubble Space Telescope 37, 64, 132, 181
   invention of 109
   James Webb Space Telescope **17**, 139
   Kepler Telescope **17**
   on moon **164**
   Multiple Mirror Telescope (MMT) 113
   observations 16, 46, 53, 100
   radio 17, 108, **164**, 180
   spacecraft 156

Spitzer Space Telescope 96
   x-ray radiation 108
Tereshkova, Valentina 180
Terraforming **168–169**
Time line **174–181**
Titan (moon) **56–57**, 154, 156, 181
Titania (moon) 58
Tombaugh, Clyde **66**, 179
Trapezium (constellation) **100**
Triangulum galaxy (M33) 130
Trifid Nebula (M20) **101**
Triton (moon) **60–61**
Tunguska region of Siberia 15

U

UFOs **160–161**
Ultraviolet light 17
Universe
   accelerating expansion **142–145**, 179
   birth of **10**, **12**, **147**
   black holes **146**
   branes (parallel universes) **147**
   end of **144–145**
   expansion **142–145**, 179
   exploration **172–173**
   supernovas 142
   unobservable **140–141**, 146–147
Unmanned missions
   Jupiter 180
   Kepler Mission 156
   Mars (planet) 154, 180, 181
   Saturn 54-55, 181
   Soyuz 180
   Voyager 180
Uranus (planet) **23**, **58–59**, 179

Ursa Major (Great Bear constellation) 90

V

Venus (planet) 22, **26–27**
   atmosphere 24–26
   brightness 24, 26, **27**, **29**
   interior structure **28**
   life on 154
   mapping 181
   phases **29**
   surface 25, 26, **28–29**
   volcanoes 28, **28–29**
Viking Lander 154, 180
Volcanoes
   Earth 77
   Mars 38, **41**
   Moon 82
   Venus 28, **28–29**
Voyager missions 180

W

Whirlpool galaxy **132**
White dwarfs
   death of stars **98–99**
   definition 104, 183
   globular clusters 124
   star sizes **102–103**
Wilson, Robert 180

X

X-ray radiation 17, 108
X-ray wavelengths of light 158

ABOUT THE AUTHORS

DAVID A. AGUILAR, author and illustrator of *Planets, Stars, and Galaxies,* is a man with his head in the stars and his feet grounded firmly on Earth. He is Director of Science Information at the Harvard-Smithsonian Center for Astrophysics in Cambridge, Massachusetts and the past Director of the Fiske Planetarium and Science Center at the University of Colorado in Boulder.

DENNIS A. TITO, foreword author, is considered the first space tourist. In 2001, at the age of 60, the multimillionaire and former NASA Jet Propulsion Laboratory employee paid to take a voyage aboard a Russian Soyuz spacecraft to the International Space Station.

CHRISTINE PULLIAM, contributing writer ("To the Stars & Beyond"), is a public affairs specialist at the Harvard-Smithsonian Center for Astrophysics in Cambridge, Massachusetts, and a freelance

science writer. She earned her B.S. in physics and her M.A. in astronomy from the University of Texas at Austin.

PATRICIA DANIELS, contributing writer ("Dreams of Tomorrow" and time lines of the solar system and astronomy), has written more than a dozen science and history books for adults and children, including the *National Geographic Encyclopedia of Space* and *Constellations: My First Pocket Guide.* She lives in State College, Pennsylvania.

ILLUSTRATIONS CREDITS

All illustrations and images courtesy of David A. Aguilar unless otherwise noted.

8 (bottom), 93 (top) Space Boy flashlight courtesy of Schylling Toys; 28-29 (bottom), 40 (top), 41 (top), 49 (middle), 49 (bottom, right), 50 (top, left), 50 (top, right), 51 (top, left), 51 (top, right), 57 (middle, right), 96-97, 97 (inset), 108: NASA/JPL; 35 (top), 36 (inset), 104: NASA/ SOHO; 36 (top, right): © JAXA/NAOJ/NASA/ STFC; 37: Joshua Strang/USAF; 40-41 (bottom): Horizon Hills/ NASA/JPL/MSSS; 41 (middle): NASA/JPL/MSSS; 49 (top, left), 49 (top, right): NASA/ LPI; 54-55 (top), 57 (middle,

left), 57 (top), 57 (bottom): NASA/CICLOPS/JPL; 56 (top, left): NASA/JPL/Univ. of AZ; 56 (right): ESA/NASA/JPL/ Univ. of AZ; 66: © Bettmann/ CORBIS; 80 (1, 2, 5, 6, 7, 9, 10, 11), 81 (12, 13): © Shutterstock; 80 (3): © Mediscan/CORBIS; 81 (4): © Douglas P. Wilson/ Frank Lane Picture Agency/ CORBIS; 81 (8): © Jack Hollingsworth/CORBIS; 88-89: © Serge Brunier; 90 (bottom): © British Library, London, UK/British Library Board/The Bridgeman Art Library; 90 (top), 126: © www.spiegelteam.de; 100 (top), 100 (bottom), 101 (bottom), 105 (top), 105 (middle), 127 (middle), 130-131: © Robert

Gendler; 101 (top, left): © Estate of Arthur Lyon Cross, University of Michigan Museum of Art; 101 (top, right): © Bibliotheque de l'Observation de Paris; 105 (bottom): Bruce Balick/NASA; 111: © Envision/CORBIS; 127 (bottom): © NOAO/AURA/ NSF; 132 (left), 132 (top, right): NASA/GSFC; 132 (bottom, right): NASA/Kirk Borne/ STScI; 133 (left): NASA/EJ Schreier/STScI; 138-139: NASA/STScI; 139 (inset): NASA/JSC; 178-179: NASA/KSC; 181 (top): still image from *A Trip to the Moon,* Georges Méliès, 1902, via David Aguilar.

ADDITIONAL READING

Baumann, Mary K., Hopkins, Will, Nolletti, Loralee & Soluri, Michael. *What's Out There: Images from Here to the Edge of the Universe.* London: Duncan Baird, 2006

Beatty, J. Kelly, Petersen, Carolyn & Chaikin, Andrew, Ed. *The New Solar System.* Cambridge, Mass.: Sky Publishing, 1999

Crelin, Bob. *There Once Was a Sky Full of Stars.* Cambridge, Mass.: Sky Publishing, 2007

Croswell, Ken. *Ten Worlds: Everything That Orbits the Sun.* Honesdale, Pa.: Boyds Mills Press, 2006

Darling, David. *The Universal Book of Astronomy.* Hoboken, N.J.: Wiley, 2004

Davis, Kenneth C. *Don't Know Much About Space.* New York: HarperCollins Publishers, 2001

Decristofano, Carolyn Cinami & Carroll, Michael. *Big Bang!* Watertown, Mass.: Charlesbridge Publishing, 2005

Dinwiddie, Robert et al. *Universe.* New York: Dorling Kindersley, 2005

Glover, Linda et al. *National Geographic Encyclopedia of Space.* Washington, D.C.: National Geographic Society, 2005

Harrington, Philip & Pascuzzi, Edward. *Astronomy for All Ages.* Old Saybrook, Conn.: Globe Pequot, 2000

Hewitt-White, Ken. *Patterns in the Sky.* Cambridge, Mass.: Sky Publishing, 2007

Odenwald, Sten. *Back to Astronomy Café.* Boulder, Co: Westview Press, 2003

Schorer, Lonnie. *Kids to Space: A Space Traveler's Guide.* Burlington, Ontario: Collector's Guide Publishing, Inc., 2006

Skurzynski, Gloria. *Are We Alone?* Washington, D.C.: National Geographic Society, 2004

Time-Life Books, Ed. *Comets, Asteroids, and Meteorites.* Alexandria, Va: Time-Life, Inc., 1990

Villard, Ray & Cook, Lynette. *Infinite Worlds.* Berkeley, Ca.: University of California Press, 2005

WEB SITES

http://antwrp.gsfc.nasa.gov/apod/astropix.html

http://www.astronomycafe.net

http://www.chandra.harvard.edu

http://www.hubblesite.org

http://www.kidsastronomy.com

http://imagine.gsfc.nasa.gov/docs/ask_astro/ask_an_astronomer.html

http://www.nasa.gov/centers/goddard/home/index.html

http://www.nineplanets.org

http://www.space.com/scienceastronomy

PUBLISHED BY THE NATIONAL GEOGRAPHIC SOCIETY

John M. Fahey, Jr.
President and Chief Executive Officer

Gilbert M. Grosvenor
Chairman of the Board

Nina D. Hoffman
Executive Vice President;
President, Book Publishing Group

PREPARED BY THE BOOK DIVISION

Nancy Laties Feresten
Vice President,
Editor-in-Chief, Children's Books

Bea Jackson
Director of Design and Illustrations,
Children's Books

Amy Shields
Executive Editor, Series, Children's Books

Carl Mehler
Director of Maps

STAFF FOR THIS BOOK

Karen M. Kostyal, *Editor*

David M. Seager, *Art Director*

Jocelyn Lindsay, *Researcher*

Lori Epstein, Annette Kiesow,
Illustrations Editors

Margo Browning and Jennifer Emmett,
Contributing Editors

Rachel Armor,
Illustrations Production Assistant

Lewis Bassford,
Production Project Manager

Jennifer A. Thornton, *Managing Editor*

Gary Colbert, *Production Director*

Susan Borke, *Legal and Business Affairs*

MANUFACTURING AND QUALITY MANAGEMENT

Christopher A. Liedel,
Chief Financial Officer

Phillip L. Schlosser, *Vice President*

John T. Dunn, *Technical Director*

Chris Brown, *Director*

Maryclare Tracy, Nicole Elliott, *Managers*

To Chesley Bonestell for graciously spending long afternoons with me in his Carmel studio, guiding me through the worlds he had created and painted...to my mother and grandmother, who realized butterfly nets, telescopes, and scuba tanks were a necessary part of a young boy's future life...and to my supporting and loving wife, best friend and nurturing critic Shirley Grace, who helped me research, write, and shape my thoughts and artwork to bring them to life.

The dynamic team at National Geographic: My dedicated editor Karen Kostyal, who always asked just the right questions while keeping this project flying straight ahead through space; science advisor, writer, and colleague at the Center for Astrophysics Christine Pulliam, who performed miracles on both even- and odd-numbered days; Vice President and Editor-in-Chief Nancy Laties Feresten, who enthusiastically embraced my vision and had the supreme confidence I could make it happen.

And especially to art director and book designer David M. Seager, who pushed my creativity to levels not realized before, while providing insight and unwavering artistic vision.
—DAA

✳

On the front cover: A comet streaks into deep space passing asteroids.
On the back cover: An alien world and its moon in the heart of the Milky Way

✳

Library of Congress Cataloging-in-Publication Information
Aguilar, David A.
Planets, Stars, and Galaxies : a visual encyclopedia of our universe / written and illustrated by David A. Aguilar.
p. cm.
Includes index.
ISBN 978-1-4263-0170-4 (hc : alk. paper) —
ISBN 978-1-4263-0171-1 (lib. bdg. : alk. paper)
1. Solar system—Pictorial works. 2. Galaxies—Pictorial works. 3. Astronomy—Pictorial works. I. Title.
QB501.A267 2007
520—dc22

2007061234

Printed in the United States

Founded in 1888, the National Geographic Society is one of the largest nonprofit scientific and educational organizations in the world. It reaches more than 285 million people worldwide each month through its official journal, NATIONAL GEOGRAPHIC, and its four other magazines; the National Geographic Channel; television documentaries; radio programs; films; books; videos and DVDs; maps; and interactive media. National Geographic has funded more than 8,000 scientific research projects and supports an education program combating geographic illiteracy.

For more information, please call 1-800-NGS LINE (647-5463) or write to the following address:

National Geographic Society
1145 17th Street N.W.,
Washington, D.C. 20036-4688 U.S.A.

Visit us online at www.nationalgeographic.com/books
For information about special discounts for bulk purchases, please contact National Geographic Books Special Sales: ngspecsales@ngs.org

For rights or permissions inquiries, please contact National Geographic Books Subsidiary Rights: ngbookrights@ngs.org